OCR →
+ Ref Plate

THE SWORD OF THE LORD

CRITICAL PROBLEMS IN HISTORY

*The University of Notre Dame Press
gratefully acknowledges the generous support
of the Dilenschneider family in the publication
of titles in this series.*

THE SWORD OF THE LORD

Military Chaplains from the First to the Twenty-First Century

edited by

DORIS L. BERGEN

University of Notre Dame Press

Notre Dame, Indiana

Manufactured in the United States of America

Library of Congress Cataloging-in-Publication Data
The sword of the lord : military chaplains from the first to the
twenty-first century / edited by Doris L. Bergen.
p. cm.
Includes bibliographical references and index.
ISBN 0-268-02175-9 (cloth : alk. paper)
ISBN 0-268-02176-7 (pbk. : alk. paper)
1. Chaplains, Military—History. I. Bergen, Doris L.
UH20.S962 2004
355.3'47'09—dc22
2003020901

∞ *This book is printed on acid-free paper.*

"Greater love hath no man than this, that a man lay down his life for his friends." How deeply poignant and meaningful, then, is the act of an individual who is willing to sacrifice himself not just for another person's corporeal life but for his soul.

Rudyard Kipling, in his masterful history *The Irish Guards in the Great War,* touched on the role of the military chaplain when he wrote that the commanding officers first advised and finally ordered the padres not to expose themselves "wantonly in forward posts or attack. . . . That the priests, to the huge content of the men, should disregard the order ('What's a casualty compared to a soul?') was most natural of all." C. S. Lewis has commented, "Courage is not simply one of the virtues but the form of every virtue at the testing point. Courage is the first virtue because it makes all the other virtues possible." Those who choose to become chaplains in their nations' armed forces have, or at least seek, that virtue. They seek it not for glory but to help their fellow pilgrims in their ultimate hour of need.

All of us recognize the apparent randomness of survival. The soldier is even more acutely aware than most of the thin line between life and death. "There are no atheists in foxholes" may be a cliché, but only fools would bet that it's untrue. Those who face death as part of their job description tend to think seriously about God. And although the force of organized religion varies with time and place, and, according to many, is diminishing across the Western world, yet few armies have ever lacked members who are priests, ministers, rabbis, or other "holy men."

I cannot think of chaplains without remembering my dear friend John Cardinal O'Connor, who spent twenty-seven years of his life serving with the United States Navy and Marine Corps, and considering it a high privilege to do so. He left the Marines to go to another combat zone—the Archdiocese of New York.

The Sword of the Lord is a history of military chaplaincy that needed to be written and that lays the foundation for other studies of this topic. It takes the reader from the pre-Christian era to the present, raising important religious, political, and philosophical issues along the way. This is a book that should be read by scholars and will be enjoyed and appreciated by the general public.

—Robert L. Dilenschneider

CONTENTS

ILLUSTRATIONS

PREFACE AND ACKNOWLEDGMENTS

The Sword of the Lord is the result of many people's ideas and efforts. It is a pleasure for me to thank some of those who contributed to the project in all of its stages. David S. Bachrach deserves the first acknowledgment. It was David's idea for the University of Notre Dame to host a conference on military chaplains, and he worked hard to turn that idea into a reality. Without his initiative and energy, the meeting in March 2000—Military Chaplains in Their Contexts—would not have taken place, and this volume would not exist. Thomas Blantz, C.S.C., John S. Conway, Margarete Myers Feinstein, Rabbi Morley Feinstein, Daniel J. Gargola, Douglass Hemphill, Ivan Jaksic, Mark Jantzen, Donald Mathews, Wilson D. Miscamble, C.S.C., Linda H. Pardo, Rabbi Arnold Resnicoff, Carol Rittner, R.S.M., John Roth, Catherine Schlegel, J. Robert Wegs, and Henry Weinfield each offered key suggestions or encouragement at crucial moments; they merit special mention here as well.

This book is a product of the University of Notre Dame in fundamental ways. With its long tradition of studies in religion and ethics and its venerable connections to the military chaplaincy in the United States, Notre Dame was an extraordinarily supportive environment for this project. One of the university's "founding fathers," William Corby, C.S.C., served as a chaplain with the Irish Brigades in the American Civil War. A building with his name, a statue, and a mural that portrays him preaching to his men are physical reminders on campus of his place in history. Another famous chaplain associated with Notre Dame is Frank Sampson, C.S.C.— "Father Sam" —who parachuted into Normandy on D-Day as chaplain to the 101st Airborne Division. Subsequently, after a tour of duty in Korea, Fr. Sampson served as chief of chaplains, Department of the Army, from 1967 to 1971. His service earned him numerous awards and decorations, even depiction in movies, including *The Longest Day* and *Saving Private Ryan.*

People currently at Notre Dame were instrumental in very direct ways, most notably by providing funds and other forms of support for the conference in 2000 and also for this book. I particularly thank Harriet Baldwin, Julia Douthwaite, Christopher Hamlin, Mary Ellen Koepfle, and Mark W. Roche. The following Notre Dame institutes and departments generously gave financial and other assistance: the College of Arts and Letters; the Institute for Scholarship in the Liberal Arts; the Nanovic Institute for European Studies; the Graduate School; the Medieval Institute; the Erasmus Institute; the Joan B. Kroc Institute for International Peace Studies; the Cushwa Center for the Study of American Catholicism; and the departments of History, Theology, and Political Science. Wendy Schrank prepared the preliminary bibliography, and Elizabeth E. Hayes did a superb job of getting the manuscript ready for publication. Daniel S. Mattern provided incisive comments on a draft of the introduction and essential editorial help at a crucial point. Barbara Hanrahan of the University of Notre Dame Press has been wonderfully accommodating and encouraging, and Rebecca R. DeBoer and Ted Wagstaff expertly moved the manuscript through copyediting into production. Jim Harink helped in every possible way.

The authors included here deserve a special word of appreciation. I cannot imagine a more cooperative, inspiring group of people—it has been a pleasure to work with every one of them. Finally, thanks also go to Paul Fussell, Patrick Geary, Margaret Hardy, Thomas A. Kselman, John A. Lynn, Per Anders Sandgren, Robert Sullivan, and Annelise Thimme. Interlocutors of the highest caliber, they helped those of us present at the conference and represented in this book to think harder and more productively about military chaplains in all their contexts.

INTRODUCTION

DORIS L. BERGEN

This is the first book to examine military chaplains and the development of the military chaplaincy across time and space, from the first through the twentieth century, and from Europe to North America.[1] The twelve chapters that follow focus on chaplains in the Western— some might add Christian—tradition, although Jewish chaplains are also part of this history, as is evident from Rabbi Max B. Wall's account of his experiences with the U.S. Army in the Second World War. The coverage is by no means complete; no single volume could address every aspect of the military chaplaincy in all its national and chronological contexts. Nevertheless, taken together, the case studies included here provide a survey of key developments from "Nero to NATO," as one contributor quipped; that is, from the Roman Empire to the end of the twentieth century.

Taking such a long and broad view reveals an astonishing fact: the military chaplaincy has existed in a recognizable form for more than sixteen hundred years. Our discussion begins in antiquity, moves through medieval Europe and the Crusades, and then considers the English Civil War of 1642–49 as perhaps the last of the early modern "wars of religion." The American Civil War and the emerging great power Prussia/Germany from 1713 to 1918 provide examples for an examination of the chaplaincy in an age of nation building and nationalism. Through a focus on Canadian, German, and American chaplains, the impact of the world wars is explored. Two chapters reflect on the last half of the twentieth century, including the Vietnam War and its legacies for the military chaplaincy in the United States. The final essay draws critical attention to some of the moral and theological dimensions of this history from one perspective within the Roman Catholic tradition.

A diverse group of people connected by an interest in military chaplains contributed to this book. Two chapters are the work of men who themselves served as chaplains: Rabbi Max B. Wall and Father Joseph O'Donnell. The spirit of their experiences vivifies our investigations and reminds us that this history is above all about human beings, about courage and fear, and about the lives and deaths of real people. The other authors are scholars—nine historians and one theologian—who study religion and war in settings as divergent as Merovingian Gaul and Canada during the Great War. Of these scholars, two are also clergy: the Reverend Gardiner H. Shattuck, Jr. and Michael J. Baxter, C.S.C. The rest are as varied in their religious, personal, and professional backgrounds as one might expect of any international group of academics. This broad range of perspectives and approaches makes it all the more significant that so many commonalities emerge among these studies of military chaplains in dramatically different contexts.

Four key themes connect the chapters in this book and provide the framework for this introductory essay. The first deals with the basic issue of historical development over time. Where and when did the military chaplaincy begin and how has it changed? How have matters such as numbers and social origins of chaplains varied across different settings? Each chapter explores these issues in a specific time and place and demonstrates how understandings of the chaplaincy's past and present are mutually illuminating.

A second theme, most evident in the two personal accounts, involves the emotionally and spiritually intense relationship between chaplains and the men and women they serve. Soldiers about to kill or possibly be killed, bereaved family members—those and others in similarly extreme circumstances are the chaplain's constituents. What do they want and expect from those charged with providing them pastoral care? How have military chaplains dealt with their enormous responsibilities, and how have their efforts been received?

The third theme has to do with chaplains' precarious position between military and religious authorities, or as Hartmut Lehmann puts it in the title to his chapter, "In the Service of Two Kings." Are military chaplains primarily morale boosters, retained by rulers and military commanders because they prepare soldiers to fight hard and face death bravely? Or are they above all pastors, ministering to the spiritual needs of the men and women in their care? Connected with these questions is what might be called a credibility gap. Sometimes assigned privileged status and distanced from the realities of combat, military chaplains often struggle for legitimacy in the eyes of the people they serve. How have chaplains sought to balance conflicting duties and demands, from their spiritual versus their secular superiors, and from officers and other authorities versus soldiers? How have chaplains' efforts been remembered and represented?

A fourth, related theme involves the profound moral and theological dilemmas raised by the chaplaincy. Military chaplains minister not only to the wounded and dying, but also to those who attack and kill. Chaplains have served heroically in wars most would consider to have been just or at least necessary; however, they can also be found on the side of dictators, tyrants, committers of atrocities, and perpetrators of genocide. Even under the least morally ambiguous circumstances, chaplains work in the midst of violence, coercion, and suffering. How have chaplains understood their tasks and carried them out in deeply troubled and brutal times? How do we begin to think about the ethical implications of their work?

Looking Back, Seeing Ahead

In August 2000, the *Neue Zürcher Zeitung*, a Swiss newspaper, carried a story about German military chaplains stationed with peacekeeping troops in the Balkans.[2] That account featured a photograph of a Protestant pastor in camouflage fatigues, standing in front of a cross. In his left hand the chaplain holds a book—perhaps a Bible—while his right hand rests on the bowed head of a young man, likewise in uniform. Two additional soldiers look on. Behind them on a low table, a candle burns next to the ritual items associated with the Lord's Supper. This scene, a baptism on the German base at Prizren in Kosovo, provides a graphic illustration of the fundamental continuities and changes in the long history of the military chaplaincy. Some of the duties of contemporary chaplains are strikingly similar to those of their predecessors far

Protestant pastor Christian Finkenstein performs a baptism at the base in Prizren, September 1999. Photograph by Walter Linkmann. Evangelisches Kirchenamt für die Bundeswehr, Bonn. Used with permission.

in the past. Since the middle of the twentieth century, however, the goals chaplains pursue and the meanings attached to their work have begun to change, quietly but nevertheless significantly.

Military chaplains in the West can claim ancient precedents, although there seems to be considerable difference of opinion as to which venerable roots are most pertinent. According to the history of the Canadian Forces Chaplaincy, as early as 7 B.C.E. "there are records of the Assyrian army having a cadre of military chaplains."[3] The website of the British Royal Army Chaplains points to a tradition of chaplains in the Roman army,[4] whereas a discussion of military chaplains from a "Scottish perspective" offers Celtic priests as forerunners.[5] The U.S. Chaplain Corps traces its heritage "far back into the dim recesses of history," citing examples from Hebrew Scripture/the Old Testament, ancient Egypt, and imperial Rome.[6]

Certainly those interested in origins can find numerous biblical accounts of priests at war. Knowing how to interpret such passages is more difficult. Indeed, Old Testament militarism has been a problem for Christian exegesis from early on. Nevertheless, national chaplaincies invoke various examples of chaplain-like functions. In an early battle against the Amalekites, the Children of Israel triumphed only as long as Moses held up his hands in prayer to God. When Moses grew weary, it was his brother, the high priest Aaron, along with his associate Hur, who stood beside him and supported his arms, thereby securing God's blessing and the subsequent victory.[7] Priests carried the Ark of the Covenant in procession around Jericho and blew their ram's horns, and the city literally fell into Joshua's hands.[8] The warrior Gideon combined in one person the roles of prophet, priest, and general. In the biblical account, he defeated a horde of Midianites with three hundred men armed only with trumpets, empty pitchers, torches, and the battle cry: "For the sword of the Lord and for Gideon."[9]

Pointing to ancient precedents lends legitimacy and prestige to modern military chaplaincies, but it does not always accurately reflect developments in the past. As Ralph Mathisen demonstrates in the first chapter of this book, it is difficult to locate anything more than the faint beginnings of the modern military chaplaincy in the Roman world. In the classical Roman army, generals often presided over rites associated with the state cult which were intended to ensure victory. Those men can hardly be called chaplains in the modern sense because they were not concerned with the spiritual well-being of individual soldiers. Priests of some popular eastern cults did minister to soldiers, but because they had no official position in the army, they cannot be called military chaplains either. Not until the fifth century did Christian clerics accompany some Roman armies and care for their men in ways that anticipate what we see in the photograph of the uniformed German chaplain baptizing a soldier.

In contrast to the ambiguities of antiquity, by the Middle Ages chaplains were an important element in what Michael McCormick calls a "liturgy of war." Not only were medieval chaplains part of an effort to achieve victory, they also represented a promise to warriors that their actions were just and good. For Christianity, these developments constituted a dramatic shift away from the attitudes of the early church, which regarded the exercise of state power and the shedding of blood as consequences of sin. According to Patrick Geary, had such a tradition continued, the church might have approached soldiers like other "tainted" professions, for example, prostitutes, and the role of the clergy would then have been similar: to love the sinner but hate the sin. Instead, in the office of the chaplain, the Carolingian army under Charlemagne produced a "marriage" of pastoral concerns with support and encouragement of warfare.[10]

Around 800 c.e., the word "chaplain," in its Latin form, *capellanus*, first appeared to describe those clerics who carried into battle the relics of the saints, including the soldier's cape (*cappa*) of St. Martin. From the eighth century through the Crusades, men performing the office of chaplains, although not necessarily called by that name, heard confessions, assigned penances, celebrated mass, and provided last rites. As David S. Bachrach shows in his chapter, a change in the idea of penance from the old "once-in-a-lifetime" occasion to a repeatable event was crucial. This development had two significant repercussions. First, it became possible for soldiers to receive absolution and then return to military life; second, repeatable penance made it necessary for soldiers to confess their sins before each battle. In the course of the First Crusade in 1095 and subsequent warfare, in particular against Muslims, the spirituality of combat and the series of rituals in preparation were further elaborated and institutionalized.

Certain aspects of the military chaplaincy—its liturgical and sacramental functions as well as its morale-boosting role—have shown remarkable continuity into the modern world. The cross, prominent in the photo from Kosovo, has been associated with military campaigns and spiritual preparation for combat since the late Roman era and the conversion of Constantine. Indeed, the words "In Hoc Signo Vinces," which, legend has it, Constantine saw in the sky next to a radiant cross, became the official badge of Britain's Royal Army Chaplains in 1930. Later, George V had the motto anglicized: "In This Sign Conquer."[11] Likewise, for more than a thousand years, since the time of the Carolingian army, chaplains have provided Christian sacraments to soldiers. The baptism depicted here follows in that long tradition. Among Germans in the Balkans in the late 1990s, however, the chaplain's task was not to rouse men to battle, but instead to help them cope with the challenges, including at times the tedium, of peacekeeping.

Another turning point in the history of the military chaplaincy in the West was surely the Reformation. The religious upheaval of the sixteenth and seventeenth centuries resulted in two and then more Christian confessions in Europe, along with a welter of smaller groups and sects. In the so-called wars of religion, Christians fought Christians, both sides accompanied by their own men of God.

In her study of the Wars of the Three Kingdoms, Anne Laurence illustrates how the dynamics of the Reformation and its aftermath complicated the situation of English military chaplains. Their work, she shows, varied widely depending on the cause they supported and the nature of the enemy they faced. In the English Civil War, Royalist chaplains emphasized absolute obedience to the king. Parliamentary chaplains, in contrast, insisted that it was right to disobey the monarch. In the war against Ireland, anti-Catholicism played a central role for Cromwell's chaplains, who found it much easier to preach violence against the Irish than against Scottish Presbyterians. Ironically, however, even the Parliamentary chaplains had to uphold authority and combat the spread of heterodoxy, so that their own cause would not be undermined.

The eighteenth and nineteenth centuries were an age of nation building, nationalism, and imperialism in Europe, North America, and wherever European power reached. Chaplains participated fully in these trends, and it is no coincidence that the consolidation of military and national power often brought with it expansion and further regularization of the chaplaincy. For example, in 1796, England's Parliament passed a royal warrant establishing the Royal Army Chaplains' Department, and chaplains accompanied the regiments sent to protect British interests in North America during the wars between France and England, the American Revolution, and the War of 1812.

John A. Lynn has suggested that chaplains may have helped define and enforce standards of behavior at a time when the armed forces were expanding rapidly, and the resources of the state were not always equal to the task. Soldiers, according to Lynn, need feedback and appreciation of their suffering from the outside world in order to persist in combat and maintain morale.[12] Chaplains were intimately related to fighting-men's lives: they gave spiritual counsel and wrote letters home for injured and illiterate men. They may also have helped teach what was right and what was wrong in the military context in ways that, although not necessarily moral, were necessary for morale and discipline. Certainly secular authorities recognized chaplains' utility: beginning in the seventeenth century, the French army provided a chaplain— un aumônier —for each regiment.[13]

In colonial America, chaplains fought alongside and ministered to their neighbors in the militia. Chaplains' relations with Native Americans were mixed at best; they missionized and baptized them, but they also took part in brutal campaigns against them. For example, the Reverend Samuel Stone of the Church of Christ in Hartford, Connecticut, served in the Pequot War of 1637, the first, large-scale conflict with the Indians in New England. According to Increase Mather, when the military leaders of an expedition against the Pequots disagreed on how to attack the tribe, they asked the Reverend Stone for his view. After a night of prayer, Stone informed the commanders it was God's will that they take a particular route. So it was, and the colonists defeated the Pequots in an extremely bloody assault.[14] More research is needed on the role of chaplains in the many wars of colonial and imperialist expansion. In the meantime, however, it seems reasonable to assume that chaplains served those causes loyally and for the most part uncritically.

And yet, as the chapter by Gardiner Shattuck on the American Civil War demonstrates, the work of chaplains could have multiple—and unintentional—impacts. Shattuck's attention to the ill-defined place of chaplains in the Union army, some of whom reported feeling like "fifth wheels," highlights the tensions between preparing men to die and strengthening their resolve to kill. Of course, all the major Christian denominations supported the war, and no one enlisted as a chaplain unless he was prepared to pray for the victory of his armed forces. Nevertheless, readying soldiers for death by focusing attention on the heavenly reward ahead may unintentionally have induced a kind of resignation, even fatalism, that weakened their fighting spirit. Thus, military chaplains occupied an ironic position, where religious faith and military efficiency could both reinforce and undercut each other.

Hartmut Lehmann's discussion of Prussian/German chaplains emphasizes collusion more than tension in the church–military relationship. Lehmann presents a remarkable encounter in 1713 between King Frederick William I and the German pietist August Hermann Francke. To mutual advantage, the two negotiated an arrangement for provision of military chaplains to the Prussian army. The king gained a steady supply of reliable, morale-boosting chaplains, whereas the pietist movement won an eager and often desperately receptive audience among soldiers for its message of salvation and renewal. Over time, however, "nationalistic rhetoric had defeated theological reflection," and by the late nineteenth century, military chaplains all over Europe subscribed to the cause of the nation in ways that often overshadowed Christianity's universal claims.

Somewhat paradoxically, the eighteenth and nineteenth centuries also brought increasing ecumenism and diversity within the chaplaincies. In order to reach out to all soldiers in mass, national armies, military leaders needed chaplains from various backgrounds. Thus, the first Jewish chaplain, Michael Mitchell Allen, began service with the American military in 1861,[15] followed in 1884 by the first African American, Henry V. Plummer. Indeed, of the eight black men the U.S. Army commissioned between the Civil War and the Spanish-American War, five were chaplains.[16]

Again, a glance at our photograph from Kosovo suggests significant continuities as well as changes. In the uniform of the German Bundeswehr, the chaplain is practically indistinguishable from the soldiers around him. A Protestant, he serves alongside Catholic clerics, something unthinkable in seventeenth-century England, possible in the American Revolutionary army, and taken for granted in Germany by the First World War, when even some Jewish clergy found a place in the war effort. Unlike all of those earlier clergymen, however, the German chaplain in Kosovo is linked to an international as well as a national cause.

Arguably, the military chaplaincy in Europe and North America reached its peak of prestige in the first half of the twentieth century, an age of total war. In the debacle of 1914–18, from Russia to Australia, chaplains stood alongside those who fought and died, with the message, "God is on our side."[17] For chaplains and Catholic "soldier priests" in France, the war provided an opportunity to show their patriotic fervor, to redeem the church in the eyes of an anticlerical state and a disenchanted public.[18]

The French case is particularly germane to the issues raised in this collection because it illustrates the tensions surrounding military chaplains in an age of de-Christianization in Europe and North America. France's anticlerical laws in the Third Republic required priests to serve in uniform and on the front lines. As a result, during the First World War they worked vigorously to fulfill both their priestly and their soldierly functions, earning widespread respect from Catholic and non-Catholic *poilus* (doughboys) alike. Arguably, the participation of lay and ordained Catholics in the French army between 1914 and 1918 contributed in substantial ways to the improved stature of Catholicism in France between the two world wars.

The situation in England and the Dominions was rather different. Duff Crerar's study of Canadian "padres" in the First World War notes the heroism of some chaplains who left the relative safety their privilege provided to accompany the men "over the top." At the same time, as Crerar poignantly shows, the horrors of that war did much to discredit chaplains, whom soldiers often associated with the "brass hats" who thoughtlessly and wastefully sent men to their deaths.[19] The interwar period produced a literature of derision and resentment that continues to shape popular views of chaplains.

Elsewhere, chaplains disappeared altogether. Certainly there would be no place for military chaplains in the armies of the Soviet Union, which was created in the wake of military defeat and devastation.[20] Arguably, some of their functions—for example, as morale boosters—were taken over by the Red Army commissars that Trotsky created after 1917.

In contrast, for Fascist Italy and Nazi Germany, Christian chaplains remained part of military efforts. German clergy accompanied the infamous Condor Legion in its deadly missions during the Spanish Civil War.[21] As I demonstrate in chapter 8, despite the open hostility of some political leaders, chaplains also served the Wehrmacht throughout the war of conquest and annihilation that Germany began in 1939. German Protestant and Catholic chaplains witnessed atrocities against civilians and Soviet POWs. Some chaplains saw for themselves and all of them knew about the mass murder of Jews.[22] Military chaplains spent the last hours of life with at least some of the estimated twenty thousand German soldiers killed by their own leadership as deserters.[23] Ultimately, the chaplains' presence served to legitimate brutality and genocide. Perhaps more starkly than any other case, the Wehrmacht chaplains expose the disastrous potential of combining a pastoral mission with absolute, unconditional service to the nation.

Rabbi Max B. Wall's account of his experience as a chaplain stands in marked contrast, in ways that illustrate the total opposition of German and U.S. aims in the Second World War. A devoted Jew and champion of ecumenism, Rabbi Wall was involved, during and after the war, not only in ministering to American soldiers of all religious faiths, but also serving surviving Jews of Europe, even at times in defiance of his military superiors. Here we can see evidence of potential new roles for chaplains, as mediators and agents of healing in a broken world.

In the second half of the twentieth century, some of those possibilities for the chaplaincy began to be institutionalized, although slowly and sporadically. In the countries of the Warsaw Pact, the chaplaincies disappeared altogether, with the exception of Poland, where some clergy retained an affiliation with the armed forces.[24] Creation of a West German military within NATO in 1955 was followed by a new military chaplaincy, but these chaplains were very different from their pre-1945 predecessors. Rather than officers and insiders to the military establishment, they were to be permanent outsiders, not cheerleaders, but critical voices of conscience.[25]

Similar changes have occurred elsewhere. In Israel, recent years have seen emergence of a new office attached to the military—not additional chaplains in a religious sense, but secular counselors, often trained in the social sciences. These people do not provide religious services, pray for victory, or enforce discipline. Instead, their job is to help men and women cope with the emotional and practical stresses of military life.[26]

For the United States chaplaincy, a decisive turning point was the war in Vietnam. According to Anne Loveland, during or shortly after the Vietnam War, U.S. chaplains surrendered the old, familiar, morale-building role and began to pursue a new and quite different goal: as moral advisers to the military. This task includes individual counseling as well as ministry to the military as an institution.[27] Father Joe O'Donnell's account of his experiences illustrates this transformation. In contrast to those who infamously exhorted their men to "kill a Commie for Christ," Father O'Donnell describes his mission in Vietnam as an effort to "be present to others in the midst of the worst possible scenarios." His recollections echo with his own troubled questions about war and his place in it. After the Vietnam War, as executive assistant to the U.S. Navy's chief of chaplains, O'Donnell became involved in making ethical policy.

Many challenges remain for a changing military chaplaincy. Father O'Donnell highlights two in the American context: integrating women and responding to demands for pastoral care from the increasing number of religious groups represented in the military. By 2002, the 874 chaplains of the U.S. Navy included three Muslims, one of whom, Abuhena Saifulislam, was charged with ministering to al-Qaeda and Taliban prisoners brought from the battlefields of Afghanistan to the camp at Guantanomo Bay in Cuba.[28] Much smaller groups are also now included. For example, the chaplains' handbook includes a guide to "Wicca," the "ancient Pagan faith of Europe."[29] It is not always easy to work together and to respect traditions that are unfamiliar or have a history of hostility toward one's own religion.

Technological changes in warfare have brought new demands for chaplains too. The role of the military chaplain was different when preparing men for set-piece battles that may have lasted several days, than when offering spiritual solace in the trenches of the First World War or dealing with floods of refugees and displaced persons as Rabbi Wall did in the Second World War. Development—and use—of weapons of mass destruction in the twentieth century created an urgent need for chaplains who would help inform moral consciences and promote clear ethical guidelines for professional military conduct.[30] Since the Vietnam War, the United States has developed a new style of warfare that tries to limit American casualties to as few as possible. In this setting, chaplains face still other kinds of obligations and responsibilities.

Loveland hints at an additional challenge for modern-day chaplains: achieving the kind of genuine independence necessary to be effective moral advisers, even when that means criticizing publicly the policies of their own governments or commanders in chief. Former NATO chaplain Rabbi Arnold Resnicoff adds yet another goal: realizing a vision of military chaplains as mediators and peacekeepers in the post–Cold War world.[31] The German chaplain pictured in Kosovo embodies something of this potential.

SERVICE AND SACRIFICE

Surveying the history of the military chaplaincy is only part of what this book does. The authors also concern themselves with more immediate questions about military chaplains in specific settings. What do chaplains do? What do those they serve want from them? Addressing these questions, one cannot help but be impressed and moved, in Paul Fussell's words, by the "appallingly difficult job" of military chaplains in increasingly secular societies.[32]

The intensity of wartime and the omnipresence of death haunt the work of the military chaplain. Perhaps a soldier's words are the best introduction to the emotional and spiritual neediness that chaplains confront. During the American Civil War, a fourteen-year-old girl asked her brother, a young Indiana lawyer fighting for the Union, what it felt like to be in battle. His reply conveyed a desperate spirituality:

> There is no man, however brave he may be, who does not when the storm begins to rage fiercest around him; when he sees a

friend on the right and another on the left, stricken down and quivering in the agonies of death; when he sees the serried ranks of his foe coming upon him undaunted and pouring their deadly fire out toward him, making the air quiver and hiss with the rapid movement of all manner of projectiles, from the keen sound of the little bullet that sings on its errand of destruction like the buzzing of a fly, to the bomb shell that goes by you like a thunder bolt, overcoming all obstacles; I say there is no man who when the first waves of such battle as this surge upon him, does not involuntarily and mentally appeal to God for protection.[33]

It may be precisely the chaos and terror of such moments that make the chaplain so important as a symbol that somehow, even in the midst of death and fear, there is meaning. That role of the chaplain—to embody courage, hope, and steadfastness in the face of alienation and destruction—may in turn explain why so many popular accounts of chaplains emphasize an almost superhuman bravery. Under the most extreme circumstances imaginable, people need heroes, and chaplains, because of their association with traditions that extend beyond the immediate horrors, are likely candidates.

All of these tendencies are evident in the story of U.S. Chaplain (Capt.) Emil Kapaun, a hero of the Korean War.[34] A diocesan priest from Wichita, Kansas, Kapaun arrived in Korea in July 1950. Four months later, Chinese forces captured him and a group of soldiers he had refused to abandon, even when he had the opportunity to escape. From the moment of surrender through his own illness and death in May 1951, Father Kapaun proved fearless in his ministry. When an enemy soldier prepared to shoot a wounded GI, Kapaun pushed the man away, pulled his comrade to his feet, and supported him along the hundred-mile trek to a POW camp. During seven months of imprisonment, Father Kapaun encouraged his soldiers, prayed with them, stole food for them, washed their undergarments, and buried them when they died.[35] A fellow POW described the chaplain's message of hope:

Father always spoke in parallels, relating the sufferings that Christ endured to those we were forced to bear. As he spoke, the agony in the garden, the road to Calvary, the Crucifixion, became very real to us who bore our own crosses of blows, and cold, and illness, and starvation. Christ endured, he told us, and we, too, must endure, for the day of our resurrection from the tomb of the prison camp would surely come, as surely as the stone was rolled away from the sepulcher.[36]

The Catholic War Veterans of the United States are seeking sainthood for Chaplain Kapaun.

The qualities stressed in stories of Father Kapaun are evident in accounts of many other chaplains as well. It is as if soldiers' anxieties—about cowardice, failure, and futility—are somehow assuaged by elevating the chaplain as their opposite: courageous, strong, the personification of meaning. Canadian veterans tell an anecdote about a chaplain in the Second World War who was determined to accompany his men through thick and thin. He had to be removed forcibly from a tank in the interests of his own safety.[37] Likewise, stories of the chaplains at Pearl Harbor highlight bravery and selflessness.

In December 1941, the U.S. armed forces had twenty-eight chaplains on Oahu. One was the Catholic priest Lt. Al Schmidt, onboard the USS *Oklahoma*. When torpedoes struck the ship, Father Schmidt helped find an open porthole and get men out. He tried to follow, but the ecclesiastical gear attached to his belt left him stuck halfway through. Realizing there were still men inside, Schmidt had those already out shove him back in, so others could escape. He never made it off the ship. A month later, at a Protestant church service in San Francisco, a Jewish sailor told how he survived Pearl Harbor because a Catholic chaplain pushed him out through a porthole.[38] Another chaplain, Elmer Tiedt, worked straight through December 7–8, ministering to the dead and wounded in the hospital at Hickam Airfield, even after receiving word that his own wife had been killed. Only when he returned home did he discover she was still alive.[39]

The image of a chaplain sacrificing his safety, his family, and even his life to stay with his men is central to U.S. Chaplain (Lt.) Eugen L. Daniel's account of his experiences as a POW in Germany during the Second World War.[40] Similarly, German Protestant chaplain Bernhard Bauerle insisted on remaining in the Soviet Union until the last POW in his unit had been released.[41] Italian director Roberto Rosellini enshrined this heroic view of a chaplain in his 1943 film, *L'uomo della croce* (*Man of the Cross*).

The film's plot bears recounting. In mid-1942, an Italian tank division arrives at the Soviet front. Wounded in an exchange of fire, an Italian soldier is unable to advance with the rest of his division. The chaplain volunteers to stay behind with him, although he realizes they will be captured. The men take refuge in a barn, where Russian peasant women are also hiding. One of the women goes into labor, and the chaplain delivers her baby. He baptizes the child and explains Christianity to the women. Meanwhile, Italian troops take the village, but the chaplain is killed as he tries to save a dying enemy soldier.[42]

Stories of heroism—real and fictional—may themselves help chaplains stand firm by creating and defining a role to play in situations that allow little time for reflection. At the same time, however, such accounts set impossibly high standards of behavior. Both Rabbi Wall and Father O'Donnell recall crushing feelings of inadequacy in the face of the colossal suffering and need around them. "Whatever I did it wasn't enough," says Wall, as he describes his tireless efforts on behalf of Jewish "displaced persons" in Germany. For thirty years, O'Donnell writes, "[I was] sure that in my own life as a priest I had not been faithful." No matter how much effort, "I couldn't stop it; I couldn't keep people from dying."[43]

Military chaplains are in a lonely position; others bring their fears and doubts to them, but to whom can they turn? The daughter of a U.S. chaplain in the Second World War told me that her father, a rabbi, had accompanied U.S. troops as they entered several concentration camps in southern Germany in the spring of 1945. With strength and dignity, he said *kaddish* for the dead, comforted the traumatized soldiers of all faiths in his unit, and arranged for local Germans to view the overwhelming evidence of atrocities committed in their name. After he returned home, however, he could not speak about his experiences, even to his wife, nor could he stop the nightmares that continued to torment him decades later.[44]

Reading the popular literature on chaplains, it is hard to avoid the uncomfortable impression that in order to be considered truly heroic, chaplains have to die. "Live with the men," enjoined the Reverend Studdert Kennedy, a British chaplain in the First World War; "Go everywhere they go. . . . The more Padres die doing Christ-like deeds, the better for the Church."[45] It seems no coincidence that the most highly decorated noncombatant in British history, Chaplain Theodore Hardy, was killed in action in France in October 1918.[46] Likewise, his most famous American counterparts, the "four immortal chaplains" of the Second World War, died, along with almost seven hundred other people, when the USS *Dorchester* went down in the North Atlantic in February 1943. Chaplains George Fox (Methodist), Rabbi Alexander Goode (Jewish), the Reverend Clark Poling (Dutch Reformed), and Father John

Washington (Roman Catholic) were among the first on deck after a German torpedo struck the ship. They calmed the men and distributed life jackets, giving away their own when supplies proved inadequate. Witnesses recall last seeing the chaplains standing arm-in-arm, praying as the ship went down. At the dedication of the Chapel of the Four Chaplains in the Pentagon, President Harry S. Truman quoted from the New Testament: "Greater love hath no man than this, that a man lay down his life for his friends."[47]

LIMINALITY AND LEGITIMACY

A third theme evident throughout this book might be summed up with the phrase "credibility gap." Military chaplains operate in a peculiar sphere between religious and military worlds. As a result, they face suspicion and criticism from all sides. Have chaplains typically served secular instead of spiritual authorities or advanced the cause of victory above the needs of the soldiers in their care? Some chaplains have been lionized, but more find themselves ignored and isolated. Often their proximity to authority—including their officers' rank in most militaries—has made them suspect in the eyes of the common soldiers they serve and forced them to struggle for legitimacy. In many cases the fact that they do not normally engage in combat leaves them open to the charge they are not "real men." All of the following chapters address these issues in various ways.

Perhaps the best way to illustrate this theme is with an example from literature. As Paul Fussell so eloquently shows in his analysis of the "soldier writers" of the First World War, literary texts often bring a kind of "emotional truth" that more literal testifiers cannot provide.[48] Works of imagination can make explicit matters that remain concealed or taboo for those directly involved. It is no surprise that a number of authors and artists introduce military chaplains into their works precisely in ways that emphasize their borderline position and its accompanying perils. *The Good Soldier Švejk*, Jaroslav Hašek's hilarious account of a Czech infantryman in the First World War; Albert Goes's short novel, *Unruhige Nacht* (*Restless Night*); Joseph Heller's *Catch 22*; *M*A*S*H*, the play and television series about the Korean War; and even Mort Walker's comic strip, *Beetle Bailey*, all depict chaplains as helpless and at times pathetic; drunk, despairing, and doubting; caught between military and religious imperatives; and mocked by the soldiers to whom they minister.[49]

One of the most poignant presentations of a military chaplain occurs in Herman Melville's novel, *Billy Budd*, written in 1891. A look at this work reveals some of the issues of credibility linked to the chaplaincy.[50] In the story, Billy Budd is a young man pressed into service on the British man-of-war, HMS *Indomitable*, in 1797, in the struggle against revolutionary France. His innocent goodness and physical beauty arouse the jealousy of John Claggart, the ship's master-at-arms. Claggart falsely accuses Budd of plotting mutiny and denounces him to the captain. Suspicious of Claggart's veracity, Captain Vere summons accused and accuser before him. Claggart repeats his lies, and Budd, unable to respond in words, strikes the master-at-arms a blow to the head that turns out to be fatal. A drumhead court convicts Budd and condemns him to death. He is hanged the next morning at sunrise.

Ineffectiveness and impotence characterize the naval chaplain in Melville's text. Neither present nor mentioned in the crucial scenes as Captain Vere and the members of the drumhead court struggle with their belief in Budd's fundamental innocence and their loyalty to military discipline, the chaplain makes his first appearance alongside death and remains associated with death throughout the novel. He presides over the burial of Claggart and then visits the imprisoned Budd before his execution. Both Budd's natural goodness and his sailor's nature make the chaplain irrelevant to him.[51] It was "in vain," Melville writes, that "the good Chaplain sought to impress the young barbarian with ideas of death akin to those conveyed in the skull, dial, and cross-bones on old tombstones."[52] Budd was wholly without the "irrational fear" of death that Melville links to "highly civilized communities."

Equally futile, in Melville's account, were the chaplain's "efforts to bring home to him the thought of salvation and a Saviour." Billy listened politely, "doubtless at bottom regarding all that in much the same way that most mariners of his class take any discourse abstract or out of the common tone of the work-a-day world." In Melville's words, "It was like a gift placed in the palm of an outreached hand upon which the fingers do not close."[53]

Having offered us a look through Budd's eyes, Melville adds his own assessment of the contradictions inherent in the military chaplaincy:

Marvel not that having been made acquainted with the young
sailor's essential innocence (an irruption of heretic thought hard
to suppress) the worthy man lifted not a finger to avert the
doom of such a martyr to martial discipline. So to do would not
only have been as idle as invoking the desert, but would also
have been an audacious transgression of the bounds of his function, one as exactly prescribed to him by military law as that of
the boatswain or any other naval officer. Bluntly put, a chaplain
is the minister of the Prince of Peace serving in the host of the
God of War—Mars. As such, he is as incongruous as a musket
would be on the altar at Christmas. Why then is he there? Because he indirectly subserves the purpose attested by the cannon; because too he lends the sanction of the religion of the meek
to that which practically is the abrogation of everything but
brute Force.[54]

The chaplain's final appearance underscores Melville's view of his
role. For a moment, some kind of unrest threatens to explode among
the sailors after Budd's execution. It is the return to discipline and routine and the chaplain's palliative rituals that prevent any disruption:
"The band on the quarter-deck played a sacred air. After which the Chaplain went thro' the customary morning service. That done, the drum
beat the retreat, and toned by music and religious rites subserving the
discipline and purpose of war, the men in their wonted orderly manner,
dispersed to the places allotted them when not at the guns."[55]

Paul Fussell, a veteran of the U.S. Army in the Second World War,
has suggested that the modern tendency to assign chaplains officer
rank "sows the seeds of bitterness" and exacerbates a sense among the
troops that their spiritual guides are estranged from their experiences
and needs. For him and his comrades, he said, their "intimate chaplain"
was the medic Juan, a sincere Christian who held informal, but effective, small religious services when things got bad. Fussell's only contact with a "real" chaplain came six weeks before the end of the war in
Europe, when he was wounded by a German shell. At the battalion aid
station, the chaplain, a first lieutenant, considered himself the men's
ethical consultant. According to Fussell, he cheered people up when
they got their morphine by telling them the lie they had done well,
and the battalion was proud of them.[56]

There is some agreement with Fussell's suggestion that one way to
"rescue the whole institution of the chaplaincy" is to give chaplains a

noncommissioned rank. In Australia, for example, there is a campaign to decommission military chaplains.[57] Others, like Patrick Geary, have pointed out that in fact it is mostly the commander on the spot, not the chaplains, who actually deals most directly with pastoral issues, like the question "Why?" on the lips of a young American soldier dying in Vietnam.[58]

In societies where manliness is often equated with soldierly qualities, chaplains face additional hurdles. The Geneva Conventions prohibit chaplains from bearing arms, although there is an old tradition extending far into the past of chaplains in combat. (Indeed, the Franciscan John Capistrano, designated patron saint of military chaplains by Pope John Paul II in 1984, led part of the Christian army at the Battle of Belgrade in 1456.[59]) Thus, chaplains—noncombatants who represent religious traditions that generally condemn killing—are sometimes viewed with contempt as irrelevant or derided as "womanly." It does not help that, according to one Finnish chaplain, in European countries such as Finland, "commitment to the Church, belief in God's existence, and frequent praying as manifestations of religiousness and ecclesiastical interests are at their lowest among men of 25–40 years of age," precisely the group that dominates the armed forces.[60]

Even laudatory accounts of the Korean War hero Chaplain Emil Kapaun raise the issue of manliness, albeit defensively. "The first thing I want to make clear is this," writes 1st Lt. Ray M. (Mike) Dowe, Jr., of Father Kapaun:

> He was a priest of the Church, and a man of great piety, but there was nothing ethereal about him, nothing soft or unctuous or holier than thou. He wore his piety in his heart. Outwardly he was all GI, tough of body, rough of speech sometimes, full of the wry humor of the combat soldier. . . . In a prison whose inmates hated their communist captors with a bone deep hate, he was the most unbending enemy of Communism, and when they tried to brainwash him, he had the guts to tell them to their faces that they lied. He pitied the Reds for their delusions, but he preached no doctrine of turn-the-other-cheek.[61]

A striking analysis of credibility within the chaplaincy appears in a letter I received in April 1991, from Major Emory Earl Toops, U.S. Air Force (retired). According to Major Toops, "the relationship between Man and God and War" was a subject "even military chaplains today are reluctant to take on." In twenty years in the Air Force, he wrote, he had never heard a chaplain address that issue. To do so, he suggested, was impossible within the parameters of the chaplaincy:

> If a chaplain takes the approach that there are just wars (or that every war his country undertakes is a just war) and thus his duty is to provide comfort and sustainment to the soldier in order to make him a soldier better able to carry out his orders, he would probably lose his accreditation from his denomination (and hence, his commission as a chaplain). And, of course, if he takes the pacifist "turn the other cheek" approach, he risks alienating his commander and his promotion recommendation suffers.[62]

The result, Major Toops concluded, was "a chaplain in the military who simply wears a uniform and performs the typical family-oriented ministry: pre-marital counseling, weddings, preaching to the family on Sundays, etc." As for theology, "you usually end up with a lowest common denominator 'General Protestant' service calculated to offend no one." To his recollection, the biggest doctrinal dispute he had seen regarded "when to put out the baby Jesus in the church manger scene—Catholics wait until December 24; Protestants will put Jesus into the manger much earlier." Toops's description of the content of sermons suggests a manipulation of biblical texts one might have expected instead in a description of the First World War:

> The closest I've come to a purely "military theology" was while I was a cadet at The Citadel (1966–70). There, mandatory chapel attendance was a panoply of flags, swords, and company guidons. One of the more memorable sermons was on "Moses and the Seven Principles of Warfare." (It took a lot to keep cadets interested and awake).[63]

DIRTY WARS, JUST WARS

Our fourth theme, connected to the preceding one, focuses on the profound moral and theological dilemmas raised by the chaplaincy. How have chaplains understood their tasks and carried them out, particularly under regimes engaged in wars of atrocity and annihilation? Almost all of the following chapters touch on this painful topic, whether they deal with the zealous cruelty of the Crusades, the viciousness of early modern warfare, modern total war, Nazi genocide, or the Vietnam War and the My Lai massacre. As the letter from Major Toops reminds us, even in less extreme circumstances chaplains face ethical questions regarding the justice of their cause. Were chaplains in the Confederate army who accepted slavery as morally legitimate culpable in the same way as the Wehrmacht chaplains who condoned Hitler's "war of annihilation"? And what do we make of chaplains who served in wars they believed to be defensible or even just but whose "side" since has been judged morally questionable?

A specific example from Latin America in the 1970s serves to illustrate the issues at stake. In the mid-1990s, Eduardo Galeano, a writer from Uruguay, discussed his country's recent emergence from a brutal dictatorship. One of the cases he cited to show how Uruguay's Dirty War had scarred both victims and perpetrators involved an officer at the School of the Navy, where some five thousand people were tortured and murdered.[64] For about two years in the late 1970s, every Wednesday, Captain Adolfo Scilingo boarded a plane that also held fifteen to twenty heavily sedated people who were deemed subversives. Inside the plane, although they were already "like zombies," a doctor gave them a second sedative. Scilingo then undressed them, opened a door, picked each person up, and heaved him or her into the South Atlantic.

Tormented by remorse, Scilingo went to see the chaplain of the School of the Navy. "At least they die a Christian death," the chaplain assured him; they did not suffer. "War is war," he added, and "even the Bible foresees separation of the chaff from the wheat." It was not only soldiers who were responsible for the regime's crimes, Captain Scilingo concluded two decades later, "a lot of people consented to what was happening."[65]

Some chaplains played similar roles in Chile. In his memoirs, former Chilean president Patricio Aylwin describes an unforgettable experience in early October 1973:

My wife and I went to Panimavida [thermal baths] to celebrate our anniversary. We were having dinner one night when we saw two military officers take a table close to ours. They were wearing fatigues and had handguns on their sides. To our surprise, one of them approached us to say hello in very cordial terms. He was a priest, Florencio Infante, a military chaplain. He told us that he had just arrived from Talca, where he had administered last rites to the intendant of that province, who had been shot by a firing squad in the afternoon. He told us this as if it were the most natural thing in the world.[66]

Chaplains also served South Africa's apartheid regime, and the *Truth and Reconciliation Commission of South Africa Report* spends considerable time discussing their influence. The churches participated in the structures of the apartheid state, the report observes, "most notably in the military chaplaincy." Chaplains came from the Afrikaans churches and the (black) Nederduitse Gereformeerde Kerk in Afrika, as well as from the Anglican, Methodist, Presbyterian, Baptist, Apostolic Faith Mission, and Roman Catholic churches. A formal agreement between the state and the churches governed chaplains' appointments.[67]

In his submission, Chaplain General Johan de Witt described the chaplains' service as the "official channel" through which churches ministered to their members in the South African Defence Force (SADF). General Magnus Malan, former defense minister and before that head of the SADF, thanked the churches for their prayers and maintained that he and his colleagues "received from the chaplains the correct guidance."[68]

The commission reached a different conclusion. It found that "Whatever the motivation of the individual chaplains, their participation served to reinforce the acceptance of the apartheid cause in the minds of church members, and often 'justified' the demonisation of the opponents," not only to members of the defense forces, but to their family and friends:[69]

The military chaplaincy gave moral legitimacy to a culture characterized by the perpetration of gross human rights abuses. It served to filter out dissenting voices, to strengthen the resolve to kill and to reassure the doubting soldier that he or she was serving the purposes of God. In spite of professions of a loyalty higher than that of the state, chaplains found themselves lending succour to persons trying to kill "enemy" soldiers who were sometimes members of their own denomination. [70]

At the same time, the *Truth and Reconciliation Report* recognized the dilemma for chaplains who sought to attend to their church members' need for pastoral care and acknowledged a range of views within the chaplaincy. At denominational levels, its authors observed, the chaplaincy was often an "embarrassment—especially to those who claimed to be against apartheid oppression." The South African Council of Churches had proposed an "independent" chaplaincy, with distinctive uniforms and no salary from the state. Some churches threatened to order their clergy not to wear military uniforms, and some also responded by supplying chaplains to the liberation movements. Others, the report noted, "incurred the wrath of their members by withdrawing their chaplains altogether."[71]

All these qualifications notwithstanding, the report's conclusion is sobering:

> In general, however, apart from the intentions of individuals within it, the chaplaincy was a tool in the hands of the military, and thus an important cog in the apartheid machine. The degree of involvement of the chaplaincy in the defence forces is a good illustration of the importance that the apartheid state attached to religion and its power to command allegiance. It illustrates, too, the complexity and interconnectedness of the social, political and cultural web in South Africa.[72]

Military chaplains everywhere are part of a complex, interconnected web of "social, political and cultural"—and military—forces. Perhaps it is unrealistic and unjust to expect them to be prophets of judgment and defiance. Still, a few counter-examples inspire hope that the chaplaincy can be, in Gardiner Shattuck's words, "a sign of contradiction." In 1941, an Italian chaplain protested to the Vatican when he witnessed mass slaughter of Jews in Transnistria by Germans, Romanians, and Ukrainians.[73] That same year, two German chaplains attempted to prevent the murder of some ninety Jewish children in Ukraine.[74] Neither the Italian nor the German clergy succeeded in halting the killing, but their efforts remind us of the potential, even in the most horrific situations, for chaplains to do right.

In his unassuming way, Rabbi Max Wall provides a brilliant example of a chaplain conscious of his ethical responsibilities. Defying military regulations, Rabbi Wall used his position, his energy, and his connections to help create a large and effective aid network in occupied Germany for Jewish survivors of the Shoah. His fellow chaplain, Abraham Klausener, even went AWOL in order to devote all his time to providing humanitarian and spiritual aid to those most in need. The work of these men reminds us that a history as long and complicated as that of the military chaplaincy in the West has multiple dimensions. The chapters that follow present military chaplains in some of their many and varied historical contexts.

NOTES

1. An extremely useful but completely different book that describes the state of the military chaplaincy around the world as of the early 1990s is Martin Bock, *Religion im Militär: Soldatenseelsorge im internationalen Vergleich* (Munich: Olzog Verlag, 1994).

2. Roland Löffler, "Militärseelsorger im Ernstfall, Einsatz von Bundeswehrgeistlichen auf dem Balkan," *Neue Zürcher Zeitung*, international edition (Aug. 25, 2000, no. 197): 8.

3. "The Canadian Forces Chaplain Branch," www.dnd.ca/chapgen/Engraph/history_e.asp?Cat=1.

4. "A Short History of the Department," www.armychaplains.com/shorthistory.htm.

5. "Indeed, when Julius Caesar invaded Angelsey he was met by an army of tribesmen who were led into battle by their religious leaders. Caesar's subsequent massacre of these Celtic Priests whom he saw as providing the backbone of the resistance was meant not just as a show of strength but as a precautionary measure which would rob the people of their spiritual direction and ensure his permanent conquest of the island." David V. F. Kingston, "The Role of the Army Chaplain in Her Majesty's Forces—from a Scottish Perspective," www.armychaplains.com/theological%20papers/Kingston%20The%20Role%20of%.

6. William J. Hourihan, comp., "A Brief History of the United States Chaplain Corps," chap. 1: "Origins of the Chaplaincy," United States Army Chaplain Center and School, Fort Jackson, S.C., 2001, 160.150.55.11/history/brief/chapter_1.htm.

7. Ex 17:8–16; see also Nm 31:6–7, where Moses sends Pinhas, son of the priest Eleasar, with holy items and trumpets into battle against the Midianites.

8. Jos 6:2–16. Also of interest is the passage in Dt 20:2–4, describing how before battle, priests exhorted warriors to courage and reminded them of God's support.

9. Jgs 7:15–22. See also I Sm 14:1–23 and I Sm 15:1–33, where the warrior king Saul consults prophets and priests to communicate God's will to him before engaging the enemy and to ensure that his sacrifices would be pleasing to the Lord.

10. Patrick Geary's comments at "Military Chaplains in Their Contexts," symposium at the University of Notre Dame, Mar. 2000; hereafter materials from those sessions referred to as MCITC. Proceedings recorded on audiotape.

11. See Kingston, "Scottish Perspective."

12. Remarks by John A. Lynn, MCITC.

13. See John A. Lynn, *Giant of the Grand Siècle: The French Army, 1610–1715* (New York, 1997); also Lynn, *Bayonets of the Republic: Motivation and Tactics in the Army of Revolutionary France, 1791–94*, 2d ed. (Boulder, Colo.: Westview Press, 1996).

14. Hourihan, "A Brief History"; see also Alfred A. Cave, *The Pequot War (Native Americans of the Northeast)* (Amherst: University of Massachusetts Press, 1996).

15. Unit Ministry Team, "Chronological History of the Chaplain Corps," www.wood.army.mil/2−101N/Originals/UMT.htm.

16. Hourihan, "A Brief History," chap. 4: "The United States Army Chaplaincy, 1865−1917."

17. See Aleksandr S. Senin, "Russian Army Chaplains during World War I," *Russian Studies in History* 32 (1993): 43−52, and Margaret Hardy, "Priests and Soldiers Too: Military Chaplaincy in the Australian Infantry Forces 1901−1919" (Ph.D. diss., Australian Catholic University, in progress).

18. Remarks of Thomas A. Kselman, MCITC.

19. For a contemporary's assessment of how the "Great War" discredited European intellectuals, including religious leadership in general, see Julien Benda, *The Betrayal of the Intellectuals*, trans. Richard Aldington (Boston: Beacon Press, 1955), chap. 3.

20. In the desperation of the Second World War, however, Soviet authorities did make an exception when they briefly permitted a rabbi to serve as chaplain for Jews in military formations of the Polish Armed Forces, formed on Soviet territory by the Polish government-in-exile. See Leon S. Rozen, *Cry in the Wilderness: A Short History of a Chaplain; Activities and Struggles in Soviet Russia during World War II* (New York and Tel Aviv: Om Publishing, 1966).

21. For a chaplain's account, see Karl Keding, *Feldgeistlicher bei Legion Condor: Spanisches Kriegstagebuch eines evangelischen Legionspfarrers* (Berlin: Ostwerk [1937]).

22. On German chaplains as witnesses to massacres of civilians in Greece, see Mark Mazower, "Militärische Gewalt und nationalsozialistische Werte: Die Wehrmacht in Griechenland 1941 bis 1944," in Hannes Heer and Klaus Naumann, eds., *Vernichtungskrieg: Verbrechen der Wehrmacht, 1941−1944* (Hamburg: Hamburger Edition HIS Verlag, 1995), 157−90. Regarding chaplains' experience with mass murder of Jews in Ukraine, see Bernd Boll and Hans Safrian, "Auf dem Weg nach Stalingrad: Die 6. Armee 1941/42," in Heer and Naumann, *Vernichtungskrieg*, 260−96.

23. See Jürgen Thomas, "'Nur das ist für die Truppe Recht, was ihr nützt ...': Die Wehrmachtjustiz im Zweiten Weltkrieg," in Norbert Haase and Gerhard Paul, eds., *Die anderen Soldaten: Wehrkraftzersetzung, Gehorsamsverweigerung und Fahnenflucht im Zweiten Weltkrieg* (Frankfurt am Main: Fischer Taschenbuch, 1995), 48.

24. See remarks regarding a Polish Protestant chaplain after 1945 in Janusz Mallek, "Evang.-Augsburgische Kirche nach dem II. Weltkrieg," paper read at a meeting of the Kirchliche Zeitgeschichte-Herausgeberkonferenz, Ustrón, Poland, Sept. 2001.

25. This new concept of the chaplaincy sparked controversy in West Germany, where some church people deemed it a betrayal of a proud tradition. Arrangements for military chaplains also deepened the divide between West and East. At the time it signed the 1957 agreement with the Bundeswehr, the Protestant Church in Germany (EKD) included Germans on both sides of the Cold War divide. East Germany's ruling Socialist Unity Party, however, considered it unacceptable for its citizens to belong to a church that furnished chaplains to the enemy, and increasingly cut East German Protestants off from the church in the West. See Joachim Heise, "Kirchenpolitik von SED und Staat," in Günther Heydemann and Lothar Kettenacker, eds., *Kirchen in der Diktatur: Drittes Reich und SED-Staat* (Göttingen: Vandenhoeck & Ruprecht, 1986), 130.

26. My thanks to Moshe Zuckermann, himself a former sociological counselor to the Israeli Defense Force, for this insight.

27. See "Chaplains try to ease pain of tragedies. February training session focuses on building counseling skills," in U.S. Army Europe News Release (Feb. 13, 2001), www.hqusareur.army.mil/htmlinks/Press_Releases/2001/February/20010214-4.htm.

28. Thomas Fields-Meyer and Don Sider, "Keeper of the Peace: Navy Chaplain Abuhena Saifulislam Tends to a Challenging Flock: Taliban Prisoners," *People* (Apr. 22, 2002): 127–28.

29. "The U.S. Army Chaplains Guide to Wicca," extract from *Religious Requirements and Practices of Certain Selected Groups: a Handbook for Chaplains*, 3 pp., U.S. Government Publication no.008-020-00745-5, www.npsnet.com/cliffe/milwicca.htm (2000).

30. On this point, see Jonathan C. Gibbs III, "The Responsibilities of an Army Chaplain," *New Horizons* (June 2000).

31. Rabbi Resnicoff correspondence with author, 2000.

32. Fussell, comments, MCITC.

33. Quoted by Mike Wilson, "Author collects war letters in book," *Red Deer Advocate*, Red Deer, Alberta, Canada, May 18, 2001, B3, from Andrew Carroll, ed., *War Letters: Extraordinary Correspondence from American Wars* (New York: Washington Square Press, 2002).

34. See William L. Maher, *A Shepherd in Combat Boots: Chaplain Emil Kapaun of the 1st Cavalry Division* (Shippensburg, Pa.: Burd Street Press, 1997).

35. See Christopher M. Riggs, "Fr. Kapaun, an Example of Love in a Prison of Hate," reprinted from *Catholic Advance, Diocesan Newspaper of the Diocese of Wichita*, www.cwv.org/kapaun1/kapaun/html, Aug. 18, 2001; also Arthur Tonne, *The Story of Chaplain Kapaun, Patriot Priest of the Korean Conflict* (Emporia, Kans.: Didde Printing, 1954).

36. Excerpt from a pamphlet written by 1st Lt. Ray M. (Mike) Dowe, Jr., in Catholic War Veterans, "Catholic War Veterans Support Efforts to Obtain Sainthood for Martyred U.S. Army Chaplain Father Emil J. Kapaun," 2001, www.cwv.org/kapaun/kapaun.htm.

37. Ruth Holt, conversation with author in Surrey, B.C., Canada, June 2001.

38. "What the Pearl Harbor Chaplains Were Doing at Pearl Harbor on December 7th 1941," transcript of an address given by Captain Dave Chambers, CHC, USN (Ret.), Dec. 1991, to the National Conference on Ministry to the Armed Forces, www.bluejacket.com/pearl_harbor_address.htm.

39. Ibid.

40. Eugene L. Daniel, *In the Presence of Mine Enemies: An American Chaplain in WW II German Prison Camps* (Attleboro, Mass.: Colonial Lithograph, 1985).

41. On Bauerle, see *Nachlass* (personal papers of) Bernhard Bauerle, in Landeskirchliches Museum Ludwigsburg, Germany (regional church museum). My thanks to Andrea Kittel and Eberhard Gutekunst for granting access to these materials. See also *Mit Gott für Volk und Vaterland: Die Württembergische Landeskirche zwischen Krieg und Frieden, 1903–1957* (Stuttgart: Haus der Geschichte Baden-Württemberg and Landeskirchliches Museum Ludwigsburg, 1995).

42. *L'uomo della croce* (*Man of the Cross*, 1943), ccat.sas.upenn.edu(italians/Amiciprize/1996/uomo.html.

43. Quoted in Andrew S. Hughes, "For God and Country: Military Chaplains Fulfill Traditional Duties even as Military Changes," *South Bend Tribune*, June 1, 2000, C1–2.

44. Conversation with author, Mt. Holyoke, Mass., 1994. For an account by a Protestant chaplain, who recalls working with a Jewish colleague in similar circumstances, see Leslie A. Thompson, "97th Infantry Division: A Personal Memory of Flossenburg," Jan. 14, 1989, www.plaisted.org / brothers / Flossenburg.html. For background, see Robert H. Abzug, *Inside the Vicious Heart: Americans and the Liberation of Nazi Concentration Camps* (New York: Oxford University Press, 1985).

45. Quoted in Royal Army Chaplains Department, "The Work of an Army Chaplain," 1999, www.armychaplains.com / chaplainwork.htm.

46. See Royal Army Chaplains Department, "A Short History of the Department," 1999, www.armychaplains.com / shorthistory.htm.

47. See the Immortal Chaplains Foundation, "The Story of the Immortal Chaplains," www.immortalchaplains.org / History / history.htm. Truman quoted in "Remarks, The Honorable Louis Caldera, Secretary of the Army, Chapel of the Four Chaplains, Legion of Honor Gold Medallion Award, Philadelphia, PA, February 1, 2000," www. hqda.army.mil / secarmy / speeches / chaplain.htm. The verse is found in Jn 15:13. On the commemorative stamp, see "Four Chaplains Stamp—The story of the original first design by Louis Schwimmer," www.schwimmer.com / fourchaplains /.

48. See esp. Paul Fussell, *The Great War and Modern Memory* (London: Oxford University Press, 1975).

49. Albert Goes, *Unruhige Nacht* (1950; Stuttgart, Philipp Reclam, 1988). Goes tells of a German Protestant chaplain assigned to accompany a soldier the night before his execution. See also Jaroslav Hašek, *The Good Soldier Švejk*, trans. Cecil Parrott (London: Penguin, 1973); Joseph Heller, *Catch 22* (New York: Simon and Schuster, 1961); *M*A*S*H*, TV series available on DVD; and Mort Walker, for example, *50 Years of Beetle Bailey* (New York: NBM Publishing, 2000).

50. Melville, *Billy Budd, Sailor* (Chicago: University of Chicago Press, 1962).

51. Ibid., chap. 25, pp. 122–24.

52. Ibid.

53. Ibid.

54. Ibid., chap. 25, p. 124.

55. Ibid., chap. 28, p. 129.

56. Fussell, comments, MCITC. On his wartime experiences in general, see Paul Fussell, *Doing Battle: The Making of a Skeptic* (Boston: Little, Brown, and Co., 1996).

57. Comments by Margaret Hardy, MCITC.

58. Comments by Geary, MCITC.

59. See Hourihan, "A Brief History," chap. 1.

60. Findings of Senior Chaplain Seppo Kangas, in Jarmo Koskela, "Army Chaplain Building Trust," Universitas Helsingiensis, www.helsinki.fi / lehdet / uh / 499d_l.html.

61. Dowe, "Efforts to Obtain Sainthood."

62. Emory E. (Earl) Toops to author, Monticello, Ill., Apr. 2, 1991; letter in possession of the author.

63. Ibid.

64. "Galeano," on CBC "Sunday morning," story by Bob Carty, Apr. 1996, CBC audiotape.

65. Ibid.

66. Patricio Aylwin Azócar, *El reencuentro de los democratas: del golpe al trifuno del no* (Santiago, Chile: Ediciones B Chile, 1998), 41. Thanks to Ivan Jaksic for translating this passage and bringing it to my attention.

67. "Institutional Hearing: The Faith Community," *Truth and Reconciliation Commission of South Africa Report*, vol. 4, chap. 3, p. 67, par. 34.

68. Ibid., p. 70, par. 48.

69. Ibid., p. 67, par. 35.

70. Ibid., p. 71, par. 52; see also p. 91, par. 120.

71. Ibid., p. 71, par. 51; see also p. 85, par. 100.

72. Ibid., p. 72, par. 57.

73. My thanks to Kevin Madigan for bringing this information to my attention. See the description of the role of Italian priest and chaplain Pirro Scavizzi, in Madigan, "What the Vatican Knew about the Holocaust, and When," *Commentary* 112, no. 3 (Oct. 2001): 46.

74. See Boll and Safrian, "Auf dem Weg nach Stalingrad," in Heer and Naumann, *Vernichtungskrieg*, 275–77; also Doris L. Bergen, "Witnesses to Atrocity: German Military Chaplains and the Crimes of the Third Reich," in Omer Bartov and Phyllis Mack, eds., *In God's Name: Religion and Genocide in the Twentieth Century* (New York: Berghahn Books, 2000), 123–38.

CHAPTER ONE

Emperors, Priests, and Bishops

Military Chaplains in the Roman Empire

RALPH W. MATHISEN

A discussion of military chaplains in the Roman imperial period, that is, from approximately 27 BC to AD 500, is fraught with difficulties, not the least of which is that the word *chaplain* itself, in its Latin form *capellanus*, is not first attested until approximately AD 800.[1] This consideration, however, provides the freedom to speculate on what the equivalent of a military chaplain in the Roman world might have been. *Webster's New Universal Unabridged Dictionary* describes a military chaplain as "a minister, priest, or rabbi serving in a religious capacity with the armed forces,"[2] so one might ask whether priests ever served with Roman armies and, if so, whether they discharged the same kinds of functions, such as tending to the spiritual needs of the troops on an individual basis, that one has come to associate with military chaplains in the modern day.

There is no doubt that soldiers in the imperial Roman army took religion seriously. It was all around them, in their personal lives and in the life of their unit.[3] Just as the Roman emperor was the commander in chief of the Roman army, he was also the head of the Roman state religion: there was no separation of church and state in the Roman Empire.[4] As *pontifex maximus*, or chief priest, the emperor had supreme responsibility for maintaining the *pax deorum* (peace of the gods) and ensuring that the gods who oversaw the welfare of the state continued to do so. This was particularly important with regard to the army, which was the most significant institution of the Roman state.

The religious life of the military was institutionalized in several ways. Every camp had a shrine for standards, called the *aedes signorum*, which was located in the headquarters area, or *principia*.[5] The shrine was attended by an honor guard and contained the "eagle" (if it was a legion), other standards, and images of the emperor or emperors. Legionary commanders, military units, and individual soldiers made multitudes of dedications, often in the form of stone inscriptions, on behalf of various kinds of deities: generalized military gods known as the *dii militares* ("military gods")[6]; gods such as Jupiter Optimus Maximus ("Jupiter the Best and Greatest," the primary Roman state god), Mars, and Victoria (the personification of "victory"); and of the divine element, *genius*, of the emperor.[7] Garrison forts also had altars dedicated to such deities along the edge of parade grounds.[8] Such dedications, however, were made on an individual basis without priestly intermediaries, so no chaplains can be found here.

Religious ceremonies involving aspects of the state cult, such as the taking of the auspices (usually by inspecting the entrails of sacrificial animals, such as sheep),[9] were intended to reassure the troops about the continuing goodwill of the gods, and did involve priests of one sort or another. Some were overseen either by the emperor himself, or by his subordinate commanders in the field.[10] For example, a scene on Trajan's Column in Rome, from the early second century, shows a sacrifice known as the *suovetaurilia*, or the "pig, sheep, and bull sacrifice." It depicts a procession with the animals going around the fort toward an altar, where a veiled priest, perhaps the unit commander or even the emperor, stands with horn players. *Victimarii*, who do the actual slaughtering, stand in the rear with axes.[11]

A number of military personnel had religious responsibilities. These included the aforementioned *victimarius* and the *turarius* (incense-keeper),[12] both relatively modest positions and ones hardly sufficient to occupy their holders full-time. In addition, the *aedituus legionis* (a "sacristan," or sexton), and the *aquilifer, signifer,* and *imaginifer* (various kinds of standard-bearers) all oversaw the shrine of the standards,[13] and the *haruspex* inspected sacrificial livers.[14] None of these individuals, however, was called a "priest" or could qualify as a "chaplain."[15] Indeed, it has been argued that the "army needed no special priests for its corporate worship" other than the commander himself.[16]

Sacrificial Procession from Trajan's Column, in Graham Webster, *The Roman Imperial Army of the First and Second Centuries A.D.* (London: Adam and Charles Black, 1969). Copyright ©. Used with permission.

This simple conclusion is belied, however, by evidence, slender but undeniable, for priests-qua-priests who functioned within the context of Roman army units. A unique early instance is T. Aelius Malcus, a member of the Praetorian Guard in Rome, perhaps in the second century AD. He also served as *antistes sacerdos* (priest) of "the temple of Mars in the camp of the praetorians."[17] But the favored status of the praetorians, not to mention the lack of similar examples, suggests that this may have been an exceptional case.[18] Nor is it clear just what was Malcus's actual function; one recent writer suggests he was merely a custodian.[19] It was not until the third century that military priests who participated in the religious life of the unit began to emerge. Around 235, in Syria, a cohort's *aedituus* (sacristan) is later attested as a *sacerdos* (priest).[20] Along with the tribune (the commanding general), the rest of the cohort, and a civilian priest, he participated in a sacrifice to gods of the city of Palmyra.[21] In this instance, however, it should be noted that the religious function involved a local cult practice, not the traditional Roman state cult, which presumably remained under the jurisdiction of the unit commander; the army priest was merely a participant, not the officiator.

A similar case is found in AD 241, when Aurelius Mucianus, described as a *sacerdos* (priest) and *miles* (soldier) of the tenth praetorian

Relief of Marcus Aurelius sacrificing in front of the temple of Jupiter Capitolinus. From the Photographic Archive of the Musei Capitolini, Rome. Used with permission.

cohort stationed at Sindrina in Bulgaria, participated in the paying off of a vow "with the citizens and fellow soldiers,"[22] which would have involved making a sacrifice. In this case, too, a military priest participated in a local ceremony, perhaps as part of the long Roman military tradition of placating local gods. Military priests are mentioned again in an Egyptian dedication, "for the safety of the legion," of 323, which, along with the unit commander, cites an "archpriest" and three "priests of the legion."[23]

In the face of the tremendous amount of material that survives regarding the kinds of positions and functions that existed in the Roman army, the sparseness of the evidence for "unit priests" suggests that they were not common in the imperial army. The most that can be said, it seems, is that soldiers acting in the capacity of priests occasionally represented military units in religious ceremonies of a local nature, just as the unit commander represented the unit in ceremonies involving the state cult. None of these kinds of ceremonies would have been tailored to meet the personal spiritual needs of individual soldiers; it is difficult, therefore, to find modern-type "chaplains" either in these ad hoc legionary priests or in the unit commander in his role of cult officiator. Nevertheless, the existence of legionary priests does seem to demonstrate an increasing role of participatory religion among Roman soldiers as of the third century.

Nor, moreover, are these the only kinds of priests who functioned in the context of Roman army units. A number of nonstate cults, especially eastern ones, gained popularity within the ranks of the army and, although they were never accepted into the official calendar of military religious celebrations,[24] they existed side by side with the traditional state and local cults. The most striking example is the cult of Jupiter *Dolichenus*, who was portrayed standing on a bull and brandishing an axe and was often unofficially assimilated to Jupiter Optimus Maximus.[25] This cult became particularly popular in the army beginning in the mid-second century. Wherever a group of soldiers worshipped, they needed a priest to carry out ritual functions.[26] It is unclear, however, whether a civilian priest had to be engaged or whether army regulations permitted a soldier to serve in this capacity. An inscription from a Dolichenum (as the places of worship were called) in Dacia notes that Flavius Barhadadi, "priest of Jupiter Dolichenus," made a dedication for the good health of the "Roman Empire and the legion Thirteen Gemina."[27] Barhadadi's status is unclear. His name would indicate that he was of eastern origin, and perhaps not even a Roman citizen. He may have been a civilian priest from the "old country" who had been engaged to serve as the unit's priest.

Circa 200, Marcus Ulpius Chresimus, a Parthian by birth but also a Roman citizen, described himself as "priest of Jupiter Dolichenus" in dedications made on behalf of "the good health of the emperor and of the *equites singulares Augusti*" (part of the imperial bodyguard).[28] Around 250, Arcias Marinus, "priest of Dolichenus," made an offering at Remagen on behalf of an army cohort.[29] A potentially more direct connection to the army is provided by a fragmentary inscription from Carnuntum, near Vienna, of ca. 235. It seems to indicate that Ulpius Amandianus, a soldier of the Thirteenth Legion, was a candidate for the priesthood of Jupiter Dolichenus.[30] In addition, an army veteran, Aelius Valentinus, is attested as a *sacerdos* of a Dacian temple of Dolichenus.[31]

Jupiter Dolchinius (Jupiter Dolichenus), a third-century stela from Wiesbaden. Copyright by Les Editions Nagel & Briquet, Geneva (Switzerland). All rights reserved in all countries. Used with permission.

Even though none of these individuals is irrefutably described as being a priest while on active duty, the pattern that emerges is of members of military units being permitted to engage in personal cult practices that included the use of priests who, one must conclude, in some way satisfied the spiritual needs of the soldiers.[32] Unfortunately, however, absolutely nothing is known of cult practices or liturgy, so one cannot say to what degree, if any, these priests might also have fulfilled the functions of "chaplains."

Aside from Christianity, which will be discussed later, the cult best attested as meeting personal spiritual needs in the Roman world as of

Mithras' killing of the bull, "Mitrasrelief" (AS I 624). Kunsthistorisches Museum, Vienna (Austria). Used with permission.

the third century was that of the Persian sun god, Mithras.[33] It offered not only a moral code, but also a baptismal initiation and a life after death, and devotees met in the contemporary equivalent of churches for communal meals. Mithraism was well suited for soldiers, having grades of membership like army ranks, training periods, and initiation rites, and it developed a large following in the army.[34] Priests played important roles as custodians of Mithraic temples and performers of the sacraments and liturgy, although there is no certain evidence that soldiers also served as priests.[35] One might speculate that Mithraic priests performed some chaplain-like functions; however, there is no indication what these might have been, with the caveat that they do not seem to have been part of the regular military command structure. The preceding discussion indicates that there was a pre-Christian tradition of priests of various sorts associated with army units. The practice appears, moreover, to have been manifested in a rather ad hoc manner, based upon local circumstances and the personal religious predilections of particular groups of soldiers. In addition, there is only very sparse evidence for such priests being soldiers on active duty.

When one is looking at the Christian Roman army of the fourth century and later, and asking whether Christian clergy appear ministering to the spiritual needs of Roman army units, the story, at first, changes little. The most often-cited source for Christian clerics being assigned to Roman army units comes from Eusebius of Caesarea, who in the early fourth century reported in his *Life of the Emperor Constantine:* "When he engaged in a war, he caused a tent to be borne before him, constructed in the shape of a church, so that in case he or his army might be led into the desert, they might have a sacred edifice in which to praise and worship God, and participate in the mysteries. Priests and deacons followed the tent, who fulfilled the orders about these matters, according to the law of the church."[36] This report suggests that the traveling chapel served a very practical purpose: to provide a place for worship "in the desert," that is, where there were no other churches available.

Eusebius's account, however, is unique; there is no other evidence for Christian clergy accompanying Roman armies from the fourth or even the early fifth century.[37] A. H. M. Jones, the only modern writer to have written on the topic of Christian chaplains in the Roman army—and only two pages[38]—doubts, however, that the practice of Christian clerics accompanying the Roman army was very widespread. Indeed, there is negative evidence, as in the *Life of St. Martin of Tours*, that army units did not have Christian priests: when Martin served in the army during the 350s, his religious activities were carried out in a solitary fashion, and there is no mention of the presence of any clerics.[39]

Beginning in the middle of the fifth century, however, one finds additional reports of Christian clerics being attached to military units. The mid-fifth-century ecclesiastical historian Sozomen, for example, provides a report about Constantine: "From him the units of the Romans, which now are called 'arithmoi,' each have their own chapel (*skēnē*) provided and priests (*hiereas*) and deacons named."[40] Only a few specific examples of this supposedly widespread practice, however, can be found.

From the same period comes a letter of bishop Theoderet of Cyrrhus (393–ca. 460), who recommended the bearer to the bishop of Ancyra, Eusebius, and noted, ". . . those deemed worthy of the priesthood direct not only provinces, cities, villages, estates and farms, but the regiments of soldiers stationed in cities and villages themselves also have consecrated shepherds. . . . Among these is the discreet deacon Agapetus, who claims as his city the metropolis of our province, and has been appointed to guide a military regiment (*tagma*) in things divine."[41] Also, in approximately 460, St. Saba encountered at Alexandria a unit of the Roman army, the "Isaurian regiment" (*numerus Isaurorum*), into which his father, John, had been conscripted when Saba was five. John, now going under the name of Conon, had risen to command the unit, and proposed that Saba "join up and become priest of the unit."[42] Saba, however, declined the invitation. And a century later, Pope Pelagius (555–60) wrote to Laurentius, bishop of Centumcellae in Italy, that the soldiers stationed there had petitioned the emperor to have a priest, a deacon, and subdeacon appointed for them.[43] This suggests that it was possible for army units to have not merely a single cleric, but a veritable band of them assigned to tend to their spiritual needs.[44]

There certainly is evidence, therefore, for the appointment of Christian priests to Roman army units as of the mid-fifth century. But, as in the case of their Principate forbears, it appears to have been done on something of an ad hoc basis. The father of St. Saba may have seen the appointment of a unit priest merely as a means of keeping his son around, and the soldiers of Centumcellae had to make a special plea to the emperor to have clerics assigned. Nor is there any reference in official records, whether in the law codes or in the *Notitia dignitatum* (the official "list of offices") of the late Roman Empire, to military priests, even though a multitude of other kinds of military offices are attested. This would suggest that army units were permitted to have their own Christian priests, just as in earlier days they had been allowed their priests of Jupiter Dolichenus or Mithras, but that such priests were not a part of the regular military hierarchy or structure. Nor did these clerics fit the mold of those who had accompanied Constantine on campaign; rather, they ministered to army units on garrison duty, who may (although this is not specifically stated) have built their own freestanding chapels or churches, and needed clerics to oversee them.

But the Romans were not the only ones in the Roman world who had armies. Barbarian soldiers who professed the Arian form of Christianity also had spiritual needs, and additional insight can be gained by looking at them.[45] Like the Romans, non-Romans made the transition from pagan to Christian practices.[46] Indeed, the earliest specific examples of Christian clerics being attached to army units come not from the Roman legions, but from barbarian units that were attached to the Roman army. For example, in 382, Ambrose of Milan reported thus to the emperor about the activities of the Arian bishop Julianus Valens, who was said to have been made bishop of Poetovio (Pettau) in Pannonia Superior after betraying his city to the Goths: "Profaned by Gothic impiety, clothed in the manner of the barbarians in a torque and armband, [he] dared to go forth in the sight of the Roman army. This, doubtless, is sacrilege not only in a bishop, but even in any Christian; indeed, he recoiled from Roman practice—unless by chance the idolatrous clerics of the Goths (*sacerdotes Gothorum*) are accustomed to go forth thus."[47] Given his close affiliation with them, Valens must have been performing his episcopal duties on behalf of the band of Goths in imperial service that he was accompanying, perhaps as a kind of religious counselor or senior chaplain.

Another example of a bishop accompanying a barbarian army is found in North Africa, where Count Sigisvult was sent in 427 to take charge of the war against the rebel Count Bonifice.[48] He and his Gothic troops were accompanied by the Arian bishop Maximinus, whom he sent on a mission to Hippo Regius in an attempt to effect a reconciliation between Boniface and the imperial government.[49]

At the same time, armies of freelancing barbarians also had Christian clerics. According to Eunapius, when the Visigoths crossed the Danube in 376, they brought with them several religious: "They all claimed to be Christians and some of their number they disguised as their bishops. . . . They also had with them some . . . so-called monks, whom they had decked out in imitation of the monks among their enemies . . . it sufficed for them to trail long grey cloaks and tunics. . . . The barbarians used these devices to deceive the Romans."[50] This conventional disparagement of Gothic motives is belied by other reports of Gothic armies being accompanied by clerics.

In the early fifth century, for example, one discovers the Arian bishop Sigesarius exercising clearly pastoral duties while ministering to the needs of the army of Alaric the Goth. In 409–10, he baptized the puppet emperor Priscus Attalus as an Arian,[51] and in 415 he unsuccessfully attempted to keep the murdered king Athaulf's children from falling victim to the sword of King Sigeric.[52] At some time thereafter, too, according to Gregory of Tours, a Visigothic army, accompanied by their "heretical clerics" (*cum hereticorum sacerdotibus*), arrived at Rions, in the Gironde in Gaul. They occupied a Nicene church and used it for their Easter services.[53]

Arian clerics would have accompanied barbarian armies for a very pragmatic reason: in the course of their travels, they were not likely to encounter any Arian churches where their spiritual needs could be met. In contrast, Nicene troops, by the fifth century, certainly could anticipate finding churches and clergy virtually wherever they were on the road. This may be why there are no specific examples of Christian clerics accompanying Nicene armies on the march.

To conclude, the evidence for priests serving with Roman armies is sparse and sporadic at best. The occasional pagan priest is found, but their use does not seem to have been a regularly established practice. In the late Roman period, Christian clerics occasionally are found attached to stationary Roman army units, but here, again, it seems to have occurred only on an ad hoc basis, and not as part of the regular army command structure. Barbarian army units seem to have made more regular use of Christian clerics, probably as a result of practical necessity. In both cases, Christian clerics serving with army units presumably carried out the same functions as priests in civilian life, and therefore would certainly seem to qualify as "chaplains." And in them one can see at least a faint foreshadowing of modern military chaplains.

NOTES

1. See Ronald E. Latham, *Revised Medieval Latin Word-List from British and Irish Sources* (London: Published for the British Academy by Oxford University Press, 1965), 68.

2. *Webster's New Universal Unabridged Dictionary*, 2d ed. (Cleveland, 1983), 303.

3. A good general account of the classical Roman army is Graham Webster, *The Roman Imperial Army of the First and Second Centuries AD*, 3d ed. (Totowa, N.J.: Barnes and Noble Books, 1985); for religion, see Alfred von Domaszewski, *Die Religion des römischen Heeres* (Berlin, 1895; New York: Arno Press, 1975). See also George R. Watson, *The Roman Soldier* (London: Thames and Hudson, 1969); Henry M.D. Parker, *The Roman Legions* (Oxford: Clarendon Press, 1928); Michael Grant, *The Army of the Caesars* (New York: Scribner, 1974); Adrian K. Goldsworthy, *The Roman Army at War: 100 BC–AD 200* (Oxford: Clarendon Press, 1996); and L. J. F. Keppie, *The Making of the Roman Army: From Republic to Empire* (Totowa, N.J.: Barnes and Noble Books, 1984).

4. See Michael P. Speidel, *The Religion of Iuppiter Dolichenus in the Roman Army* (Leiden: Brill, 1978), 44.

5. See Watson, *Roman Soldier*, 277, and Domaszewski, *Religion*, 111. For the shrine, see Tertullian, *Apologia* 16: "religio Romanorum tota castrensis signa veneratur, signa iurat, signa omnibus deis praeponit."

6. Domaszewski, *Religion*, 1–3; for examples, note *Corpus inscriptionum Latinarum* (CIL) 3.3472 (from Aquincum, AD 212–22), 3.3473 (from Aquincum), and 3.7591 (from Novae): "Dis militaribus Genio Virtuti aquilae sanctae signisque legionis I Italicae Severianae M. Aurelius Iustus . . . primus pilus dono dedit . . ."

7. Domaszewski, *Religion*, 4, 22 ff.; Webster, *Roman Imperial Army*, 275.

8. Watson, *Roman Soldier*, 277–78; they were buried to prevent desecration when a camp was abandoned.

9. Watson, *Roman Soldier*, 193; Webster, *Roman Imperial Army*, 275. In Tacitus, *Annals* 1.62, Germanicus, as augur, laid the first sod of the funeral mound for those slain at the Battle of the Teutoberg Forest in AD 9.

10. A third-century painting from Dura-Europus shows a sacrifice being overseen by Julius Terentius, tribune of the Cohors XX Palmyrenorum ("Twentieth cohort, of Palmyrenes"): Franz Cumont, *Fouilles de Doura-Europos (1922–1923), Texte, Atlas* (Paris: P. Geuthner, 1926) 49–50.

11. Watson, *Roman Soldier*, 120; Speidel, *Dolichenus*, 46. The *victimarii* are included in a list of army specialists who have immunity from "heavy duties": *Digest* 50.6.7 (citing the jurist Tarruntenus Paternus), "Quibusdam aliquam vacationem munerum graviorum condicio tribuit, ut sunt mensores, optio valetudinarii, medici, capsarii . . . in eodem numero haberi solent lani (butchers), venatores, victimarii, optio fabricae . . ." One notes that there is no entry for priests. See also, e.g., CIL 6.31149; Watson, *Roman Soldier*, 76, 181–82, and Speidel, *Dolichenus*, 44.

12. E.g., CIL 6.3236, 31164, 31150; also Speidel, *Dolichenus*, 75, and Robert O. Fink, A. D. Hoey, and W. F. Snyder, eds., "The Feriale Duranum," *Yale Classical Studies* 7 (1940): 1–222, no. 1007.

13. E.g., CIL 3.5822 = *Inscriptiones Latinae selectae* (ILS) 2526, of the second or third century from Augusta Vindelicorum, "Dis manibus Victorini Longini equitis alae II Flaviae singularis, Claudius Latinus, aedituus singularium, heres faciendum curavit." For the *aedituus* as "sacristan of the legion," see Speidel, *Dolichenus*, 51–52. Note also Pap. Dura 82 = Fink et al., "Feriale Duranum," 47, where the *aedituus* is among those who stand guard at the standards (*excubant ad signa*). For the standard-bearers, see Domaszewski, *Religion*, 10–13.

14. See Domaszewski, *Religion*, 111, no. 173 = CIL 8.2586, from Lambaesis in Africa ca. 200: "qui imagines sacras aureas fecerunt cornicularii (2 men), comment(arienses) (2), speculatores (4), beneficiarii co(n)s(ularis) (30), quaestionarii (5), benef(iciarii) t(ribuni) sexm(estris) (5), haruspex (1), cura agente C Memmio Victore (centurione) leg(ionis) III Au(gustae)." It is unclear, however, how extensive this practice was, although the use of haruspices is still attested in 439, when the Roman general Litorius supposedly "trusted the responses of the haruspices and the monitions of the demons" (dumque haruspicum responsis et daemonum significationibus fidet) (*Monumenta Germaniae historica, Auctores antiquissimi* 11.23).

15. Watson, *Roman Soldier*, 120, notes, "But their duties were not like those of our service chaplains, to help soldiers with personal problems, but to officiate at the sacrifices and other ceremonies."

16. Speidel, *Dolichenus*, 44.

17. Speidel, *Dolichenus*, no. 87, p. 47 = CIL 6.2256: "T. Aelio Malco tectori equiti praetorian(o) coh(ortis) III pr(aetoriae) qui et urb(anicianus) item antistes sacerdos templi Martis castror(um) pr(aetoriorum)." Here, the role of *sacerdos* was just one more position to be included in a résumé.

18. As the only large body of troops stationed in Italy, and often attendant upon the emperor, the emperor had to be careful to keep them happy. Note their possession of not just an altar, but also of a temple within their camp.

19. Speidel, *Dolichenus*, 53, supposes that here *antistes* (priest) was equivalent to *aedituus* (custodian).

20. See Speidel, *Dolichenus*, 53, n. 171, who suggests, "The change in title from *aedituus* to *sacerdos* seems to be due to the sacristan's functioning as a priest for the cohort."

21. Speidel, *Dolichenus*, 53; see Pap. Dura 89 = Robert O. Fink, *Roman Military Records on Papyrus* (Cleveland: Published for the American Philological Association by the Press of Case Western Reserve University, 1971), 50. For a "priest of a legion" ("hiereus legionarios") at Dura before 256, see Cumont, *Fouilles*, no. 113, 376.

22. CIL 6.30685: "Numini sancti Aesculapi Sindrinae regionis Philippopolitanae, Aurelius Mucianus, sacerdos, miles cohortis X praetorianae piae vindicis Gordianae 7 Severi votum quod susceperat libens solvit cum civibus et commilitionibus suis . . ."; see Speidel, *Dolichenus*, no. 174, 54.

23. Joseph G. Milne, *Greek Inscriptions* (Catalogue Général des Antiquités Egyptiennes du Musée de Caire) (Oxford, 1905), no. 9238b, 45, from Aswan or Luxor; see also Speidel, *Dolichenus*, 53, n. 173.

24. For an example of a religious calendar from the mid-third century, see Watson, *Roman Soldier*, 276–77, and Fink et al., "Feriale Duranum," 1–222, a papyrus list of forty-one festivals observed by the Cohors XX Palmyrenorum from Dura-Europus, including, e.g., those celebrating paydays; the day of discharge; the deities Jupiter, Apollo, Mars, Neptune, and Hercules; the standards; and the accession of emperors.

25. Dolichenus is depicted standing on a bull, grasping a double ax and thunderbolt, and sporting the Phrygian cap and a sword. See Speidel, *Dolichenus*, 1–2; Franz V. M. Cumont, *The Oriental Religions in Roman Paganism* (Chicago: Open Court Publishing Company, 1911), 113; Domaszewski, *Religion*, 145; and Eve and John R. Harris, *The Oriental Cults in Roman Britain* (Leiden: Brill, 1965), 64. The cult faded after the 250s, when the New Persians destroyed the cult temple at Doliche in Commagene.

26. See Speidel, *Dolichenus*, 46–54: "the oriental religious needed holy men of special birth or initiation . . . to direct the rites of worship . . ." (p. 46).

27. Speidel, *Dolichenus*, no. 28, 50: "Iovi optimo maximo Dolicheno et deae Suriae magnae caelesti pro salute perpetui imperii Romani et legionis XIII Geminae Flavius Barhadadi sacerdos Iovis Dolicheni ad legionem supra scriptam votum libens merito posuit."

28. CIL 6.31187 = ILS 2193: "M(arcus) Ulp(ius) Cresimu⌈s sa⌉cer(dos) I⌈ovis Dolicheni⌉ | natione Parth|us et ex gener|osis MHNA tur(ma)|Issii | fecit pro salu|te imp et sing(ularium) | Aug(ustorum) et omni|bus amici(s) | mei(s). | Q.Mar| cius.Ar|temido|rus . . . | . . . templa . . . ," the first line also could be read as "M VLP CRESIMVSS eXERCI⌈tator⌉." Another inscription of same person, dated to the mid-second century but perhaps later, reads "Soli invicto pro salute imp(eratorum) et genio n(umeri) | eq(uitum) sing(ularium) eorum, M(arcus) Ulp(ius) Chresimus | sace⌈r(dos)⌉ Iovis Doliche⌈ni⌉ v(otum) s(olvit) l(aetus) l(ibens) | ⌈m(erito)⌉": see CIL 6.31181 = Domaszewski, *Religion*, no. 134. Note also ILS 2193*, "Iovi | Dolicheno | pro salute n. | eq. sing. Aug. | Q. Marcius | Artemidorus | medicus cas | trorum aram | posuit."

29. Domaszewski, *Religion*, no. 133, 64: "in h(onorem) d(omus) d(ivinae) Arcias Marinus sacerdos Dolicheni donum donavit equitibus cohortis I F . . . Decio et Grato cos."; see Speidel, *Dolichenus*, 49, who, without explanation, questions whether he was a soldier.

30. Pierre Merlat, *Répertoire des inscriptions et monuments figurés du culte de Jupiter Dolichenus* (Paris-Rennes, 1951) = Speidel, *Dolichenus*, no. 26, 48: "Iovi optimo maximo Dolicheno pro salute imperatoris Caesaris Caii Iulii Veri Maximini Pii felicis invicti Augusti, Ulpius Amandianus, miles legionis XIIII Geminae librarius numeris, custos armorum signifer optio octavi principis prioris candidatus numini cum Ulpio Amando veterano [his father?] legionis supra scriptae posuit(?)." Speidel, *Dolichenus*, 49, notes, "Not all restorations in this much mutilated text are reliable, but . . . it is obvious that Amandianus was still in active service."

31. Speidel, *Dolichenus*, no. 29, 54: "Iovi optimo maximo Dolicheno, pro salute imperatoris, Aelius Valentinus, veteranus, sacerdos templum impedio suo restituit," an altar found near Apulum.

32. Domaszewski, *Religion*, 64, for example, suggests that these examples represent a break with a past policy of not having army priests. Speidel, *Dolichenus*, 53, proposes that a "growing intensity of religious feeling brought . . . a trend for more and more units to have their own priests," and that soldiers could work their way up in the priestly ranks, going from *colitor* ("worshipper"); to *candidatus* ("candidate"); to *sacerdos*, *antistes*, or *hiereus* ("priest").

33. See Michael P. Speidel, *Mithras-Orion: Greek Hero and Roman Army God* (Leiden: Brill, 1980), and Franz V.M. Cumont, *Die Mysterien des Mithra* (Darmstadt, 1975), who notes: "Die mithrische Religion ist vor allem Soldatenreligion . . ." (p. 36).

34. Along with the *miles* ("soldier"); others grades included *decurions*, the ten highest-ranking of whom were called *decemprimi*, along with *magistri* ("Masters"), *curatores* ("Care-Takers"), *defensores* ("Defenders"), and *patroni* ("Patrons") (Cumont, *Mithras-Orion*, 155–56).

35. Speidel, *Dolichenus*, 47–51; Watson, *Roman Soldier*, 278.

36. *Vita Constantini* 4.18–9: *Nicene and Post-Nicene Fathers* (New York, 1890), 1:544–45.

37. Christian bishops certainly counseled Roman emperors in the field, however, as when the Arian bishop Valens of Mursa predicted a victory for Constantius II in 351 (Sulpicius Severus, *Chronicle* 2.38).

38. A.H.M. Jones, "Military Chaplains in the Roman Army," *Harvard Theological Review* 46 (1953): 239–40.

39. *Vita Martini* 2–4, "He was regarded as a monk rather than as a soldier"; he was baptized at 22 years old, but there is no indication of by whom.

40. Sozomen, *Ecclesiastical History*, 1.8.

41. J. Sakkelion, ed., *Forty-eight Letters of Theodoret of Cyrrhus* (Athens, 1885), no. 2.

42. *Vita s. Sabae* 9. Jones, "Military Chaplains," translates it as "chaplain of the unit."

43. "Principali [sic] devotissimorum militum qui illic in civitate Centumcellensi consistunt, relatione ad nos directa sacram se insinuant clementissimi principis impetrasse quae eis presbyterum diaconum et subdiaconum fieri debere praecepit" (*Patrologia graeca* 69.416).

44. Note also U. Wilcken, L. Mitteis, *Grundzüge und Chrestomathie zur Papyruskunde* (repr. Hildesheim, 1963) 1.6, a petition to the emperor Theodosius II (402–50) and Valentinian III (425–55), addressed "to Apion, bishop of the legion of Syene and Kenes Syene and Elefantine," although Jones ("Military Chaplains") suggests he "appears rather to be bishop of the garrison town than of the unit."

45. See Ralph W. Mathisen, "Barbarian Bishops and the Churches 'in barbaricis gentibus' during Late Antiquity," *Speculum* 72 (1997): 664–97.

46. Pagan non-Roman armies also had their priests. Tacitus (*Germania* 7) reports that German armies were accompanied in battle by priests carrying insignia taken from sacred groves. In the fifth century, the Huns were said to consult soothsayers before battles (Jordanes, *Getica*, 195–97): the haruspices "examined the entrails of cattle and certain streaks in the bones that had been scraped."

47. "qui etiam torquem, ut asseritur, et brachiale, Gothica profanatus impietate, more indutus gentilium, ausus sit in conspectu exercitus prodire Romani: quod sine dubio non solum in sacerdote sacrilegium, sed etiam in quocumque Christiano est, etenim abhorret a more Romani, nisi forte sic solent idolatrae sacerdotes prodire Gothorum . . ." (Ambrose, Letters 10.9–10).

48. Possidius, *Vita Augustini* 17.7, notes that Maximinus had come to Africa "with the Goths," and at this time, of course, it was not unusual for western military units under barbarian command to be heavily barbarian. See John B. Bury, *History of the Later Roman Empire*, 2 vols. (London: Macmillan, 1923), 1:245.

49. See Ralph W. Mathisen, "Sigisvult the Patrician, Maximinus the Arian, and Political Strategems in the Western Roman Empire ca. 425–40," *Early Medieval Europe* 8 (1999): 173–96.

50. Eunapius, fr. 48.2: Karl Müller, ed., *Fragmenta historicorum Graecorum* (FHG) (Paris, 1885) 4.55; *The Fragmentary Classicising Historians of the Later Roman Empire*, trans. R. C. Blockley (Liverpool: F. Cairns, 1981–83), 75–78; see also Eunapius, *Vitae sophistarum* 476C.

51. Sozomen, *Ecclesiastical History*, 9.9.1; see Herwig Wolfram, *History of the Goths* (Berkeley: University of California Press, 1988), 158, 166.

52. Olympiodorus, fr. 26: Karl Müller ed., FHG 4: "He slew the children who had been born to Athaulf by a former wife, seizing them by force from the protection of bishop Sigesarius."

53. Gregory of Tours, *Glory of the Confessors*, 47.

CHAPTER TWO

The Liturgy of War from Antiquity to the Crusades

MICHAEL McCORMICK

Historians are naturally inclined to dig into the past for the deep roots of modern phenomena. The pioneering study of Byzantine military religiosity, for instance, stemmed from a German army chaplain's experiences on the Western Front in 1914.[1] But the editor of this volume deserves special recognition for doing the inverse, for putting into practice Marc Bloch's oft-forgotten precept: to study well a phenomenon in the past, one must understand it in the present.[2] The medievalist may learn as much from the modernist as vice versa.

What can a specialist in late antiquity and the early Middle Ages contribute to the historical experience of military religiosity and of the chaplains themselves in this regard? For this question, the era from about AD 300 to the First Crusade is particularly rich; of all the things that characterize the societies of this lengthy period, religion and warfare are surely among the most abundant, and the most abundantly attested. And, long dead though they may be, those societies have left their mark on the modern world. After all, our term *chaplain* is itself a Carolingian coinage. A ninth-century scholar who had served as a royal chaplain records that the Latin word *capellanus* derives from the great royal relic of the patron saint of the Franks, the *cappa*. This was the very soldier's cape, which, according to the story, St. Martin's sword

45

sliced in half to share with a naked homeless man who turned out to be Christ.[3] I quote: "Originally, chaplains (*cappellani*) got their name from the *cappa* of St. Martin, which the kings of the Franks were accustomed to keep by them during battles to help in victory; the clerics who carried and cared for it, along with other relics of the saints, started to be called *cappellani*."[4]

Walafrid Strabo was likely writing down an oral tradition he had heard in the royal chapel. His account of the military vocation of that soldier's relic finds indirect confirmation in a canonical decision formulated almost a century earlier. The first stirrings of reform in the Carolingian church had excluded ecclesiastics from military expeditions, except for those appointed ("qui . . . electi sunt") for divine ministry, that is, saying mass, prescribing penance, and carrying the saints' relics. Ideally, these army clergy were to be limited to a bishop or two, the ruler's *capellani* (the customary spelling today), and one priest for every great leader (*unusquisque prefectus*).[5]

The medievalist can contribute more than etymologies. My purpose here is modest, but it may prove useful to the broader conversation about the historical experience of army religion. I would like to capitalize on earlier work on the celebration of victory and on the origins of the ritual face of crusading in order to supply some deeper background for more recent developments. First, I summarize briefly what we know today about the development of Christian war rituals from the time of Emperor Constantine to their apotheosis in the First Crusade, seven centuries later. Second, I inventory some key rituals and practices devised, we must think, by early medieval chaplains. This medieval interaction of religious behavior and warfare may prove interesting in two ways: practices that foreshadow those of later chaplains raise the question of historical origins and development; those that are without parallel pose the question of the originality of medieval civilization, or of its modern descendants. By way of conclusion, we will hear from an early medieval chaplain, as it were, by listening to the words of a ninth-century homily for warriors.

What exactly were our chaplains doing in and around combat? An important part of the answer is what I have called the liturgy of war. Broadly construed, the liturgy, and especially its social context and function, offers a rich area of investigation for those who are not frightened by its strange bestiary of sacramentaries, missals, pericopes, homeliaries, *ordines*, and so forth. This is because in its development and its nature, the liturgy both reflects and shapes the society from which it emanates. It bears emphasizing that the early medieval liturgy was not an inert collection of immutable texts inherited from the re- mote past. Such a vision of liturgical constancy owes more to the print- ing press and the canons of Trent than to familiarity with the fluidity of medieval textual traditions. The manuscripts are full of inventive, innovative texts. When we take the trouble to compare one ancient book to another, we see how much the liturgical celebrants changed their services. The very prayers evolve; my favorite is an elaborate, eighth- century biblical allusion to the Angel of Light and shadows of conflict, which in the eleventh century mutates into a prayer for clear weather for combat.[6]

For the historian of medieval chaplains, a second advantage of litur- gical texts stems from their practical nature. We can and should talk about the theologians' analyses of war; with the liturgy, however, we leave behind the schoolroom and approach the battlefield. The liturgy takes us to the rites and words expressed by and to the warriors them- selves. In the liturgy, gesture articulates the word and acts out ideas. We have no idea whether late Roman soldiers heard a word of St. Au- gustine's theology of war, but we can be sure that they wept and took communion before charging the enemy, that they cried, "Nobiscum Deus!" — "God is with us!" — as they rode into combat against the bar- barians.[7] We can believe that Frankish warriors and their king trudged around their camp in procession, singing *kyries* and responding to their assembled priests' chant: "To Lord Charles and his army of the Franks, long life and victory!" with the proto-Romance refrain, "Tu lo juva!" "(O God) Help him!"[8] In a word, with the liturgy of war, we observe in action the men entrusted with the spiritual care of warriors, and we can begin to explore how their rites shaped the warriors' self-understanding. It is, I think, no accident that the early medieval liturgy constantly called the faithful *fideles*, and that this word emerged as a favorite term for what we call "vassals."[9]

In the development of Christian military religious practices, research to date indicates three critical turning points down to the First Crusade. The first occurred in late antiquity; the second came in the Carolingian period, around 800; and the last emerged from the First Crusade itself, in 1099. That the alliance between the Christian religion and warfare marked the decisive moment in the conversion of the Roman Empire is well known. Marching against Rome in 312, the upstart emperor,

Constantine, received divine reassurance that a phenomenon that had appeared in the heavens presaged Christ's help; if the emperor's legionaries painted that symbol on their shields, Christ would give him victory.[10] It is clear that Constantine connected his commitment to the new God with this and subsequent military successes; that commitment launched the Christianization of the empire as a whole, and the Roman army in particular. But the very familiarity of the episode and its consequences perhaps dulls our sensitivity to just how shocking the development must have seemed to many Christians in 312. Within the new religion, a powerful strain of thought had been, at best, hostile to the imperial army, its gods (or demons, as the Christians saw them), and its violent defense of the empire: the acts of the early martyrs include recruits or soldiers who paid the death penalty for refusing military service.[11] This kind of thinking helps explain why specifically Christian rituals of victory developed rather gradually near the bloodshed of the battlefield.[12] At Rome, for instance, the pagan triumph ceremony appears to have lost its old pagan features, but Christian ones replaced them only slowly, so far as we can tell. Even in the more Christian capital of Constantinople, it would be two hundred years before an emperor would fully and explicitly incorporate a visit to a Christian shrine into his triumphal entry.[13] Why and how this happened seems to me complex; but the essential point is that specifically Christian victory rituals emerged rather gradually between about 300 and 550.

That gradual change surely reflects the deepening Christianization of late Roman society at large, a process that had reached new levels by the sixth century. To my eyes, the sixty or so years after 541 look like the decisive turn in the history of the later Roman Empire. The brilliant military successes of Justinian's armies dissipated into wars of attrition and stalemate; conditions worsened when the terrifying hammer blows of the great plague caused further disorder to the fragile late Roman economy, and Persian armies were able to drive deep into the east Roman heartland. The cascade of defeats and death destabilized the late Romans' view of the world and themselves, unleashing the destructive forces of riot, revolution, and religious persecution around the *mare nostrum*. The soldiers of a tottering army—which itself must have suffered heavy losses to the recurring waves of the Justinianic plague—needed all the inspiration they could get. Morale boosters came in the form of new, victory-producing relics, in special litanies just before combat, in paintings of the Virgin on the sails of Roman ships, and in the ubiquitous display of the symbols of Christianity in the trappings of the Roman army. Christian rituals of warfare reached a kind of high-water mark in approximately 600.[14] And they did so in a way that underscores the institutional identification of the Roman army with the state religion. The army's priests did not officiate alone: the commander and his officers joined them in leading the troops' litanic service of *kyrie eleisons* just before combat.[15]

The deployment of the imperial forces and their Christian trappings along the provincial frontiers relayed the innovations to the Germanic kingdoms that still bordered imperial territory; Germanic mercenaries serving in the Roman army got to know them firsthand.[16] Visigothic Spain and Lombard Italy shared frontiers with the empire around 600 and thus were particularly influenced by the contemporary imperial model. Frankish Gaul, in contrast, had moved further away from the imperial edge much earlier, and consequently borrowed less at this late date. This meant that there was more room for innovation later, when the Carolingian dynasty, bent on both military expansion and reforming the liturgy, reached the apex of its power.

Merovingian Gaul certainly saw some military rites of Roman origin. A few scraps of prayer books from the earlier eighth century show that here and there, at least, priests prayed for the king's victory. Whether they did so amidst the royal warriors or from the safety of their monastic fortresses is not clear. It is also unclear whether the prayers preserved in service books like the sacramentary from Reichenau or the Bobbio Missal were something new, or something old of which we are seeing the earliest surviving witnesses.[17] Careful liturgical and philological study of the formulas of the prayers might answer this question. How such a hypothetical continuity may have occurred can be imagined, mutatis mutandis, from the analogy of archival records in early eighth-century central Italy. The language and formulas of the earliest Lombard charters make plausible the local preservation of late Roman notarial traditions stretching back to the sixth century. Presumably, such traditions were handed down from master to apprentice.[18] Whether a comparable chain of tradition stands behind the early eighth-century war masses is uncertain. Nonetheless, their general characteristics fit well enough with what we can discern of more ancient, local liturgies of war, exemplified, for instance, by Leodegarius of Autun. This seventh-century bishop fasted and staged a noteworthy procession to bless his city defenses in anticipation of enemy attack.[19]

Even if some eighth-century war prayers embody deeper historical continuities, the rise of the Carolingian monarchy marks a decisive change in the history of war rituals. That change arose from at least three factors. The first was human: the Carolingian dynasty and the elite out of which they ascended were intensely interested in the performance of the liturgy and strove to make it more splendid, more uniform, and more authentically oriented on the model of Rome. Bishops and abbots counted among the king's closest personal advisers. Whether or not they themselves actually fought—the canons that Charlemagne and his successors honored forbade this, yet some Carolingian bishops surely died on campaign, or made the grass run red with Viking blood—these professional liturgists rode by the king's side, a ready source of advice and ideas to extend the ritual reach of their faith.[20]

Second, the nature of warfare had changed, and the fighting itself expanded considerably, to the point that the court annalists remarked on the rare years in which the Franks did not go to battle.[21] From hindsight, Charlemagne's conquests look inevitable. Contemporaries knew better. Charlemagne's armies suffered serious structural problems. Marshalling his grandees to fight when and where, and especially as long as the king wanted, was an extremely complex political task.[22] Early in the reign, the invasion of Italy was a much closer call than is often realized. For this is surely the meaning of Charles's efforts to buy his way out of the invasion, and of the fact that his warriors planned to head for home just as the tide was turning, as we learn only from the Italian evidence.[23] Nor was the problem confined to a young king, still learning the craft of rulership. Late in Charlemagne's reign, at least one campaign had to be called off because the warriors who had been mobilized simply failed to show up.[24] Obviously, these Frankish armies differed fundamentally from those of ancient Rome. For better or for worse, they were an extension of aristocratic society and its inveterate lifestyle, rather than a separate, professional, and specialized war-fighting institution. The military historian John Keegan may have overstated the case, but there is something to his view that they constituted "crowd armies," whose essential characteristic was to be "formidable only by reason of their size and because of the variable military skills of their individual members."[25]

For this kind of army, conditioning and high morale were essential, and practices that enhanced them were of great value. Any doubt on that score is quickly laid to rest by the detailed reconstruction of later medieval combat made possible by the casualties from the Battle of Visby (1361), on Gotland, and driven home by the photographs of the remains of the fallen fighters. The clinical analysis of the horrific wounds wrought in face-to-face combat by powerful right arms is numbing, as is the fact that they are still visible on some of the 1,185 casualties excavated in the mass graves from the battle. The killing field allows rare insight into the demographics of a medieval battle, which include a good number of women, and so confirm, for instance, mention of females among the Crusaders.[26] More than twelve hundred years after the fact, the trauma wrought by a powerful right-handed sword blow is still plain on the skull of a Carolingian warrior buried in Hesse. It throws chilling light on the horror of eye-to-eye war in the eighth century.[27]

The last factor stems from the Carolingians' newly ambitious monarchy. These kings show every sign of believing both that their activities were divinely sanctioned and that the ruler bore personal responsibility for subjects' minds and souls. For a few generations, the Carolingians had the means and desire to expand their power through violence and law, and they did not fail to do so.

In the revival of sacred rituals of warfare, the 790s were a watershed, as they were for so much else in Carolingian history. The decade of innovation that ended in Charlemagne's imperial coronation saw the building of the palace at Aachen and the coalescence of a more sedentary court society; court art and poetry luxuriated, and the king's advisors voiced an aggressively novel definition of religious orthodoxy in the *Libri Carolini*. It was a time when the European commercial economy was experiencing a new and remarkable dynamism, as I show in a recent book, even as Charles the Great introduced a new and heavier coinage, and opened diplomatic relations with the Caliph of Baghdad.[28] In these years, the Carolingian family and its supporters were experimenting with showy new ceremonies on a grand scale, for instance in the spectacular welcome staged by—and for—the aristocratic warriors of the imperial army when, in 799, the toppled Pope Leo III arrived at Charles's headquarters in Paderborn.[29] It was also a decisive time for the liturgy of war: in a great expedition of 791, Charlemagne and his army first celebrated a spectacular series of litanic processions to obtain victory, and enjoined a similar ceremony on the royal court, behind the lines. The expedition was a splendid success, which guaranteed the future of the revived combat-related rituals.[30]

The manuscript books that have preserved many of these services would reward closer codicological and cultural scrutiny from the perspective of this volume. Some will have been the very books that Carolingian chaplains carried with them on campaign; insofar as every medieval manuscript is a unique, hand-crafted object tailored to the needs of its owner, these ancient service books mirror the men who made and used them. In the Western tradition, they are the oldest physical objects connected with the practice of military chaplaincy to survive.[31] Two sacramentaries are plausible candidates for this honor. One is connected with Charlemagne's court and, apparently, his battle-hardened kinsman, Count William of Aquitaine. The other sacramentary may well come from the entourage of his son, Louis, when he was a sub-king warring against the Muslim "pagans" on the empire's southern frontier. A third book from the next generation is even more intriguing.[32] This manuscript stems from Louis the Pious's imperial court of the 820s.[33] It is written in stenography—a sign that may connect it with the emperor's writing office—and contains the text of a remarkable homily preached to the troops as they set out for war. From it, we shall hear how an early medieval chaplain managed to recapitulate key points of Christian doctrine, even as he admonished his listeners not to fight for earthly profit or glory, but for the defense of Christianity and the faith, to insure God's help in their moment of danger.[34]

Although the empire he had created failed, Charlemagne's civilization lived and set the pattern, or at least the ideal, for the next generations of Europeans. This was particularly true of things liturgical. Carolingian forms of worship came to dominate in the Ottonian empire of tenth- and eleventh-century Germany. From there, they were transplanted to Rome, and hence to the universal church. Like his other liturgical innovations, the Carolingian ritual apparatus of warfare did not disappear with Charlemagne. On the contrary, it flourished and even expanded its reach in successive generations. For instance, in the territories that would one day become France, the old Carolingian "Mass for the King on the Day of Battle against the Pagans" became now a lordly mass for use "Against Pagan Persecution."[35] Across the Rhine, whether we read the Ottonian historians or the liturgical books themselves, we find just the sort of army rites that the Carolingians had developed.[36] The tradition of the Carolingian liturgy of war, in other words, was unbroken in the tenth and eleventh centuries.[37]

It continued down to the time of the First Crusade. The remarkable panoply of liturgical and paraliturgical procedures deployed by the Crusaders was no spontaneous invention of the disheveled and disoriented mass of soldiers, as some have argued. These rituals did not just grow out of pilgrim customs nor borrow from Byzantium, as others would have it. I have analyzed elsewhere how the old Carolingian liturgical customs converged with homesickness, mental habit, fear and religious (and physical) delirium, radical alienation, and pilgrimage to fuse the old rites into the new phenomenon of the Crusade in the course of the extraordinary events of 1098 and 1099. To their novel and desperate situation, the leading prelates of the "army of God" (as they called themselves) applied the liturgical traditions of the Carolingians, whether the starving warriors were fasting and staging litanic processions before combat or following a miraculous relic into battle.[38]

These then are the key stages that have so far emerged in the development of the ritual apparatus of combat between its inception in late antiquity and the First Crusade: invention and slow elaboration under the Christian Roman Empire, revival under the Carolingians, and application to a wholly new kind of warfare in the Middle East by the warriors of the First Crusade. The unbelievable success of that tiny band of fighters in a foreign land would fire the imagination of the European warrior class for generations. Their victory gave birth to a new kind of war, a crusade, and with it, the liturgical rites that appeared to have stood the warriors of God in such good stead. Swathed in the success of the conquest of Jerusalem, the future of the liturgy of war was assured.[39]

Even this brief sketch makes clear that studying what late antique and medieval chaplains were actually doing opens up a broad series of questions. They turn on a complex and extensive series of practices that issued from the ways in which religion and the military life interacted both at home and in the field. Some examples, which deserve more scrutiny than I can give them here, illustrate what remains to be done.

In the early Middle Ages, social groups expressed their identity in their shrines. Now and then we catch a glimpse of a church that seems to have had a military clientele.[40] This might be the implication, for instance, when military men figure prominently in the hagiographical texts connected with a shrine. One example may well be the very large basilica of Sant'Apollinare in Classe, outside Ravenna, to judge from the late antique historical novel about St. Apollinaris. It depicts pagan Roman Ravenna as a duchy that was practically one large military base. The *Passion* attributes Apollinaris's entry into Ravennate society to his host, "an Asian soldier." The saint's breakthrough miracle restores an officer's ailing wife to good health. Before curing her, St. Apollinaris insists that the officer summon his soldiers to witness the miracle. The tribune complies, the soldiers see the miracle, and exclaim: "He who can do such things is truly God! He is powerful enough, if he is loved, to help us even in combat!" The message presumably did not fall on deaf ears among the embattled Byzantine garrison of Ravenna.[41] Some warriors also venerated distinctively military saints. Byzantium's professional soldiers seem to have favored holy military heroes, such as St. Theodore or St. George.[42] But the early medieval West also had its military saints. A warrior cult of the Archangel presumably explains the proliferation of votive masses to St. Michael; the belief that such masses produced victory led to unspecified "unreasonable" abuses and their prohibition by the bishops of Ottonian Germany.[43]

Religion supplied the symbols and insignia of late Roman and medieval armies; we have already noted that a symbol of Christ decorated the shields of Constantine's army. Whatever that symbol's form, the chrismon would become the Roman forces' emblem for centuries, and we can still see it on the shields of the elite troopers depicted in the famous mosaic of Justinian at Ravenna. But the chrismon faced increasing competition from that other Christian sign that had so troubled earlier Roman sensitivities. As its connotation of torture and infamy receded from public consciousness, the cross loomed ever larger in the public symbolism of the Roman Empire and its successors. Relics of the True Cross ensconced in golden processional crosses led Byzantine, Visigothic, and Frankish armies to war; by the eleventh century, crosses covered Crusader trappings and reinforced among warriors the christomimetic strain of contemporary spirituality.[44] Especially in the age of crisis, religious sentiment had seeped into unlikely objects of late Roman army life. For example, the official seals of the Roman army of Italy bore the legend "Deus adiuta!"—"May God help us!"— the sort of slogan whose ambivalence did not escape contemporary commanders.[45]

As combat loomed, early medieval chaplains sought to maintain the morale of their fighters and seized the moment to accomplish their broader mission of pastoral care. Imminent death focused men's minds. Before battle, the chaplains and their flock staged spectacular and participatory liturgical services, including special votive masses. The belief that war arose out of sin, and that the outcome of battle was a form of divine judgment reinforced the menace of death to encourage peni-

Mosaic, Ravenna, S. Vitale. Emperor Justinian with guards, court officials, and eccle-siastics, ca. AD 547. Alinari 18224. Courtesy of Art Resource.

tential rites of purification and supplication. Thus, we see the Frankish army poised on the edge of the central European forest, marching bare-foot around their encampment as they intoned the litanies of the saints. As paradoxical as it appears to the modern military historian, the Carolingian warriors fasted for three days to purify themselves before battle. The Crusaders did similarly at Antioch, feasting only on the Eucharist. The gestures of the rites themselves, and the army's chant-ing of the litanic refrains, conveyed their sense even to those who had little Latin; the meaning of the moment was also made explicit in the homilies preached to the troops, whose few surviving specimens re-ward closer scrutiny.[46]

The blessing of the standards, or the related custom of following a processional cross or a prized relic—the Crusader's Holy Lance offers a splendid example—served the dual purpose of encouraging the war-riors and sacralizing the standards that were a vital tool of communi-cation in the chaos of combat, and therefore needed special protection.[47] Battle cries offer a kind of litmus test for religion in the mindset of a group of warriors at a specific moment. For instance, the deepening re-ligious sentiment of the fighters of the First Crusade can be read in this phenomenon. At the beginning of the Crusade, a contingent from southwestern France rode into battle shouting "Toulouse!" The distinctive regional rallying cry proclaimed their local identity. By its end, the Crusaders were shouting "God wills it!" and the like.[48]

Death is a natural outcome of war. In early medieval Christendom, postcombat thanksgiving services mirrored the litanic supplications that had preceded them, and they were naturally followed by funerals of the fallen warriors. We hear of the latter, for instance, in 842 after the carnage of Fontenay, in the Carolingian civil war. Various penitential measures accompanied the funerals. This is something of a special case, however, in that Fontenay was a major engagement in a civil war (a novel experience at the time) that was ostentatiously depicted as an appeal to divine judgment, apparently even before battle was joined.[49] I know of no exact late Roman or medieval equivalents of the civic monuments that are the war cemeteries that dot the battlefields of the United States and Europe, although we have already met at least one late medieval mass grave directly connected with a battle.[50] The closest medieval equivalent of our memorial cemeteries is probably the practice of founding a religious house on the site of a great battle. Best known from the Normans' Battle Abbey in England, the custom can be traced back to the seventh century.[51] The liturgical books also record the social memory of death in combat. Medieval men and women took prayer associations and their commitments very seriously, and the commemoration of those killed in battle was no exception. Thus, an annual feast memorialized the Byzantine soldiers who died on the disastrous Bulgarian campaign of 811; they were still venerated as martyrs in the liturgy of the Hagia Sophia in Constantinople a century later.[52] Similarly, the heavy casualties of the great Ottonian defeat at Colonna in southern Italy motivated a prayer commemoration at Fulda, and earlier examples are likely.[53] Emperor Henry IV also founded a liturgical commemoration of his fallen fighters.[54] The extent and nature of these collective commemorations may be a useful index of the standing of the army within society; the specifics of their services yield insight into how societies construed the searing experience of defeat and destruction.[55]

What was it like? We cannot, thank God, recreate the experience of warfare fused with religious sentiment as it occurred in the early Middle Ages. We can, however, listen to the words of someone who was there. The atmosphere of a Carolingian service for Franks preparing to go into battle against "pagans," presumably Muslims, is palpable in the homily for warriors that I have already mentioned. To make that atmosphere more widely available to scholars engaged, notably, in comparative work, I have translated the text in the appendix to this chapter.

When we read that homily, or when we look at the spectrum of special services with which early medieval chaplains prepared their spiritual charges for battle, we cannot help but be struck. Their ingeniousness found scope to invent ways of bolstering the spirits of their charges in terms that appealed to—and therefore suggest—the mentality of ninth-century warriors. In terms of the chaplains' pastoral function, what is perhaps most striking is the imagination and creativity that the clergy of the early Middle Ages deployed. In so doing, they brought the values of the Christian religion into a most unlikely place, but one where it was sure to command the attention and penetrate the hearts and minds of men about to face death. It is hard for me to escape the impression that the development of specialized rites for and about fighting-men played a role in forging their growing consciousness of themselves as a class apart, as a group of Christians specially dedicated to a particular code and a particular lifestyle of combat that, in later centuries, would come to be known as chivalry.

Appendix

Translation of a Homily for Warriors Preserved in a Chaplain's Book from the Carolingian Court (Vat. Reg. lat. 846).

This text was presumably preached to Frankish warriors in some campaign during the first fifteen years of Louis the Pious's reign.[56] Although it is labeled "Letter of Consolation to those Going off to War" in the manuscript, the text does not formally resemble a medieval letter.[57] The tone and content are clearly homiletic.[58] Beyond its presence in this manuscript, the work offers few clues to the author's identity. The best evidence lies in its language.

Various stylistic and grammatical infelicities confirm what the homiletic tone suggests, and what stenographic notation would allow: the text is very close to what we may take to be Carolingian spoken Latin.[59] The language of the homily brings nothing to mind so much as the contemporary transcriptions of dispute settlement proceedings and their echoes of spoken testimony (and which deserve more detailed linguistic scrutiny than they have received). Word order, lexical choices, and grammatical features lie on the frontier between Vulgar or Popular Latin and Proto-Romance.[60]

I do not know whether a skilled ninth-century Latinist would have deployed his accustomed classicizing language in dictating a hasty homily to little-lettered warriors. In any case, the sermon's language does not point to a very unusual literary culture: the speaker uses a number of stock phrases that echo the Bible, the liturgy, perhaps a biblical preface of Jerome, and some reading of Gregory the Great, Caesarius of Arles, or Leo I.[61] A reminiscence of Benedict's *Rule* hints at a monastic background. The very simplicity and directness of expression indicate that the author meant to be understood by Proto-Romance speakers of an age when Latin was just separating from the vernacular.[62]

The Sermon

Men, brothers, and fathers,[63] you who *have the Christian name* and *bear the standard of the cross on* your *brow,*[64] pay attention and *listen! Consider carefully*[65] at *what cost you have been redeemed,*[66] whose *name you have on you,*[67] because you, Christ *redeemed* you[68] *by blessed blood* to the *eternal inheritance*[69] from which you were thrown out for *the sin of our first kinsman*,[70] Adam. By our Savior's redemption, the human race was put back there. Consider this carefully, when you are moving out and you are going to fight against your enemies, that, with God's help, you defend the Christian name. And beware, with all your cunning and cleverness, lest *you bear in vain* what has been given to you through God's gift.[71] Abstain from evil deeds, *abstain from carnal desire*,[72] *put God in front of your eyes with* love *and fear*.[73] And in your prayers, always call on God to help you. Act on this campaign in such a way that God does not desert you *on the day of tribulation*,[74] and strive with all forethought, that you do not want to fight the war for earthly profit or secular glory, but (rather) for the defense of the Christian name and God's churches, and that *faith*, which you have accepted, *remains intact* in you.[75] When you are under way, don't pillage or lead [people? animals?] off with you,[76] nor act against Christian law, but take only what necessarily[77] pertains to victualing, when it is necessary, with all reverence and all fear, so that you do not offend God. For if on this campaign which you are going on now, you want *to fight for God*,[78] keep to the law of God on it and act in a way that it might please God to *send his angel with you*,[79] who can defend you with strength and protect your camps with the help of his piety, so that he will be a weapon against your enemies. Let the *shield of his piety*[80] protect you and defend you from your opponents. If you want to know only one thing, that it is an important thing to bear the Christian name and to live here [on earth] with the greatest *discipline in the fear of God*[81] and afterward to rejoice forever with God *in the delights of paradise*,[82] know that *God does not desert* you,[83] because your opponents who battle against you, are *battling* not only against you, but *against God*,[84] because these persecutors of Christians and the churches despise the standard of the holy cross.

So, if you want to keep your faith firmly and fulfill the will of God, do not fear your opponents, but with all daring and all the *strength of the arm of God*[85] be ready to defend the name of your Christianity. Know that he who *gives up his body* and soul *for God's sake*, without a doubt will either be *crowned* here,[86] in the present age if he conquers or, something much better, if he commits his soul or his body onto death, let him know that he will have profited for his soul and he will receive the reward of his labor in eternal life with the Lord, and rest with the other heirs in paradise. Think just about this, that in your every act and your every deed, you do what pleases God, so that it pleases God to move with you and protect you with his piety. Know that if you want to go with fear and reverence and call on God for help, God will be with you against your enemies, as he was with Joshua when he battled against Amalech.[87] Let each man get ready according to his conscience, let him remember his sins which he committed earlier, let him not take them with him into the combat of Christ, but let him devoutly confess his sins beforehand to a priest and before God and, freed of those great sins, safe from past deeds, with God's favor, you can stand in battle without any hesitation and any sin on the day of the Lord, because if you are clean, as the Lord says, "*I will stay with you* and *my angel will precede you* and *he will be your protection.*"[88] Act so that your heart does not tremble, and do not reckon your body more precious than your soul. Whatever you do, do it for God and God will fight for you. End. Amen. Thanks be to God!

Notes

1. A. Heisenberg, "Kriegsgottesdienst in Byzanz," in *Aufsätze zur Kultur- und Sprachgeschichte vornehmlich des Orients: Ernst Kuhn zum 70. Geburtstage . . . gewidmet* (Breslau, 1916), 244–57, reminiscing about Christmas 1914 at Jolimont, Belgium; so too Peter Partner, *God of Battles: Holy Wars of Christianity and Islam* (London, 1997), which aims to relativize the otherness of modern Islamic *jihad* movements by comparing them notably with the Western medieval phenomenon.

2. Marc Bloch, *The Historian's Craft,* trans. Peter Putnam (New York, 1962), 45–46.

3. Sulpicius Severus, *Vita sancti Martini,* 3, in J. Fontaine, *Sulpice Sévère: Vie de saint Martin,* Sources chrétiennes, 133 (Paris, 1967), 1:256–58.

4. Walafrid Strabo, *De exordiis et incrementis quarumdam in observationibus ecclesiasticis rerum,* ed. Victor Krause, Monumenta Germaniae historica (hereafter MGH), Capitularia regum Francorum 2 (Hanover, 1897), 515.29–32: "Dicti sunt autem primitus cappellani a cappa beati Martini, quam reges Francorum ob adiutorium victoriae in proeliis solebant secum habere, quam ferentes et custodientes cum ceteris sanctorum reliquiis clerici cappellani coeperunt vocari"; cf. Josef Fleckenstein, *Die Hofkapelle der deutschen Könige,* MGH Schriften, 16.1 (Stuttgart, 1959), 10–11 and next note. For a fine (though slightly different) translation and an excellent introduction and commentary, including on Walafrid's life, see Alice L. Harting-Correa, *Walahfrid Strabo's Libellus de exordiis et incrementis quarundam in observationibus ecclesiasticis rerum* (Leyden, 1995), here 193.

5. Boniface, *Ep. 56,* ed. M. Tangl, MGH Scriptores rerum Germanicarum, 2d ed. (Berlin, 1955), 99.24–100.2; cf. Friedrich Prinz, *Klerus und Krieg im früheren Mittelalter,* Monographien zur Geschichte des Mittelalters, 2 (Stuttgart, 1971), 8 ff.

6. Michael McCormick, "Liturgie et guerre des Carolingiens à la première croisade," in *"Militia Christi" e Crociata nei secoli XI–XIII,* Miscellanea del Centro di studi medioevali, 13 (Milan, 1992), 211–38, here 223, n. 45; for the biblical references

(all to the Vulgate), see, e.g., Nm 20:16; Jgs 2:1. The volume contains a number of germane studies, notably Friedrich Prinz, "Primi stadi della militia Christi altomedioevale nella tarda antichità e nel sistema ecclesiastico imperiale del periodo carolingio e degli Ottoni," ibid., 49–63; J. Flori, "De la chevalerie féodale à la chevalerie chrétienne?" ibid., 67–99; M. Brett, "Warfare and its Restraints in England, 1066–1154," ibid., 129–44; F. Cardini, "La guerra santa nella cristianità," ibid., 387–99; and K. Elm, "Die Spiritualität der geistlichen Ritterorden des Mittelalters," ibid., 477–518.

7. For Augustine's theology of war, see esp. his *Ep.* 138, 2, ed. A. Goldbacher, *Corpus scriptorum ecclesiasticorum latinorum* 44 (1904), 139.18–142.1, and *Ep.* 189, ibid., 57 (1911), 133.12–135.19; late Roman soldiers' conduct: Michael McCormick, *Eternal Victory. Triumphal Rulership in Late Antiquity, Byzantium and the Early Medieval West*, 2d ed. (Cambridge, 1990), 246–47.

8. Michael McCormick, "The Liturgy of War in the Early Middle Ages: Crisis, Litanies, and the Carolingian Monarchy," *Viator* 15 (1984): 1–23.

9. Thus, *fidelis* occurs ca. 120 and 100 times, respectively, in the Propers of the Carolingian Sacramentaries of Autun and Angoulême, judging from the CETEDOC's *Instrumenta lexicologica latina*, series A: 21: *Liber sacramentorum Augustodunensis* (Turnhout, 1984), and ibid., series A: 39: *Liber sacramentorum Engolismensis* (Turnhout, 1987). For the use of *fidelis* in the sense of "vassal," see François Louis Ganshof, *Feudalism*, trans. Philip Grierson (New York, 1964), 52 and 69. In OFr, *feel* et *feelté* occur in the same sense as *vassal, vassalage*; for the analogous term *hold* in OHG, see Dennis H. Green, *The Carolingian Lord: Semantic Studies on Four Old High German Words* (Cambridge, 1965), 140–63.

10. See the important argument of Peter Weiss, "Die Vision Constantins," in *Colloquium aus Anlass des 90. Geburtstages von Alfred Heuss*, ed. Jochan Bleicken, Frankfurter Althistorische Studien, 13 (Kallmünz, 1993), 143–69, about the celestial phenomenon of Constantine's vision; for the previous state of the question: Jochan Bleicken, *Constantin der Grosse und die Christen*, Historische Zeitschrift, Beihefte, n.F. 15 (Munich, 1992), 23–33; to the latter's discussion of the triumph of 312, add McCormick, *Eternal Victory*, 100–105.

11. In AD 295, St. Maximilian of Africa, for instance, went to his death rather than be conscripted into the Roman army for, said he, he was a Christian, and could do no evil. Even so, this does not mean that all Christians avoided the army, as the prosecuting magistrate pointedly observed to Maximilian. *Acta Maximiliani*, 2, 9–10, ed. Antonius A.R. Bastiaensen, *Atti e passioni dei martiri*, ed. Bastiaensen et al. (Vicenza, 1987), 242.25–32; Eng. trans., e.g., in John Helgeland et al., *Christians and the Military: The Early Experience* (London, 1987), 58–59, which work also offers further references and a convenient historical theological overview of the changing attitudes and behavior of early Christians, which were not monolithic. The bibliography on the theme is enormous; see Peter Brock, *The Military Question in the Early Church: A Selected Bibliography of a Century's Scholarship, 1888–1987* (Toronto, 1988); Adolf von Harnack, *Militia Christi. The Christian Religion and the Military in the First Three Centuries*, trans. David M. Gracie (1905; Philadelphia, 1981) remains fundamental.

12. McCormick, *Eternal Victory*, 108–9.

13. Ibid., 100–111.

14. Ibid., 244–48. Almost a century after Constantine's victory, the new sermons of St. Augustine refer gushingly to imperial veneration of the tomb of Peter when, in

late 403 and the spring of 404, Emperor Honorius visited Rome for many months to celebrate a triumph and assume his sixth consulate. Although Augustine's effusions have led some to assume that Honorius visited St. Peter's tomb in the course of his triumphal parade into the city, Augustine does not explicitly say this. Insofar as we can reconstruct it from Claudian, the parade's itinerary leaves no place for so lengthy and sensational a deviation from the usual route. See F. Dolbeau, ed., *Augustin d'Hippone, Vingt-six sermons au peuple d'Afrique* (Paris, 1996), 6 and 245–46, and H. Ingelbert, "Universalité chrétienne et monarchie impériale dans les nouveaux sermons d'Augustin découverts à Mayence," in G. Madec, ed., *Augustin prédicateur (395–411): Actes du Colloque international de Chantilly (5–6 septembre 1996)* (Paris, 1998), 450–51, about Dolbeau Sermons 22,4 and 25,26, ed. Dolbeau, *Augustin d'Hippone*, 557 and 266, respectively. In Dolbeau Sermon 22,4, I would not follow Ingelbert in translating *pergere* as "aller directement." During his stay, Honorius will surely have visited the great shrines, not least at Christmas and Easter, and he will have had ample opportunities for the demonstration of piety trumpeted by Augustine: McCormick, *Eternal Victory*, 102, n. 95.

15. Maurice, *Strategicon*, 1, 18, ed. George T. Dennis, *Das Strategikon des Maurikios*, Corpus Fontium Historiae Byzantinae, 17 (Vienna, 1981), 138.13–19; George T. Dennis, "Religious Services in the Byzantine Army," in Ephrem Carr et al., eds., *Eulogema. Studies in Honor of Robert Taft, S.J.*, Studia Anselmiana, 110 (Rome, 1993), 107–17. For the later Byzantine rituals of war, see also Athena Kolia-Dermitzake, *Ho byzantinos "hieros polemos"* (Athens, 1991), and in general, Tia M. Kolbaba, "Fighting for Christianity. Holy War in the Byzantine Empire," *Byzantion* 68 (1998): 194–221.

16. McCormick, *Eternal Victory*, 231–37, 252–59.

17. Ed. A. Dold and A. Baumstark, *Das Palimpsestsakramentar im Cod. Aug. CXII*, Texte und Arbeiten, 1.12 (Beuron, 1925), 37, and Elias A. Lowe, *The Bobbio Missal. A Gallican Mass-Book*, Henry Bradshaw Society, 53 (London, 1917), 64–65; cf. McCormick, *Eternal Victory*, 344–46.

18. Herbert Zielinski, *Studien zu den spoletinischen "Privaturkunden" des 8. Jahrhunderts und ihre Überlieferung im Regestum Farfense*, Bibliothek des Deutschen historischen Instituts in Rom, 39 (Tübingen, 1972), esp. 213–14.

19. B. Krusch, ed., *Passio Leodegarii*, MGH Scriptores rerum Merovingicarum 5 (1910): 304.2–6; for Roman antecedents, see McCormick, *Eternal Victory*, 241–42.

20. See above, n. 5; for example, Angilram, archbishop of Metz and archchaplain, and Sindpert, bishop of Regensburg, both died on campaign in 791: S. Abel and B. Simson, *Jahrbücher des Fränkischen Reiches unter Karl dem Grossen*, 2 (reprint, Berlin, 1969): 27–28; Viking gore: Sedulius Scottus, *Carmina*, 8.29–36, ed. I. Meyers, *Corpus Christianorum, series latina* (hereafter CCL), *Continuatio Mediaevalis* 117 (Turnhout, 1991): 21–22.

21. E.g., *Annales regni Francorum*, a. 790, ed. Friedrich Kurze, MGH Scriptores rerum Germanicarum (Hanover, 1895), 86.

22. Consensus and adhesion to the king's plans were never established once and for all; they had to be hammered out anew for almost every enterprise. On this theme, see G. Tellenbach, "Die geistigen und politischen Grundlagen der karolingischen Thronfolge," *Frühmittelalterliche Studien* 13 (1979): 184–302; although his general point runs rather differently, see on indirect reflections of those who were less than

enthusiastic about the new dynasty, Jürgen Hannig, *Consensus fidelium*, Monographien zur Geschichte des Mittelalters, 27 (Stuttgart, 1982), 150.

23. *Liber pontificalis*, ed. L. Duchesne, 2d ed. (Paris, 1981) 1:495.13–14; cf. ibid., 515–16, n. 21.

24. A. Boretius and Victor Krause, eds., MGH Capitularia no. 50, 2, 1 (Hanover, 1883): 137.16–21, with François L. Ganshof, *Frankish Institutions under Charlemagne*, trans. Bryce and Mary Lyon (New York, 1970), 161, n. 73.

25. John Keegan, *The Face of Battle* (reprint, London, 1988), 175–76.

26. B. O. Ingelmark, "The Skeletons," in B. Thordeman, ed., *Armour from the Battle of Wisby* (Stockholm, 1939), 149–209, on wounds, 160–209; from a sample of 155 remains examined for sex, he estimates that 5 percent (that is, 63) of the total recovered casualties were women; for women in the First Crusade, see J. A. Brundage, "Prostitution, Miscegenation, and Sexual Purity in the First Crusade," in Peter W. Edbury, ed., *Crusade and Settlement* (Bristol, 1985), 57–65. There is, however, some reason to think that the special circumstances at Visby may make its overall demography somewhat atypical.

27. M. Kunter, "Die Sachsenkriege," in Christoph Stiegemann and Matthias Wemhoff, eds., *799. Kunst und Kultur der Karolingerzeit: Katalog der Ausstellung*, pt. 1 (Mainz, 1999), 281–82, no. V.21.

28. Court: Donald A. Bullough, *"Aula Renovata*: The Carolingian Court before the Aachen Palace," *Proceedings of the British Academy* 71 (1985): 267–301; orthodoxy: A. Freeman, "Carolingian Orthodoxy and the Fate of the Libri Carolini," *Viator* 16 (1985): 65–108, here 65–75; economic dynamism: McCormick, *Origins of the European Economy* (Cambridge, 2001); Baghdad: M. Borgolte, *Der Gesandtenaustausch der Karolinger mit den Abbasiden und mit den Patriarchen von Jerusalem*, Münchener Beiträge zur Mediävistik und Renaissance-Forschung, 25 (Munich, 1976), 45–61; coins: P. Grierson and M. Blackburn, *The Early Middle Ages (5th–10th Centuries)* (= Medieval European Coinage, 1) (Cambridge, 1986), 208–9.

29. McCormick, "Paderborn 799: Königliche Repräsentation—Visualisierung eines Herrschaftskonzepts," in Stiegemann and Wemhoff, *799. Kunst und Kultur der Karolingerzeit: Beiträge zum Katalog* (Mainz, 1999), 71–81.

30. McCormick, "Liturgy," 8–13.

31. *Liber sacramentorum Gellonensis*, ed. A. Dumas, CCL 159 (1981): 431, no. 2750; *Liber sacramentorum Engolismensis*, ed. P. Saint-Roch, CCL 159C (1987): 358; on their court connections, McCormick, *Eternal Victory*, 347–49, and "A New Ninth-Century Witness to the Carolingian Mass against the Pagans," *Revue bénédictine* 97 (1987): 77.

32. See the text translated in the Appendix to this article.

33. I am deeply grateful to the late Donald Bullough for alerting me that, in an unfinished study, the late Bernhard Bischoff concluded that this book (Vat. Reg. lat. 846) belonged to a group of "manuscripts produced for Louis's Court but apparently by Tours-related scribes, and in all probability while Alcuin's pupil Fridugis was chancellor in the 820s"; letter of May 26, 1994.

34. The contents are edited and reproduced by W. Schmitz, *Miscellanea tironiana aus dem Codex Vaticanus latinus reginae Christianae 846 (fol. 99–114)* (Leipzig, 1896). According to Schmitz, Vatican City, B. Apost., Reg. lat. 846 is a composite codex; our part comprises only the last sixteen folios and is damaged at the end, as well as,

apparently, the beginning. The miscellany looks like a kind of manual whose Latin is laced with Proto-Romance features. It includes excerpts from Defensor of Ligugé; the military sermon; "Sententiae deflorate de diversis causis," which is a very interesting kind of catechism, inc. "Homo pro quid dicitur? R(esponsio): Homo dicitur ab humum (!), quia de limo terre formatus est. Int(errogatio): Quibus substantiis constat homo? R. Duabus, mortale et immortale . . ." whose questions include reference to the Filioque (30.18–20) and to Christ's equality with the father (30.25 ff); a glossary mention of the type of spears used by Bretons (43.16; an echo of Louis the Pious's Breton campaigns of 818 and 824?); a summary of biblical history and inventions; extracts from Eucherius of Lyons; names of patriarchs; an orthographic excerpt from Isidore of Seville, *Origines*, 1, 27; and medical recipes. The overall impression is of some kind of vademecum for a teacher of court chaplains.

35. McCormick, "A New Witness."

36. Significantly, Widukind of Corvey's idea of holy war against the pagans seems to derive from the liturgy. See H. Beumann, *Widukind von Korvei* (Weimar, 1950), 207–8.

37. McCormick, "Liturgie et guerre," 222–33; and, in general, the classic study of C. Erdmann, *Die Entstehung des Kreuzzugsgedankens* (Stuttgart, 1935), partially trans. as *The Origin of the Idea of Crusade*, trans. M. W. Baldwin and W. Goffart (Princeton, N.J., 1977).

38. McCormick, "Liturgie et guerre," 218–20; on the developing idea of death in combat as martyrdom, see C. Morris, "Martyrs on the Field of Battle before and during the First Crusade," in D. Wood, ed., *Martyrs and Martyrologies*, Studies in Church History 30 (Oxford: Blackwell, 1993), 93–104.

39. See, for instance, the English developments traced by Brett, "Warfare," 141–44; cf., e.g., D. M. Webb, "Cities of God: The Italian Communes at War," in W. J. Sheils, ed., *The Church and War*, Studies in Church History 20 (Oxford: Blackwell, 1983), 111–27; and A. K. McHardy, "The English Clergy and the Hundred Years War," ibid., 175.

40. This seems to have been true of the Praetorian church in Visigothic Toledo: McCormick, *Eternal Victory*, 308–12; cf. for the later Roman army, e.g., A. H. M. Jones, *The Later Roman Empire, 284–602*, 2 (reprint, Baltimore, 1986), 1263, n. 55.

41. *Passio Apollinaris*, 3 and 5–6, ed. *Acta sanctorum*, Iulii 5 (Paris, 1868), 345B–E. The Bollandists print "militem Astaticum," but report the variant "Asiaticum." Debate continues on whether that legendary *Passio Apollinaris* dates from the seventh, sixth, or even fifth century, e.g., Eligius Dekkers, *Clavis patrum latinorum*, 3d ed. (Steenbrugge, 1995), no. 2166. The role of soldiers (including that "miles Asiaticus") and their families as its protagonists, the officers' titles (*dux, comes, patricius*, and *consul*), and the fact that Ravenna itself is called a *ducatus* all point toward the Byzantine period. For the contemporary Greek text, which apparently translates the Latin, see E. Follieri, "Vite e inni greci per i santi di Ravenna," *Rivista di studi bizantini e neoellenici*, n.s., 2–3 (1965–66): 193–203.

42. A. Kazhdan, "Military Saints," in *Oxford Dictionary of Byzantium*, 3 vols. (Oxford, 1991), 2:1374; Alba M. Orselli, *Santità militare e culto dei santi militari nell'impero dei Romani (secoli VI–X)* (Bologna, 1993), with further references.

43. Synod of Erfurt, 932, ed. E. D. Hehl and H. Fuhrmann, MGH Concilia 6 (1987), 112.14–18; cf. McCormick, "Liturgie et guerre," 232; for its possible Lombard antecedents, see *Eternal Victory*, 295, n. 159.

44. On the early Roman perception of the cross, witness, e.g., Justin Martyr's efforts to argue that the shape was not inherently ignoble since it was used for ships' masts and yardarms, and even the imperial standards: *Apologia pro Christianis*, 55, ed. M. Marcovich, *Patristische Texte und Studien*, 38 (Berlin, 1994), 110–11; McCormick, *Eternal Victory*, 247, 308–11, and 358; on the imitation of Christ, G. Constable, *Three Studies in Medieval Religious and Social Thought* (Cambridge, 1995), 145–217; and, for a specific case of widespread cross iconography, V.H. Elbern, "Crucis edita forma. Gestalt und Bedeutung des sogenannten Jerusalemer Kreuzes," in F. J. Felten et al., eds., *Vita Religiosa im Mittelalter: Festschrift für Kaspar Elm zum 70. Geburtstag* (Berlin, 1999), 261–82.

45. Seal: G. Zacos and A. Veglery, *Byzantine Lead Seals*, 1.1 (Basel, 1972), 583–84, no. 807; similarly for Byzantine Africa, sixth century: "Deus adiuta Leontii (!) magistro militum Uuzacenae": J. Nesbitt and N. Oikonomides, *Catalogue of the Byzantine Seals at Dumbarton Oaks and in the Fogg Museum of Art* 1 (Washington, D.C., 1991), 35, no. 6.2. The phrase is the Latin analogue to the ubiquitous "Kyrie" or "Theotoke boethei" of the empire's Greek-language seals. Maurice, *Strategicon*, 1, 18, 138.1–12, shrewdly observed that hearing the battle cry *Nobiscum deus* increased the anxiety of some soldiers even as it excited others. In the broadcasting of religious sentiment, the military followed a broader trend in society; see, e.g., the Christian symbolism on plates and lamps produced in the pottery shops of Roman Africa: J. W. Hayes, *Late Roman Pottery* (London, 1972), 286–87.

46. McCormick, "Liturgy of War," 8–10, and "Liturgie et guerre," 215–16. For a Carolingian sermon, see below.

47. Standards: McCormick, *Eternal Victory*, 246–47, 309–12, and 358–59; Lance: C. Morris, "Policy and Visions. The Case of the Holy Lance at Antioch," in John Gillingham and J.C. Hart, eds., *War and Government in the Middle Ages: Essays in Honour of J. O. Prestwich* (Bury St. Edmunds, 1984), 33–45.

48. McCormick, "Liturgie et guerre," 215.

49. Nithard, 3, 2, ed. Philippe Lauer, *Histoire des fils de Louis le Pieux* (reprint, Paris, 1964), 80–82; cf. Ferdinand Lot and Louis Halphen, *Le règne de Charles le Chauve*, 1 (Paris, 1909), 26, 28, and 32 (from Nithard) and 37–38.

50. See above, n. 26; another case is possible, though still debated. In the late Roman Christian complex of 270 tombs excavated at Portogruaro in 1873–75, some forty apparently contemporary sarcophagi bear inscriptions identifying the entombed as Roman soldiers. They may have honored casualties from the Battle of Cold River on September 5–6, 394: D. Hoffmann, "Die spätrömischen Soldatengrabschriften von Concordia," *Museum Helveticum* 20 (1963): 22–57, whose interpretation has been challenged by R. Tomlin, "Seniores-Iuniores in the Late-Roman Field Army," *American Journal of Philology* 93 (1972): 253–78, here 269–72.

51. McCormick, *Eternal Victory*, 294–95, and E.M. Hallam, "Monasteries as 'War Memorials': Battle Abbey and La Victoire," in *Church and War*, 47–57.

52. McCormick, *Eternal Victory*, 252, and E. Follieri and I. Dujčev, "Un'acolutia inedita per i martiri di Bulgaria dell'anno 813," *Byzantion* 33 (1963): 71–106; for another ninth- or tenth-century commemorative liturgical office for the souls of Byzantine soldiers killed in battle, T. Detorakes and J. Mossay, "Un office byzantin inédit pour ceux qui sont morts à la guerre," *Le Muséon* 101 (1988): 183–211.

53. E.g., Karl Leyser, *Rule and Conflict in an Early Medieval Society. Ottonian Saxony* (Oxford, 1989), 58, with other examples. Possible Carolingian forerunners: *Eternal Victory*, 362.

54. K. Schmid, "Salische Gedenkstiftungen für fideles, servientes und milites," in L. Fenske et al., eds., *Institutionen, Kultur und Gesellschaft im Mittelalter: Festschrift für Josef Fleckenstein* (Sigmaringen, 1984), 245–64.

55. For an evocative account of private initiatives and state interventions to bury and commemorate the casualties of the ferocious battle for Berlin in 1945, see Alf Lüdtke, "Histories of Mourning: Flowers and Stones for the War Dead, Confusion for the Living," in G. Sider and G. Smith, eds., *Between History and Histories: The Making of Silences and Commemorations* (Toronto, 1997), 149–79.

56. Translated from the revised text published by Koeniger, *Die Militärseelsorge*, 72–74, with such corrections as I have noted below. See notes 32–33 to this chapter.

57. "Incipit epistola consolatoria ad pergentes in bellum," ed. Schmitz, 26. It is possible that the incongruous rubric reflects some specific circumstance of the text's genesis, e.g., someone whose words were appreciated by the Frankish host, but who was physically unable to travel to the army's assembly. For the usual formats of medieval letters, see G. Constable, *Letters and Letter Collections*, Typologie des sources du moyen âge occidental, 17 (Turnhout, 1976), 16–20.

58. As previous scholars have noted, e.g., Koeniger, *Die Militärseelsorge*, 52, n. 1.

59. Thus, the repetitious use of pronouns, which I would ascribe not to copyist's error, but to the pleonasm typical of informal speech, and which should not therefore be emended out of the text.

60. For the settlements, see, e.g., the essays by P. Fouracre, J. L. Nelson, W. Davis, and C. Wickham in W. Davies and P. Fouracre, eds., *The Settlement of Disputes in Early Medieval Europe* (Cambridge, 1986). Regarding grammatical features, e.g., *apud* = Fr. *avec;* "contra conscientiam suam" = "according to his conscience"; a masculine comparative modifies a neuter noun: "pretiosiorem corpus vestrum."

61. See notes to the translation.

62. See, e.g., Roger Wright, *Late Latin and Early Romance in Spain and Carolingian France* (Liverpool, 1982).

63. "Men . . . fathers" and "listen": Acts 7:2 and 22:1.

64. See Caesarius of Arles, *Sermones*, 13, 1, ed. G. Morin, CCL 103 (1953), 64; cf. also Jerome, *Prologus in libro Iob*, in *Biblia sacra iuxta vulgatam versionem*, ed. R. Weber et al. (Stuttgart, 1984), 732.45–46.

65. E.g., Caesarius of Arles, *Sermones*, 24, 5, and 131, 4, CCL 103: 110 and 541.

66. Cf., e.g., Leo I, *Tractatus 97, 55*, ed. A. Chavasse, CCL 138A (1973), 326:83–85; 1 Cor 6:20.

67. E.g., Jas 2:7.

68. I have restored this *vos*, suppressed by Koeniger.

69. For the language, cf., e.g., *Liber sacr. Gellon.*, CCL 159: 300, no. 2102; Heb 9:15.

70. Cf., e.g., *Liber sacramentorum Augustodunensis*, ed. O. Heiming, CCL 159B (1984), 13, no. 93.

71. Cf., e.g., Gregory I, *Moralia in Iob*, 7, 29, ed. M. Adriaen, CCL 163 (1979), 363.1–3.

72. 1 Pt 2:11 and 1 Thes 4:4.

73. Benedict, *Regula*, 7, 10, ed. A. de Vogüé and J. Neufville, *La règle de Saint Benoît*, 1, Sources chrétiennes, 181 (Paris, 1971), 474.

74. E.g., Ps 49:15.

75. E.g., Augustine, *Sermo* 64A, ed. G. Morin, *Sancti Augustini sermones post Maurinos reperti*, Miscellanea Agostiniana 1 (Rome, 1930), 312.16.

76. "... neque apud vos deducere." The verb implies animate objects that can be led. The most likely meaning therefore is the kidnapping of people (presumably to sell them as slaves) or the theft of animals. However, it is worth noting that in Old French, the cognate *déduit* can refer to sexual intercourse; see A. Rey, ed., *Dictionnaire historique de la langue française* (Paris, 1998), 1:1014.

77. The Tironian notes for *n(ecessi)-tas* are clear. I have nonetheless emended the text to *necessitate*, since the clause is otherwise quite difficult to construe, and I have not noticed for this period any parallels in the *Patrologia Latina Database*.

78. E.g., Gregory I, *Homiliae xl in Euangelia*, 1, 10, 6, and *Patrologia latina* 76: 1113B.

79. Gn 24:20; cf., e.g., *Liber sacr. August.*, CCL 159B: 224, no. 1816 (a prayer for travelers).

80. Eph 6:16.

81. Prv 15:33; cf. Sir 1:34.

82. Ez 28:13.

83. Ps 93:14.

84. 2 Chr 13:12; cf. 2 Mc 7:19.

85. Cf., e.g., Ps 88:4.

86. Office, Vespers Response, Vigil of multiple martyrs, "Tradiderunt corpora sua propter Deum ad supplicia, et meruerunt habere coronas perpetuas," ed. R. J. Hesbert, *Corpus antiphonalium officii*, 4, Rerum ecclesiasticarum documenta, Series maior, Fontes, 10 (Rome, 1970), 434, no. 7772, attested in Carolingian antiphonaries, e.g., the court Antiphonary of Compiègne (Paris, B.N. lat. 17,436).

87. Ex 17:9–16.

88. Jer 7:3 and 7; Ex 23:20, cf. 32:34; Ps 120:5.

CHAPTER THREE

THE MEDIEVAL MILITARY CHAPLAIN AND HIS DUTIES

DAVID S. BACHRACH

During the campaigning season of 1245, Herbert FitzMatthew, an officer in King Henry III of England's invasion force in Wales, was tormented by visions of his own death in battle. In order to combat his fears, Herbert summoned one of the chaplains serving with his company to whom he made a full confession of his sins and received the *viaticum*, that is, the consecrated host given to the very sick and dying as a part of the ceremony of last rites. When questioned by his fellow officers about this behavior, Herbert responded that he was sure that he would die in the approaching battle. From the chronicler's point of view, Herbert's actions helped to prepare him to meet his death on the next day at the hands of the Welsh.[1] The unnamed priest who heard Herbert's confession and gave him the Eucharist was simply one of countless military chaplains providing pastoral care to soldiers across Latin Europe and the eastern Mediterranean. This chapter examines the chaplain's office from its well-developed form in the mid-thirteenth century back to its origins during the early Middle Ages, and considers both prescriptive and descriptive or circumstantial evidence produced by contemporaries.

By the mid-thirteenth century, the sacramental and moral aspects of the chaplain's office had achieved a firm basis in law. In 1238, Pope

Gregory IX (1227–41) provided a detailed list of the military chaplain's duties in a papal bull—a legally binding expression of the papal government's religious authority—issued to the Dominican and Franciscan orders on August 9 of that year. Gregory authorized the service of mendicant friars in the Hungarian royal army and emphasized that they were to hear confessions, assign penances, and carry out the other sacraments, very likely meaning the celebration of mass and, when necessary, the provision of last rites.[2] In addition to these sacramental duties, Pope Gregory also ordered the chaplains to provide moral encouragement to the men through sermons. Indeed, he even included instructions about what the mendicant priests were supposed to say to the troops to make them feel better about their military service.[3] First, the pope stressed that the Hungarian soldiers were fighting against heretics and schismatics, namely, the Bulgarian supporters of John Asen who had defied Pope Gregory by attacking the Latin empire of Constantinople. Second, Gregory emphasized that the Hungarian ruler, on whose behalf the soldiers were fighting, was a most Christian king and Catholic prince who chose to act on behalf of the church with the aid of God. Finally, the pope authorized the mendicant chaplains to grant the soldiers remission of their sins.[4]

It is clear that Pope Gregory IX spelled out a role for military chaplains that was already well established in law. Twenty years earlier, Pope Innocent III (1198–1216) issued his own authoritative statement on the nature of the military chaplain's office in the context of the Fourth Lateran Council celebrated in 1215. Under Pope Innocent's leadership, more than four hundred bishops and eight hundred abbots, as well as numerous other ecclesiastical and lay dignitaries, gathered at Rome to discuss and ratify a program of reform, and to organize a crusade to aid the Christians living in the Holy Land. Consequently, this council has justly attracted wide attention from medieval historians as a pivotal moment in the history of the medieval church.

Pope Innocent enunciated the duties of military chaplains in the last canon of the council, which specifically dealt with the organization of a new crusade to aid the Holy Land. *Ad liberandum*, as the text dealing with the projected crusade came to be called, authorized the recruitment of priests and bishops to serve with the army for three years, clearly intending that there be continuity of pastoral care over the entire course of the campaign.[5] Pope Innocent divided the moral obligations of these chaplains into two parts. They were required to exhort

the men to behave properly as Christian soldiers, and they were supposed to teach the troops by example to maintain a proper spirit of
Christian fear of God.[6] When discussing the sacramental duties of the
priests, Pope Innocent emphasized their role as confessors, insisting
that, "if at any time [the troops] should fall into sin, they should recover through a true penance."[7]

Those who have studied the events of 1215 and the immense influence of Pope Innocent on the subsequent history of the church have
become accustomed to claiming great changes as a result of the Lateran
Council. Those scholars who do not see Innocent as a revolutionary at
least give him credit for structuring much that had been less structured and less well organized prior to his pontificate and his council.[8]
However, the Fourth Lateran Council did not bring revolutionary
change to the office of military chaplain. One cannot even claim that
it gave a firmer structure to what had already existed in a loosely organized fashion. About a century before the celebration of the Fourth
Lateran Council, Bishop Ivo of Chartres (1090–1115) laid out in great
detail the canonical responsibilities of military chaplains in the armies
of the West, including both their moral and sacramental duties.

Ivo began his discussion of a chaplain's duties by noting that there
was a longstanding canonical prohibition in effect against priests and
bishops carrying arms or fighting. He juxtaposed these forbidden behaviors with the actual duties of the chaplains. First, they were required
to celebrate mass for military forces in the field. The priests also were
required to hear the confessions of the soldiers and to assign them
penances. Ivo emphasized that priests serving in the army had to be
competent to carry out these two tasks.[9] In addition, the chaplains had
to provide spiritual care to the wounded and the dying through the rite
of extreme unction. Ivo explained, "the chosen priests should know
how to care for the ill and to grant unction with sacred oil and holy
prayers."[10] He emphasized that this was important so that no one die
without having received the sacred *viaticum*.[11] As well as these rituals,
which canon lawyers of the later twelfth century would define as sacraments, Ivo assigned four other pastoral duties to the chaplains. First,
each army was to have bishops or priests who were responsible for
bringing sacred relics into the field; although, this duty does not have
a place in the thirteenth-century legal texts, or for that matter in the
modern obligations of chaplains.[12] Also, each army was to have two or
three bishops who were required to offer blessings to the army, preach

to the troops, and work for the reconciliation of the soldiers, most likely through the rite of confession.[13]

When comparing Ivo's definition of the chaplain's role in the army to that later outlined by Pope Innocent III in 1215 and Pope Gregory IX in 1238, it is quite clear that the bishop of Chartres was determined to emphasize the sacramental—or what would come to be the sacramental—aspects of the office. As would be true of these two thirteenth-century popes, Ivo insisted that priests serving with the army had to be able to hear confessions and assign penances. But he went further in emphasizing the important part played by the celebration of mass and final unction in the chaplain's ritual repertoire.

One might postulate that the great religious upheavals of the eleventh century, particularly the launching of the First Crusade in 1095, stimulated Ivo's detailed focus on the office of the military chaplain. Clearly, the emergence of the crusading movement did have profound effects on such matters as remissions of sin, penance, and even the nature of monastic life through the foundation of orders of fighting monks.[14] However, while Ivo may well have been motivated by the contemporary military and religious situation to deal in detail with the office of military chaplain, he was no innovator. Already a century earlier, Bishop Burchard of Worms (1000–1025), the most noted canonist of his time, had considered the matter of military chaplains in exceptional detail within the context of his *Decretum*, which he wrote as a handbook intended to teach clerics how to be bishops.[15] As would be true of his successors in the twelfth and thirteenth centuries, Burchard's manual included provisions detailing both the sacramental and the moral components of the chaplain's office. In dealing with the former, he emphasized that the army have bishops and chaplain priests capable of saying mass, and that each officer in the army should have on staff a priest trained in hearing confessions and assigning penances.[16] Furthermore, Burchard insisted that the priests chosen to serve with the army should not only know how to celebrate mass and assign penances, but also that they were responsible for carrying out the rite of final unction and ensuring that no soldier died without benefit of the *viaticum*.[17]

Burchard shared with both his medieval and modern successors the view that chaplains had an obligation to provide spiritual comfort beyond that found in the rites of mass, confession, penance, and final unction. He emphasized that the bishops in the army should preach to the men and offer them blessings.[18] In addition, Burchard insisted that bishops, along with their chaplain priests, should bring sacred relics into the field, almost certainly for the purpose of providing the men with an extra source of spiritual comfort.[19]

Burchard's detailed treatment of the military chaplain's office was clearly the source for Ivo's own discussion of the office a century later, when he used a verbatim copy of the older bishop's text to express his own views about the duties of priests serving with the army. When compared with works coming out of the thirteenth-century legal tradition dealing with military chaplains, Burchard offered a fuller consideration of the priest's sacramental or proto-sacramental duties, particularly the celebration of mass, final unction, and *viaticum*, than would be true of either Pope Innocent III or Pope Gregory IX. However, like Ivo's *Decretum*, Burchard's work shares with thirteenth-century tradition a concern for extra-sacramental pastoral care, including blessings and prayers.

Some might argue that Burchard's attention to the details of soldiers' spiritual lives developed out of the terrors of the year 1000, which, if they had a significant impact upon large numbers of lay people, would undoubtedly have been of importance to soldiers as well.[20] However, Burchard was not the first churchman to provide a detailed legal outline of the duties of military chaplains. He based his treatment of the chaplain's office on a body of canons emanating from the Carolingian era.[21] Around 850, a man whom modern scholars call Benedict the Levite compiled a corpus of royal and imperial edicts, some of which were genuine and some of which were forgeries, for the purpose of creating a dossier of arguments against the improper exploitation of church resources and personnel by the secular government.[22] These documents were intended to express a maximum limit of priests' obligations, priests whose time and resources might otherwise have been abused by secular authorities. Consequently, those duties specifically mentioned in these documents are likely to have been common rather than extraordinary. In the present context, it is important to note that the compiler included texts in his dossier that dealt specifically with the question of a chaplain's duties while serving with military forces on campaign. The most detailed of these documents, ostensibly drafted to prohibit the military service of bishops and priests in the army, not only provides a list of the military chaplain's duties, but also describes in detail the reasons why chaplains were so essential to the war effort.[23]

The text begins with an injunction against priests serving in the army that was drawn from prohibitions against such behavior issued by the papal see and by numerous episcopal synods.[24] However, the author then added that two or three bishops, chosen by their fellow prelates, along with a select group of priests, could serve with the army in order to provide pastoral care. The bishops were required to preach to the troops and to offer them blessings as well as reconciliation. The specially picked group of priests was to have a thorough knowledge of the rites of penance, mass, final unction, and *viaticum*.[25] After enjoining the priests to abstain completely from bearing arms or shedding blood, the author emphasized again that their role was to carry out the sacred mysteries, that is, the celebration of mass, and to pray on behalf of the troops.[26] He then compared the pastoral care to be provided to soldiers by chaplains serving with the army on campaign to the religious work of priests who remained in their home parishes. He insisted that this second category of clerics should celebrate masses, carry out litanies, give charitable donations, and pray to God on behalf of the army.[27]

The author of the text emphasized that both kinds of religious service—by chaplains serving in the field and by priests remaining at home—were intended to help the army win victories. He noted explicitly that the purpose of providing pastoral care to soldiers, particularly the celebration of mass and saying prayers for them, was to secure God's aid in obtaining victory.[28] Similarly, the purpose of the religious celebrations by priests remaining at home was to achieve military success through God's aid.[29]

This ninth-century legal text provides the fullest description of the medieval chaplain's duties that we have seen thus far. Not only does the text record both the chaplain's proto-sacramental and moral obligations, but it also includes an explanation for the purpose of these duties, namely, that pastoral care helped to ensure God's aid for the army. Furthermore, the author added a detailed list of duties incumbent upon priests not actually serving with soldiers in the field, but who, nevertheless, had an obligation to provide religious support. The enunciation of this last duty goes far beyond anything prescribed by Burchard, Ivo, Pope Innocent III, or Pope Gregory IX. Moreover, the author's decision to explain the purpose of military pastoral care has no analog in the later legal texts I have addressed.

Having worked back to the mid-ninth century, we are very close to the origin of the office of the military chaplain. As we learn from Ralph Mathisen, in the late Roman Empire and its successor states, Christian clerics accompanied the army, as did cadres of pagans equipped with a broad spectrum of rites and ceremonies that were intended by military leaders to maintain the religious life of soldiers in the field. But there were no chaplains. However, in 742, the official status and duties of priests serving in the armies of the *regnum Francorum* underwent significant change.

During the fourth and fifth centuries, it was widely accepted at the highest levels of the church that once a soldier confessed his sins and received penance he would have to leave the military life. Pope Leo I (d. 461) made this point explicitly in a letter to Bishop Rusticus of Narbonne, stating, "it is completely contrary to all the rules of the church for a soldier to return to duty after receiving penance."[30] This system of penitential discipline had gradually changed, however, as the older idea of once-in-a-lifetime penance gave way to repeatable penance under the influence of Irish missionaries, who, in the seventh century, brought with them to the mainland the innovative tariff books.[31] These pastoral manuals were essentially schedules of sins with corresponding penances. The underlying theory was that every sin had a specific means of satisfaction attached to it, and that once this penance had been satisfied, the sinner could rejoin the Christian community. It was no longer necessary for soldiers either to wait until their final days to confess their sins or, if they chose to confess earlier, to enter a secluded or monastic life.[32]

This major development in Christian doctrine fundamentally altered the need for and duties of clerics serving with Christian soldiers. It was now necessary to provide thousands, and in some cases, tens of thousands, of soldiers with the opportunity to confess their sins before they went into battle. The earliest surviving evidence of a governmental response to this problem comes from the *Concilium Germanicum* held in 742, under the direction of Carloman, Carolingian mayor of the palace, and Boniface, the papal legate to the Frankish court. In the second canon of the council, the bishops dealt with the religious care to be provided to soldiers, and gave explicit guidance concerning the pastoral responsibilities of bishops and priests serving with the army. According to the text of the canon, the commander of the army was to have on his staff one or two bishops with their attending chaplains who were responsible for celebrating mass and carrying relics. In addition, every unit commander was required to retain a priest who was capable of hearing confessions and assigning penances to the soldiers of that command.[33] It is in this final requirement that we can see the first major expansion of the duties of the military chaplain to include the provision of individual pastoral care to all of the soldiers serving in the army.

Pope Gregory IX's description of the duties of the military chaplain in 1238 was simply the latest manifestation of a five-hundred-year legal tradition dealing with the pastoral care of soldiers. The military chaplain's office predated the Fourth Lateran Council of 1215, the First Crusade launched in 1095, the religious tumult occasioned by the turn of the millennium, and even the re-establishment of the western empire in 800 under Charlemagne's rule. Indeed, it is proper to identify the *Concilium Germanicum* as the legal origin of the chaplain's office in the Latin West.

As we have seen, prescriptive sources are especially useful in coming to understand the nature of a particular office, as they set forth in explicit terms, and often in some detail, what it was that people in authority wanted to be done. Nevertheless, such sources can easily be misinterpreted as representations of the real rather than the ideal. It is, therefore, useful to contextualize the worldview contained within prescriptive documents by considering them in relation to circumstantial or descriptive evidence that shows which elements of the ideal were actually put into practice, and which elements remained a dead letter.

A variety of eighth-century sources dealing with Frankish military operations describe the activities of Carolingian chaplains in some detail. For example, in a letter dated between 784 and 791, Pope Hadrian I (772–95) emphasized to Charlemagne (768–814) that although the papal government opposed the military service of clerics, the Frankish king was well within his rights to continue to mobilize bishops and priests to serve with Carolingian military forces for religious purposes. For his part, the pope stressed that he was most concerned that chaplains should perform their duties by preaching to the troops and hearing their confessions.[34]

That Charlemagne shared Pope Hadrian's concerns for the proper provision of pastoral care to his troops is demonstrated in a letter that he sent to his wife, Fastrada, at the commencement of a campaign in 791 against the Avars, a central Asiatic people settled to the southeast of the Frankish realm. Charlemagne reported that his men, led by priests in camp, performed three days of litanies from the fifth through the seventh of September. During the ceremonies, everyone in camp begged for God's mercy and for his aid. They specifically asked that God grant them victory in the approaching battle and keep them safe and free from danger.[35] Furthermore, each priest celebrated a special mass unless he was prevented by some infirmity, and every cleric who could do so sang fifty psalms.[36] The *Annales regni Francorum*, which served as a semi-official court history, likewise recorded that as the soldiers waited to invade the Avar lands, they held litanies for three days and participated in special masses that were carried out by priests serving with the troops for the salvation of the army (*pro salute exercitus*).[37]

Such sources record the chaplain's duties from the perspective of the secular and ecclesiastical leadership. We are fortunate also to have a *reportatio* or transcript of a sermon delivered in the late eighth century by a priest serving with Carolingian military forces. This document sheds light on one chaplain's own understanding of his office.[38] The major theme of the sermon was that soldiers should take every advantage of the religious care made available to them in camp by their chaplains, particularly the opportunity to confess their sins. According to the surviving text, the preacher made explicit the role played by priests, particularly their efforts to ensure the personal salvation of the soldiers and the success of the army as a whole. The preacher returned throughout his sermon to the efficacy of the rite of confession in reconciling penitent Christians to God, and at one point compared the confession of one's sins to standing in a battle line (*acies*) with Christ. He emphasized that just as it was crucial for each soldier to do his duty in the battle line so that the entire force would hold together, so too the soldier should perform his obligations to Christ in order to keep that union strong.[39]

The preacher demonstrated considerable persuasive skills by adducing those arguments most suited to convincing soldiers that they should participate in the rites of confession and penance. First, he reminded the troops that no person could predict how long he would live, and that it was therefore necessary to confess while time still remained. Then he emphasized that if confession were necessary for everyone, it was even more important for soldiers because they went into battle against their enemies every day.[40] After making this point, the preacher again called upon the men to confess their sins to priests because they were specialists who could heal the wounds of sin.[41] The remainder of the sermon reiterated the previous points and stressed the vital connection between confession and salvation.[42] This text and its content are clear evidence that pastoral care was actually provided to at least some Carolingian soldiers in the field.

If we move from the Carolingian empire to its eastern successor state in Germany, we have a variety of narrative accounts that describe in detail the pastoral efforts of priests and bishops serving with soldiers in combat situations.[43] One of the earliest battles to receive extensive attention during the period after the final partition of the Carolingian empire in 887 was the siege of Augsburg by a Hungarian army in August 955. In his description of Bishop Ulrich of Augsburg's actions during the siege, Gerhard, the provost of St. Mary's Cathedral in that city, sheds considerable light on the complex of religious rites carried out by the bishop on behalf of the troops under his care.

Before the beginning of battle on the second day of the siege, Bishop Ulrich celebrated a public mass for the soldiers. After consecrating the host, Ulrich saw to it that every soldier received the Eucharist. Gerhard described this event in a particular manner, claiming that the bishop "brought them all back to life with the sacred *viaticum*."[44] Gerhard's terminology is important here, because by the tenth century, the word *viaticum* had taken on two specific meanings in the liturgy celebrated in the eastern portions of the old Carolingian empire. It could either signify a health-bringing rite designed for those who were ill, or it could be used to describe the Eucharist that was taken when an individual was about to die and after he had made his last confession.[45] As was noted above, Benedict the Levite, in his mid-ninth century collection of texts, emphasized that chaplains should be diligent in their efforts to ensure that no one die without receiving the sacred *viaticum*. It would appear that the technical term utilized in these legal texts had achieved some popularity as the term used to describe the Eucharist received by soldiers before battle.

Following the celebration of mass, Bishop Ulrich preached to the men in order to comfort and inspire them as they prepared to risk their lives in battle. We are fortunate that Gerhard not only recorded the fact that Ulrich preached a sermon, but also gave a short description of its content. According to the chronicler, the basic premise of the bishop's address was that the soldiers should maintain their faith and place their trust in God. Ulrich quoted from Psalm 23, saying, "Though I walk in the valley of the shadow of death I will fear no evil because you are with me."[46] This psalm was of particular value for soldiers going into battle. It claimed for them the support of God who, the psalmist wrote, would lead them over the roads of justice for the sake of his name and protect them with his staff and rod.[47] By focusing upon this text, Bishop Ulrich let the soldiers know that respect for Christ, whose name they shared as Christians, would protect them in battle. In addition, the psalm offered God's mercy for all the days of one's life and eternal rest in the home of the Lord.[48] This theme was particularly important for men who faced the possibility of imminent death. In Gerhard's view, the bishop's actions were successful in convincing his men to stand and fight, as is clear from the author's observation that the men were prepared to go into battle both *interius* and *exterius*.

The pastoral role ascribed to Ulrich by his biographer corresponds very closely to the duties enunciated for priests serving with soldiers in the Carolingian period. In particular, Gerhard's emphasis upon preaching, leading prayers, and the celebration of mass is familiar. The same concern to provide soldiers with adequate pastoral care is evident in an early eleventh-century account of a battle that had been fought between German forces and Slavs a few decades earlier. In 982, a major force of Slavs invaded the Saxon March and caused enormous damage, including the destruction of the settlement at Hamburg. A field army was quickly mobilized under the command of Margrave Theoderic, who served as the district commander for the northeastern frontier. Bishop Thietmar of Merseburg (1009–18), whose father served as an officer in the campaign, reported that following their atrocities, the Slavic army regrouped on the Tanger River, a tributary of the Elbe. It was there that Margrave Theoderic caught the Slavs and dealt their army a serious defeat at a place called Belxem, between the Tanger and Milde rivers.[49]

In his description of the pre-battle activities, Thietmar emphasized the importance Theoderic placed on ensuring the spiritual preparation of his men.[50] According to the bishop of Merseburg, the Ottonian commander insisted that the priests in his army lead the troops through a complete regimen of religious preparation before going into combat. First, mass was celebrated in view of the entire Saxon force, very likely led by Bishops Gisilher and Hilward, whom Thietmar identified among the leading figures in the army. Following the celebration of mass, Theoderic ordered that every soldier fortify himself with the sacrament of the Eucharist (*corpus animamque celesti sacramento muniunt*).[51] This almost certainly meant that the soldiers confessed their sins to priests serving with the army. By the late tenth century, it had already been an established element of Christian practice that lay people should purify themselves through the rite of confession before receiving the host.[52] Only after completing these rites did the soldiers assemble with their units into battle lines and engage the enemy.

As was true of their counterparts east of the Rhine, the western successors of the Carolingian *imperium* also employed chaplains in military campaigns. When Anglo-Norman historians discussed Duke William II of Normandy's invasion of England in 1066, they consistently remarked upon the important role played by priests serving with the invading army in assuring the participation of the soldiers in confession, mass, and communion. When William of Malmesbury, writing about sixty years after the Battle of Hastings, sought to contrast the behavior of the Anglo-Saxon army under Harold Godwinson's command with the Christian piety of the Norman troops, he emphasized the latter's participation in religious rites led by priests. In particular, William of Malmesbury reported that Duke William's men spent the entire night confessing their sins, whereas Harold's troops indulged in drunken revelry.[53] Orderic Vitalis, widely considered to be one of the most reliable twelfth-century English historians, focused upon William and his command staff and reported that on the morning of the battle, William heard mass and received the host.[54] Wace, the twelfth-century historian who was commissioned to write a metrical history of the Norman Conquest by King Henry II of England (1154–89), may be a better witness for the service of military chaplains in the second half of the twelfth rather than the mid-eleventh century.[55] Nevertheless, it is important to note that like his earlier counterparts, Wace described priests, particularly Bishop Geoffrey of Coutances, moving among the Norman troops before battle, hearing their confessions, assigning penances, and then granting absolution.[56]

In addition to organizing the personal religious acts of confession and communion, priests serving in the Norman army also offered intercessory prayers on behalf of the soldiers in an effort to raise their morale. Wace reported that while William's men slept, the priests remained in vigil all night long, praying, chanting litanies, and singing psalms and kyries. Then, during the battle itself, the priests were called upon to continue to pray for victory.[57] Orderic Vitalis likewise noted the presence of numerous priests and other religious, including monks, who were serving with Duke William's forces. He concluded that William had brought these bishops, priests, and monks to England in order that they might fight with their prayers.[58]

As is suggested by Wace's emphasis upon the pastoral care provided by priests to the Conqueror's troops at Hastings, military chaplains of the Norman type were quickly incorporated into the new Anglo-Norman fighting forces that were developed under the Conqueror and his successors. In 1138, during the campaign that culminated in the famous Battle of the Standard, Anglo-Norman troops under the overall command of Archbishop Thurstan of York were amply supplied with chaplains. Two contemporary chroniclers detailed the duties of the priests serving with the Anglo-Norman army in the course of describing the major events of the campaign. Richard, first a canon and then prior at Hexham in Northumbria, wrote his account of the Battle of the Standard shortly after 1139. Not only was his canonry included in the area from which soldiers were mobilized to serve in the war, but also Hexham itself was attacked by the Scots. As a result, Richard had ample opportunity to interrogate eyewitnesses to the battle.[59] Aelred of Rievaulx also lived through the Battle of the Standard and later served as abbot of Rievaulx from 1147 to 1167. Aelred composed his text about seventeen years after the battle (between 1155 and 1157) and is likely to have known Richard of Hexham's account of the conflict. However, the abbot also had access to sources of information that were unavailable to Richard of Hexham. In particular, Aelred was a close friend of Walter of Espec, one of the leading lay commanders on the English side.[60]

According to both chroniclers, at his first meeting with the barons of northern England, Archbishop Thurstan promised that he would accompany the Anglo-Norman army and provide spiritual support during the course of the campaign. However, Richard of Hexham recorded that when the army began its departure from York, the barons begged him to remain behind because they were worried about his health. They requested that rather than risking his life to no purpose, he remain at York and support the soldiers with prayers, vigils, fasts, and "everything else that pertained to God."[61] Thurstan acceded to their wishes, but insisted that the army commanders take into the field his personal cross and a banner bearing the image of St. Peter.[62] He also sent Bishop Ralph of Orkney in his place, along with one of his archdeacons and a complement of his priests for the expressed purpose of assigning penances and granting absolution to the militiamen who were then pouring into the English camp at Northallerton.[63] Both Richard and Aelred also reported that Archbishop Thurstan committed himself to sending parish priests into the field to serve alongside the rural levies being mobilized to fight the Scots. According to Richard of Hexham, these parish priests were required to bring crosses into the field.[64] Abbot Aelred of Rievaulx emphasized that these priests were to bring relics and banners in addition to their crosses.[65]

After these initial preparations, the troops finally readied themselves for battle on the morning of August 22, 1138. But before the actual start of the fighting, the Anglo-Norman army commanders sought to raise the morale of their men through a series of ceremonies focused on religious and sacred objects kept in the care of the army's priests. They first raised a ship's mast from the middle of a battle wagon on which they hung sacred banners bearing the images of St. Peter the Apostle and two Northumbrian saints, Bishop John of Beverley and Bishop Wilfrid of Ripon, both of whom were renowned as confessors. They then placed a placard onto the base of the standard on which was written, "The task of soldiers is either to conquer or die."[66] On the very top of the wooden pole, the commanders placed a silver pyx containing a consecrated host.[67]

Then, as the men were drawn up for battle standing shoulder-to-shoulder and shield-to-shield, priests dressed in their white vestments walked among the soldiers carrying crosses and saints' relics. According to Aelred, the clerics intended to strengthen the morale of the men through sermons and prayers.[68] After the battle began, Bishop Ralph of Orkney and the other priests serving with the army climbed onto a high point behind the lines. Aelred reported that the bishop granted a final remission of sins to those who were fighting, after which he and his fellow priests raised their arms to heaven and prayed to God to give aid to the army. Finally, Aelred recorded that Ralph gave the soldiers his blessing, and the priests responded saying "amen amen."[69]

Chronicles composed in the thirteenth century, just prior to and after the celebration of the Fourth Lateran Council, likewise demonstrate that the description of the chaplain's office in legal documents had close analogs in the actual practice of priests on the field of battle. Two of the most reliable and informative narrative sources for the Fourth Crusade (1202–4)—Geoffroi de Villehardouin's *La conquête de Constantinople* and Henry of Valenciennes's *Histoire de l'Empereur Henri de Constantinople*—both emphasize the important role military chaplains (*li chapelain*) played in the crusader army.[70] Geoffroi de Villehardouin, a noble of very distinguished lineage, was one of six legates sent by Count Thibaut of Champagne, Count Louis of Blois, and Count Baldwin of Flanders to Venice in order to organize the transportation of the crusader army in which he led a large contingent. Villehardouin's chronicle reflects his interest in the overall state of the army and the efforts necessary to maintain it as a cohesive fighting force, including the provision of pastoral care to the troops.[71] Henry of Valenciennes was himself a chaplain in the service of Henry, the brother of Count Baldwin of Flanders and his successor as Latin emperor of Constantinople. He was therefore in an ideal position to observe the religious duties performed by the priests in the army.[72]

In his account of the first major assault carried out by the Latin crusaders against Constantinople (July 5, 1203), Villehardouin reported that on the day before the main action, bishops and priests addressed the army and emphasized the importance of each man confessing his sins before going into combat. In explaining this summons to participate in the sacrament of confession, Villehardouin recorded that the chaplains had emphasized that no one knew God's plans for him, so it was better to be prepared for one's end.[73] Villehardouin himself shared this view of the importance of confession and, furthermore, believed that the bishops and priests succeeded in communicating their message to the soldiers. In fact, he reported that the entire army participated in the sacrament eagerly and with great devotion.[74]

The crucial role played by military chaplains during the Fourth Crusade is made even clearer when we consider the crusaders' and priests' behavior, during the spring of 1204, in the wake of their betrayal by the crusaders' erstwhile protégé, Emperor Alexius. This scion of the Byzantine imperial family broke his agreements with the Latin army under pressure from his court. He was subsequently deposed by one of his own generals, who then attacked the crusaders camped outside of the city. However, despite the grim necessity of again besieging and then assaulting Constantinople, the morale of the army remained high, in part because of the energetic efforts of the priests serving with the troops. Henry of Valenciennes reported that on the night of April 8, 1204, after military commanders had decided upon a major assault to capture the city, the army was assembled to hear a sermon intended to encourage them for the next day's action. The officers chose a chaplain named Philip to lead the army in prayer and to exhort them to make the proper sacramental preparation before battle. Philip, speaking in French to his French audience, stressed that the soldiers depended upon God's aid in the upcoming fight because they had no refuge and nowhere to run. But he reassured them that they would be worthy of this aid because they would make true confessions of their sins.[75] Philip's sermon could have left no doubt in the minds of the crusaders that their spiritual well-being, as well as their physical safety, depended upon their participation in the sacrament of confession. In fact, the men were commanded by the preacher to participate in the rite.

The next day saw the celebration of the full panoply of rites and ceremonies appropriate for priests accompanying an army into battle.

At the break of dawn, the chaplains celebrated mass and prayed that God would grant them honor and victory over their enemies. Following the end of mass, the soldiers confessed and received the host.[76] Then, after the crusaders had formed their battle lines, Philip again addressed the army. On this occasion he stressed that the troops had confessed and were therefore washed clean of all their sins.[77]

The crucial moment in the development of the chaplain service came in 742 when the Frankish government formally established the office of the unit chaplain, whose incumbent was obliged to hear confessions and assign penances to soldiers under his care. Moreover, the bishops gathered at the *Concilium Germanicum* instituted a second reform that required each army to have a headquarters' chaplain unit consisting of one or two bishops with their attendant priests. By the mid-ninth century, after the successful implementation of these reforms, the office of military chaplain had a well-defined legal status, including both proto-sacramental and moral obligations. Over the course of the eleventh, twelfth, and thirteenth centuries, ecclesiastical authorities, including a number of popes, adapted the original Carolingian chaplain's office by emphasizing those elements that fit their own needs and concerns. The continuing and important role of military chaplains in medieval armies over this half millennium, which is indicated by these legal documents, is confirmed by the appearance of priests in numerous narrative accounts that stress their service on the battlefield. Consequently, it is clear that soldiers in the armies of medieval Europe, like their counterparts in the early modern and modern eras, could depend upon priests to see them through the terrors and moral dilemmas inherent in warfare.

NOTES

1. Concerning this account, see Matthew Paris, *Chronica Majora*, ed. Henry Richards Luard, 7 vols., Rolls series 57 (London: Longman and Co., 1872–83), 4:407–9.

2. Johanis Hyacinth Sbaraleae, ed., *Bullarium Franciscanum Romanorum Pontificum*, 4 vols. (Rome, 1759–68), 1:249.

3. See Christoph T. Maier, *Preaching the Crusades: Mendicant Friars and the Cross in the Thirteenth Century* (New York: Cambridge University Press, 1994), 117–20.

4. Sbaraleae, *Bullarium Franciscanum*, 1:249.

5. *Conciliorum Oecumenicorum Decreta*, 3d ed. (Bologna: Instituo per le Scienze Religiose, 1973), 267.

6. Ibid., 267.

7. Ibid.

8. Concerning the role of the Fourth Lateran Council as an agent of change, see John W. Baldwin, "Paris et Rome en 1215: les réformes du IVe concile de latran," *Journal des savants* 1 (1997): 99–124; Nicholas Vincent, "Two Papal Letters on the Wearing of the Jewish Badge, 1221 and 1229," *Jewish Historical Studies: Transactions of the Jewish Historical Society of England* 34 (1997): 209–24; Peter von Moos "Occulta cordis; contrôle de soi et confession au Moyen Age," *Médiévales: langues, textes, histoire* 30 (1996): 117–37; Richard M. Fraher, "IV Lateran's Revolution in Criminal Procedure: The Birth of *Inquisitio*, the End of Ordeals, and Innocent III's Vision of Ecclesiastical Politics," in Rosalius Josephus Castillo, ed., *Studia in honorem eminentissimi Cardinalis Alphonsi M. Stickler* (Rome: Libreria Ateno Salesinno, 1992), 97–111; Pierre-Marie Gy, "Les définitions de la confession après le quatrième concile du Latran," *L'Aveu: Antiquité et Moyen Age: Collections de l'Ecole Française de Rome* 88 (1986): 283–96; and Leonard E. Boyle, "The Fourth Lateran Council and Manuals of Popular Theology," in Thomas H. Heffernan, ed., *The Popular Literature of Medieval England* (Knoxville: University of Tennessee Press, 1985), 30–43.

9. Ivo of Chartres, *Decretum*, Patrologiae Cursus Completus (= PL) 161: 424.

10. Ibid.

11. I follow here Frederick S. Paxton, *Christianizing Death: The Creation of a Ritual Process in Early Medieval Europe* (Ithaca: Cornell University Press, 1990), 192–95.

12. I have found one important exception regarding the use of relics in modern armies. During the First World War, Russian Orthodox priests serving in the Russian imperial army routinely brought relics to the front. See Aleksandr S. Senin, "Russian Army Chaplains during World War I," *Russian Studies in History* 32 (1993): 43–52.

13. Ivo of Chartres, *Decretum*, PL 161: 424.

14. Concerning the developing role of indulgences in the period after the First Crusade, see Maier, *Preaching the Crusades*; James A. Brundage, *Medieval Canon Law and the Crusader* (Madison: University of Wisconsin Press, 1969); and Jean Richard, "Urbain II, la prédication de la croisade et la définition de l'indulgence," in Ernst-Dieter Hehl, Hubertus Seibert, and Franz Staab, eds., *Deus qui mutat tempora: Menschen und Institutionen im Wandel des Mittelalters: Festschrift für Alfons Becker zu seinem fünfund-sechzigsten Geburtstag* (Sigmaringen: J. Thorbeck, 1987), 129–35. Concerning the changing views of penance and their effect on crusading warfare, see Jonathan Riley-Smith, *The First Crusaders, 1095–1131* (Cambridge: Cambridge University Press, 1997), and Marcus Bull, *Knightly Piety and the Lay Response to the First Crusade: The Limousin and Gascony c. 970–c. 1130* (Oxford: Clarendon Press, 1993). Works dealing with the military orders include Jonathan Riley-Smith, *Hospitallers: The History of the Order of St. John* (London: Hambledon Press, 1999), and Malcolm Barbor, *The New Knighthood: A History of the Order of the Temple* (Cambridge: Cambridge University Press, 1994).

15. Burchard of Worms, *Decretum*, PL 140: 612–13. Burchard's purpose in writing the *Decretum* is discussed by Paul Fournier, "Études critiques sur le décret de Burchard de Worms," *Nouvelle Revue Historique de Droit Français et Étranger* 34 (1910): 41–112, 213–21, 289–331, and 564–84.

16. Burchard, *Decretum*, PL 140: 612.

17. Ibid., 612–13.

18. Ibid., 612.

19. Ibid.

20. The fullest account of the terrors of the year 1000 is Richard Allen Landes, *Relics, Apocalypse, and the Deceits of History: Ademar of Chabannes, 989–1034* (Cambridge: Harvard University Press, 1995).

21. For the identification of this text as the work of Benedict the Levite, see Hartmut Hoffmann and Rudolf Pokorny, *Das Dekret des Bischofs Burchard von Worms* (Munich: Monumenta Germaniae Historica [= MGH], 1991), 181.

22. Concerning Benedict's use of sources, see Gerhard Schmitz, "Die Waffe der Fälschung zum Schutz der Bedrängten? Bemerkungen zu gefälschten Konzils- und Kaptilarientexten," in *Fälschungen im Mittelalter: Internationaler Kongress der Monumenta Germaniae Historica*, 5 vols. (Hanover: MGH, 1988), 2:79–110. Schmitz argues specifically (92) that Pseudo-Benedict created his collection from previously existing materials.

23. *Capitularia Spuria*, MGH Legum 2 pars altera, ed. G.H. Pertz (Hanover: MGH, 1837), 110, no. 141.

24. *Capitularia Spuria*, 110, no. 141.

25. Ibid.

26. Ibid.

27. Ibid.

28. Ibid.

29. Ibid.

30. Pope Leo I, *Epistolae*, PL 54: 1206–7.

31. See Bernard Poschmann, *Penance and the Anointing of the Sick* (New York: Herder and Herder, 1964), 131–38; Raymond Kottje, "Die Tötung im Kriege: Ein moralisches und rechtliches Problem im frühen Mittelalter," *Beiträge zur Friedensethik* 11 (1991): 1–21 passim; and H. Lutterbach, "Die Bußordines in den iro-fränkischen Paenitentialen: Schlüssel zur Theologie und Verwendung der mittelalterlichen Bußbücher," *Frühmittelalterliche Studien* 30 (1996): 151–53.

32. Concerning the important role of penitential manuals in lay religious life, see Rob Meens, "The Frequency and Nature of Early Medieval Penance," in Peter Biller and A.J. Minnis, eds., *Handling Sin: Confession in the Middle Ages* (Woodbridge: York Medieval Press, 1998), 35–63; Michael S. Driscoll, "Penance in Transition: Popular Piety and Practice," in Lizette Larson-Miller, ed., *Medieval Liturgy: A Book of Essays* (New York: Garland Publishing, 1997), 124–38, see note 5 for a useful introduction to the literature; Kottje, "Die Tötung im Kriege," 1–21; and Allen J. Frantzen, "The Significance of the Frankish Penitentials," *Journal of Ecclesiastical History* 30 (1979): 409–10. Frantzen forcefully rejects Rosamond Pierce's (McKitterick) argument in "The 'Frankish' Penitentials," *Studies in Church History* 11 (1975): 31–39, that penitential handbooks had only a brief history of use in the Frankish church. See also Bernhard Poschmann, *Buße und Letzte Ölung* (Freiburg: Herder, 1951), 71–77.

33. Albert Werminghoff, ed., *Concilia Aevi Karolini*, vol. 1, pt. 1, MGH Concilia, vol. 2, pt. 1 (Hanover: MGH, 1906), 2–4.

34. *Epistolae Merovingici et Karolini Aevi*, 8 vols. (Berlin: MGH, 1892–1939), 3:625.

35. Ibid., 4:528.

36. Ibid., 4:529.

37. Friedrich Kurz, ed., *Annales Regni Francorum*, MGH Scriptores Rerum Germanicarum 10 (Hanover: MGH, 1895), 88.

38. This sermon appears in the appendix to Michael McCormick's "The Liturgy of War from Antiquity to the Crusades," in this volume. Albert Michael Koeniger, *Die Militärseelsorge der Karolingerzeit: Ihr Recht und ihre Praxis* (Munich: Verlag der J.J. Lentner Buchhandlung, 1918), 51, n. 1.

39. Ibid., 69.

40. Ibid.

41. Ibid.

42. See ibid., 69–70.

43. Examples of the celebration of a range of religious rites by soldiers and priests include Widukind of Corvey, *Rerum Gestarum Saxonicum*, ed. Paul Hirsch, MGH Scriptores Rerum Germanicarum 60 (Hanover: MGH, 1935), 52–53, 157; Gerhard von Augsburg, *Vita S. Oudalrici Episcopi Augustani*, ed. Walter Berschin and Angelika Häse (Heidelberg: Universitätsverlag C. Winter, 1993), 196; *Die Chronik des Bischofs Thietmar von Merseburg*, ed. Robert Holtzmann, MGH Scriptores Rerum Germanicarum, n.s., 9 (Berlin: MGH, 1935), 48, 120; and D.G. Waitz, ed., *Annalista Saxo*, MG SS 6 (Hanover: MGH, 1844), 638.

44. Gerhard, *Vita S. Oudalrici*, 196.

45. See Paxton, *Christianizing Death*, 192–95.

46. Gerhard, *Vita S. Oudalrici*, 401.

47. Boniface Fischer, ed., *Biblia Sacra iuxta Vulgatam Versionem* (Stuttgart: Deutsche Bibelgesellschaft, 1983), 794.

48. Ibid.

49. *Die Chronik des Bischofs Thietmar von Merseburg*, 120.

50. Ibid., 122.

51. Ibid.

52. On this point, see Regino of Prüm, *Libri Duo de Synodalibus Causibus et Disciplinis Ecclesiasticis*, ed. F.G.A. Wasserschleben (Leipzig, 1840), 156, c. 329. The connection between confession and communion is stressed by Joseph Avril, "Remarques sur un aspect de la vie religieuse paroissiale: la pratique de confession et de la communion du Xe au XIVe siècle," in *L'encadrement religieux des fidèles au moyen-âge et jusqu'au concile de Trente* (Paris: Ministère de l'éducation nationale, 1985), 348, 352, and Rob Meens, "Frequency and Nature of Early Medieval Penance," 38.

53. William of Malmesbury, *Gesta Regum Anglorum*, ed. R.A.B. Mynors, R.M. Thomson, and M. Winterbottome, 2 vols. (Oxford: Clarendon Press, 1998), 1:454.

54. Orderic Vitalis, *The Ecclesiastical History of Orderic Vitalis*, ed. Marjorie Chibnall, 6 vols. (Oxford: Clarendon Press, 1969–80), 2:172.

55. Concerning the value of Wace's text for the history of the Norman Conquest, see Elisabeth van Houts, "The Memory of 1066 in Written and Oral Traditions," *Anglo-Norman Studies* 19 (1996): 167–80, and Matthew Bennet, "The Roman de Rou of Wace as a Source for the Norman Conquest," *Anglo-Norman Studies* 5 (1982): 21–39.

56. Wace, *Le Roman de Rou*, ed. A.J. Holden, 2 vols. (Paris: 1971), 2:157.

57. Ibid.

58. Orderic Vitalis, *Ecclesiastical History of Orderic Vitalis*, 2:172.

59. Richard of Hexham, *De Gestis Regis Stephani et de Bello Standardii*, ed. Richard Howlett, 4 vols., Rolls series 82 (London: Longman and Co., 1884–89), 3:139–78. The house at Hexham was attacked by the Scots during their invasion and three of the canons were killed. See D. Whitelock, M. Brett, and C.N.L. Brooke, eds., *Councils and*

Synods with Other Documents Relating to the English Church AD 871–1204, 2 vols. (Oxford: Clarendon Press, 1981), 2:767–68.

60. Aelred of Rievaulx, *Relatio Venerabilis Aelredi Abbatis Rievallensis de Standardo,* ed. Richard Howlett, 4 vols., Rolls series 82 (London: Longman, 1886), 3:181–99.

61. Richard of Hexham, *De gestis Regis Stephani,* 161.

62. Ibid.

63. Ibid., 162.

64. Ibid., 161.

65. Aelred of Rievaulx, *Relatio de Standardo,* 182.

66. Richard of Hexham, *De gestis Regis Stephani,* 163–64.

67. Ibid.

68. Aelred, *Relatio de Standardo,* 192.

69. Ibid., 195–96.

70. Geoffroi de Villehardouin, *La conquête de Constantinople,* ed. Edmond Faral, 2 vols. (Paris: Société d'édition les belles lettres, 1938–39); Henri de Valenciennes, *Histoire de l'Empereur Henri de Constantinople,* ed. Jean Longnon (Paris: P. Geuthner, 1948).

71. Concerning Villehardouin's perspective and reliability, see Edmond Faral, "Geoffroi de Villehardouin: La question de sa sincérité," *Revue Historique* 176 (1936): 530–82, and Jeanette M. A. Beer, *Villehardouin: Epic Historian* (Geneva: Droz, 1968), 2–3.

72. Henri de Valenciennes, *Histoire de l'Empereur Henri de Constantinople,* 7–8.

73. Villehardouin, *La conquête de Constantinople,* 1:152.

74. Ibid.

75. Henri de Valenciennes, *Histoire de l'Empereur Henri de Constantinople,* 37–38.

76. Ibid., 38.

77. Ibid., 44.

CHAPTER FOUR

Did the Nature of the Enemy Make a Difference?

Chaplains in the Wars of the Three Kingdoms, 1642–49

ANNE LAURENCE

From the years 1642 to 1649, the English Parliament raised an army that fought wars against three different sets of enemies in three wars: one civil war and two wars of conquest. Religious matters played a central role in all three conflicts, and for all three, Parliament made provisions for chaplains to be part of the army. Chaplains served on both sides of the civil war that split England in the period from 1642 to 1649, with the army of the Parliament of England and with the Royalist troops of King Charles I. They also served in the struggles in Ireland and in Scotland, both of which concluded with the conquest and occupation of those countries by English forces. The English Civil War and the contemporary wars in Scotland and Ireland—known as the Wars of the Three Kingdoms—offer us the opportunity to examine whether chaplains served a different function if the nature of the war, and of the enemy, differed.[1]

THE WARS OF THE THREE KINGDOMS

Relations between the king and Parliament deteriorated into war in 1642 after King Charles I's flagrant disregard for the rights of his subjects and his abuse of what Parliament considered to be its legitimate powers. Charles had been forced to call Parliament to ask for money to quell rebellions in both Scotland and Ireland, each of which was a kingdom in its own right with its own Parliament. The English Parliament declined to give the king funds until he redressed grievances closer to home. Charles had also tried to enforce conformity within the established church—the Church of England—to ceremonies that many clergy and laity regarded as popish and that challenged the Calvinist theology of the Anglican church. There were those, known as Puritans, who believed that the Anglican church settlement contained too many remnants of the pre-Reformation Roman Catholic church and who wanted to move the church in a more Protestant direction by abolishing bishops, removing the emphasis on the sacraments, allowing extempore prayer and preaching by men not ordained as ministers, and giving the laity a greater part in church government.

When civil war broke out, dissent from Anglican theology and practices was a punishable offence in England, so the character of the church was a matter of intimate concern to everyone. Moderate Puritans who wanted the church to be more Protestant were ultimately prepared to take up arms for that cause. Over the course of the Civil War, a growing range of radical Protestant views was aired among the Parliamentary forces, as was the idea of religious pluralism or toleration, an abhorrent concept to many moderates. Against them were ranged Anglicans—members of the established Church of England—who believed that resistance to the monarch was wrong. Those moderate Anglicans who were not prepared to resist their lawful ruler, the king, found themselves allied, against their will, with Roman Catholics.

Contemporary commentators in England saw religion as a fundamental casus belli. A Parliamentary army chaplain, writing twenty years after the war, said that "the generality of the stricter diligent sort of Preachers" joined Parliament, and that "it was principally the differences about Religious matters that filled up the Parliaments Armies, and put Resolution and Valour into their Soldiers, which carried them on in another manner than mercenary Soldiers are carried on."[2] But not all chaplains shared his views. The Baptist Hanserd Knollys, writing his autobiography at the age of ninety-three, thirty years after the war, said he left the school at which he was teaching "to go into the Parliaments Army, and preached freely to the common Souldiers, till I did perceive the Commanders sought their own things more than the cause of God and his People, breaking their Vows and solemne Engagements. Whereupon I left the Army."[3]

Charles's attempts four years earlier to impose the Anglican prayer book on the Scots, whose established church was considerably more Calvinist than the Church of England, were a major cause of the war that broke out in Scotland in 1638. Meanwhile, in Ireland in 1641, the Catholic Irish rebelled against the Protestant English government and engaged in guerrilla tactics against the settlers, or planters, from England and Scotland who occupied much expropriated Irish land. The war in Scotland was largely concluded by 1651, but the war in Ireland continued until 1653. Both conflicts provide a counterpoint to events in England. The antagonists in Scotland and Ireland were not necessarily divided by the Royalist/Parliamentarian split that separated the warring parties in England, and religious issues came into play differently in these wars of conquest.

The wars that took place in the British Isles from 1642 to 1649 were part of a wider European conflict, a series of confessional wars that pitched Protestants and Catholics against each other. Religious and political differences divided antagonists in ways that are frequently difficult to disentangle, regardless of whether the wars were national, tribal, or civil. The extent to which the Wars of the Three Kingdoms are regarded as confessional has an important bearing upon how we understand the role that religion played in the various warring armies. Recent discussion about whether the English Civil War was the last of the early modern wars of religion or the first European revolution provides a larger landscape in which to consider the role of religion in armies in general and the role of chaplains in particular.[4]

When the English Parliament raised an army against the King, its soldiers were initially volunteers—locally recruited Englishmen—but within a year, conscription was introduced, as it was for the king's army. Chaplains were not conscripted. By the end of 1642, each side had several armies in different parts of the country. A good many ordinary soldiers fought for both parties, not for ideological reasons, but because prisoners were often encouraged to change sides. Parliamentarians made a point of claiming the moral high ground for the behavior of their soldiers; when they were unruly, they were compared to the king's army. A Parliamentary chaplain, writing after the war, commented that "Though none could deny but the Earl [of Essex, commander in chief of the first army of the Parliament] was a Person of great Honour, Valour, and

Sincerity: yet did some Accuse the Soldiers under him of being too like the King's Soldiers in Profaneness, lewd and vitious Practices, and rudeness in their Carriage towards the Country."[5] In contrast, the Royalists, unruly though their soldiers were, asserted the inconceivability of rebelling against the rightful king.

Apart from forces raised in England, the Scots provided an army to support Parliament, and the king brought over troops from Ireland (many of them English Protestant settlers, though the Parliamentarian press often characterized them as savage Irish Catholics). The civil war in England continued until 1646, when Parliament captured the king's headquarters at Oxford. In 1648, war was renewed; this time the Scots supported the king. The Royalists in England were finally defeated at the Battle of Preston in 1648, and five months later the king was executed. Having defeated their enemies at home, the Parliamentarians set about subduing Ireland and then Scotland, where there had been warfare sporadically throughout the 1640s.

The theological complexion of the Parliamentary forces in England was extremely heterodox, ranging from moderates who supported some kind of an established church, and who would even have tolerated bishops, providing no *jure divino* claims were made, to people who proclaimed themselves to be Seekers, who would accept no formal ecclesiastical organization at all. During this period, "gathered congregations," whose members believed in the supremacy of the individual congregation over any form of church hierarchy, flourished. In these years, Baptists and Congregationalists (or Independents, as they were then known) emerged as denominations. Within the Parliamentary army, these formal distinctions had no official validity, although they provoked considerable debate and sometimes hostility between members of the army.

When it came to sending an army in 1649 to subdue Ireland, however, the only requirement was that it be Protestant. The doctrinal and ecclesiological divisions that had wracked the army in England were of little account in 1649. For the most part, English troops were highly resistant to going to Ireland, however much the expedition was advertised as a crusade against popery. In contrast, the military force that went to Scotland in 1650 went less unwillingly, even though the religion of the Scots enemy, Presbyterianism, was closer to that of members of the Parliamentary army than was that of the English Royalists, let alone the Irish Catholics.

Although there had been a transformation in military tactics in Europe, warfare was still a matter of physical contact. Soldiers for the most part had to look the enemy in the eye. Nor had the military revolution altered the way in which appointments were made in armies; patronage continued to govern the recruitment of officers and chaplains. Although the Parliamentary army was reformed in 1645 to create the New Model Army, an army more open to talent than its predecessors, officers and chaplains were still clients of the commander of the regiment or garrison who appointed them. But perhaps the most important characteristic of this kind of war was that it was, in one historian's words, an "untidy, mobile affair, conducted by troops who were often literally interchangeable, a war profoundly integrated with civilian society and only intermittently a matter of set-piece battles."[6]

CHAPLAINS IN THE WAR IN ENGLAND

Numerous Pamphlets there are abroad . . . broacht by the seducing Chaplains of the Army and their accomplices . . . yea, these Army Chaplains have so corrupted their hearers and disciples from the simplicity of the Gospel that the whole Army now contends for Toleration by the Sword in the Field.[7]

The wars of the mid-seventeenth century were really the first wars in which it was possible to mobilize the press to advertise the virtues of one side and the vices of the other. Chaplains were both subjects of the propaganda war conducted in the press between the two sides and a part of each side's own propaganda effort. Their job in this role was to sustain men who had to face their neighbors in a war over political and religious differences. Weekly newspapers (known as newsbooks) gave news of the war, their titles proliferating as factions on each side multiplied. In the newsbooks, chaplains were used as a metaphor for dissatisfactions with the religious temper of the armies in England. They also served as an ideological symbol for armies fighting in the wars in Scotland and Ireland.

Tom Tell-Troth, pseudonymous author of the above account of the role played by chaplains in the Parliamentary army, was not one of the Royalist enemy, but a disaffected Parliamentarian pamphleteer.

Appearing in 1647, after the first civil war had ended, this pamphlet was characteristic of the vociferous criticism of Parliament and its armies by its own supporters, as dissatisfied groups and individuals sought to make their voices heard in the negotiations over a peace settlement with the king. Intemperate though Tom Tell-Troth's words are, they reflect a theological position that was commonly found among moderate supporters of Parliament.

On the other side, although those who supported the king were for the most part Anglicans, some had had to swallow their dislike of the king's attempts to increase the amount of ceremonial in the church. However wrong he might be, they believed, nothing justified resistance to the monarch. The duty of absolute obedience to the king, therefore, was perhaps the most distinctive feature of the sermons of the Royalist clergy.[8] One of the few surviving Royalist tracts addressed to soldiers characterizes the Parliamentarians as fighting for base silver, whereas Royalists had right on their side. However, the author continued, the king's soldiers behaved "as if their loyalty to their Prince would excuse their Rebellion against God."[9] This was a reference to the notorious lack of discipline of the Royalist soldiers. Among other subjects the author touched on was the difference between justly claimed spoils of the battlefield and unjustified plunder (a crime against civilians).[10]

A comparable publication from the Parliament sought to provide, in a somewhat casuistical fashion, justification for taking up arms against the king. According to a sermon originally given to volunteer soldiers in Norwich, and printed by order of the House of Commons, "There is much difference between taking up of Armes against the Kings Person, and taking up of Armes for the defence of the Kingdom, without the Kings command."[11] The protection of the Protestant religion, it was argued, justified the war: "If things go ill, the worst is death, and what great matter it is to dye for your God, a little before your time, who would live when Religion is dead? . . . Can you lose too much for Christ who hath lost so much for you?"[12] Simeon Ashe, a chaplain in the Parliamentary forces in the early years of the war, reported an instance of chaplains taking up a matter of discipline. After the Parliamentary victory at Marston Moor, one of the few, big, set-piece battles of the war, some of the Parliament's troops had taken flight, but had "by their Ministers and others been so sharpely reproved . . . that there is hope they will regain their credit, by good service upon the next occasion."[13]

Parliamentary army chaplains were noted for their preaching.[14] This reputation is indicative of the differences between the Royalist and Parliamentary armies, and the role of religion in them—none of the men known to have served as Royalist chaplains was celebrated for what he did in the army, but rather for other aspects of his career.[15] Nevertheless, many of those Parliamentary chaplains who served in the early months of the war soon returned home to their parishes. The chaplain Richard Baxter, with hindsight, blamed them for allowing the spread of heterodoxy, "by forsaking the Army, and taking themselves to an easier and quieter way of life."[16] From the start of the war there was a grave shortage of chaplains; the notional establishment of one per regiment was never achieved. Even if it had been, the dispersal of forces in small numbers in garrisons meant that there could never have been an adequate supply.[17]

Chaplains frequently asserted the special place that the Parliament's army held in God's eyes. In a thanksgiving sermon to Parliament for the victory in 1644 over the Royalists at Cheriton, Obadiah Sedgwick, who had served as a chaplain in the early months of the war, argued that this special place was the result of the soldiers' godliness: "O Sirs! An Humbling Army, a praying Army, a God-trusting Army, that is the army which is able (in some sense) to overcome God, that is the Army which is most likely to overcome men."[18]

Simeon Ashe told a story of how, after the Parliament's victory at Marston Moor in 1644, some troops came out of a wood and, seeing a group of foot soldiers, approached them, "but hearing them sing Psalms, they swore, that thereby they know them to be their enemy." This, he claimed, must be "our discriminating character. . . . That it is our constant practise to sing forth the praises of our God."[19] William Sedgwick, who had served as chaplain to the Parliamentary garrison at Ely, asserted that the "Army is a peculiar Ordinance of God wherein he hath a speciall delight."[20] Sedgwick was perhaps more extreme in his views than most, for he left the army in order to berate the high command for betraying the ideals of their troops by putting "the world" before "godliness."[21]

The range of religious views to be found among the supporters of Parliament increased month by month as press censorship and control of the pulpit lapsed, allowing unprecedented freedom of expression and conscience. The Puritan Anglicans who started the war were soon joined by Presbyterians (who opposed divine right episcopacy), Independents

(Congregationalists, who believed in the congregation as the central organizing principle of the church), and Baptists (who believed in adult baptism and who had existed only in very small numbers before the war). Further groups emerged as the war continued: there were Muggletonians, Ranters, and, most important for subsequent events, Quakers, whose original strength was within the Parliamentary armies. (They did not become pacifist until the later seventeenth century.) It was this religious free-for-all, promoted chiefly by soldiers (laymen) preaching in the army, that was of such concern to Parliament and to the more orthodox members of the army command.

The spread of heterodoxy would, it was believed, undermine the ideological purity of the Parliament's cause. Increasingly, the task of chaplains was to control the spread of heterodox religious views among the soldiers in the interests of military discipline, a task that became harder as high-ranking officers such as Colonels Hewson and Pickering joined the common soldiers and noncommissioned officers who preached. A Presbyterian critic wrote: "Our Armies are the Nurseries of all errours and all our evills, and hence we may see the true cause why all the Sectaries are so for warre and keeping up the Armies, cannot abide to hear of disbanding, because their Kingdome is inlarged and maintained thereby."[22] And, in the words of the chaplain Richard Baxter, "My life among [the soldiers] was a daily contending against Seducers, and gently arguing with the more Tractable."[23] He deplored the "hot-headed Sectaries" of the Parliamentary forces, but he also commented, "All the sober men that I was acquainted with, who were against the Parliament, were wont to say, 'the King hath the better Cause, but the Parliament hath the better men.'"[24] For both writers, the danger came from preaching laymen, not from chaplains.

As the war in England progressed, larger political claims were made for the Parliamentary army, often by chaplains. The substance of the chaplains' political message derived from the idea that God had chosen the Parliament's army. The radical group of civilians and soldiers known as the Levellers exploited the democratic political implications of this doctrine. Hugh Peter took part in the Putney Debates; a number of chaplains and former chaplains were present at the Whitehall Debates a year later, though only Peter, Thomas Collier, and William Erbury of the currently serving chaplains spoke there. Few chaplains went as far as the Levellers' position, and those who did spoke out only after leaving the army. William Sedgwick, for example, declared, a few months after his departure, that the soldiers were "rightly and truly the people, not in a grosse heape, or in a heavy dull body, but in a selected choice way."[25] "The Army," he argued, "are truly the people of England, and have the nature and power of the whole in them."[26] Chaplains attracted special criticism because people outside the army believed they disseminated radical religious views that had implications for any political settlement. This was, for the most part, a misapprehension; chaplains in the Parliamentary forces were not raving extremists, despite their exceptionally bad press.[27] It was laymen such as Henry Denne and Paul Hobson who gave the army a reputation for radical sectarianism; the further association of religious radicals with the chaplains was almost entirely independent of the chaplains themselves.[28]

CHAPLAINS IN IRELAND AND SCOTLAND

The Battle of Preston in 1648 signaled the end of war in England and left the victorious Parliamentarians free to subdue Ireland and Scotland. An English army invaded Ireland in 1649 and gradually defeated the Catholic forces and their Royalist Protestant allies. Meanwhile, Scotland was invaded in 1650. Here, the conquest took rather less time, concluding with Cromwell's victory at the battle of Worcester in 1651. Both Ireland and Scotland, however, were occupied by an English army throughout the 1650s.

Within the Wars of the Three Kingdoms, the identity of the enemy made a significant difference for chaplains. The theological preferences of the chaplains in Parliamentary forces in England were judged to a nicety, while in Ireland, the provision of chaplains to the expeditionary force was never independent of the English government's desire to promote Protestantism.[29] Little attention was paid to the kind of theological divisions that had wracked the English Parliamentarians: in Ireland in 1649, it was sufficient that a man be Protestant. Well over half of the chaplains of the expeditionary force and army of occupation stayed on to further the government's policy of supplying the country with a godly (that is, Protestant) ministry whose chief task was to keep the settlers Protestant rather than to convert Irish Catholics.[30] Generally, troops intended for Ireland loathed the thought of going there, however much the war was advertised as a righteous struggle against popery. One of the most active recruiters for the Irish expedition was the chaplain Hugh Peter, who was a sufficiently trusted servant of the

Parliamentary army command to be sent to deal with a mutiny among embarking soldiers.[31]

The military expedition to Scotland in 1650 was made up of members of the Parliamentary army who had not gone to Ireland the year before. Attempts were made to give the invading army a sense of mission, despite the contradictions of going to war against co-religionists on the grounds that they supported Charles II, who had been declared king in Scotland after his father's execution. A letter signed by three chaplains, and sent out to all units by the army, sought to appeal to popular religious fervor: "Let both you and us be instant in Prayer, for the uniting of the hearts of all that fear the Lord . . . that there may not be found any of the generation of the just, joyning Issue with those that support the Beast."[32] Even though theologically there was much for English Puritans and sectaries to approve of in Scottish Presbyterianism, these enemies were associated with the Antichrist because they favored the king. Thus, war against the Scots was justified. The chaplains' job in this conflict was to keep English soldiers committed to the political aims of the English government and to dissuade them from any ecclesiastical fellow-feeling with the Scots, especially once the Scots had been defeated on the field and the English were merely an army of occupation.

The war against the Scots posed a different order of problem from that in Ireland. Soldiers had to be persuaded to go to war against their co-religionists whose only fault was to support the monarchy. Only by appealing to sectarian distinctions could attacks on fellow anti-episcopal Protestants be justified. The army that went to Scotland was accompanied by chaplains from the same range of denominations as those who had served in England, but Baptists were better represented than they had been previously. It was easier for them to justify a war against Presbyterian Scots than it was for the moderate Independents (Congregationalists) and Presbyterians who had made up the majority of chaplains in the army hitherto. Politically, it was desirable for the English army to support the gathered congregations of the religious radicals to emphasize their difference from the Scots. Troops in Scotland were isolated from the English civilians whose religious beliefs were regarded as politically suspect. Chaplains to the English forces in Scotland were not engaged on a mission, as those in Ireland were, but in servicing a field army which was transformed into an army of occupation. No attempt was made to alter Scots' religious sensibilities.

Chaplains' appointments reflected the political concerns of the Parliament. Early in the war, the army command required chaplains who could explain to the troops why it was right to fight and kill their neighbors and disobey their king. Later, within the Parliament's army, chaplains had to combat the spread of religious heterodoxy lest the religious justification for the war be undermined. In Ireland and Scotland, it was much easier to characterize the enemy as "other." In Ireland, the enemy was, above all else, Catholic. Popular pamphlet literature in England had long raised the population's conviction that Catholics and all they stood for were abhorrent. Thus, esprit de corps arose from nothing more than shared Protestantism, of whatever complexion. In Scotland, according to Parliamentary interests, the native population had damned itself by supporting the king. Their Presbyterian theology was opposed to the English Royalists' divine right episcopacy, but it was equally opposed to the gathered congregations of the English sectaries.

Confessional Wars and Civil Wars

In the succession of European wars that followed the Protestant Reformation, confessional differences between Roman Catholics and Protestants to a large extent determined allegiances. It has been argued that the English Civil War was the last of these western European wars of religion, rather than the first European revolution.[33] This suggests approaches we might take to examine the role of religion in these wars and the part played by chaplains in the armies.[34]

A feature of the Continental religious wars of the period was the cruelty with which combatants treated one another. The English Protestants saw this as Catholic cruelty. Descriptions of the atrocities supposedly committed against Protestants in the Thirty Years' War (1618–48) fueled an already extensive anti-Catholic literature.[35] The alleged murder of two hundred thousand Protestants at the outbreak of the rising in Ireland, described with lurid detail in illustrated pamphlets, was simply an extension of a familiar theme.[36] Another recurrent subject was priests granting absolution to Catholic troops on the battlefield. War for religion conjured up images of bloodbaths, and Parliamentary propaganda made much of the presence of Roman Catholics among the king's forces. The invasion of Ireland was justified on the grounds of the atrocities allegedly committed against Protestants there.

In the wars that took place in England and Scotland, however, there seems to have been a sense of the enemy as someone who was, if not a spiritual brother, at least a spiritual cousin. It is hard to imagine a civil war chaplain using the words of an English First World War chaplain, "The soldier's business is to kill the enemy . . . and he only tries to avoid being killed for the sake of being efficient."[37]

The wars in Scotland have been characterized as differing from earlier Anglo-Scottish conflicts. "Sharing a common sovereign and Protestant beliefs," Mark Charles Fissel writes, "the Scots and English did not manoeuvre to exact revenge, inflict maximum damage or deliver a lightning blow, but prepared cautiously, sometimes reluctantly, neither side wishing to fight unless forced to do so by the other."[38] On these grounds, the Bishops' Wars might also be distinguished from other European confessional wars. Another historian has characterized the English Civil War as "unusually benign."[39] It was in neither side's interests to advocate wholesale slaughter of the enemy. A Royalist chaplain preached to the king's army, "Perhaps you expect that . . . I should stir you up to be cruell . . . I durst never excite men to fight up to the back in blood."[40]

One of the largest battles was at Naseby, a Parliamentary victory involving around 25,000 men that resulted in about 1,000 fatalities from the king's forces and about 150 from Parliament's. The battle is almost as notorious, however, for the massacre of 100 women of the Royalist baggage train, many of whom were said to be Irish.[41] Likewise, the justification for the slaughter of civilians at the siege of Basing House, owned by the Catholic Marquis of Winchester, was that they were Catholic.[42] In 1644, a parliamentary order forbade giving quarter to Irish soldiers captured from the Royalist forces.[43] They were not accorded the protection of Christians. This was regarded as a low point of the first civil war, but it is believed that standards of conduct overall declined and that the behavior of all troops in the second civil war was worse than it had been earlier.[44]

Was this atmosphere of relative (though declining) restraint attributable to religion, to military discipline, or to common prudence? For many contemporaries, not all of them supporters of the Parliament, it was religion that inspired the seemly conduct of the troops. Prisoners were exchanged as they were in a foreign war, and people were not executed as traitors. The author of the *Souldiers Catechisme* argued that if Parliament was not successful, the Protestant religion would "be utterly supprest . . . and the Popish Religion again advanced."[45] He

expressly described the enemy as "for the most part Papists and Atheists . . . Cursers and Blasphemers" and encouraged soldiers to regard
the enemy not "as Country-men, or Kinsmen, or fellow-Protestants,
but as enemies of God and our Religion, and siders with Antichrist."[46]
Yet this clarion call was not heeded when the enemy were fellow Protestant Englishmen. Common prudence dictated that antagonists deal
with one another in a way that would allow them to live side by side
when the war was over.

Let me return to my original question: Did the nature of the enemy
make a difference? It is clear that denominational divisions between
Protestants were of much greater concern in some armies than in others. It is also clear that if the enemy was, or could be, construed as
being Roman Catholic, a greater degree of violence was believed to be
justifiable, violence supported by chaplains who identified the enemy
with the enemies of God. In debates about the English Civil War, the
role of religion and the role of chaplains has been much discussed.[47] It
is clear that the development of more radical varieties of Protestantism
in the Parliamentary armies in the early days of the war owed much to
chaplains, but the pressures of patronage and the anxieties of the army
command about heterodoxy increasingly removed chaplains from these
debates and replaced them with mechanic preachers. The armies did not
lack chaplains of moral influence, but ministers who became chaplains
often were not men of stature in civilian life. It generally seems to be the
case that ministers, some of whom had great spiritual influence outside
the army, could not reconcile the conflicting requirements of persuad-
ing men to fight and quashing religious heterodoxy, or those of a hier-
archical military and an egalitarian church polity.

A civil war made the difference between it being possible for a chaplain to argue for out-and-out victory and the need to urge restraint on
soldiers. Where the enemies were Roman Catholic rebels, with a reputation for brutality, it was easier for chaplains to deliver a simple message. Where the enemies were politically disloyal co-religionists, chaplains had to tread carefully. But in each case, there was a strong sense
that different kinds of chaplains suited the war. In England, religious
divisions within the army were potentially damaging. In Ireland, any
Protestant minister could do the job, whereas in Scotland, chaplains
who had been regarded as radical troublemakers in England helped the
army command to escape from the difficulties of explaining the need to
fight brother-Protestants. Thus, chaplains' appointments in the Wars
of the Three Kingdoms show a high degree of ideological pragmatism.

NOTES

1. Conrad Russell, "The British problem and the English Civil War," *History* 72 (1987): 397. Russell's article is a revised and expanded version of his inaugural lecture as Astor Professor of British History at University College London, delivered in 1985.

2. Matthew Sylvester, *Reliquiae Baxterianae: Or, Mr Richard Baxter's Narrative of the Most Memorable Passages of his Life and Times*, pt. 1 (London, 1696), 31.

3. *The Life and Death of That Old Disciple of Jesus Christ, and Eminent Minister of the Gospel, Mr Hanserd Knollys* (London, 1692), 20.

4. See, particularly, John Morrill, "The Religious Context of the English Civil War," in John Morrill, *The Nature of the English Revolution* (London: Longman, 1993), 45–68, originally published in *Transactions of the Royal Historical Society*, 5th ser., 34 (1984).

5. Sylvester, *Reliquiae Baxterianae*, pt. 1, 47.

6. Barbara Donagan, "Did Ministers Matter? War and Religion in England, 1642–1649," *Journal of British Studies* 33 (1994): 123.

7. Tom Tell-Troth, *Works of Darkness Brought to Light* (London, 1647), 11.

8. Donagan, "Did Ministers Matter?", 144.

9. Henry Ferne, *The Camp at Gilgal, or A View of the Kings Army, and Spirituall Provision Made for It* (Oxford, 1643), 9.

10. Ibid., 43.

11. William Bridge, *A Sermon Preached unto the Voluntiers of the City of Norwich and also to the Voluntiers of Great Yarmouth* (London, 1642), 17.

12. Ibid., 16.

13. Simeon Ashe, *A Continuation of True Intelligence from the English and Scottish Forces in the North . . . no. 5* (London, 1644), 6.

14. Sylvester, *Reliquiae Baxterianae*, pt. 1, 43.

15. There is a case to be made that it was the Royalist clergy *outside* the army who were more important for their efforts in recruiting men to the king's army. See Ronald Hutton, *The Royalist War Effort, 1642–46* (Harlow: Longman, 1982), 13. This book makes no mention of Royalist chaplains or of religion in the Royalist army.

16. Sylvester, *Reliquiae Baxterianae*, pt. 1, 51.

17. Anne Laurence, *Parliamentary Army Chaplains, 1642–51*, Royal Historical Society Studies in History 59 (Woodbridge: Boydell and Brewer, 1990), 7, 14, 17.

18. Obadiah Sedgwick, *A Thanksgiving Sermon Preached before the Honourable House of Commons at Westminster* (April 9, 1644) (London, 1644), 23.

19. Simeon Ashe, *A Continuation of True Intelligence from the Armies in the North . . . no. 6* (London, 1644).

20. William Sedgwick, *A Second View of the Army Remonstrance* (London, 1649), 13.

21. Ibid., 12.

22. Thomas Edwards, *The Third Part of Gangræna: Or, A New and Higher Discovery of the Errors . . . of the Sectaries* (London, 1646), 266.

23. Sylvester, *Reliquiae Baxterianae*, pt. 1, 53.

24. Ibid., 50, 33.

25. Sedgwick, *A Second View*, 13.

26. Ibid., 11.

27. Laurence, *Parliamentary Army Chaplains*, 86–87. See also Ian Gentles, *The New Model Army in England, Ireland and Scotland, 1645–1653* (Oxford: Blackwell, 1992), 87–119.

28. Laurence, *Parliamentary Army Chaplains*, 78.

29. Ibid., 62.

30. Ibid., 63–64

31. Ibid., 164.

32. "The Letter of the General Council of the Army to their Brethren in their several Quarters and Garrisons, upon their march into Scotland 1650," in *The Fifth Monarchy or Kingdom of Christ in Opposition to the Beast's, Asserted* (London, 1659), 9–10.

33. Morrill, "Religious Context of the English Civil War," 67–68. However, like Anthony Fletcher in *The Outbreak of the English Civil War* (London: Edward Arnold, 1981), 405–6, he argues for the significance of religion in the breach between king and Parliament, rather than in the taking of sides subsequently. François Guizot, in 1826, identified the English Civil War as a revolution. "Previous to the French revolution," he wrote, the English revolution "was the greatest event which Europe had to narrate . . . our revolution, in surpassing, did not make that of England less great in itself; they were both victories in the same war." F. Guizot, *History of the English Revolution of 1640* (London, 1890), ix. Guizot argued that there was nothing in either revolution that could not have been found already; "they advanced civilization in the path it has been pursuing for fourteen centuries"—that is, the people supplanted the feudal aristocracy, the church, and the monarchy in the possession of power (xii–xv).

34. Glenn Burgess, "Was the Civil War a War of Religion?" *Huntington Library Quarterly* 61, no. 2 (2000): 178, 181. Glenn Burgess has argued that religion was not the informing ideology of the Civil War; rather, it was used to defend an already legitimate war. In this sense, the English Civil War was a just war rather than a holy war, but a just war in which one of the institutions under attack was religion.

35. *Lachrymae Germaniae: Or, the Tears of Germany. Unfolding her woefull Distresse by Jerusalem's Calamity* (London, 1638).

36. Richard Baxter repeated this widely advertised figure. See *Reliquiae Baxterianae*, pt. 1, 28–29. Also see *The Teares of Ireland Where is Lively Presented as in a Map, a List of the Unheard of Cruelties and Perfidious Treacheries of Bloud-thirsty Jesuits* (London, 1642). See Barbara Donagan, "Codes and Conduct in the English Civil War," *Past and Present* 118 (1988): 74.

37. George A. Birmingham, *A Padre in France* (London, 1918), 64, quoted in Joanna Bourke, *An Intimate History of Killing: Face-to-Face Killing in Twentieth-Century Warfare* (London: Granta Books, 1999), 1.

38. Mark Charles Fissel, *The Bishops' Wars: Charles I's Campaigns against Scotland, 1638–1640* (Cambridge: Cambridge University Press, 1994), 5–6.

39. Barbara Donagan, "Atrocity, War Crime, and Treason in the English Civil War," *American Historical Review* 99, no. 4 (1994): 1137.

40. Edward Symmonds, *A Militarie Sermon* (Oxford, 1644), 24.

41. Gentles, *New Model Army*, 60.

42. Ibid., 77.

43. Donagan, "Atrocity, War Crime," 1148.

44. Ibid., 1139.

45. Robert Ram, *The Souldiers Catechisme: Composed for the Parliaments Army* (London, 1644), 3.

46. Ibid., 11, 14–15.

47. See, particularly, Leo F. Solt, *Saints in Arms* (Stanford, Calif.: Stanford University Press, 1959); Mark A. Kishlansky, *The Rise of the New Model Army* (Cambridge: Cambridge University Press, 1979), 70–73; Austin Woolrych, *Soldiers and Statesmen* (Oxford: Clarendon Press, 1987); and Donagan, "Did Ministers Matter?"

CHAPTER FIVE

Faith, Morale, and the Army Chaplain in the American Civil War

Gardiner H. Shattuck, Jr.

I want to begin this essay with a personal statement and an admission of bias. As a male American who came of age in the 1960s, it is difficult for me to think and write about the military chaplaincy without recalling memories of life in the United States at the time of the Vietnam War. This fact was brought home to me as I prepared for the talk I delivered at the "Military Chaplains in Their Contexts" symposium at Notre Dame in March 2000. During my research for that gathering, I reread Anne Loveland's excellent study, *American Evangelicals and the U.S. Military* (1996). In her discussion of the Vietnam era, Loveland mentions a United Church of Christ (UCC) report, released by a task force of that denomination in 1973, that was highly critical of the way in which army regulations defined the chaplain's duties. The report charged that the army required chaplains to subordinate their religious mission as faithful Christians and Jews to the secular goals of the military establishment. As a result of such misdirected priorities, army chaplains were often prevented from exercising their proper role as prophets preaching "God's judgment on the policies and practices of the nation." The UCC task force argued that the chaplain, rather than merely blessing the actions of his government, ought to be a "sign of contradiction" within the military—a religious figure who symbolized the inherent contradictions between the expectations of the church and the expectations of the state regarding a soldier's responsibilities in wartime.[1]

I remember reading excerpts from that report when I was in seminary, and it certainly made an impression on me when it was first released. Considering it again three decades later, I now realize that its theological reasoning also significantly affected my thinking as a historian in the ensuing years, encouraging me to consider the subtle and decidedly ambiguous ways in which religious faith might influence a soldier in battle. I thus risk the charge of "presentism" by admitting the impact of that Vietnam-era document on my own scholarly work on the American Civil War, especially on the thesis I presented in my first book, *A Shield and Hiding Place* (1987), and on the arguments advanced in this essay.[2] As I suggest here, the Civil War chaplain operated not only as an official representative of the war effort of his nation, but also as a religious "sign of contradiction," at times implicitly undermining the martial aspirations of his country's leadership.

In one of the most thorough and perceptive accounts of a chaplain's experiences in the American Civil War, Baptist minister Frederic Denison described the duties he performed in the two Union regiments in which he served. Denison was elected chaplain of the 1st Rhode Island Cavalry in the fall of 1861, and he accompanied that unit when it campaigned in Maryland and Virginia in 1862. After the rigors of army life caused his health to fail in early 1863, he was assigned to a less active post, transferring to the 3rd Rhode Island Heavy Artillery, stationed on the South Carolina coast. During the period he spent in the Union army, Denison completed a multitude of tasks, practical as well as spiritual. He not only conducted worship services, prayed, preached, and counseled his men, but he also cared for the sick and wounded, buried the dead, guarded prisoners, delivered the mail, chronicled the activities of his regiment, functioned as its librarian and treasurer, taught freed slaves how to read and write, and even assisted officers as an aide-de-camp.

Despite the relatively successful career that he enjoyed, Denison complained that Union chaplains as a whole labored under a "serious impediment." They were placed in a very "awkward and uncomfortable position," he thought, for they had "no appointed or recognized place . . .

on a march, in a bivouac, or in a line of battle." In order to illustrate this problem, he mentioned a troubling battlefield encounter with a group of chaplains considerably less resourceful than he. Denison ran into his colleagues during the chaos surrounding the Union collapse at Second Bull Run in September 1862. Separated from their units and obviously lost, the chaplains were looking thoroughly bewildered when Denison spotted them. They were in great distress and "tearfully" asked him what they should do. Although Denison assumed those chaplains were "good men, anxious to do their duty," he believed they were virtually useless at that critical moment in the battle. Since they had received no clear instructions about their responsibilities, most never really knew what was expected of them in the field. As a consequence, Denison con-cluded, the typical chaplain felt like "a supernumerary, a kind of fifth wheel to a coach, being in place nowhere and out of place everywhere." Despite the expectation that they were meant to do all they could to aid the Union cause, chaplains were often unsure about their role as re-ligious figures in a military setting, especially when the army was on the march or engaged in combat.[3]

During the four years of the Civil War, a total of approximately 2,500 men served as chaplains in the Union army, and the problems Frederic Denison described were representative of what many of them experienced.[4] Clergy, of course, were by no means the only men to feel disoriented when they entered the army, for as historian James Mc-Pherson observes, "amateurism and confusion" characterized the early months of the war, and "trial and error . . . played a larger role than theory" throughout much of the conflict.[5] Unlike ordinary soldiers, however, Civil War chaplains had few obvious models on which to pat-tern themselves. Prior to the attack on Fort Sumter, the 16,000 soldiers in the U.S. Army had been served by just thirty chaplains, and some of those men held concurrent civilian pastorates while others were not even formally ordained. With the flood of volunteers surging into the army in the spring of 1861, the War Department dramatically increased the number of chaplains, mandating the appointment of one Christian clergyman for each thousand-man regiment in federal service. (Although Congress modified this requirement in 1862 and sanctioned the selection of regularly ordained clergy from *all* religious bodies in the United States, chaplains in the Civil War era not only were almost exclusively Christian, but they were also overwhelmingly Protestant: just one rabbi and approximately forty Roman Catholic priests are known to have

Union 9th Corps chaplains near Petersburg, Virginia. Courtesy of the Library of Congress, Washington, D.C. LC-B8171-7049.

served in the Union army.[6]) Yet because they were accorded no formal military rank—receiving the pay, but not the authority, of a captain of cavalry—and were expected to wear uniforms bare of any military insignia—simply a plain black hat, coat, and pants, most chaplains were indistinguishable from civilian clergy. Constitutional principles about the separation of church and state required, moreover, that the chaplains' exact duties had to remain vague. Army regulations obliged them to hold Sunday morning worship services whenever possible and to maintain a proper moral tone in their regiments by discouraging gambling and profanity among the men; other than that, however, individual chaplains were free to do as much or as little as seemed appropriate to them. As a result, the most competent chaplains were ministers like Frederic Denison, clergy who were comfortable serving as spiritual handymen in the uncharted pastoral waters of Civil War army life.[7] They enjoyed a good deal of freedom and, viewed in the best possible light, the eclectic nature of the chaplain's role allowed them to develop, in the words of nineteenth-century church historian Leonard Bacon, "a right apostolic sense to become all things to all men."[8]

Bacon's hopeful tone notwithstanding, some chaplains had a very difficult time earning the respect of the men under their care, for ac-

ceptance of the gospel that a chaplain preached did not mean that soldiers, even pious ones, invariably admired the minister or priest himself.
In fact, while numerous Americans affirmed the reality of the supernatural and embraced religious movements and beliefs throughout the
antebellum period, many of them simultaneously rejected and ridiculed
the authority of traditional ecclesiastical institutions.[9] When the war
began, in fact, chaplains were often forced to battle the unflattering notion that as clergy, they were much less competent than other men to
serve effectively in the army. Writer Louisa May Alcott, for instance,
hinted at this idea in her popular postwar novel, *Little Women* (1868),
when the character Meg speaks about the military service of her ministerial father: "I think it was so splendid in father to go as a *chaplain*
when he was too old to be draughted, and not strong enough for a soldier."[10] Indeed, some skeptics worried that Christianity itself encouraged "feminine" qualities in men and that as a consequence, committed
Christians, whether ordained or lay, usually made ineffective soldiers.
As southern diarist Mary Boykin Chesnut noted when she saw a group
of generals at prayer in a Richmond church in March 1864, "less piety
and more drilling of commands" might have been a more suitable activity for the defenders of her capital on that Sunday.[11] Thus, despite
the pervasiveness of religious belief in the United States at the time of
the Civil War, the ordained leadership of the country's major religious
bodies, Protestant and Catholic alike, sometimes felt it was an uphill
struggle to gain the trust and cooperation of the people to whom they
ministered; this attitude inevitably influenced the perceptions of chaplains about their experiences in the army.[12]

The several hundred Protestant ministers and the handful of Roman
Catholic priests who served as chaplains in the Confederate military
forces faced an even more difficult situation than the one with which
their counterparts in the North contended. Unlike the United States
government, Jefferson Davis and others in authority in the Confederacy at first recoiled from the idea of providing any state-supported
chaplaincy. Instead, Confederate leaders urged the major denominations in the South to select their own clergy and send them as volunteers into the military. Although protests from church members soon
forced a change in policy, the Confederate Congress merely authorized
the appointment of an indeterminate number of chaplains for regiments
and brigades without any stipulations as to their ecclesiastical standing,
rank, uniform, or duties. Since the chaplain's pay was eventually set at

the same level as a second lieutenant's—the lowest-ranking officer in the army—southern clergy sensed that the pastoral, liturgical, and spiritual work they performed was a low priority to their government. This official indifference so rankled them that many were tempted to quit the army altogether, and by the midpoint of the war only about half the Confederate regiments still had active chaplains.[13]

Nevertheless, the southern military forces were hardly bereft of clergy. As the Confederate government had hoped, the Southern Baptist Convention, the Presbyterian Church, and the Methodist Episcopal Church, South, all made the evangelization of soldiers a high priority, and together they sent over two hundred missionaries to minister to the army's spiritual needs. Bishops of the Episcopal Church also regularly visited troops campaigning within the geographical boundaries of their dioceses, and Lutheran synods in several states appointed missionaries to serve in the army. As a result of these individual denominational efforts, most prominent clergymen in the South were involved at one time or another in ministry to the Confederate military forces.[14] In addition, the southern denominations published tracts and newspapers, Bibles, hymnals, and prayer books that were distributed widely among the troops. Despite the generally debilitating effects of the conflict on most religious institutions in the South, this missionary effort proved to be highly successful. Church leaders reported that because of their evangelistic labors, spiritual interest actually seemed to be far stronger in the army than in parishes at home during the final months of the war.[15]

The most positive feature of military life—a phenomenon on which chaplains and clergy on both sides commented at length—was the remarkable series of evangelical revivals that took place in the armies in the field. Since scholars generally accept that southern soldiers, if not intrinsically more devout, were at least more candid about their piety than northerners, the revivals in the Confederate armed forces have received significant attention in recent studies about common soldiers in the Civil War.[16] Roughly 10 percent of the men in the Army of Northern Virginia, for example, underwent some sort of religious conversion during "the Great Revival" that swept their ranks in the winter of 1863-64.[17] In one account of the revival, a soldier in the 21st Virginia Regiment described the amphitheater his brigade constructed on a hillside near their encampment. Two thousand soldiers, most of the men in the brigade, gathered there every night, and chaplains led them in prayer and hymn-singing over the course of several weeks.[18] As a soldier in the 42nd Mississippi Regiment observed, moreover, the chapel his brigade erected not only provided a warm, sheltered place where comrades could gather for prayer, but it also became "the very gate of Heaven" for those who were about to die in battle.[19] And according to William Bennett, a minister who headed the Soldiers' Tract Association of the Methodist Episcopal Church, South, revivals were a "blessed work of grace" that not only transformed the army into "a school of Christ" in wartime, but also helped ease the pain of military defeat for southern whites during the Reconstruction period.[20]

Southern Baptist J. William Jones was by far the most important (and self-conscious) postwar publicist of the Confederate army revivals. Known as "the fighting parson," he had enlisted as a private in the 13th Virginia Regiment at the outbreak of hostilities, and he later became the chaplain of his regiment as well as a missionary chaplain in A. P. Hill's corps. Rising to even greater prominence after the war, Jones served for many years as secretary of the Southern Historical Society and as chaplain-general of the United Confederate Veterans. In 1887, he published his highly influential book, *Christ in the Camp*, which was a collection of upbeat tales about religious life in Lee's army. Writing within a culture that was becoming increasingly concerned with the concept of manliness, Jones intentionally cultivated the idea of a "muscular" Christianity, stressing the practical, worldly value of a committed religious faith.[21] He sought not only to demonstrate the spiritual significance of the revivals, but also to counter the view that too much religious enthusiasm feminized a soldier and, as some skeptics had charged, undercut his will to fight. *Christ in the Camp* is filled with stories of diligent chaplains, devout generals, and pious privates, men whose faith enabled them to enter combat fearlessly and who, if struck down on the battlefield, triumphantly surrendered their souls to God. Presenting images of manly soldiers with robust religious views, Jones labored to prove that true believers made the most disciplined and effective fighting-men.[22]

Though less widely publicized and studied than religious events in the Confederate armies, revivals were a significant part of the experiences of northern soldiers as well. The revivals in the Union army were clearly an extension of the so-called Business Men's Prayer-Meeting awakening, which began in New York City in September 1857 and spread to other urban areas of the United States over the next months.[23] Inspired

by those prewar revivals—religious exercises that were themselves part
of a conscious effort to stress the practical value of a masculine piety—
a group of leaders from Protestant denominations in the North organized the United States Christian Commission in an effort to evan-
gelize the thousands of young men entering the army in 1861. The
Christian Commission was independent of the federal government,
but the swarms of volunteer "delegates" it supported, clergy, lay men,
and a few lay women, were usually allowed free access to the troops
by military officials. These workers assisted chaplains by distributing
Bibles and other religious literature and by providing nursing care to
sick and wounded soldiers. Similar to the attitudes expressed by regimental chaplains, Christian Commission delegates believed that their
main work was spiritual, but recognized the value of offering material
aid on occasion as well.[24] As George Stuart, the head of the commission, wryly observed, "there is a good deal of religion in a warm shirt
and a good beefsteak."[25] The results of this coordinated evangelistic
effort became apparent in 1864, when reports began to circulate about
the outbreak of revivals among the Union troops in both the eastern
and western theaters of the war. Like the Confederate soldiers who
faced them, northerners constructed wooden chapels for worship, engaged in private and public prayer, organized Bible-reading groups,
and baptized numerous converted comrades during the last year of
the war.[26]

As George Stuart and J. William Jones both maintained, religious
work among Civil War soldiers had temporal as well as heavenly dimensions. Because of this dual pastoral emphasis, chaplains sometimes
argued that the spiritual authority they exercised not only enabled individuals to grow in the faith, but also enhanced the fighting spirit
of their units. One of the most dramatic illustrations of the supposed
bond between religious devotion and combat morale is found in William
Corby's memoirs of his service in the Irish Brigade. Corby, a Roman
Catholic priest, was chaplain of the 88th New York Regiment, which was
posted on Cemetery Ridge during the Battle of Gettysburg. Late in the
afternoon of July 2, 1863, the Irish Brigade was ordered to advance and
meet the attacking Confederate force. Before the soldiers went forward,
however, Corby climbed onto a nearby boulder and, exposing himself to
enemy fire, stood up and pronounced the absolution of sin on every man
he saw. He later claimed that all the soldiers in the brigade, whether
Catholic or not, knelt solemnly in front of him as cannonballs exploded
and bullets whistled over their heads. Sustained by their own prayers

Paul Henry Wood, *Absolution under Fire*, 1891. Courtesy of the Snite Museum of Art, University of Notre Dame.

and by the priest's benediction, the troops then joined the battle and bravely risked death in defense of the Union position.[27]

The Irish Brigade and the other units supporting it blunted the Confederate assault against Cemetery Ridge and Little Round Top, and Gettysburg ultimately became the most significant Union victory in the war. Veterans of the Irish Brigade never forgot the courage their chaplain had displayed at that critical moment in the conflict, and nearly fifty years after the event, they erected a bronze statue of the priest, his right hand raised in blessing, on the Gettysburg battlefield. The post-humous tribute Corby received was unique, for unlike the many generals, colonels, and other soldiers commemorated by monuments at Civil War sites, he was the only chaplain so honored. Although as a Roman Catholic, Corby was hardly representative of the several thousand clergy, mainly evangelical Protestant, who labored in the Union and Confederate armies, the man, his public gesture, and the monument his bravery inspired have come to symbolize the highest ideals of the American military chaplaincy.[28]

In an important collection of essays entitled *Religion and the American Civil War* (1998), a group of historians have argued that religious concepts and ideas were central to the experiences of most Americans between 1861 and 1865. Virtually everyone at that time—politicians and ordinary people, soldiers and civilians, slaveholders and slaves—sought divine favor and interpreted the war's events within the context of his or her own religious beliefs.[29] Because of the prevalence of religious themes in the civic discourse of the nineteenth century, some observers have, over the years, assumed that the public statements of Civil War-era ministers, priests, and rabbis were, in the words of historian James Silver, merely "unvarnished appeals for patriotism," chauvinistic pleas designed to impel their people into battle.[30] In discussing religion as a form of "propaganda" in the South, for example, Silver envisions white southern Protestantism as "a powerful social organization," which, in spite of the North's overwhelming material advantages, was "the major resource of the Confederacy in the building and maintenance of . . . morale" during the war.[31] As historian Willard Wight also notes, no one in the South did as much as the leadership of the major Protestant denominations—Baptist, Methodist, Presbyterian, and Episcopal—in rallying support for Confederate war aims.[32] Though somewhat less shrill than their Confederate counterparts, northern clergy, too, are said to have had a vital part in contributing to the sectional strife before 1861 and in sustaining the martial ardor of those to whom they ministered during the war itself.[33] Moreover, according to Warren Armstrong, the author of a book on Union chaplains, the courage and commitment of the men he studied motivated soldiers from a variety of denominational backgrounds to sacrifice themselves for the sake of the Union cause. Disregarding the cynic's adage that "God is always on the side of the heaviest battalions," Armstrong argues that chaplains were "in a very real sense the morale officers of the army," who together made an inestimable contribution to the success of the United States war effort.[34]

Other scholars, examining not clergy and chaplains, but the ordinary fighting man in the Civil War, have arrived at remarkably similar conclusions about the role of religious faith in motivating soldiers in combat. James McPherson, for instance, speaks at length about the importance of religion in his prize-winning book, *For Cause and Comrade* (1997). McPherson thinks the Civil War armies were probably the most religious in history. The majority of soldiers trusted that God watched over them on the battlefield, and those with the strongest religious faith usually entered battle buoyed by a "positive religious fatalism." McPherson is particularly impressed by the revivals among the Confederate troops, and he claims that they were a major factor in sustaining the army's fighting spirit, thereby prolonging the war and temporarily warding off the South's inevitable defeat.[35] Drew Gilpin Faust is another historian who has linked religious faith and military morale. In her analysis of the southern army revivals, she emphasizes how religion helped internalize discipline and molded inexperienced recruits into a highly effective fighting force. Indeed, "the comradeship of the regenerate," Faust says, "encouraged . . . the group solidarity that modern military analysts have identified as critical to the maintenance of morale." Whenever the trauma of battle threatened to deflate morale, revivals functioned as "the obvious cultural resource" that nurtured resistance and inculcated a useful "spirit of discipline and subordination" among the outnumbered southern soldiers.[36]

There is certainly much truth in these observations about religion's social and psychological relevance in encouraging Americans to wage a long and bloody civil war. The overwhelming majority of the soldiers were Christians, and the leadership of all the major denominations officially supported the military struggle. And surely no man enlisted as a chaplain unless he was prepared to work for the victory of his own armed forces. Nevertheless, despite the plausible correlation between religion and patriotism, the ministry of chaplains and the religious beliefs of soldiers may not have played quite as one-sided a role as scholars like Silver, Armstrong, and McPherson have assumed.

According to anthropologist Clifford Geertz, religion represents a powerful "system of symbols" that, in the face of the ambiguities of human existence, gives meaning to the world in which people live. Although pain, destruction, and death raise the disturbing notion that life is fundamentally meaningless, religion fashions a context or "cultural system" in which men and women are able to see coherence in the universe. Religion especially helps resolve the problem of suffering, Geertz writes, by showing believers "how to suffer, how to make of physical pain, personal loss, worldly defeat, or the helpless contemplation of others' agony something bearable, supportable."[37] Based on this sociological reasoning, the principal responsibility of the Civil War chaplain was clear: to posit and sustain a worldview in which the maiming and death of comrades, the results of battle, the imminent threat of a soldier's own demise, and all the incidents of army life had a recognizable moral purpose. Making sense out of immense suffering and violence—demonstrating how, as William Corby said, "in the presence of death, religion gives hope and strength"—was, therefore, the most

Sunday morning mass in camp of 69th N. Y. Regiment. Courtesy of the Library of Congress, Washington, D. C. LC-B8184-4132.

important pastoral task for which clergy and lay evangelists in the Civil War armies held themselves accountable.[38]

Viewed from this perspective, the writings and memoirs of some Civil War participants suggest that religious assurance and soldierly efficiency did not always work in concert, but sometimes were at cross-purposes. Although most Civil War chaplains undoubtedly wished to make men into better soldiers, morally as well as militarily, they also emphasized that their primary mission was supernatural rather than temporal, saving souls rather than killing enemy combatants. As Frederic Denison stressed when he preached on the eve of a battle, the Christian soldier, like Jesus, might not only pray, "Father, save me from this hour," but he also understood that "for this cause came I unto this hour." To be in harmony with God's will, this chaplain implied, required believers to accept the inevitability of their own suffering and death.[39] Christian theology, furthermore, has never been the ideological servant of the secular state, and few American religious leaders, then or now, have ever suggested that patriotism is simply interchangeable with piety.[40] Looking at a soldier's combat readiness, as Denison did, from the standpoint of Jesus' passion and sacrificial death, one might conclude that this classic Christian theological emphasis could well have detracted from, not enhanced, the soldier's desire to kill other men.

George Cary Eggleston's remarkable memoir, *A Rebel's Recollections* (1874), provides a demonstration both of this phenomenon and of problems inherent in an overabundance of religious enthusiasm among the troops. Eggleston argued that the widespread revivals in Lee's army contributed significantly to "the general despondency" and "gloomy fatalism" that gripped the Confederate forces at the end of the war. While Eggleston conceded, as historians McPherson and Faust have emphasized, that evangelical Protestant beliefs strengthened the resolve of individuals and enabled them to face death with equanimity, he also thought "a sort of religious ecstasy" had permeated the ranks of his army, fostering the "superstitious belief that Providence would in some way interfere" and redeem the Confederacy from impending defeat. This religious conviction led some men to take unnecessary, even suicidal, risks in battle. "My time is coming, that's all," one soldier said, when asked why he was willing to expose himself to enemy fire. An hour later, Eggleston dourly noted, "the poor fellow's head was blown from his shoulders." Viewed from a strictly religious perspective, the man's life had come to a premature, but not inappropriate end, for the army revivals had prepared him to entrust his body and soul wholly to God's care. As Eggleston recognized, however, a dead soldier, whether spiritually regenerate or not, was of little practical use to the outnumbered armies of the embattled Confederacy.[41]

Sam Watkins's well-known and colorful account of the war, *"Co. Aytch"* (1882), illustrates this religious paradox from the standpoint of a person sympathetic to the army revivals. Watkins described the revivalistic fervor that gripped the Confederate army encamped in northern Georgia early in 1864. One night, during an especially intense prayer service around a bonfire, an old decayed tree caught fire and came crashing down on ten men, killing them instantly. Despite the unsettling nature of this accident, Watkins and other soldiers who had been involved in the revival professed to find it an encouraging omen. God had answered the prayers of the men who had been crushed by the tree, he wrote, for they had been released from their service in the Confederate ranks and had joined "the army of the hosts of Heaven" instead.[42] In a similar vein, Robert Stiles, a Confederate artillery officer and son of a Presbyterian minister, recounted how God could transform a soldier's battlefield death into a personal religious victory. In his memoir, *Four Years under Marse Robert* (1903), Stiles explained how he had helped convert one of his comrades in the spring of 1863. When that soldier was later killed at Gettysburg, Stiles described the death in particularly gruesome detail: struck by an enemy cannonball, the man lay on the ground, his "body gashed with wounds, the top of the skull blown off and the brain actually fallen out upon the ground in two bloody, palpitating lobes." Although the soldier's fate might have seemed pathetic and revolting to an unbeliever, Stiles insisted that it was an experience from which a Christian could gain hope. Bolstered by his faith in God's power over death, the man had embraced his fate and, like the biblical prophet Elijah, a "chariot and horses of fire had caught him up into Heaven."[43]

Scenes of death and dying akin to these represented a staple of Victorian fiction, and consolation literature was an enormously popular genre throughout the nineteenth century. Books with titles such as *Agnes and the Key of Her Little Coffin* (1857) and *The Empty Crib* (1873) sought to demonstrate that a life cut short in youth was of far greater worth, both for the individual and for family members, than a long but spiritually uneventful existence.[44] The appalling casualty rate in the Civil War presented a not unwelcome opportunity for American Christians to add to this literature, and in their writings clergy and devout lay people regularly reflected on the meaning of religious faith for soldiers who were killed in battle or who died from disease in camp.[45] In the postwar period, moreover, Elizabeth Stuart Phelps's extraordinarily popular novel, *The Gates Ajar* (1868), helped answer the spiritual needs of many who had lost sons, brothers, and husbands during the war. Phelps offered reassurance to thousands of readers that although death had claimed their loved ones, those men were at peace with God in heaven.[46]

In the latter stages of the war, such religious literature took on special significance for white southerners, who sought consolation regarding not only the eternal fate of individual soldiers, but also the moral worthiness of their entire society. Failure on the battlefield and immense hardship at home notwithstanding, white southern Christians insisted that the misfortunes they suffered were part of God's providential plan for humankind. As a Presbyterian minister in Petersburg, Virginia, observed in 1865, worldly success was a poor measure of Christian righteousness, for just as saints in past eras had undergone affliction, so adversity provided an invaluable opportunity for believers in modern times to experience divine grace. The disastrous outcome of the Civil War, he believed, would prove to be "the very impress of a Father's loving kiss," the mark of God's enduring but chastening love for the South.[47] Abram Joseph Ryan, a Roman Catholic priest and former Confederate army chaplain, also wrote prolifically on this theme. Known as "the Poet Priest of the Lost Cause," he sought to demonstrate how, unlike the victorious North, the South had been consecrated by its wartime losses.[48] And Stonewall Jackson, the pious Confederate general who had been mortally wounded in 1863 at the Battle of Chancellorsville, became one of the leading exemplars of southern religious virtues at the end of the Civil War. Rather than interpreting his untimely end as symptomatic of God's displeasure with the slaveholding South, church leaders presented Jackson as a Christian martyr and celebrated the religious stoicism he displayed on his deathbed.[49]

Operating within a theological framework in which death was regarded not only as inevitable (the condition of sinful humanity), but also as theoretically desirable (the hope of resurrection and eternal life), chaplains on both sides of the conflict were called to preach with confidence about the spiritual value of their soldiers' daily sacrifices. Yet how effective could this emphasis have been in boosting the fighting spirit of the troops? The primary purpose of an army, after all, is to destroy rather than to be destroyed, and Civil War soldiers were drilled in methods of avoiding death and slaying the enemy, not in rituals of Christian resignation and martyrdom. As the consummate soldier, George Patton, quipped in 1944: "No bastard ever won a war by dying for his country," but "by making the other poor dumb bastard die for his."[50] Nineteenth-century clergy continually heard the gibes of cynics like Patton whom they encountered in the army camp and at home. Was it possible, then, to increase the spiritual vitality of the men in their units and prepare them for death in combat without decreasing in some measure their desire to kill opposing soldiers? Perhaps most chaplains thought this was not an insurmountable dilemma, but in the eyes of some skeptical soldiers and civilians, a comrade's conspicuous piety or a general's resignation in the face of death was more worrisome than inspiring.

William Corby's feat at Gettysburg was arguably one of the most courageous public gestures made by a chaplain in the Civil War, and his heroism was rightly honored by the proud veterans of the Irish Brigade. With the placing of a statue on the spot where Corby delivered the priestly absolution of sin, army chaplains as a group symbolically entered American sacred space and national memory.[51] Yet not all chaplains were either as resourceful or as lucky as Corby. His actions were remarkable, and a clergyman standing ramrod straight with an upraised arm and extended hand represents a fitting subject for a battlefield monument. No memorial will ever be erected to commemorate the "fifth wheel," the redundant and slightly irrelevant figure that Frederic Denison described. Denison's metaphor, however, mirrors well the difficult and ambiguous position in which many Civil War chaplains found themselves. Despite their bravery and numerous expressions of patriotism, the most important aspect of their ministry as clergy—strengthening the faith of their men and preparing them spiritually to accept death— may well have undercut the military goals of their nation. As the foregoing evidence suggests, religious faith and military efficiency were sometimes at cross-purposes during the Civil War, and at such times chaplains functioned as the distinctive "sign of contradiction" to which a later generation of church leaders referred.

NOTES

1. Report of the Task Force on Ministries to Military Personnel of the United Church of Christ, quoted in Anne C. Loveland, *American Evangelicals and the U.S. Military, 1942–1993* (Baton Rouge: Louisiana State University Press, 1996), 96–97.

2. Gardiner H. Shattuck, Jr., *A Shield and Hiding Place: The Religious Life of the Civil War Armies* (Macon, Ga.: Mercer University Press, 1987), 1–12.

3. Frederic Denison, "A Chaplain's Experience in the Union Army," in *Personal Narratives of Events in the War of the Rebellion: Being Papers Read before the Rhode Island Soldiers and Sailors Historical Society*, 4th ser., no. 20 (Providence, R.I.: The Society, 1893), 1–45 (quotations on 11, 16, 23).

4. Roy J. Honeywell, *Chaplains of the United States Army* (Washington, D.C.: Office of the Chief of Chaplains, Department of the Army, 1958), 120–22, and Shattuck, *Shield and Hiding Place*, 62–63.

5. James M. McPherson, *Battle Cry of Freedom* (New York: Oxford University Press, 1988), 308–33 (quotations on 331–32).

6. Shattuck, *Shield and Hiding Place*, 54–55.

7. Herman A. Norton, *Struggling for Recognition, 1791–1865*, The United States Army Chaplaincy, vol. 2 (Washington, D.C.: Office of the Chief of Chaplains, Department of the Army, 1977), 82–112, 168–69; Earl F. Stover, *Up from Handymen* (1865–1920), The United States Army Chaplaincy, vol. 3 (Washington, D.C.: Office of the Chief of Chaplains, Department of the Army, 1977), v, 2; Randall M. Miller, "Catholic Religion, Irish Ethnicity, and the Civil War," in Randall M. Miller, Harry S.

Stout, and Charles Reagan Wilson, eds., *Religion and the American Civil War* (New York: Oxford University Press, 1998), 264–65; Warren B. Armstrong, *For Courageous Fighting and Confident Dying: Union Chaplains in the Civil War* (Lawrence: University Press of Kansas, 1998), 2–14; and Shattuck, *Shield and Hiding Place*, 51–63.

8. Leonard Bacon, *A History of American Christianity* (New York: Christian Literature Co., 1898), 349.

9. Nathan O. Hatch, *The Democratization of American Christianity* (New Haven, Conn.: Yale University Press, 1989), 9–10, 22, 44, 212–13.

10. Louisa May Alcott, *Little Women* (1868; New York: Oxford University Press, 1994), 11 (emphasis added).

11. Mary Boykin Chesnut, *Mary Chesnut's Civil War*, ed. C. Vann Woodward (New Haven, Conn.: Yale University Press, 1981), 585–86.

12. Kurt O. Behrends, "'Wholesome Reading Purifies and Elevates the Man': The Religious Military Press in the Confederacy," in Miller, Stout, and Wilson, eds., *Religion and the American Civil War*, 136, and Shattuck, *Shield and Hiding Place*, 23–24. For further background on popular perceptions of clergy and religion in antebellum America, see Ann Douglas, *The Feminization of American Culture* (New York: Knopf, 1977), and Jon Butler, *Awash in a Sea of Faith: Christianizing the American People* (Cambridge, Mass.: Harvard University Press, 1990).

13. Charles F. Pitts, *Chaplains in Gray: The Confederate Chaplains' Story* (Nashville, Tenn.: Broadman, 1957), 39–44; Herman Norton, *Rebel Religion: The Story of Confederate Chaplains* (St. Louis, Mo.: Bethany, 1961), 115–34; and Shattuck, *Shield and Hiding Place*, 63–71.

14. W. Harrison Daniel, "Southern Protestantism and Army Missions in the Confederacy," *Mississippi Quarterly* 17 (1964): 179–83.

15. Daniel W. Stowell, *Rebuilding Zion: The Religious Reconstruction of the South, 1863–1877* (New York: Oxford University Press, 1998), 15–27, and Shattuck, *Shield and Hiding Place*, 45–49.

16. Reid Mitchell, "Christian Soldiers? Perfecting the Confederacy," in Miller, Stout, and Wilson, eds., *Religion and the American Civil War*, 297–98.

17. Herman Norton, "Revivalism in the Confederate Army," *Civil War History* 6 (1960): 410–24; Shattuck, *Shield and Hiding Place*, 99; and Drew Gilpin Faust, "Christian Soldiers: The Meaning of Revivalism in the Confederate Army," *Journal of Southern History* 53 (1987): 63–73.

18. John H. Worsham, *One of Jackson's Foot Cavalry*, ed. James I. Robertson, Jr. (Jackson, Tenn.: McCowat-Mercer Press, 1964), 113–14.

19. LeGrand James Wilson, *The Confederate Soldier*, ed. James W. Silver (Memphis, Tenn.: Memphis State University Press, 1973), 146–48.

20. William W. Bennett, *A Narrative of the Great Revival which Prevailed in the Southern Armies* (Philadelphia: Claxton, Remsen, and Haffelfinger, 1877), 16, 73, 426–27.

21. George M. Fredrickson, *The Inner Civil War: Northern Intellectuals and the Crisis of the Union* (New York: Harper and Row, 1965), 166–70, 217–25, and Stuart McConnell, *Glorious Contentment: The Grand Army of the Republic, 1865–1900* (Chapel Hill: University of North Carolina Press, 1992), 106–7.

22. J. William Jones, *Christ in the Camp; or, Religion in the Confederate Army*, new ed. (Atlanta: Martin and Hoyt, 1904), [3]-8, 13–16, 463–64, and Mitchell, "Christian

Soldiers?", 298–303. For additional background on Jones, see Charles Reagan Wilson, *Baptized in Blood: The Religion of the Lost Cause, 1865–1920* (Athens: University of Georgia Press, 1980), 119–38.

23. Kathryn Teresa Long, *The Revival of 1857–58: Interpreting an American Religious Awakening* (New York: Oxford University Press, 1998), 87–90, 119–20.

24. Lemuel Moss, *Annals of the United States Christian Commission* (Philadelphia: J. B. Lippincott, 1868), 64–68, 476–79, and Joseph O. Henry, "The United States Christian Commission in the Civil War," *Civil War History* 6 (1960): 374–88.

25. George H. Stuart, *The Life of George H. Stuart,* ed. Robert Ellis Thompson (Philadelphia: J. M. Stoddart, 1890), 129.

26. James H. Moorhead, *American Apocalypse: Yankee Protestants and the Civil War, 1860–1869* (New Haven, Conn.: Yale University Press, 1978), 68–71, and Shattuck, *Shield and Hiding Place,* 88–92.

27. William Corby, *Memoirs of Chaplain Life: Three Years with the Irish Brigade in the Army of the Potomac,* ed. Lawrence Frederick Kohl (1893; New York: Fordham University Press, 1992), 180–86.

28. Corby, *Memoirs of Chaplain Life,* 397–400, and Miller, "Catholic Religion, Irish Ethnicity, and the Civil War," 264–65, 284–86, 393–96. After the war, Corby served as president of the University of Notre Dame, and a replica of the Gettysburg monument—later dubbed "fair-catch Corby" by football fans—was erected on the campus of the school. A painting of the chaplain's dramatic battlefield gesture (*Absolution under Fire* by Paul Henry Wood) also hangs inside the entrance to Corby Hall at Notre Dame.

29. Randall M. Miller, Harry S. Stout, and Charles Reagan Wilson, "Introduction," in Miller, Stout, and Wilson, eds., *Religion and the American Civil War,* 4.

30. James W. Silver, "The Confederate Preacher Goes to War," *North Carolina Historical Review* 33 (1956): 499–509 (quotation on 504).

31. James W. Silver, *Confederate Morale and Church Propaganda* (1957; New York: W. W. Norton, 1967), [8–9], 93–101 (quotations on [8], 101).

32. Willard E. Wight, "The Churches and the Confederate Cause," *Civil War History* 6 (1960): 361–73. For a similar argument, see W. Harrison Daniel, "Protestantism and Patriotism in the Confederacy," *Mississippi Quarterly* 24 (1971): 117–34.

33. David B. Chesebrough, *"God Ordained This War": Sermons on the Sectional Crisis, 1830–1865* (Columbia: University of South Carolina Press, 1991), 1–13, 221.

34. Armstrong, *For Courageous Fighting and Confident Dying,* 106–7, 121, 125 (quotation on 121).

35. James M. McPherson, *For Cause and Comrades: Why Men Fought in the Civil War* (New York: Oxford University Press, 1997), 61–76 (quotation on 66).

36. Faust, "Christian Soldiers," 81–88 (quotations on 82, 88). For a similar argument, see Samuel J. Watson, "Religion and Combat Motivation in the Confederate Armies," *Journal of Military History* 58 (1994): 29–55.

37. Clifford Geertz, "Religion as a Cultural System," in *The Interpretation of Cultures: Selected Essays by Clifford Geertz* (New York: Basic Books, 1973), 89–90, 103–4, 108.

38. Corby, *Memoirs of Chaplain Life,* 6, and McPherson, *For Cause and Comrades,* 70–71.

39. Denison, "Chaplain's Experience," 18–19. Denison was commenting on Jesus' farewell discourse to his disciples in Jn 12:27.

40. Drew Gilpin Faust, *The Creation of Confederate Nationalism: Ideology and Identity in the Civil War South* (Baton Rouge: Louisiana State University Press, 1988), 23.

41. George Cary Eggleston, *A Rebel's Recollections* (1874; Baton Rouge: Louisiana State University Press, 1996), 177–79. For a far-reaching discussion of the possible role of religion in hastening Confederate defeat, see Richard E. Beringer et al., *Why the South Lost the Civil War* (Athens: University of Georgia Press, 1986), 268–93, 351–67.

42. Sam R. Watkins, *"Co. Aytch," Maury Grays, First Tennessee Regiment; or, A Side Show of the Big Show* (Nashville, Tenn.: Cumberland Presbyterian Publishing House, 1882), 116–17.

43. Robert Stiles, *Four Years Under Marse Robert* (New York: Neale Publishing, 1903), 145–51.

44. Douglas, *Feminization of American Culture*, 240–72.

45. Drew Gilpin Faust, "The Civil War Soldier and the Art of Dying," *Journal of Southern History* 67 (2001): 3–38.

46. Paul A. Carter, *The Spiritual Crisis of the Gilded Age* (DeKalb: Northern Illinois University Press, 1971), 74–77.

47. John Miller, "Comfort for the Saints," *Central Presbyterian* (Dec. 21, 1865): 1, and John Miller, "Comfort for the Saints," *Central Presbyterian* (Dec. 28, 1865): 1.

48. Abram Joseph Ryan, *Poems: Patriotic, Religious, Miscellaneous* (Baltimore: John B. Piet, 1880), 27–28, 98–99, 137, 140, 273–75, and Wilson, *Baptized in Blood*, 58–59.

49. Robert Lewis Dabney, *Life and Campaigns of Lieut.-Gen. Thomas J. Jackson* (New York: Blelock, 1866), 706–28, and Daniel W. Stowell, "Stonewall Jackson and the Providence of God," in Miller, Stout, and Wilson, eds., *Religion and the American Civil War*, 200–202.

50. George S. Patton, Jr., "Third Army Speech" (May 31, 1944).

51. For the multiple levels at which this event can be interpreted, see Miller, "Catholic Religion, Irish Ethnicity, and the Civil War," 285–86.

CHAPTER SIX

IN THE SERVICE OF TWO KINGS

Protestant Prussian Military Chaplains, 1713–1918

HARTMUT LEHMANN

Military chaplains are confronted with complicated theological questions of far-reaching consequences: They minister spiritually to those
whose task it is to fight for their country and who, if need arises, have to
kill those who have attacked their people, and who may be killed themselves in the process. This means that military chaplains have to interpret the fifth commandment—thou shalt not kill—in a way that does
not burden the souls of soldiers for whom the Christian faith is something meaningful, but in a manner that leaves enough room at least for
theories of just wars, that is, for theories of wars of self-defence.

   In the following essay, I concentrate on one specific case, namely, the
case of Protestant Prussian military chaplains from the early eighteenth
to the early twentieth century.[1] With the help of this example, it is possible to discuss some of the more general questions concerning religion and war as this delicate relationship is reflected in the very special work of military chaplains. There also were a few Catholic priests
serving as military chaplains in the Prussian army between 1713 and
1918. But their numbers were small, and always remained so. Considering the anti-Catholic tradition of the Prussian house of Hohenzollern since the Reformation, the task of these Catholic military chaplains was particularly difficult. They deserve a study of their own, as do

the few rabbis who were affiliated with the Prussian army during the First World War.

Let me begin with an episode that took place in Halle in the year 1713.[2] In that year, the new Prussian king, Frederick William I (1713–40), made his first visit to the city of Halle and to the famous educational and social institutions that had been founded in a suburb of Halle two decades earlier by one of the most influential leaders of Pietism, August Hermann Francke. Pietism has to be considered the most significant reform movement within German Lutheranism since the Reformation. Since the 1690s, key exponents of Pietism received significant support from the Prussian authorities. And since the sixteenth century, there had been pastors affiliated with the Prussian army on an irregular basis. As Frederick William I began to replace the traditional militia and build a professional army, by contemporaries called a "standing army," he also made a new start in recruiting military chaplains, and he looked for assistance from Halle.

In 1713, as the Prussian king walked through the Franckesche Stiftungen (Francke Foundations), he asked the Pietist patriarch: "What do you think of war?" ("Was hält er vom Kriege?"). "Your majesty is obliged to defend the country," Francke responded, "but I am called to preach that God blesses the peaceful." The king: "This is certainly good. But does He not forbid His people from taking part in war?" (Perhaps one could also translate this as "from doing military service?") The Pietist patriarch replied: "Students of theology are suited, as your majesty knows, to fill positions in church and school." The king: "But does He not tell His people that if they become soldiers they will become the devil's prey?" The Pietist patriarch: "I know many Christian soldiers. I have more supporters among soldiers than among the clergy."[3]

After Frederick William I had left Halle, Francke must have felt that the king was not satisfied with the answers he had given. Therefore, he sat down and wrote the king a letter. As regards his view of war, Francke explained, he would like to add that he knew not only of pious kings in the Old Testament who, following God's commands, had conducted war, but that he was also aware of the fourth verse of the thirteenth chapter of Paul's Letter to the Romans in the New Testament, in which Paul called for strict obedience to authority and had taught that governments carried the sword because as God's servants they had the duty to punish evil-doers. It was clearly not against God's word to conduct war, Francke continued, but as businesspeople should not commit sins while trading, soldiers should not use excessive violence or do injustice while going about their work.[4] In this brief exchange of 1713, the Prussian king asked direct questions, whereas the Pietist patriarch answered cautiously. As can be demonstrated from a series of encounters in the years that followed, both the king and the Pietist patriarch had a clear view of the agenda they tried to pursue. Let me first say a few words about the Pietist agenda.

In the tradition of the founder of Pietism, Philipp Jakob Spener (1635–1705), Francke set out to build God's Kingdom. Francke's followers, a relatively large group of people from all walks of life who considered themselves to be reborn Christians, awaited the return of Christ in the not-too-distant future. They were convinced, however, that God in his overwhelming mercy had granted an extra and last period of grace (*eine zusätzliche und letzte Gnadenfrist*), which His faithful children should and could use in order to spread His message and in order to start building His son's realm. Francke and his disciples hoped that God would accept the charitable and educational institutions at Halle as a first step toward His Kingdom, and that He would reward their labors in establishing these institutions on the day of the Last Judgment. As Francke told his followers, they needed no other protection as long as they firmly believed in God.[5]

In theological terms, Francke expressed the strong eschatological convictions of the Halle Pietists. In political terms, Francke knew, of course, that if he wanted to maintain his institutions and if he wanted to expand their influence beyond Halle, he needed the support of the Prussian king.[6] There is much proof that Francke had ambitious plans reaching far beyond Halle. He was not content to establish an orphanage, several schools, a pharmacy, and a print shop at Halle and to send some missionaries to foreign lands. Rather, he hoped to start a *General-reformation*, a general reformation of humankind as he called it, and this goal meant that he also wished to include the Prussian army in his sphere of influence. He even hoped to win the king completely for his cause. Francke would have been overjoyed if one of his disciples, serving as a military chaplain, had been able to influence the king spiritually, thus transforming the Prussian ruler into a reborn Christian. It is in this context that he cherished the idea of providing Halle-trained military chaplains for the Prussian army.

The Prussian king's agenda was quite different. Frederick William I planned to create a strong standing army consisting of long-serving, well-disciplined, committed, loyal, professional soldiers. He was convinced that firm religious belief would help to discipline his soldiers and bolster their morale. As the king argued, military chaplains who held strong religious views themselves would occupy a kind of key position, or at least a position no less influential than that of commanding officers. In short, with the help of Halle-trained military chaplains, the king hoped to lower the number of desertions, raise ethical standards, and improve the performance of his army. Furthermore, the Prussian king liked the idea of having a body of clergymen under his direct command. Traditionally, the Protestant church had been closely linked to the Prussian estates. The church was, therefore, part of the opposition against the plans of the king to rule in an absolutist manner. By contrast, the newly created corps of military chaplains would be part of the power structure of the king's absolutist rule.

Several high-ranking officers served as intermediaries between the Hohenzollern king and the Pietist patriarch. Their task was not too difficult, because both sides were eager to cooperate. Several incidents demonstrate that Francke was careful to avoid any conflict between Pietist circles and the Prussian army. Meanwhile, the king's protection helped Francke to expand his influence rapidly. In 1718, for example, one of Francke's radical followers openly criticized the violent manner in which Prussian regiments recruited young men into their ranks.[7] Even in Halle itself, he claimed, there had been cases of forcible impressments. Francke quickly distanced himself from this critic of the king. Some time later, when another radical Pietist published a pamphlet that supposedly encouraged soldiers to desert,[8] Francke was again quick to respond: he provided no fewer than a thousand copies of the New Testament and a hymn-book for the Prussian army, thus demonstrating that he wanted to bolster the morale of the king's army, not oppose it.

The king, in turn, on several occasions gave Francke the opportunity to preach at the court and to his officer corps. More important, Frederick William I was deeply convinced of the loyalty and the quality of Halle-trained military chaplains. Some he chose to become his court-preachers, others he promoted to the position of superintendent-general of the Lutheran church in Prussia. By the time of Francke's death in 1727, Halle had provided no less than 151 military chaplains to the Prussian army; by 1740, when king Frederick William I passed away, the total came to 307.[9] Within less than thirty years, Halle had managed to acquire an almost complete monopoly in this respect. Even in peacetime, the Prussian army was better equipped with military chaplains than any of its counterparts. As long as Frederick William I supported Halle, and as long as the Halle Pietists wanted to transform the whole of Prussia into a cornerstone of God's future Kingdom, Halle-trained Prussian military chaplains could believe that although they were serving two lords, they would indeed have one mission.

Soon after the death of Frederick William I, however, Prussian military chaplains were confronted with a completely new situation. Whereas the old king had given many privileges to Halle Pietists, the new king, Frederick II (1740–86), openly ridiculed Pietism and publicly supported the radical French idea of Enlightenment. Soon, the Halle-trained military chaplains faced an additional dilemma: the old king, although he loved soldiers, had never gone to war. In 1740 the new king decided to attack Austrian-held Silesia; this was just the first of a series of wars in which Prussia would be involved between 1740 and 1763.

To date, no research has been done on the role of military chaplains in those crucial years. Nevertheless, I do not think that it would be incorrect to assume that they must have been deeply disturbed. Which king should they serve? Which king could claim their ultimate loyalty? The wars started by Frederick the Great, Prussia's enlightened despot, produced a crisis not only for the Holy Roman Empire and in international politics, but also very specifically for those pious military chaplains who attempted to serve this king in the spirit in which they had been trained at Halle. Future research will have to show in detail how many military chaplains served in the wars between 1740 and 1763, whether the tone of their sermons changed as they experienced the death of hundreds upon hundreds of soldiers, and how many of them lost their lives themselves.

After 1763—following the wars of Frederick the Great—Prussia enjoyed a period of peace under the same ruler, a time in which the Enlightenment triumphed. Indeed, enlightened spirits even conquered Pietist Halle, so that the tradition of Pietism came to an end there. After the French Revolution in 1789 and Napoleon's rise to power, Prussia experienced a new series of wars. First, the Prussian army suffered a bitter defeat at the hands of the French in 1806. A few years later, in 1813, the Prussians joined the coalition that defeated Napoleon. Prussian Protestant preachers, those close to the Enlightenment as well as those close to the *Erweckungsbewegung*—the German variety of the Great

Awakening—regarded the victory over France as divine intervention.[10] As far as we know, Prussian military chaplains did so as well.[11] The two kings, the Prussian sovereign and the God of the Bible, had joined hands in this victory, so the Prussian Protestant clergy believed, and military chaplains had no difficulties in explaining that soldiers' lives lost in the war against Napoleon had been sacrificed in a holy cause.

In those early nineteenth-century wars, the line between good and evil seemed to be sharp and clear. On the one side stood Napoleon, the embodiment of enlightened arrogance; a man who had seized power illegally and tried to conquer all of Europe. On the other side, Prussian preachers portrayed Frederick William III (1797–1840) as a God-fearing king who had initiated the regeneration of his people after the defeat of 1806 and thus led Prussia to victory. In retrospect, the political rebirth of Prussia and the religious renewal of the Prussian people seemed like two sides of the same coin. While the Prussian monarchy could be stabilized in the post-Napoleonic era, the *Erweckungsbewegung* revived the belief in God's coming Kingdom. Renewed harmony seemed to exist between the two kings whom military chaplains served.

Half a century after the fall of Napoleon, in 1870–71, and a century later, in 1914–18, the Prussian army again went to war with France. By 1870, popular German belief held that France was the archenemy (*der Erbfeind*) of all Germans. It is not surprising, therefore, that the sermons preached by Prussian military chaplains in 1870–71 were full of anti-French sentiments. These sermons contain some new elements, however, that deserve our attention.[12] First, in reading these sermons, we learn that Protestant chaplains regarded this new German–French military encounter as the fulfillment of the German people's mission.[13] Second, according to these sermons, the unity of the German people possessed something like a sacred quality.[14] Third, the sermons announce that the true example that reborn Germans should follow is that of the people of Israel in the Old Testament.[15]

In most Protestant sermons preached in 1870–71, the Germans appear as a chosen people. Moreover, in some sermons, the bonds holding the Germans together are depicted not as the result of common heritage and tradition, but as bonds of kinship, or blood. The sermons equate defending the *Volksgemeinschaft* and fighting for the *Blutsgemeinschaft*— that is, defending the German people and fighting for a community based on race—with striving for the Kingdom of God. As one historian put it during the First World War, when he was able to observe a similar phenomenon: it is not religion that is the source of national power in these sermons of 1870–71, but, by contrast, it is national sentiments that are used to test the validity of religion.[16] To date, the social background, theological training, and political views of the military chaplains who served in the Franco-Prussian War of 1870–71 have not been studied in detail. However, to my knowledge, there is no indication that they were any less influenced by aggressive modern nationalism than were the rest of the German Protestant clergy or the well-educated German upper class in general, the German *Bildungsbürgertum.*

In 1870–71 the newly discovered notion of *Volksgemeinschaft* did a great deal to shape the way the Old Testament legacy was interpreted. Prussian Protestant pastors did not search for specific lessons in the Hebrew Bible; rather, they projected nationalistic, and in some cases even chauvinistic, militaristic, and racist, notions into the story of God's relationship with the people of the covenant. In short, nationalistic rhetoric had defeated theological reflection. By 1870–71, the term *Volk* had acquired a dangerous meaning among German Protestants. They no longer understood *Volk* to be the community of God's faithful children, but rather they believed the German *Volk* to be a biological entity, especially chosen by God since Luther's time, and blessed by God in the victory over France in 1813 and again in 1870–71. At the same time, in the minds of pious German Protestants, the French were transformed into a pagan, non-Christian people. In 1870–71, therefore, according to German pastors, the Germans were not involved in battles between two Christian nations, but in a confrontation between a Christian nation, namely, Germany, and a non-Christian one, one that had betrayed Christianity, that is, France.

In order to illustrate these tendencies, let us hear a few remarks by Pastor Schepers, who served as a voluntary military chaplain in the summer of 1870. Schepers described how a German farmer responded when told that his son had been killed in action. According to Schepers, the farmer said: "If I have raised him so that he sacrificed his life for a good cause, so be it in the name of God. As long as our people, our *Volk* is reborn spiritually and morally through this war, I shall not object."[17] Schepers also compared the demeanor of French and German soldiers who had been wounded. The French, Schepers noted, were constantly complaining and crying; the Germans, in contrast, suffered silently and with dignity. In dealing with pain, wounded German soldiers appeared to Schepers like "the members of a higher race as compared to a lower one."[18] Injured Germans eagerly read edifying religious pamphlets, Schepers recalled, and one severely wounded man used to sing Christian hymns, thus demonstrating the true spirit of a fighting, cheerful, victorious Christian.[19] Schepers remembered another episode that sums up his view of the war. Upon entering a barn full of wounded Germans, Schepers explained to the men that they had been chosen by God from many thousands so that they would make the sacrifice necessary for victory. God would never forget what they had done.[20] According to Schepers, the soldiers seemed very content with this explanation. In Schepers's interpretation, France had been defeated by her own sinfulness and by the spirit of truth, love, and decency on the German side,[21] and there is no doubt that his views were typical of the way German Protestant military chaplains as a whole understood the events of the Franco-Prussian War.

Whereas the war of 1870–71 ended within a few months, the First World War lasted more than four years. During those four years, the German Protestant churches became heavily involved and made an all-out effort to contribute to German victory. At the beginning of the conflict, and then at certain intervals, pastors were active on the home front, arranged *Buß- und Bettage* and *Kriegsfeiertage*, that is, days of repentance and prayer and days of celebrating the war effort. After German victories, they rang the church bells and held special thanksgiving services, *Dankgottesdienste*. In addition, there were special prayer meetings in which God was implored to grant victory to the Germans because they were his true and loyal children. In the Protestant parts of Germany, pastors also arranged *Vaterländische Gemeindeabende*,[22] which can perhaps best be translated as "meetings to uplift the patriotic spirit."[23] On such occasions, some pastor or teacher reported of the progress of the German army or, in later phases of the war, of the heroic efforts in defending the fatherland. Patriotic hymns, many of which had originated in 1813, were sung; donations were collected; and even the prayers that asked God for peace were interpreted to mean peace after a victory over Germany's enemies.

During the First World War, more Protestant pastors served the German military as chaplains than ever before, well over a thousand in all; in some branches of the Lutheran church, more than 10 percent of all pastors joined the chaplaincy.[24] Early in the war, as victory seemed imminent, spirits were high, and the services arranged by military chaplains were well attended. The longer the war lasted, however, the more difficult the task of the military chaplains became. On the one hand, they were confronted with the horrors of modern warfare: hundreds upon hundreds of soldiers were killed and mutilated, and even those soldiers who escaped combat without physical harm were often severely traumatized. On the other hand, chaplains learned that soldiers cherished their own forms of piety: they carried amulets, they believed in miracles, or they accepted whatever happened in a fatalistic manner. What the soldiers seemed to care the least about was the Christian message of God's promises and of the meaning of a Christian life. Most military chaplains had their own way of coping with this situation. Many of them delivered what an observer has labeled *Durchhaltepredigten*, that is, sermons in which soldiers were admonished to continue fighting, to carry on to the bitter end, and to stick it out through thick and thin. Instructive examples can be found in a volume published by a prominent Protestant theologian just a few years after the First World War.[25]

In the fall of 1918, the German army collapsed. Military chaplains, with few exceptions, faced widespread hostility. Unable to perform any services and deeply depressed, they returned home. In the view of many military chaplains, what had started in the summer of 1914 and at first had been organized and experienced as a kind of national reawakening, a national revival, ended as a moral disaster of enormous proportions.[26] For too long, German soldiers had been told that "Kriegsdienst ist jetzt Gottesdienst," to fight in war is to take part in a religious service, and that "Heldentod," a hero's death for the fatherland, secured eternal salvation.[27] By the fall of 1918, the military chaplains, as representatives of the two kings, the Prussian ruler and God's future Kingdom, had lost all credibility.

Keen observers had anticipated this outcome as early as 1917. What we were witnessing, one military chaplain reported home in that year, was the total moral collapse of both churches. Everyone who was near the front knew that the churches were completely powerless, he wrote, that they had lost all influence and were no longer able to speak to the mind of the fighting soldiers. The reason, this observer concluded, was not that military chaplains were not trying hard enough; on the contrary, the real explanation, he maintained, was the desperate situation of German soldiers. For 99 percent of the soldiers on the front, the military chaplains preached in vain. If one looked at the spiritual needs of these soldiers, one was filled with endless grief; meanwhile, the institution called to minister to their souls was wasting its efforts to no effect.[28] In 1915, the German army started gas warfare on the Western Front; by 1916, the year of the battle of Verdun, in which more than a million German and French soldiers lost their lives, attacks were supported by tanks and airplanes, while human lives counted less and less. It is indeed hard to imagine how a Protestant military chaplain who had been raised in a decent, middle-class family would be able to cope with such horrors.

In the fall of 1918 the German Kaiser and Prussian King William II was forced to abdicate. As the revolution triumphed in many German cities, the last Hohenzollern fled to the Netherlands. At the same time, Germany's Protestant churches fell into a deep crisis. Not only had the churches lost their feudal overlords, but also because they had supported the war effort even at the time when a continuation of the war meant only more sacrifices and more losses of lives, a significant segment of the German people distrusted what pastors attempted to say. As a result, the number of people leaving the church skyrocketed within a few months,[29] and the public authority of the church hit an all-time low. After 1918 most former military chaplains joined anti-democratic, reactionary parties and subsequently supported Hitler's rise to power. Those, like Paul Tillich, who supported democracy, were rare exceptions. It is symptomatic that in 1933 when Hitler handpicked the first leader of the newly founded Reichskirche—the United German Protestant Church—he chose Ludwig Müller, a former military chaplain.[30]

If one attempts to grasp the lesson that this unique, though certainly not encouraging, story seems to tell, several aspects seem worth remembering. First, it is a legitimate duty of Christian churches to minister spiritually to those whose lives are in danger and to console those who, as a result of military conflict, have been wounded. Soldiers, if they wish, deserve a Christian burial; their families need spiritual care and the assistance and support of their congregations. In this sense, military chaplains perform an important task, and they do so in the spirit of all Christians. I should add that the same is also true for military chaplains of all other religions.

Second, the story of Prussian military chaplains shows that as they got involved in politics, they began to neglect their pastoral and spiritual responsibilities. At first, it seemed that by preaching nationalism, military chaplains would gain new authority and their message take on additional meaning. Such was the case in the Franco-Prussian War of 1870–71, when military chaplains appealed to German nationalism and to the Germans as a "chosen people," and when national rhetoric dominated most of their sermons. But already in 1870–71, many military chaplains appear to have crossed a crucial line: rather than consoling those whose lives were endangered, and caring for those in agony and pain, they attempted to inspire the soldiers to fight. They thereby became agents of political propaganda. The chaplains transformed their role into that of missionaries of another faith, namely, the belief in the special role of the German *Volk*. This kind of nationalistic evangelization had far-reaching consequences.

Already in 1870–71, it seems, the danger arose that military chaplains regarded both kings whom they served—the German Kaiser and God's future Kingdom—as less important than the idea of a united and strong German *Volk*. Over the course of the First World War, however, all efforts spent in winning battles for this German *Volk* resulted in the opposite of what they were intended to achieve. Chaplains' prayers imploring God for victory asked for earthly glory, not for salvation. By obediently serving in the Prussian king's army, even when the war aims of the king and his military and political advisers were extremely shortsighted and directed against the best interests of the Germans themselves, the military chaplains undermined the Christian notion of forgiveness. All of their efforts corrupted both the belief in God and the loyalty to the Prussian king. By misinterpreting their task, by delivering *Durchhaltepredigten* rather than *Trostpredigten*, "hold on" sermons rather than sermons of consolation, Protestant military chaplains assumed a heavy burden of responsibility in relation to those who still trusted their words.

From these observations, one may derive a general conclusion. In order to fulfill their task properly, military chaplains need to keep a distance from politics. The agenda of the two kings whom they serve cannot and should not be merged, nor should the spiritual task they are called to perform depend on anything other than the religious inspiration of their faith. In this sense, the early eighteenth-century Pietist patriarch from Halle, August Hermann Francke, knew exactly what the role of military chaplains should be. After the wars of the twentieth century, it is more important than ever before to reflect on the necessary distance between the world of politics and war, on the one side, and the world of spiritual care and consolation, on the other.

I conclude with the example of one pastor who served as military chaplain during the First World War and who later became one of the leading and most influential Protestant theologians of the twentieth century, Paul Tillich.[31] His example shows how deeply he was influenced by the older Prussian tradition and how he struggled to define the kind of service that he believed he owed to each of the two kings.

First, I quote from a sermon Paul Tillich delivered in October 1914.[32] Here, he argued that German soldiers had gone to war as patriotic fighters. The crown that they tried to win was the victory for German arms. Germany should expand, Tillich said. Germany's greatness was the laurel wreath that should adorn every German soldier's head. In order to succeed, Germans needed the right kind of arms and the right leaders, and they had to have just one goal in mind: victory. Furthermore, according to Tillich, German soldiers had to overcome three enemies: the lack of discipline, immoral thoughts, and egoism. "Vaterlandskämpfer sind wir und Gotteskämpfer," Tillich exclaimed: "we are fighting for our fatherland and we are fighting for God." At the beginning of the war, Tillich seemed to have no doubt that God was on the German side. By fighting for their fatherland, he implied, German soldiers would gain eternal salvation.

In January 1915, Tillich elaborated the theme of love.[33] True love was the readiness to sacrifice one's life for those one loved, he explained. Love meant serving and helping others. Love was the spiritual unity with those one loved, even if these persons were far away; love provided unity through thoughts, letters, and prayers. Tillich admonished the soldiers listening to him that love meant fighting evil thoughts, fighting evil behavior, and acknowledging goodness, thus creating a better community. Perhaps one could characterize this sermon of Tillich as a typical example of a sermon in which the pastor attempts to bolster first and foremost the fighting spirit and the morale of the troops (a moral *Durchhaltepredigt*).

On the birthday of Emperor William II, on January 27, 1915, Tillich gave a sermon in which he explained Matthew 22:21: Render unto Caesar what is Caesar's, and unto God what is God's.[34] This passage was most important. According to Tillich, Germans should thank the Kaiser, because he carried the heaviest burden of responsibility in the conflict in which they were engaged. Therefore, they owed William his due, and this, according to Tillich, included not only their worldly possessions, but also their lives. God had given the Germans an emperor whom they could love. On the day of his birthday, they should renew their oath of loyalty to the Kaiser. Here again, we hear Tillich the military chaplain, who believed in German victory and who had no second thoughts about the Kaiser as leader of the German people in the conflict.

Less than half a year later, Tillich expressed radically different views. At Easter 1915, he preached that Jesus was the king of kings.[35] No king had more loyal servants than Jesus, he told the soldiers who listened to him, and no king had won more victories. It had been this way throughout the centuries. Jesus was the true lord, Tillich added, and the ultimate judge. His Kingdom was not of this world; his Kingdom was above all the kingdoms of this world. The soldiers should bow their knees as they approached Jesus, the powerful king.

In the summer of 1916, while still serving on the Western Front, Tillich preached a sermon that dramatically demonstrated his new position. He began by saying that all endeavors had two aims, one earthly, the other heavenly.[36] He then explained to his listeners that the true goal of every effort should be God's Kingdom. Wherever he looked, Tillich said, the world was in ruins. But there was one mighty empire that no one had ever defeated, and in this empire the Lord was king. It was the soldiers' duty to fight for this king; Jesus should be the king in their hearts and among their people, on earth and in heaven. The Lord should be king. Tillich's sermon is a moving testimony to the increasing cruelty of warfare in 1915 and 1916.

A final example from the spring of 1917 confirms Tillich's transformation.[37] In this sermon, Tillich for the first time mentioned widespread suffering and misery. He added that soldiers should always remember that the Lord's Kingdom was not of this world. This fact had been forgotten for much too long, he insisted. Their generation had believed that hatred and injustice could be overcome by steam power and by electricity, with the help of modern medicine and social legislation. But then the Great War had come, with unheard of hatred, misery, and injustice all over Europe. In this situation, Tillich said, his listeners should remind themselves that the Lord's Kingdom was a realm of justice, peace, and joy, that it was the aim of all their desires, their hopes, and their prayers. At the same time, they should know that this was not a distant empire, but one that existed right in the middle of the world in which they lived, and everyone who strove for justice, peace, and joy belonged to this Kingdom.

Tillich's sermons from those years demonstrate in an impressive manner how this exceptional theologian found his way from national chauvinism to belief in Christ, or, differently put, from ultimate loyalty to one king to ultimate loyalty for the other. I should add that Tillich's case is unique. In the 1920s he was one of the very few among German theologians who supported religious socialism and pacifism. After Hitler came to power in 1933, Tillich lost his professorship at the University of Frankfurt. In the mid-1930s, he was forced to emigrate to the

United States, where he did not hesitate to admonish his new American countrymen to fight against Hitler's evil regime. After 1945, Tillich pleaded for reconciliation and support for a new and better Germany. But these aspects of Tillich's later career lead far beyond the topic of this volume. It was only in the 1950s, and on the basis of the experience of the Second World War, that the German churches developed a new understanding of the role of military chaplains. In doing so they arrived at similar insights to those that Tillich had gained during the First World War, but had not been able to convey to his co-religionists in the interwar period.

Notes

1. Cf. Martin Richter, *Die Entwicklung und die gegenwärtige Gestaltung der Militärseelsorge in Preussen* (Berlin: Druckerei des Sonntagsblattes, 1899; Osnabrück: Biblio, 1991); Julius Langhäuser, *Das Militärkirchenwesen im kurbrandenburgischen und königlich preußischen Heer: Seine Entwicklung und derzeitige Gestalt* (Metz: P. Müller, 1912); Hartmut Rudolph, *Das evangelische Militärkirchenwesen in Preußen: Die Entwicklung seiner Verfassung und Organisation vom Absolutismus bis zum Vorabend des I. Weltkriegs* (Göttingen: Vandenhoeck & Ruprecht, 1973); Albrecht Schübel, *300 Jahre Evangelische Soldatenseelsorge* (Munich: Evgl. Presseverband, 1964); and Franz Blanckmeister, *Die sächsischen Feldprediger: Zur Geschichte der Militärseelsorge in Krieg und Frieden* (Leipzig: Fr. Richter, 1893).

2. For the background, see Carl Hinrichs, *Preußentum und Pietismus; Der Pietismus in Brandenburg-Preußen als religiös-soziale Reformbewegung* (Göttingen: Vandenhoeck & Ruprecht, 1971), 155–60; see also Klaus Deppermann, *Der Hallesche Pietismus und der preußische Staat unter Friedrich III.* (Göttingen: Vandenhoeck & Ruprecht, 1961); Friedrich Schloemann, *Siegmund Jacob Baumgarten: System und Geschichte in der Theologie des Übergangs zum Neuprotestantismus* (Göttingen: Vandenhoeck & Ruprecht, 1974), 30–32; Peter Schicketanz, ed., *Carl Hildebrand von Canstein: Der Briefwechsel Carl Hildebrand von Cansteins mit August Hermann Francke* (Berlin: De Gruyter, 1972); Mary Fulbrook, *Piety and Politics: Religion and the Rise of Absolutism in England, Württemberg, and Prussia* (Cambridge: Cambridge University Press, 1983), 167; and Richard L. Gawthrop, *Pietism and the Making of Eighteenth-Century Prussia* (Cambridge: Cambridge University Press, 1993), 224–26.

3. Hinrichs, *Preußentum und Pietismus*, 126.

4. Ibid., 126–27.

5. See Martin Brecht, ed., *Der Pietismus vom siebzehnten bis zum frühen achtzehnten Jahrhundert, Geschichte des Pietismus*, vol. 1 (Göttingen: Vandenhoeck & Ruprecht, 1993), 440–539.

6. See Hinrichs, *Preußentum und Pietismus*, passim.

7. Victor Christoph Tuchtfeld. See Hinrichs, *Preußentum und Pietismus*, 136–47.

8. Johann Daniel Herrnschmidt. See Hinrichs, *Preußentum und Pietismus*, 160–62.

9. I am grateful to Benjamin A. Marschke, University of California at Los Angeles, for providing me with these numbers. Marschke is preparing a dissertation on "The Chaplaincy in Early Eighteenth-Century Brandenburg-Prussia" on the basis of new material that he has found. Marschke will not only give comprehensive and detailed information, he will also show how Frederick William I used the military chaplains to build an additional ecclesiastical hierarchy which depended on him and not, like the Lutheran church in Prussia, on the estates.

10. Johannes Bauer, *Schleiermacher als patriotischer Prediger: Ein Beitrag zur Geschichte der nationalen Erhebung vor hundert Jahren* (Giessen: Töpelmann, 1908); Alfred Uckeley, ed., *Königsberger patriotische Predigten aus den Jahren 1806 bis 1816 von D. Ludwig Ernst von Borowski* (Königsberg: Beyer, 1913).

11. By 1800, Prussian military chaplains were no longer exclusively recruited from Halle, and most of them were no longer close to Pietism. See Joseph Freisen, "Die Jurisdiktion des preußischen katholischen und evangelischen Feldpropstes," *Deutsche Zeitschrift für Kirchenrecht* 25 (1915–16 [Tübingen 1917]): 271–342, and Heinrich Pohl, *Die katholische Militärseelsorge Preußens, 1797–1888* (Stuttgart: Enke, 1926).

12. For an excellent analysis, see Paul Piechowski, "Die Kriegspredigt von 1870/71" (Theol. diss., University of Leipzig, 1916).

13. Ibid., 62–65.

14. Ibid., 65–76.

15. Ibid., 76–78.

16. Ibid., 75.

17. C. Schepers, *Bilder und Eindrücke aus einer achtwöchigen Dienstzeit als freiwilliger Feldprediger im Sommer 1870* (Bonn: Adolph Marcus 1871), 4.

18. Ibid., 29: "Sie erschienen darin wirklich wie die höhere Rasse gegenüber einer niedrigeren."

19. Ibid., 40.

20. Ibid., 55.

21. Ibid., 96.

22. Paul Schian, *Die Arbeit der evangelischen Kirche in der Heimat* (Berlin: E.S. Mittler, 1925), 210; see also 212, 265–69.

23. During the First World War, Protestant pastors did things that can truly be called grotesque. For example, they expunged foreign expressions from ecclesiastical texts and preached that goods made of British steel should be replaced by German products. Schian, *Kirche in der Heimat*, 287.

24. Paul Schian, *Die Arbeit der evangelischen Kirche im Felde* (Berlin: E.S. Mittler, 1921), 467–68. See also the "Volksschriftentum zum großen Krieg," nos. 101–27, ed. the Evangelischer Bund.

25. Ibid., 100–127, 130–41, 218–22.

26. Ibid., 128–30, 141–43.

27. Ibid., 223, 225.

28. Ibid., 513.

29. Schian, *Kirche in der Heimat*, 11–12.

30. Thomas Martin Schneider, *Reichsbischof Ludwig Müller. Eine Untersuchung zu Leben, Werk und Persönlichkeit* (Göttingen: Vandenhoeck & Ruprecht, 1993).

31. See Paul Tillich, *Frühe Predigten* (1909–18), ed. Erdmann Sturm (Berlin and New York: De Gruyter, 1994), especially "Feldpredigten," 355–645. For a critical analysis of Tillich's sermons as a military chaplain during the First World War, see Erdmann Sturm, "Zwischen Apologetik und Seelsorge. Paul Tillichs frühe Predigten (1908–1918)," *Theologische Literaturzeitung* 124 (1999): 251–68.

32. Tillich, "Feldpredigten," 359–61.

33. Ibid., 380–82.

34. Ibid., 383–86.

35. Ibid., 391–94.

36. Ibid., 461–63.

37. Ibid., 541–43.

CHAPTER SEVEN

"WHERE'S THE PADRE?"

Canadian Memory and the Great War Chaplains

DUFF CRERAR

In his 1930 memoir, *And We Go On*, Will Bird, a Nova Scotian who had served since 1917 on the Western Front, portrays a bitter debate between billet-mates one night in camp. "Where's the padre?" asked the student. "Before I came over I fancied that they were always with the soldiers, helping the wounded ones and having little services every chance they got." "Don't," said Tommy, "start that argument. I was a member of the Methodist Church when I enlisted. Now I don't know or care about anything connected with it." Bird's cynical comrade then offers a fairly representative sample of what other soldiers were starting to write in the late 1920s and early 1930s. "Preachers and padres are not any better than brass hats. They're out of touch with the men, and they've lost their hold." "Don't you believe in God?" asks the student. "I do," said Tommy gravely and reverently. "If I didn't I'd quit everything. But I'm going to have my own belief in my own way. . . . Bah padres, I'm sick of them. They say just what the brass hats want them to say, there's not a sincere man among them. If there was he'd be out between the lines trying to stop both sides from killing each other."

Later, when invited by a chaplain to stay for a service in the camp canteen, Bird's disillusioned veteran explodes in wrath: "'No,' said Tommy, 'I don't want to hear any more twaddle. I've had to go on church parades but this isn't compulsory, and once I'm out of this rig no man will ever make me listen to your stuff.' The padre tried to argue. 'We're going to teach a real gospel now,' he said. 'The war's over and we're going to, first of all, prove to the people what a horrible crime it is.' 'Don't do that,' cried Tommy. 'You'll lose the few you've still got if you turn hypocrite. The war hasn't changed. If it's wrong now it was wrong in '14, and what did you shout then?' The padre's eyes flooded full. He could not talk."[1]

The Canadian memory of the Great War, as its veterans called it, is profoundly ambivalent: public triumph contends with tragic personal memories of waste and loss. For some Canadians, this anger and pride mingled with deep disillusionment when the high hopes of the war were dashed in the subsequent peace. The same phenomenon has indelibly marked the Canadian perspective of the military chaplain. Several generations later, most Canadian authors echo only the soldiers' rejection that Bird eloquently portrayed. And yet, historical inquiry shows that this vivid and influential memory is an unhistorical caricature. In surveying their wartime work, this essay argues that the Canadian padres were not cloistered from battlefield experience and usually did not react to the horrors of the war with shock or religious disillusionment. Nor did the Canadian soldiers who wrote about the war universally or immediately reject their padres, before or even for a decade after the Armistice. It is not historical reality, but the post-1920's climate of Canadian veterans' rage, and its appeal to subsequent generations of Canadian scholars of religion and war, that nurtures the persistence and power of this predominant, yet distorted portrait.

THE GREAT WAR GENERATION: A WAR AND A PEACE ENDURED

From the Fenian raids in 1866 to the outbreak of the Great War, Canadian governments had improvised their religious ministry to soldiers on active service, inevitably accompanied by a welter of political controversy and interdenominational jealousy. Finally, in 1897, Ottawa did authorize a peacetime, honorary, unpaid, regimental chaplaincy to help legitimize the militia for church folk alienated by stories of drink and dissipation and to provide an outlet for adventurous, extroverted, and mostly Protestant clerics. The widely publicized exploits of a few brave chaplains in the Northwest Rebellion of 1885 and the South African War (1899–1902) created the image of the ideal military chaplain as a brave, fighting cleric.[2]

Thus, it was inconceivable in 1914 that the government would leave chaplains out of the Canadian Expeditionary Force (C.E.F.). But the man who handpicked Canada's first regular chaplain corps, the manipulative and unruly militia minister, Sam Hughes, was more interested in the political and personal loyalty of his appointees than in pastoral merit or denominational balance. The result was a shortage of Roman Catholic chaplains in the field—Hughes was a Methodist Orangeman—and a growing number of surplus and often incompetent padres cluttering up camps in Great Britain. This inefficiency and neglect provoked outright mutiny in the summer of 1916, when Roman Catholic chaplains overseas decided that rather than wait for church officials in Canada to come to the rescue, they would work out their own escape from the scheming war minister's clutches.[3] It took the rest of the year, and determined lobbying in Ottawa by a Catholic padre back from the Somme, to persuade Prime Minister R.L. Borden to dismiss Hughes and his entourage and appoint a new Chaplain Service director. Borden chose John M. Almond, an Anglican veteran of the South African War who had been at the front since 1915.[4] By then, many Canadian officers viewed their Chaplain Service as a laughingstock, while the British War Office and the Army Chaplains Department dismissed the Canadian service as troublesome and incompetent.

Throughout 1917, Almond's tough but fair-minded approach eventually restored the honor and efficiency of the service. By the end of that year, chaplain casualty and reinforcement problems at the front had been rectified, and cases of moral failure and incompetence had been disciplined. The reformed Canadian chaplaincy reassured kinfolk that their men were not dying without religious consolation and that soldiers were not morally deteriorating overseas. The service earned impressive political clout with the government and convinced home churches that chaplains were devoted soldier-priests, whose experiences, insights, and influence with the soldiers would spearhead a national religious revival after the war. Before its demobilization in 1921, at least 524 clergymen had worn the Chaplain Service uniform, 447 of them overseas.

In addition to their administrative reforms, the chaplains added major ministry breakthroughs at the front. During the chaotic opening months of the war and in defiance of British army regulations,

Canadian field padres worked their way from the rear area to the forward edge of the battle zone.[5] By persistently visiting the trenches and dugouts, Canadian chaplains, such as Anglican Canon F. G. Scott, wore down the opposition of senior officers to padres in the trenches, even during combat. Their exploits under fire at Ypres, and in other engagements, earned tributes from soldiers. By the end of 1915, therefore, many Canadian officers at the front had decided they could count on the padres.

This credibility grew in 1916, as chaplains, pushing themselves frequently into combat areas, were sometimes wounded, taken prisoner, or gassed.[6] Finally, on the eve of the Somme campaign, Canadian Corps commander Julian Byng authorized their frontline presence. Canadian padres thus rose in army estimation from awkward and perhaps unnecessary baggage to useful assets integrated into first-class attacking formations. Their battlefield contributions became evident in the 1917 corps offensives. At Vimy, Lens, and Passchendaele, chaplains manned the most advanced dressing stations and aid posts and accompanied medical officers into captured dugouts and trenches. Space and resources were allotted specifically for the Chaplain Service in the offensive planning of every Canadian operation from Vimy onward. Divisional senior chaplains reported that their men sustained wounds and earned combat decorations and citations in ever-increasing numbers that year.

In 1918, the padres earned what many had requested since 1915: a place in the attack. Eighteen brigade chaplains went over the top with first-wave troops at the Battle of Amiens, and even more—up to one-third of all chaplains with the Canadian Corps—followed suit in the last battles of the war. During the final offensive, chaplain attrition rates approached those of other corps officers.[7] Padre casualties included gunshot as well as shell wounds, exposure to gas, and what was later dubbed "battle exhaustion" (then "neurasthenia," or more commonly, "shell-shock"). By war's end, several had been killed in action or died of wounds or exposure, one had been a prisoner of war for two years, and dozens were returning from duty sick or crippled.

In their progress from parish to trench and back, padres shared many stressful, bitter, and triumphant experiences with officers and men. Some writers charge that chaplains were cloistered from all the harsh and dangerous experiences of the Great War. But service records indicate that, except for killing, chaplains participated in almost every routine or hideous aspect of war. From Canadian military records it

Tea and coffee for the wounded: Canadian Chaplain Service coffee stall behind the lines at battle of Hill 70, August 1917. National Archives of Canada. NAC-PA1600.

appears that many rose to those occasions, though some were indeed bedeviled by personal weaknesses, age, family, or parish problems. However, any failure had disastrous results for the honor of the service and was soon the talk of the army. Examination of the human side of the padres' experience reveals that while most found war service harrowing, relatively few failed in their duty. Most chaplains returned from the war believing they had made a faithful pilgrimage to the painful field and returned, like their men, scarred but intact.

Chaplains' letters, reports, and diaries show little disillusionment or loss of faith. Even after prolonged overseas service, although many had given up the optimistic assumption that the church would weather the storms unchanged, most who expressed their views about the war, the Gospel, and the mission of the church echoed the militant idealism of prewar days. The small minority who opposed crusading rhetoric often met with incomprehension or rebuffs from their own church leaders and fellow chaplains. In published sermons, articles, and letters,

Heroes: three disabled Canadian chaplains receive their distinguished service order decorations at Buckingham Palace after the Armistice. From right to left: Alexander M. Gordon, Senior Chaplain, 4th Canadian Division; Canon Frederick G. Scott, Senior Chaplain, 1st Canadian Division; and Edward E. Graham, 3rd Canadian Infantry Brigade. National Archives of Canada. NAC-PA-7601.

they ascribed a providential mission to Canada and the Allies. Under the influence of atrocity propaganda, outraged by the use of poison gas on Canadian troops, and the torpedoing of the *Lusitania* in 1915, padres told the men that winning the war would certainly advance the Kingdom of God on earth; Germany embodied the forces of the Antichrist. The war was Canada's crucible of regeneration. Military service was the highest of Christian duties in this critical hour. The urge to go to the front was the call of God. To serve and suffer in the assault on the citadel of evil was Christlike.[8]

But service at Casualty Clearing Stations, with artillery and engineer units, and of course with the infantry, took its toll on rhetorical allusions to Marathon or Armageddon. Canon Scott, for example, found that his patriotic preaching underwent a profound shift toward the personal and devotional as he developed from a crusading, fighting padre to admiring fellow-sufferer with the troops. Chaplains had to abandon peacetime moralism; and, because they identified with the men, they came to appreciate, even admire and idealize, the trench ethic of comradeship. But preaching at the front between 1916 and 1918, while it usually shifted from prophetic to devotional themes, nevertheless resolutely pointed to the world-historic significance of the war. Field troops, too, were told that their hardship was service in the army of Christ, that they were waging a war to abolish war itself, and that the whole world, especially Canada, would be transformed by their sacrifices.

In an effort to make Christianity appeal to the soldier, the padres repeatedly drove home their convictions about the regenerative nature of self-sacrifice and the courageous, comradely Christ. The Canadian padre's portrait of Jesus, in fact, often emerged from the writings of American modernists such as Walter Rauschenbusch and Harry Emerson Fosdick, and his call for a moral equivalent to war from the work of William James. Despite conditions that seemed to mock the nobility of these sentiments, the Canadian Great War padre reported no tension between saving individual souls and saving the whole world through military service. They were there to convince the soldier to dedicate himself utterly to the Kingdom of God and the Lordship of Jesus, the captain of his and the world's salvation. Although a small minority of chaplains rejected such an optimistic assessment, most expected that the seeds of religion planted in many soldiers overseas would flower when the veterans returned to Canada.[9] Thus, their experience of soldier nobility and self-sacrifice raised their expectations of the peace.[10]

It was rarely the war, but more often the peace that disillusioned the padres. They returned, in early 1919, to find a Canada very different from the one they had left. Once united by war, some chaplains found themselves on opposite sides of postwar disputes. Some tried to tone down veterans' labor demonstrations: in British Columbia and Winnipeg, they played a major part in encouraging many to resist "Bolshevist" agitation. The few who sided with the protesters, especially Canon Scott, found military authorities ruthlessly unsympathetic. Although chaplains normally made the transition out of uniform with a minimum of difficulty, more than one grew bitter and angry upon discovering that his denomination did not recognize his war sacrifices, sentencing him to begin his career again in poor missions, rural parishes, and extension work.

Those who anticipated receiving church leadership positions usually discovered, with other veterans, that their country had learned to get along without them. Churchmen told ex-padres that the war was not a unique training for ecclesiastical leadership, but an abnormal interlude that they ought to get over as quietly as possible. Those who turned to the army to recover their equilibrium learned that determined efforts to save the Canadian Chaplain Service from demobilization had been abandoned by 1920. The chaplaincy was returned to its prewar status as an honorary regimental office in the Non-Permanent Militia. Most, therefore, made their peace with their denominations, but many left the ministry and took up careers in penal, legal, journalistic, sociological, and civil service professions. A few entered politics. Others left the country entirely for mission fields and work in American or British churches.[11]

Surprisingly, a significant number held to their wartime idealism in the first decade of the peace. Not only Presbyterians and Methodists, but also Baptists, Anglicans, and some Roman Catholics led social reform projects and spoke out on the same issues that had been part of their prewar and wartime visions. Most Presbyterian ex-chaplains led the campaign to create the United Church of Canada, and though a few colleagues vigorously opposed them, none cited the war as the cause of their opposition. Such cases suggest that Canadian scholars should not exaggerate the speed with which wartime idealism died down. By the end of the 1920s, the optimistic expectations former padres held of the peace had soured, first into frustration, then into disenchantment. The disappointing outcome of Church Union, the nation's return to traditional party politics, economic instability, and new war clouds on the international horizon all dimmed their hopes as they stood around the cenotaphs each November. H. R. Nobles, a Baptist ex-chaplain, while walking past the Regina war memorial on November 11, 1929, confronted the bleak prospects ahead. That night he drafted a poem where the ghosts of the fallen asked, "Have we failed? / Have we failed? / Did we die in vain?"[12] By then, a few strident critics of the padres and their war, veterans themselves, were also being heard. To many padres, it was the most bewildering and unkind development of all.

As the 1930s brought the worst of the Great Depression at home and the rise of dictatorial governments overseas, quiet re-evaluations of their war led many idealistic ex-padres to an emotional and sometimes theological crossroads. Though some in prominent ecclesiastical positions continued to crusade for various reform movements and

A hasty field burial: Canadian chaplain and troops at the Somme, October 1916. National Archives of Canada. NAC-PA-652.

the League of Nations Society, only a minority replaced the crusade or just-war theology with Christian pacifism. Most re-associated with veterans' groups; many grimly donned militia uniforms and solemnly prepared for another conflict. In 1936, during the veterans' pilgrimage to Vimy, and especially at the dedication of the war memorial on Hill 145, their words of commemoration betrayed divided minds and hearts. Bishop A.E. Deschamps, a lieutenant-colonel in the militia, spoke in the traditional vein of the men who had died for others, who, practicing "the higher form of Christian Charity . . . will live again in the heavenly home."[13]

Speaking for the United Church, ex-chaplain George Fallis paraphrased the New Testament letter to the Hebrews, substituting the Canadian soldiers who died overseas for the ancient heroes of the faith.[14] Just minutes earlier, however, they had heard another ex-chaplain, Cecil Owen, with longer and closer experience of the front, and who had left a son buried in France, voice the uncertainties of many a veteran nerving himself for the future: "Returning to France and Flanders' Fields gives us a feeling that we are treading on sacred ground as we think of the countless thousands who lie sleeping here. To many who thought that the Great War would end war, we can only say that One, and only

One, can make men live together in love and peace. We must educate our children in the finer aspects of courage and sacrifice which emerged during the war so that they will remember the heroism and the deeper lessons which should have resulted from it."[15]

By 1939, such hopes were in ashes. As Canada declared war against Germany, only one ex-C.E.F. chaplain joined the "witness against war" movement begun by a few members of the United Church.[16] Others volunteered for active service. On October 18, 1939, the Canadian government appointed Bishops George A. Wells (Anglican), a veteran senior chaplain of the Great War, and C.A. Nelligan (Roman Catholic) as heads of their respective branches of a brand-new Canadian Active Service Force Chaplain Service.[17] It was now clear that though their war had been won overseas, it was lost in the peace that followed.

FROM RESPECT TO REJECTION:
WAR WRITERS RECALL THE PADRES

If any Canadian padres remembered the Great War with disillusionment and a spirit of revolt, very few admitted to it on paper or in public. Neither, at least at first, had most Canadian veterans and war writers. The initial public memory of the war was affirmative and consoling. As Jonathan Vance has shown in his study of Canadian writers and artists, the national memory, especially in the first decade after 1918, but also long afterward, was based on continuity with wartime mythical elements and motifs. Even when some critics and a few Canadian war writers tried to shake this consoling viewpoint, the defensive fury of the reaction by readers and most critics revealed the public's desire to give the war an explanatory and consoling purpose; the cost had been too great to view it otherwise.[18]

Consequently, the initial public image of the chaplain during the first decade after the war was, on the whole, positive. Most early Canadian war books followed, albeit in more subdued tones, the patriotic and optimistic themes that had been part of wartime propaganda. Wide-eyed personal accounts of "ripping padres" were succeeded by more sober books of commemoration and comradeship, though the attempt by the Chaplain Service to write its own official history was deemed by Colonel A.F. Duguid, Canada's official war historian, as too cliché-ridden for publication.[19] The standardized battalion histories—usually written by an officer—gave a stereotypical view of the chaplain based upon the regimental war diary and official documents. They allotted only two or three paragraphs to the padre: mentioning if he earned any citations or decorations and noting his role as a fellow-officer and contributor to unit life. Usually, he was portrayed as the medical officer's alter ego, the spiritual affairs officer who was brave, devoted, patriotic, and above all, useful, whether with the medical officer in the aid post, censoring letters, umpiring a baseball game, passing out cigarettes, or managing carrying parties.[20] In this genre, brave chaplains were regarded with both warmth and some equivocation as "more man than cleric."[21]

When there was an angry objection to such portraits, as in L.M. Gould's *From B.C. to Basieux*, a history of the 102nd Battalion—written, significantly, by one who had served in the ranks—it revealed ambivalence. Gould denounced church parades, which "were the grimmest and ghastliest of service jokes, and were provocative of more blasphemy and discontent than any active operation." Canadian soldiers were extremely proud of the fact that most of them were volunteers. Thus, church parades (following a lengthy inspection and usually accompanied by profane comments from NCOs fussing about uniform violations and cleanliness), after which the men were marched off to a compulsory worship service, created extreme resentment. Chaplains found such services a special challenge throughout the war, as they tried to break through the natural resistance of men compelled by army regulations to exercise their religious freedom. Here, the padre found himself forced to play the role of an officer, not a soldier's comrade. Staff officers were hated, because they demanded such parades after combat (despite the padre's objection) instead of sending the men to the baths.

In Gould's depiction, the YMCA welfare workers carry off most of the laurels, yet the unit's padre, Roman Catholic chaplain Charles Fallon, is above reproach, even if all other padres are not. He had redeemed himself by rescuing wounded under fire during the 1918 fighting.[22] Gould's book revealed a widespread military phenomenon remarked on by other padres, notably Canon Scott: soldiers (and veterans) routinely denounced all padres except the ones they had known in their own unit.[23] But few echoed Gould's revolt against the conventions of military religion until 1929, when W.B. Kerr struck out at patriotic smugness. Although Kerr, an artilleryman, admits that padres like Canon Scott were brave and devoted, his opinion of the underside of the chaplaincy is scathing: "Each Brigade had a chaplain; ours stayed at the wagon lines and held services there Sunday morning; rarely, if ever, did we see any of them at the guns. . . . Most kept well out of danger, made friends only with the officers, knew nothing of the men, they who ought to have acted as a link between the commissioned and the noncommissioned ranks with the confidence of both. The chief interest of some seemed to be in getting themselves promoted or moved back to England or the base; such conduct was viewed with disgust and regarded as entirely unworthy of the men's profession." [24] To Kerr, although some chaplains had, at times, helped the troops by running canteens and through social work, they generally failed in their religious role. [25]

Any balance between grudging credit and repudiation was completely upset during the next decade. The recollections of more junior officers and ex-privates injected anger and bitterness into the literature. Their long-suppressed rage at the entire war immediately reflected on the chaplain. The 1930 release of Charles Yale Harrison's *Generals Die in Bed* caused a storm of controversy among Canadian readers. Although a few critics praised his account of service with the 14th Canadian Infantry Battalion as the first authentic private's version of the war, most were outraged at the shocking portrayal of the war's moral and spiritual impact on soldiers. [26] Harrison depicted most of his peers as godless, cynical, and profane. Harrison's religious soldiers were an unpopular minority, millennialist cranks whose narrow morality and censoriousness drew constant ridicule, and who often proved cowardly at critical moments. Prayer made soldiers uneasy and irritable, for it seemed to draw fire. God was just another absent and arbitrary general who sent men to die, then abandoned them to the shelling. After a barrage, parade divine service was a puny and pathetic exercise. [27]

Significantly, some Canadian veterans were as outraged by the book as were the critics. Disgusted with Harrison's portrayal, "putrid with so-called realism," Will Bird began his own chronicle of war. In 1930, a small run of *And We Go On* was released to the Canadian public, with moderate financial and far more critical success than *Generals Die in Bed*. To him, writers like Harrison misrepresented the soldier as a morally and spiritually contaminated survivor. In spite of all the death and disillusionment, most Canadian soldiers had come back with their moral and spiritual integrity damaged, strained, or even irretrievably alienated from their former civilian lives, but still intact. [28] Nevertheless, his view of Christianity's representatives in the army during the war also bluntly challenged the facile rhetoric of officers, church, and war leaders. Chaplains were noncombatant officers, and therefore more mascot than fellow-soldier.[29] "Padres, as a rule, were scorned, for only sincerity could live with the 'other ranks,' and they knew, whatever the showing, that he was not one of them. Our own padre was not disliked. Sometimes on the crater line he came at night with cigarettes and warm drinks and talked with a private, but he was apart from the men, and usually with, perhaps through circumstances, an officer [the Medical Officer] whom the majority cordially hated."[30]

Bird's worm's-eye recollections are especially interesting, and yet, on the surface, perplexing. We know his battalion (the 42nd), his private thoughts, and those he placed in the mouths of his comrades — we even know the hated medical officer's name — and so we can also identify Bird's padre. He was George Kilpatrick, D.S.O., a veteran with frontline service in battles ranging from Vimy Ridge and Passchendaele to Amiens and Mons in November 1918 (the Distinguished Service Order was only awarded to officers who risked their lives under fire). Brother-officers, according to the battalion's deputy commander and regimental historian, C. B. Topp, praised Kilpatrick for being athletic, brave, and devoted to the regiment.[31] Canadian Expeditionary Force military records corroborate this impression.[32] But Bird's view is that of a man in the ranks, which helps to account for the appeal of his characterization to subsequent Canadian war scholars. Like his view of Kilpatrick, Bird's opinion of Topp's account of the battalion is entirely dismissive. To him, it was written "For Officers Only."[33]

Other writers reacted to Harrison by shifting the focus from padre and crusade to simple comradeship. Kim Beattie, another veteran and chronicler, gave some credit to some padres, but noted that their religious work was continuously offset by soldiers' contempt for conventional religion. In the 48th Battalion:

The stress of life was such that religion had little chance to enter the round of their days. The war-wise padre had realised long ago that care of the men's bodies was the greatest work he and their officers could do, and their souls would take care of themselves. The spirit of the front-line was the spirit of sacrifice . . . all of them unconsciously felt that daily about them were instances of sheer unselfishness and a purer, more honest Christianity than that of civil life. There was a greatness about the spirit of the front-line such as they had never sensed before and were never, perhaps, to feel again. It was the spirit of sacrifice and comradeship, never spoken of, yet always there and most surely found when Death and Dread strode over the world.[34]

Thus, by the early 1930s, Canada's war literature on padres had parted into two streams, one commemorative and the other vehemently critical. Against such strong and vivid denunciation, the handful of sympathetic accounts that followed had little effect.[35] Philip Child wrote that every veteran writer who followed Harrison's depiction "lies, or has forgotten," but H.M. Urquhart claimed that YMCA officers influenced the 16th Battalion more than chaplains. To soldiers, padres were just more brigade officers, except, as usual, for Canon Scott.[36] In 1937 former stretcher-bearer F. Noyes added a new and influential charge.[37] To him, the padre who "pharisaically prays for victory for our side and disaster for the enemy" was contemptible: "We remember only too well how often we were compelled to chase this type of chaplain from our advanced dressing dugouts, to make room for the wounded. We never could understand why this sort of bible-thumper was reluctant to face Death if he really believed all the stuff he poured in our ears."[38] Even the nurses had their say. Mary Clint wrote that any interdenominational unity overseas was not produced by revival but by patriotism. It was the Cause that united, not the Faith. Furthermore, she added, in the light of the denominational bickering between politically appointed padres she had witnessed overseas: "One might suggest, however, that in another war *all* chaplains should be specially selected to honour their creed and cloth."[39] As war clouds gathered again, such sentiments cast a dark shadow on the Canadian padre—as buffoon, coward, or hypocrite. From then on, few writers would get clear of its influence.

Ambivalent Legacy: Recent Canadian Scholars View the Padre

Although the majority of Canadian chaplains of 1939 were veterans, by 1945 almost every chaplain overseas was too young to have been a soldier, much less a padre in the Great War. The next generation of active service chaplains brought to their ministry a new style and tenor of preaching, though much of the hospital, camp, and forward-area ministry resembled that of their forebears. After the Second World War, padres, especially those of the Great War, moved to the shadowy periphery of Canadian war memory. Except for occasional mention by soldiers, the Great War chaplains became virtually invisible. The 1962 official history of the Canadian Expeditionary Force devoted more attention to the veterinary and dental branches than it did to padres.[40] In Canada, the most well-known reference to Great War padres was the denunciation by Will Bird, repeated in his re-published memoirs, entitled *Ghosts Have Warm Hands*.[41]

Only in the 1980s did scholars turn to the original sources to re-assess the chaplain. When they did, it was the critical stream that shaped their conclusions. One of Canada's most knowledgeable and prolific military historians, Desmond Morton, found in the organizational chaos of the service ample illustration of Canada's lack of military preparation in 1914, the Byzantine evolution of Canadian forces overseas, and the ludicrous results of political appointees, especially padres, being given military rank and privileges.[42] Although he noted several false stereotypes of Canadian soldiers, when he turned to the chaplain, his portrayal often relied on Bird and on British war writers such as Guy Chapman, Robert Graves, and C. E. Montague, who described the Great War soldiers as "the sheep who were not fed" by their padres.[43]

Likewise, Canadian church historians barely noticed chaplains until the 1960s. Then, what struck them most forcefully was their militant idealism. Students of the Social Gospel had no difficulty, for example, in finding chaplains' statements that, to them, proved the war's heightening effect on religious nationalism and reform.[44] Nevertheless, in these studies, chaplains were sampled, not studied, useful only in supporting accounts primarily of the wartime role and idealism of home-front churches. Padres remain in the background most of the time, relegated to the role of consoling soldiers and their kin, or endorsing home-front calls for reform.[45]

The tone and focus of Canadian religious scholarship on the Great War changed, however, in the early 1980s, influenced by provocative books from Great Britain and the United States on the psychological and cultural effects of the war. Studies by Eric Leed, Robert Wohl, and especially Paul Fussell, burst like star shells on a cohort of graduate students poring over long-neglected documents and researching topics such as Canadian secularization, neo-orthodoxy, fundamentalism, and "Christian realism." The most exciting aspect of this scholarship, to them, was the convincing presentation of the tremendous break the war represented in modern culture. Consequently, the war's impact on

Canada, especially its impact on clergymen, came to be interpreted in a new light.

To these scholars, the Great War confronted disillusioned Canadian padres with fatalistic, semi-pagan soldiers—deeply cynical, hating civilians, rendered silent by the obscenity, humiliation, and depersonalization of "trenchland"—the war they got instead of the war they had been led to expect. To Michael Gauvreau, who acknowledged his debt to Fussell, Leed, and Wohl, the interaction of padre and soldier brewed a new religious concoction, a blending of anti-ecclesiastical mysticism and comradeship, which he called "Christian Realism." Soldiers abandoned the old institutions of religion, padres noted, but the generous spirit of Christianity remained. Soldiers found meaning only in the cross, and gave credence to miracles, myths, and tales of the supernatural. Rather than divorce personal faith from social action, the lessons of "trenchland," with its emphasis on experiential religion and fellow-suffering with Christ, gave birth to some of the central tenets of the postwar evangelical mind.[46]

Studying Canadian Methodism and Presbyterianism, however, David Marshall argued, in the mid-1980s, that the war had a shattering effect on chaplains, clerics, and seminary students. Instead of amplifying their idealism, the spirit of revolt drove them away from formal Christianity or back to older-style evangelicalism, which denied the naive historical theology of their teachers and leaders. Thus, the war helped secularize the churches, shake their credibility with Canadians, and shock the clergy into mutually hostile liberal and fundamentalist camps by the 1920s. When it came to their influence, padres were unsure how the soldiers responded to their preaching, but religious individuals in the ranks frankly declared they were not getting through to the men. The padres, like miners' canaries, had discovered the religious toxicity of modern war as they toured the dugouts.[47] It was not an optimistic picture of Canada's war, and certainly not an optimistic picture of the Canadian Great War padres.

The streams of Canadian military and cultural historiography eventually merged in the work of Jonathan Vance. He questioned the wholesale transfer of Paul Fussell's analysis to the Canadian context. According to Vance, the soldier-writers Fussell examined, who shaped the modern memory of the war, were simply unrepresentative of the majority of the troops. The anti-heroic, ironic, discontinuity-modernity tradition was only one, and not the dominant memory of Canadians between the wars. Most Canadians were not captured by Harrison's account, but by Bird's, or the more optimistic versions from the front, including the padres'.[48] Postwar Canadians, including most of those who served in the trenches, intensified instead of discarded the wartime patriotic verities in pulpit, page, and sculpture. "High Diction" was heard right up to 1939. Harrison's shattering version was vehemently rejected, even by other veterans, who may have resented official military religion and historical theology, but kept their spiritual and moral selves whole. Most important, these veterans believed they had done it on their own, without a padre's help.[49]

Jonathan Vance, like Desmond Morton, views the Canadian Great War padre heritage with a blend of skepticism and disdain. In the tradition of Will Bird, most post–Second World War Canadian scholars find themselves unable to empathize with the beliefs of pre–First World War days. Vance notes, "Canadians who lived through the war may have had a very different understanding of it than we expect them to." Yet, like Marshall, Vance and other writers of his generation cannot see how prewar historical theology could be reconciled with modern war.[50] To them, if most padres and Canadians between the wars were not repentant, perhaps they should have been. "The acceptance of any version of memory is as much about forgetting as remembering," wrote Vance, who obviously wants to set the record straight about Canadian culture, but still accepts uncritically the persuasive and largely unsubstantiated chaplain critiques by war writers.[51] Taking the lead from Bird, Kerr, and others, he concludes that padres were well meaning, but widely despised by the troops. Attempts to show that padres were willing to take risks and share discomforts he has dismissed as unconvincing.[52]

Vance criticizes scholars who use as history Fussell's study of the chronicles of disillusionment by the war generation. He wisely chastens those who forget that *The Great War and Modern Memory* was no more an attempt to be a history of the Great War "as it really was" than any other veteran's memoir of the trenches. Fussell's work was mainly a study of war recalled, "conventionalized," and "mythologised" by a select group of Englishmen who survived one phase of the war: the hideous trench deadlock between the Somme and Passchendaele. If taken as attempts by the "lost generation" to convey with verisimilitude their war, Canadian and other scholars miss what Fussell himself pointed out: soldier memoirs are not diaries, in fact they are, as literature, closer to first novels than autobiographies. Fussell knew that the claims of a Blunden, Graves, or Sassoon must be tested against historical sources as carefully as Will Bird's or Charles Yale Harrison's. War writers, Canadian or otherwise, were not dispassionate recorders of reality, but, consciously or not, weavers of constructed memories and crafters of more-or-less works of fiction.[53] The irony is that Vance himself continues to echo the negative stereotypes of the padre from these very sources. Thus, Canadian scholars who are aware of the distorting effect are nevertheless unable to see clearly through the psychological and literary prism of the veterans' culture of late 1920s and 1930s.

In fact, scholars studying any of the military religious ministries of any war must be forewarned of the pitfalls found in postwar complaints by veterans and veteran-writers about chaplains' absence from danger. As the other essays concerning twentieth-century chaplaincies in this volume demonstrate, all scholars must weigh veteran pronouncements about their padres against both actual historical records, such as casualty returns, and a more realistic assessment of service conditions. In any of the twentieth century's countless battles, chaplains were not likely even to be seen by memorialists, unless from a stretcher. The chaplain, even when he jumped off from the front line at zero hour, rarely made it to the final objective with the first wave: too many men fell en route that needed looking after. When men were wounded and dying, his place was in the dugout, for that was where both padre and medical officer did their frontline work. For every sardonic aesthete, there were many more soldiers who drew courage and reassurance from traditional Christian piety, the Bible (and *Pilgrim's Progress*), and turned to the padre. The padre's, and the soldier's, version of truth should be judged by literary, intellectual, even theological canons; it should also, however, be judged by careful historical reconstruction. At no time should scholars fail to take into account the distorting impact of the love-hate relationships veterans have with their war memories, lest they, too, experience the present in the past. If there were fewer true believers in the ranks than the chaplains believed, neither were there as many atheists or agnostics as veterans later claimed.

Although they do not get much credit for it, the historical record shows that Canadian padres served with soldiers in the field. Given the high expectations of the peace, which chaplains encouraged, there was, inevitably, great bitterness among veterans after vainly waiting over a decade for the Kingdom of Heaven, or at least a world fit for heroes. Today, as then, among Canadian war writers, the padre is an easy tar-

Back of the line: a Canadian chaplain and one of countless divisional burial parties at work. National Archives of Canada. NAC-PA4352.

get, the subject of lively and generally injudicious pronouncements in Canadian literature and Canadian Legion branches. To recapture the mutual dependence that padres and fighting-men had, Canadian scholars must keep trying to reach back past the psychological watershed of the Great War created by veteran-memorialists, and the hollow peace that ensued.

NOTES

1. Will R. Bird, *And We Go On* (Toronto: Hunter-Rose, 1930), 337; see also 279–81, 297–300.

2. For this and the following, see Duff Crerar, *Padres in No Man's Land: Canadian Chaplains and the Great War* (Montreal: McGill-Queen's University Press, 1995).

3. Duff Crerar, "Bellicose Priests: The Wars of the Canadian Catholic Chaplains, 1914–1919," Canadian Catholic Historical Association, *Historical Studies* 58 (1991): 21–39.

4. In March 1917, a new establishment was created by the Canadian Forces Overseas, giving Almond command of 276 chaplains (three times the size of the Australian

chaplain contingent). By the summer, there were 62 chaplains on the Continent outside of the 70 serving with the Canadian Corps, while over 140 served in Britain in Canadian camps, depots, and hospitals. Crerar, *Padres*, 130.

5. Initial British regulations allotted only five chaplains to an infantry division. The Canadians insisted on, and were granted, eleven chaplaincies in February 1915. British practice soon followed suit. In December 1917, the Canadian quota went up to seventeen per division. Ibid., 39, 66.

6. Along with the shell wounds came seven cases of "nervous shock" or shell-shock, among corps chaplains in 1916. Ibid., 119.

7. In the last hundred days of the war, 17.8 percent of Canadian Corps chaplains were taken out of action, one by death in action, the rest from wounds, exposure, exhaustion, or battle fatigue. One chaplain, Ambrose Madden, was wounded in action for the third time. Ibid. 131–34.

8. Ibid., 163–68.

9. Ibid., 167–74.

10. The diaries of Julian Bickersteth, M.C., a British Army chaplain, indicate that similar experiences occurred in British and Imperial forces. John Bickersteth, ed., *The Bickersteth Diaries, 1914–1918* (London: Leo Cooper, 1995).

11. Crerar, *Padres*, 195–201.

12. Poem in the possession of the author, provided by Mrs. Anita Nobles, his daughter, in 1983.

13. D.E. MacIntyre, *Canada at Vimy* (Toronto: Peter Martin, 1967), 190; of the nearly eight thousand Canadian veterans who went on the pilgrimage, thirteen had been C.E.F. chaplains, see Murray, *The Epic of Vimy* (Ottawa: Canadian Legion, 1936), 183–217.

14. *New Outlook*, July 29, 1936, 711.

15. C.C. Owen, July 26, 1936, quoted in MacIntyre, *Canada at Vimy*, 189.

16. Rev. M.N. Omond, a United Church minister who had served in the C.E.F. as chaplain during the war, endorsed the "Witness Against War," *United Church Observer*, Oct. 15, 1939, 21; see David R. Rothwell, "United Church Pacifism, October 1939," *Bulletin of the United Church of Canada Archives*, 1973, 37, and T. Socknat, *Witness Against War* (Toronto: University of Toronto Press, 1987), chap. 7. Other veteran padres countered with justifications of the use of force and the right to defend Christendom, e.g., James Faulds in *Observer*, Oct. 1, 1939, 21.

17. Canada, Department of National Defence, *Canadian Active Service Force Routine Orders*, R.O. #69, Oct. 18, 1939; *United Church Observer*, Dec. 15, 1939, 3; also Tom Sinclair-Faulkner, "For Christian Civilization" (Ph.D. diss., University of Chicago, 1975), 83–89, 156–59.

18. The best assessment of mainstream Canadian war memory is Jonathan Vance, *Death So Noble: Memory, Meaning and the First World War* (Vancouver: University of British Columbia Press, 1997).

19. *Canada in the Great World War*, 6 vols. (Toronto: United Publishers, 1917–1921), 1:100; also 5:70. "Passchendaele Preparations," and "Battle of Passchendaele Ridge," in ibid., 4:209, 226, 232, 245; J.F.B. Livesay, *Canada's Hundred Days* (Toronto: Allen, 1919), 77–79; see also 128, 140, 166, 270. See also C.L. Foster and W. Smith-Duthie, *Letters From the Front*, 2 vols. (Toronto: Southam, 1920), 1:43, 123. On the stillbirth of

the Chaplain Service History, see National Archives of Canada (NAC), MG 30 E 4, William Beattie papers, "History of the Canadian Chaplain Services," 1922, 345.

20. *The Story of the 65th C.F.A.* (Edinburgh: Turnbull and Spears, 1919), 114, 123; C.S. Grafton, *The Canadian "Emma Gees"* (London: Hunter, 1938), 117, 212; also D.J. Corrigall, *The History of the Twentieth Battalion* (Toronto: Stone and Co., 1935), xi, 150, 291, 298–300. Typical were the series compiled by R.C. Fetherstonhaugh, *The Royal Montreal Regiment* (Montreal: private, 1927), 23, 20, 69, 153, 275–77; also, *Thirteenth Battalion* (Montreal: 1925) 12, 22, 120, 201, 254, 284, 301, and *The 24th Battalion* (Montreal: *Gazette*, 1930). See also Fetherstonhaugh with G.R. Stevens, *Royal Canadian Regiment*, 2 vols. (Montreal: *Gazette*, 1936), 1:364, 431, and Fetherstonhaugh, *#3 Canadian General Hospital* (Montreal: *Gazette*, 1938), 11, 20, 85–86, also 190, 67, 273, 53, 210, 234; Ralph Hodder-Williams, *The Princess Patricia's Canadian Light Infantry* (London: Hodder-Stoughton, 1923), 2:271 and note, 378, 405; also Weatherbe, *From the Rideau to the Rhine and Back* (Toronto: Hunter-Rose, 1928), and Ken Cameron, *#1 Canadian General Hospital* (Sackville: Tribune Press, 1938), 83–84, 113, 187, 233, 235. See also Singer and Peebles, *History of the Thirty-First Battalion* (Calgary: private, 1939), 213, 282, 458.

21. John Anthony MacDonald, *Gun-fire* (Toronto: Greenway, 1929), 54, 61, 99, 117, 170, 188, 208.

22. L.M. Gould, *From B.C. to Basieux* (Victoria: private, 1919), 34, 62–63, 88, 109.

23. F.G. Scott, *The Great War As I Saw It* (Toronto: Goodchild, 1921), 116.

24. W.B. Kerr, *Shrieks and Crashes* (Toronto: Hunter-Rose, 1929), 146–47; another memoir that echoes Kerr is J.H. Pedley, *Only This* (Ottawa: Graphic, 1927), 99–100, 118, 367.

25. Kerr, *Shrieks and Crashes*, 71, 156, 162, 200–201.

26. On the controversy over Harrison, see Jonathan Vance, *Death So Noble*, 193–97. A similar British denunciation of disillusioned war books by Hemingway, Barbusse, Graves, Remarque, and Jünger is Douglas Jerrold, *The Lie About the War* (London: Faber and Faber, 1930).

27. Charles Yale Harrison, *Generals Die in Bed* (New York: W. Morrow, 1930), 3, 6–7, 26, 41, 58, 82, 85, 99–105, 131, 138–39, 194–96. Not all Canadian war writers were so bitter, though, significantly, Philip Child does not include a chaplain in his war novel, *God's Sparrows* (1937; Toronto: McClelland & Stewart, 1979), 146, 276–82.

28. Bird's most significant religious experiences overseas are his encounters with the ghost of his brother, killed in action in 1915. Will Bird, *Ghosts Have Warm Hands* (Toronto: Clarke, Irwin, 1968), 41, 139.

29. Will R. Bird, *And We Go On*, 3–6. See also Bird, *Ghosts*, 119; and 23, 75–94, 100–101, 162–63, 186–87 ff.

30. Ibid., 192–93.

31. Topp relied on Kilpatrick's war diary for much of the human interest in the battalion history, C.B. Topp, 42nd Battalion, C.E.F., *Royal Highlanders of Canada* (Montreal: private, 1931), vii, 69, 84, 91, 130–31, 169, 176, 282.

32. Crerar, *Padres*, 126–28, 144, 156, 161–62.

33. Will R. Bird, *The Communication Trench* (Toronto: Briggs, 1932), 132.

34. Kim Beattie, *48th Highlanders of Canada, 1898–1921* (Toronto: private, 1932), 154–55.

35. Arthur Lapointe, *Soldier of Quebec*, trans. R. C. Fetherstonhaugh (Montreal: Garand, 1931 [1919]), 10, 50, 85. To W. W. Murray, the padres were mostly just good for a laugh, though, yet again, Canon Scott merits respect, *Five Nines and Whiz Bangs* (Ottawa: Legionary Library, 1937), 132–34, 140–41, 145–46, 212.

36. H. M. Urquhart, *The History of the 16th Battalion* (Toronto: Macmillan, 1932), 222–26.

37. *Stretcher-Bearers . . . At the Double!* (Toronto: Hunter-Rose, 1937), 89–90, 115, 168, 198.

38. Ibid., 16, 168–69.

39. Mary Clint, *Our Bit* (Montreal: Barwick, 1934), 47, 98; also J. J. Mackenzie, *#4 Canadian General Hospital* (Toronto: Macmillan, 1933), 46, 99–100, 124, 216, 228.

40. The only reference was a footnote commemorating Canon Scott: G. W. L. Nicholson, *Canadian Expeditionary Force, 1914–1919* (Ottawa: Queen's Printer, 1962), 451. For Second World War Canadian chaplains, see W. T. Steven, *In This Sign* (Toronto: Ryerson, 1948); Duff Crerar, "In the Day of Battle: Canadian Catholic Chaplains in the Field, 1885–1945," Canadian Catholic Historical Association, *Historical Studies* 61 (1995): 53–77. For post–Second World War Protestants, see Major Albert Fowler, *Peacetime Padres* (St. Catharines: Vanwell, 1996).

41. Bird, *Ghosts*, 139. For an example of the visibility and acceptability of his criticisms to other writers and editors, see Heather Robertson, *A Terrible Beauty* (Toronto: J. Lorimer, 1977), 136.

42. Desmond Morton, *A Peculiar Kind of Politics* (Toronto: University of Toronto Press, 1982), 99, 114–16.

43. Morton, *When Your Number's Up* (Toronto: Random House, 1993), 242–43. Similarly, see Pierre Berton, *Vimy* (Toronto: McClelland & Stewart, 1986), 186, 195–96, 211.

44. M. Bliss, "The Methodist Church and World War I," *Canadian Historical Review* 49, no. 3 (1968): 213–33; John Webster Grant, *The Churches in the Canadian Era* (Toronto: McGraw-Hill Ryerson, 1972); A. Richard Allen, *The Social Passion* (Toronto: University of Toronto Press, 1972); E. A. Pulker, *We Stand on Their Shoulders* (Toronto: Anglican Book Centre, 1986); John S. Moir, *Enduring Witness: A History of the Presbyterian Church in Canada* (Toronto: Presbyterian Publications, 1974).

45. J. H. Thompson, "'The Beginning of our Regeneration': The Great War and Western Canadian Reform Movements," *Canadian Historical Association Historical Papers*, 1972; also Brian Fraser, *The Social Uplifters: Presbyterian Progressives and the Social Gospel in Canada, 1875–1915* (Waterloo: Wilfrid Laurier University Press, 1988).

46. Gordon Martell's discussion of Fussell, Leed, Wohl, and John Keegan in "Generals Die in Bed: Modern Warfare and the Origins of Modernist Culture," *Journal of Canadian Studies* 6, nos. 3–4 (fall–winter 1981), was especially significant to Michael Gauvreau, "War, Culture and the Problem of Religious Certainty: Methodist and Presbyterian Church Colleges, 1914–1930," *Journal of the Canadian Church Historical Society* 29, no. 1 (Apr. 1987). See also Gauvreau, *The Evangelical Century* (Montreal: McGill-Queen's University Press, 1991), 260–65.

47. David Marshall, "Methodism Embattled: A Reconsideration of the Methodist Church and World War I," *Canadian Historical Review*, 66, no. 1 (Mar. 1986). See also his *Secularizing the Faith: Canadian Protestant Clergy and the Crisis of Belief* (Toronto: University of Toronto Press, 1992), chap. 6. Marshall paid very close attention to the

work of Eric Leed, *No Man's Land: Combat and Identity in World War I* (Cambridge: Cambridge University Press, 1979); as well as John Keegan, *Face of Battle* (London, 1976), and Dennis Winter, *Death's Men: Soldiers of the Great War* (London, 1978).

48. Vance, *Death So Noble*, 56–58, 71–72.

49. Ibid., 93–96, 163, 186–97.

50. Ibid., 9, 36.

51. Ibid., 260.

52. Jonathan F. Vance, "'Donkeys' or 'Lions'? Re-examining Great War Stereotypes," *Canadian Military History* 6, no. 1 (spring 1997): 125–28.

53. Paul Fussell, *The Great War and Modern Memory* (London: Oxford University Press, 1975), 321, also 310–13, 240.

CHAPTER EIGHT

GERMAN MILITARY CHAPLAINS IN THE SECOND WORLD WAR AND THE DILEMMAS OF LEGITIMACY

DORIS L. BERGEN

In his memoir, German chaplain Hans Leonhard describes a visit to a military hospital during the Second World War. Leonhard entered a ward full of men with sexually transmitted diseases. "So you're a pastor?" one patient jeered. "We don't need someone like you. You just want to tell us those stories about cattle breeders and pimps."[1] The phrase came from the Nazi ideologue Alfred Rosenberg: in *The Myth of the Twentieth Century*, he dubbed the Old Testament a collection of "stories of pimps and cattle traders."[2] Members of the pro-Nazi "German Christian" movement popularized Rosenberg's phrase in church circles.[3] Leonhard, accustomed to hostile reactions, answered the taunt with a challenge: "Tell me just one such story," he said to the man. "If you can tell me even one, I'll leave the room immediately and never bother you again." All the patients looked at their comrade. "I can't think of any right now," the soldier finally said. The others laughed, but he did not give up. "You probably want to tell us something about praying," he accused Leonhard. "Well, a real man doesn't pray." The chaplain countered with another question: "Were you at the front?" There was a pause before the man muttered, "We from the reserves have done our duty, too." According to Leonhard, that admission ended the exchange. The chaplain sat down with the rest of the men and talked about the Old Testament and about prayer. The next day, his memoir reports, they all showed up at the worship service.[4]

A skeptic might raise doubts about the veracity of Leonhard's account, with its stereotypical antagonists—the stalwart Christian chaplain, the Nazi reservist infected by cynicism and disease—and its happy ending. Indeed, it seems safe to assume that Leonhard, writing almost half a century after the fact, used familiar narrative patterns, contemporary vocabulary, and wishful thinking to give coherence to memories that must have been incomplete. Nevertheless, the general outline of the encounter resembles many other descriptions of German chaplains' work in the Second World War, as recorded in their diaries, letters, and wartime reports to military and ecclesiastical superiors.[5] Like Leonhard's memoir, those sources show chaplains fighting for credibility, both in the eyes of the men they served and with the authorities to whom they answered. This essay explores some of the issues of legitimacy that confronted German military chaplains during the Second World War.

Approximately one thousand clergymen, Protestant and Catholic, served the German military as chaplains during the Second World War.[6] Like their counterparts elsewhere, they preached, administered the sacraments, soothed the sick and wounded, and buried the dead. Their defensive posture was not unique; other chaplains in other places and times have faced critics of their own. But the nature of Nazism and the hostility toward Christianity of top leaders like Adolf Hitler, Heinrich Himmler, Joseph Goebbels, and Martin Bormann made the Wehrmacht chaplains particularly vulnerable. Paradoxically, that vulnerability may have increased their effectiveness as enablers of Nazi German slaughter. In order to protect themselves from their detractors, military chaplains in the Third Reich labored to prove and reprove that they met a real need of the troops and boosted morale. Yet the more successfully they did so—and especially on the Eastern Front, it appears, they were successful[7]—the more they helped legitimate a war of annihilation. Merely the presence of chaplains, at sites of mass killing in Poland, Yugoslavia, Greece, Byelorussia, and Ukraine,[8] offered Germany's warriors the comforting illusion that despite the blood on their hands, they remained decent people, linked to a venerable religious tradition.

Poland 1941: a Catholic German chaplain gives mass before the invasion of the Soviet Union. Bundesarchiv, Koblenz. 356.363/623.415.

REDEEMING THE CHURCH?
THE LEGACY OF THE SECOND WORLD WAR

The historian Gerhard L. Weinberg has pointed out that military and political leaders tend to fight every war based on lessons they think they should have learned from the previous war.[9] Certainly the shadow of the First World War hung over many aspects of the Second World War, including the efforts of German military chaplains. In some ways, the earlier conflict lent authority to their work; it gave important front-line experience to at least some of the men in the chaplaincy,[10] and it provided a model of confessional unity, however mythical, that could be invoked to unite Protestant and Catholic Germans against their new foes.[11] Most German gentiles conveniently forgot that in the First World War, German Jews had fought alongside their Christian coun-trymen.

The legacy of the Great War created its own dilemma of legitimacy for the Second World War chaplains in Germany, and for that matter, throughout Europe. Between 1914 and 1918, the Christian churches had eagerly served the national cause.[12] German, British, and French clergy alike had urged their people to sacrifice themselves for the father-land and had promised that God was on their side. The carnage of the war and the assault on old values that resulted took its toll on the churches as well.[13] Wehrmacht chaplains were not alone in their ef-forts to salvage Christianity from the widespread perception that it was at best irrelevant during wartime and at worst numbed the masses into accepting bloodshed, including their own. But what could they preach in the new world war? No longer acceptable were the sermons typical of the Great War, with their message that one chaplain in 1942 summed up as: "hold on, hold out, and hold your tongue."[14]

Nor would "cheap, hurrah-patriotism" do. In December 1941, a Prot-estant chaplain accompanied the 7th Armored Division in the Soviet Union on its first retreat of the war. His response suggested he had learned from the debacle of the First World War: "In the events that have occurred," he cautioned, "we can see a sign from God, who is warn-ing us not to puff ourselves up because of our ongoing victories. The war will not be won by printer's ink but by blood, and the home front needs to learn that lesson as well."[15] For German chaplains of the 1940s, to borrow Paul Fussell's words, "the second war was silent."[16] Repre-sentatives of a church discredited by mass death and tainted by associa-tion with what many Germans considered the treacherous home front in 1918,[17] the Wehrmacht chaplains faced both universal and particu-lar challenges based on the legacy of the Great War.

"BE MANLY AND BE STRONG"—DILEMMAS OF MASCULINITY

As Paul Fussell and others have pointed out, the fear of appearing "un-manly in front of their friends" can motivate men at war to do terrible things.[18] In the hyper-masculinist world of war, chaplains face particu-lar problems of credibility. How can chaplains convince men under arms that they too are "real men," worthy of respect, in societies that define manliness in terms of soldierly qualities and associate piety with femininity?[19]

Specific regulations handicapped the Wehrmacht chaplains' expres-sions of manliness. They did not carry arms, although German regu-lations permitted them a small pistol when in enemy territory. Accord-ing to 1941 regulations, military chaplains wore the same uniform as "all other military administrators," except without side arms such as daggers.[20] Clergy selected for the chaplaincy tended to be older than most of the men to whom they ministered. Military regulations stipulated that chaplains had to have been born in 1909 or earlier.[21] The intention presumably was to avoid wasting prime fighting power. Younger Protestant pastors were drafted into the regular military; Catholic priests below the designated age, exempted from combat by the terms of the 1933 concordat, served in the medical corps.[22] There were exceptions, particularly on the Catholic side, but many chaplains were in their forties or fifties during the war; some were even older. In 1943, a Protestant military pastor described a gathering of chaplains from over fifty field hospitals. "Everyone in the room," he observed, "had grey or white hair."[23]

German chaplains developed a range of strategies to promote a manly image calculated to win the respect of men under arms. They paid great attention to their uniforms, making sure that they looked as soldierly as possible. For example, in 1940, a deputy Protestant base chaplain complained that the men in his jurisdiction did not take him seriously because he was not entitled to wear military uniform.[24] Instructions from chaplains in supervisory positions and military authorities emphasized the need for a manly bearing, manly music at religious services, and even a manly celebration of Christmas.[25] Only in these ways, they stressed, could chaplains reach out to a clientele that with rare exceptions—the occasional wedding or correspondence with widows and mothers—was exclusively male. A 1942 workshop featured a presentation on preaching to soldiers. It called for language that was "manly and genuine, simple and sober."[26] At a 1943 meeting of base chaplains, the highest praise given to one of their number was that he spoke as "a man, who in long years of service had earned the respect and honor of officers and men, because he possessed the ability to communicate to the longing, fighting hearts of men a manly Christian faith."[27]

Above all, instructions to chaplains stressed the importance of experience at the front: only a man who was a genuine comrade-at-arms could minister to military men. The 1941 guidelines for German military chaplains made the point clearly: "Himself a soldier by nature, the military chaplain will always strike the right tone for the soldiers and thus find the right way to the soldiers' hearts. . . . For that reason, for the past year already, only clergy have been appointed as military chaplains

Marriage ceremony with a Protestant German chaplain in a French church, November 1942. Bundesarchiv, Koblenz. J 20 026.

who have been soldiers themselves and served at least six months at the front."[28]

Chaplains themselves echoed that conviction. "Recently, I met a young fellow-clergyman in uniform," wrote Protestant Chaplain Bernhard Bauerle in a newsletter of August 1942 to chaplains at the front:

> He had been a soldier for only six weeks, and still he was no soldier! As he saw me, he doffed his cap in greeting—like a civilian— raising his cap! How embarrassing! Hopefully no one saw it! . . . Then he started to whine: How hard it was for him as a theologian among the men! When he spoke to them about the Word of God or pointed out their immoral behavior, they laughed in his face. . . . I told him, "I wouldn't be impressed by you either or let you minister to or convert me as long as you're such a pathetic soldier! First put your honor and all of your energy into making yourself a real, topnotch soldier and a good comrade. Leave the preaching and missionizing alone for the time being, by God! Maybe later they'll let you tell them something and take you and what you have to say seriously."[29]

In public and in the press, chaplains presented themselves as strong, manly fighters who performed acts of heroism. In 1942, for example, a German military chaplain near Sevastopol reported that he single-handedly captured sixteen armed Soviets. There was, he wrote, "great joy among the officers and the men over the bold deed of their pastor."[30] Chaplains' obituaries extolled the dead in a vocabulary of masculinity: "He was one of our best," proclaimed a death notice in April 1941, "a selfless priest after God's own heart, a faithful idealist and a manly, courageous soldier."[31] He died a "hero's death" in the "fight against bolshevism," read the obituary of another chaplain, a year later. "His powerful, manly ways made him much loved by officers and enlisted men alike."[32]

"Comrades," proclaimed the Catholic military bishop Franz Justus Rarkowski in 1939, shortly after the attack on Poland, "the issue is your homeland and your people! 'Be manly and be strong!'"[33] In 1940, a Protestant periodical called *Mann und Kirche* (*Man and Church*) printed a special feature on a military chaplain who had received the Iron Cross, First Class. Pastor Schumann from Chemnitz had braved deadly French fire to rescue his wounded comrades. "God helps those who have courage,"

Protestant chaplain Bernhard Bauerle preaches to German soldiers on Pentecost in Suwalki, East Prussia, June 1941. Bundesarchiv, Koblenz. 25/1982.

the article quoted him as thinking, as he strode onto the field alone. He returned alive, to the wonder of his men. "All of them spoke to him with admiration and pride," the reporter noted, "regardless of which confession they belonged to or whether they were unaffiliated pagans."[34]

Chaplains presented themselves as paragons of Christian manliness, role models for the soldiers around them. Fear, they preached, was not manly, and Christian faith drove out fear. In the words of a Catholic chaplain writing from France in February 1942: "May all those who heard me in this time from the pulpit and who received the Lord's Supper from me . . . go the iron way of duty with firm steps and heads held high, for fear is something ugly that befits no man."[35]

German chaplains were not unique in the need to legitimate themselves as men. But in the case of Nazi Germany, hostile regulations from military and political authorities exacerbated the situation. Efforts to undermine the chaplaincy often took the form of attacks on the trappings of masculinity. For example, chaplains could not visit the men in their barracks.[36] Sometime after 1942, military authorities ruled that base and military hospital chaplains could not receive the Iron Cross, although it appears that they permitted some exceptions.[37] By 1944, chaplains writing to family members were prohibited from using the word "manly" to describe how German men condemned for treason, self-mutilation, or desertion met their deaths. For example, National Socialist staff in Army High Command reprimanded one chaplain for telling a woman that her brother, a German soldier condemned to death, had died "brave as a soldier."[38] Like all clergy, chaplains were excluded from the so-called Volkssturm—the people's militia—of 1944, as Hitler rallied the forces of German manhood in defense of the fatherland.[39] German chaplains eager to prove themselves "real men" frequently found the means to do so wrenched from their grasp.

THE "URIAH LAW"—NAZI HOSTILITY TO MILITARY CHAPLAINS

As Leonhard's experience in the hospital ward suggests, chaplains in Hitler's military faced problems particular to Nazi Germany. Servants of both church and state, they nevertheless encountered considerable hostility from military, state, and party authorities. Hitler and his inner circle expressed in private, if not publicly, their contempt for Christianity, a religion they considered nothing but diluted Judaism propagated in a conspiratorial effort to weaken the so-called Aryan race.[40] Any form of Christianity, even the national religion of the chaplaincy, threatened Nazi claims to spiritual monopoly. Like the churches, the chaplains were to be allowed to survive until the war was over; Nazi leaders considered it too risky to attack Christian institutions when the full support of the home front was needed to avoid the "stab in the back" they believed had lost them the previous war.[41]

Attempts to weaken the chaplaincy took many forms.[42] Neither the Luftwaffe nor the SS had chaplains assigned to their units.[43] Numbers of chaplains were reduced; the 480 Protestant military chaplains in service during the Second World War provide a telling contrast to the figure of 2,000 for the First World War.[44] A 1942 command announced that no new chaplains would be appointed; chaplains who died, left due to illness, or were taken prisoner were not replaced.[45]

Protestant military bishop Franz Dohrmann's files are full of orders from the Supreme Command and Army High Command imposing new restrictions. In 1941, for example, Field Marshal Wilhelm Keitel forbade Wehrmacht chaplains from ministering in any way to men who had not explicitly requested their care.[46] Chaplains could only bury dead soldiers if the papers of the deceased clearly showed they were church members.[47] At the same time, clergy were prohibited from giving soldiers forms requesting last rites and a Christian burial.[48] Nor could chaplains be the first to inform family members of the death of a loved one at the front. The commanding officer or the military doctor was to break the news of death to family members.[49]

A 1942 order even required chaplains to situate themselves in areas of heaviest action, where their morale-boosting effects, and presumably the risk to their lives, would be maximized. "In combat," the order stipulated, "the military chaplain will be found in the hottest part of the battle and at the main dressing station, unless—and this will be the exception—he has received a special assignment from divisional command."[50] Chaplains called the measure the "Uriah Law," after the general in the Bible whom King David sent on a suicide mission so that the king could have Uriah's wife, Bathsheba.

Hostility from above proved contagious. Chaplains frequently complained, usually in private, that the men in their care challenged them and their authority. Descriptions of hostile soldiers, officers, and even doctors and nurses appear throughout the chaplains' reports and correspondence.[51] As chaplains discovered, soldiers raised and trained in the Nazi worldview had learned to distrust Christianity with its Jewish roots. One chaplain reported that hostile men asked him embarrassing questions about Christianity: for example, about the witch trials or the mission to the Jews.[52] Viciously anti-Semitic propaganda such as that found in *Der Stürmer* provided soldiers with a vocabulary with which to mock representatives of the churches. According to the Catholic military vicar Georg Werthmann, anti-Christian and anti-religious literature abounded at the front; Christian publications, in contrast, were almost impossible to get.[53]

It was particularly the younger men, chaplains reported, and those farthest from the demands of battle, who were most cruel in baiting the clergy and least interested in genuine spiritual engagement. One chaplain wrote that he did encounter many men who were thankful for his services, but the situation in the military hospitals was always precarious: "The attitude and the mood of a room were often determined by a few people or even one individual, and the clergy learns very quickly to figure out which spirit has the upper hand right then. There is no doubt that one sees a great deal of alienation from Christianity, and an extraordinary amount of indifference. . . . Openly Christian characters who know the Bible are rare."[54] Regardless of their own political views, and they varied considerably, chaplains in Hitler's military found themselves on the defensive against both their masters and their clients.

BLESSING THE CANNONS? LEGITIMATING NAZI WARFARE

The hostility of their employers notwithstanding, German military chaplains showed intense loyalty to their nation's cause. Declarations of love for the fatherland and commitment to Hitler and his war were no mere rhetorical flourishes; they informed every aspect of the chaplains' work. As individuals and collectively, chaplains devoted considerable time and energy to proving their value to the German war effort. They compiled statistics and testimonies from members of the armed forces to illustrate their effectiveness in boosting morale and building spirits on both the home and fighting fronts. In 1940, Protestant church officials assembled an entire packet of materials, clippings about chaplains who had been decorated for bravery, protestations of loyalty to "Führer, Volk, und Vaterland" (leader, people, and fatherland),

and excerpts from soldiers' letters to try to prove to Hitler and the Reich Ministry for Church Affairs how useful and loyal were the chaplains.[55]

Typical of efforts to justify the existence of the chaplaincy is a report by a Catholic chaplain with the 2nd Infantry Division (motorized), from the summer of 1940. He detailed his activities in ways that emphasized his utility to the war effort and the enthusiasm for his work among the men: "In the Easter season I heard confessions and held worship services with communion. Participation: 80–90 percent, and among some units even 100 percent. . . . There was not a single case in which spiritual ministry was rejected. Bless me! Thank you! Will you greet my friends and my family members? I will die for Germany and our Führer! Those were the parting words of the dying men. On the days off, at the wish of the commander, I held three services (one outdoor mass, one mass in a French church, and one communal worship service) before the onset of a new offensive. In the masses I pronounced a general absolution and afterward there was communion with 100 percent participation."[56]

Wehrmacht chaplains served the National Socialist regime, but few were themselves hardcore Nazis. Prospective chaplains required clearance from military, church, and Gestapo offices.[57] All of those agencies did their utmost to keep out potential troublemakers, although they defined the term in different ways. Therefore, if it was impossible for anyone with a record of opposition to National Socialist policies to receive an appointment to the chaplaincy, aggressively pro-Nazi politics and even strident antisemitism of the wrong kind could disqualify a candidate as well. Prospective chaplains could be disqualified for defeatism. In 1940, one potential chaplain received black marks in the Security Service report, and was ultimately rejected, because he had once said that he did not believe Hitler could win the war. The enemies were too numerous, he contested: "the Jews, the church, England, France, and America."[58] Meanwhile, members of the exuberantly pro-Nazi German Christian movement complained that Protestant Bishop Dohrmann blocked their more outspoken adherents from the chaplaincy.[59] The net result was a chaplaincy dominated by conservative, nationalist Christians.

That national conservatism may precisely have made German military chaplains effective voices to sooth qualms of conscience on the part of men engaged in an unconventional war. In March 1943, in the wake of Stalingrad, a Protestant chaplain hinted that only Christianity could save Germany: "The extraordinary challenges of the struggle in the east and the increasingly heavy demands on the spiritual and personal attitudes of the troops may have opened the eyes of many an officer, precisely the most experienced, to the fact that any weakening of the religious basis of our people means opening the way for Bolshevism. And on the other hand, every promotion of Christian faith among the soldiers contributes considerably to the German army's power to fight back and redounds to the strength of the German Volk."[60] "The German soul," wrote another chaplain for Advent 1943, "cannot be satisfied by the miserable, empty surrogates that it is being fed these days." It hungered not for Nazi propaganda, he implied, but "for the bread of life, as only Jesus Christ can give it."[61]

Only rarely did chaplains' reports allude to the "special nature" of the war in the east and the pressures created for the German men who fought it. Acknowledgments of German brutality were always vague and oblique. One such cryptic reference to atrocities committed by the Wehrmacht may be in a 1942 report from a Catholic chaplain. He listed nine particular problems he faced during the reporting period from his vantage point with a tank division in the east. In addition to cold, mud, danger from partisans, and lack of adequate hosts and wine, he mentioned "the unique nature of the action and the relations with the enemy."[62]

A Protestant pastor attached to an armored division in the Soviet Union in the summer and autumn of 1941 described the many, searching conversations he had with his men, "even on the particular problems that are part of this struggle against the Soviet Union." The next sentence suggests that those discussions addressed the viciousness of German troops in the east: "Again and again," he wrote, "everyone comes back to the question of the future of the German spirit and of religion."[63]

Chaplains themselves answered that question in conventional ways that denied the radical nature of the Nazi war effort. They echoed and invoked the patriotism of the Wars of Liberation against Napoleon and the First World War. The Catholic military bishop Rarkowski, for example, decried assaults from neopagan publicists on what he called the "religious tradition of the German army." The problem, he maintained, was not that such publications attacked "Christianity as such," but rather that they mocked "the Christian, heroic death of German soldiers." In Bishop Rarkowski's mind, German heroism and Christianity

Religious services with an armored division on the Soviet front near Smolensk, August 1941. Bundesarchiv, Koblenz. B 9522.

were inseparable and mutually reinforcing.[64] Chaplains' labors helped promote the illusion that this struggle too was a continuous development of German military and ecclesiastical traditions. In the words of the 1941 guidelines to chaplains from the Army High Command's office for spiritual care (Gruppe S): "As in earlier wars, in this war too the military chaplaincy is an important handmaid of the troop leadership: educating the men to enthusiastic willingness to give their utmost, including their very lives; training warriors who are ready to sacrifice, and by so doing, contributing to the spiritual strength of the German soldier at the front."[65]

It is difficult, perhaps impossible, to measure the chaplains' impact on the troops. We know that some Nazi killers, like Franz Stangl, commandant of Sobibor and Treblinka, seized on the involvement of Christian clergy in attacks on the handicapped and Jews as a way to justify their own roles in murder.[66] But Stangl recorded no encounters with military chaplains. We also know that after the war, at least some German veterans remembered with bitterness that the chaplains assigned to promote their spiritual life had raised no voice of protest against the murder of civilians. Looking back on his experience on the Eastern

Field services in a German garrison in the East, June 1941. Bundesarchiv, Koblenz. 19/1212/35a.

Front after forty years, the theologian Hans Richard Nevermann wrote that throughout the entire war, no officer, no comrade, and no chaplain ever had anything to say about German atrocities other than that the war was terrible.[67]

Many soldiers' letters and diaries say nothing at all about chaplains, an indication either that chaplains were too few in number to have much impact or that they seemed irrelevant. Still, we know from chaplains' own records that men did approach them with questions of conscience. Reflections from a Catholic priest stationed in the Crimea illustrate the issues that faced clergy who ministered not only to death but also to killers. A wounded man confided to him about his past: "He had been ordered to take part in a shooting commando in Sevastopol. The guy was completely ruined by this experience. Line up the Jews, clothes off, naked before his eyes, women, children, men, and then the machine guns. He had to man one of the guns himself. I can say I did not hit any of them. I always shot in the air. But the experience, how the people fell backwards, earth over them, and then the next row, until the anti-tank trench was full. . . . 40,000 people."

"What should I have done?" the man wanted to know. He had a wife and family. Should he have refused? The clergyman was beside himself. "And I am expected to respond as a priest!" he exclaimed. His answer echoed both the rationalizations and the restless conscience familiar from so many postwar German utterances: "I do not know how I would have reacted in that situation. Am I supposed to tell the soldier that he was a coward and should have stood up against it? He would immediately have been put in the same row and shot along with them. Is that what God wants? For us that was the first time that we heard anything about the shooting of Jews. The commanders of the Wehrmacht who were in charge should have refused to have anything to do with it."[68]

As ministers to their countrymen at arms, German chaplains had an immensely difficult job. Hostile military, state, and party authorities made their work even harder. Some chaplains showed fortitude in bypassing and even defying orders that limited their freedom of operation. Nevertheless, most weighed in on the side of the perpetrators, condoning and blessing their acts through words, actions, and silence. One of the most obvious manifestations of this function was the provision of group absolution for soldiers, a practice that occurred frequently enough to warrant a warning against overuse from the Catholic military bishop in 1944.[69] In the midst of what Omer Bartov has called the "barbarisation of warfare,"[70] the chaplains' presence provided a kind of spiritual relief, a moral numbing for the men in their care, a haven of normalcy that harked back to the religious practices of childhood. In this role, the chaplains performed a task shared by many women in the Third Reich and usually coded as feminine: providing a cozy home, domestic or spiritual, where killers could find peace, rejuvenation, and support.[71]

NOTES

This article appeared previously in *Church History* 70, no. 2 (June 2001): 232–47, and is being reprinted with permission.

1. Hans Leonhard, *Wieviel Leid erträgt ein Mensch? Aufzeichnungen eines Kriegspfarrers über die Jahre 1939 bis 1945* (Amberg: Buch & Kunstverlag Oberpfalz, 1994), 41–42. All translations from the German are mine unless otherwise specified.

2. Alfred Rosenberg, *Der Mythus des 20. Jahrhunderts: Eine Wertung der seelisch-geistigen Gestaltenkämpfe unserer Zeit* (Munich: Hoheneichen Verlag, 1935), 614.

3. In November 1933, Reinhold Krause, a Berlin high school teacher of religion and "German Christian," gave a speech in the Berlin Sports Palace. Before twenty thousand cheering people, Krause demanded "liberation from the Old Testament with its cheap Jewish morality of exchange and its stories of cattle traders and pimps." Krause, "Rede des Gauobmannes der Glaubensbewegung 'Deutsche Christen' im Groß-Berlin,

gehalten im Sportpalast am 13. Nov. 1933 (nach doppelten stenographischen Bericht)," 6–7, Landeskirchenarchiv Bielefeld (hereafter LKA Bielefeld) 5,1/289,2.

4. Leonhard, *Wieviel Leid*, 42.

5. Published diaries and memoirs of chaplains include: Rüdiger Alberti, *Als Kriegspfarrer in Polen: Erlebnisse und Begegnungen in Kriegslazaretten* (Dresden and Leipzig, 1940); Wilhelm Schabel, *Herr, in Deine Hände: Seelsorge im Krieg* (Bern, 1963); Josef Perau, *Priester im Heere Hitlers: Erinnerungen, 1940–1945* (Essen: Ludgerus-Verlag, 1963); Dietrich Baedeker, *Das Volk das im Finsternis wandelt: Stationen eines Militärpfarrers, 1933–1946* (Hanover, 1987); and Leonhard, *Wieviel Leid*. See also Hans Jürgen Brandt, ed., *Priester in Uniform: Seelsorger, Ordensleute und Theologen als Soldaten im Zweiten Weltkrieg* (Augsburg: Pattloch Verlag, 1994), and materials in Albrecht Schübel, *300 Jahre Evangelische Soldatenseelsorge* (Munich, 1964). The most extensive collection of personal papers of a German Second World War chaplain that I have found is the Nachlaß Bernhard Bauerle, held at the Landeskirchliches Museum, Ludwigsburg (hereafter LKM Ludwigsburg). Thanks to Eberhard Gutekunst and Andrea Kittel for permission to see these papers. There are relevant materials in the papers of Pastors Hans Stempel and Ludwig Diehl in Zentralarchiv der Evangelischen Kirche der Pfalz, Speyer (hereafter ZASP Speyer). A valuable source is chaplains' activity reports prepared at the division and army levels. Many of these are held at the Bundesarchiv-Military Archiv in Freiburg/Br. (hereafter BA-MA Freiburg); many are also on microfilm at the National Archives in Washington, D.C., in the Captured German Documents, series T-312, Records of German Field Commands: Armies; and T-315, Records of German Field Commands: Armies (hereafter T-series/roll/frame). See also Reich Church Ministry files, especially regarding appointments of chaplains, which I saw in the Bundesarchiv Potsdam (hereafter BA Potsdam), 51.01/23846 and 23847. (Materials from that archive have since been relocated within the German federal archive system.) Some materials on Catholic chaplains are at the Archiv des Katholischen Militärbischofsamts (hereafter AKM Bonn).

6. The estimate of one thousand chaplains total is based on a figure of 480 Protestants who served throughout the war, and an assumption that about equal numbers of Catholics held positions in the chaplaincy. See "Zusammenstellung der eingesetzten Pfarrer," [1941] BA-MA Freiburg, RH 15/281, 35; "Kriegsdienst der evang. Geistlichen Deutschlands, nach den statistischen Angaben der Deutsch-Evangelischen Kirchenkanzlei Berlin, Stand 1.10.1941," in Landeskirchenarchiv Nürnberg (hereafter LKA Nuremberg), Kreisdekan Nürnberg/121; and "Aufstellung an der Soll- und Iststärke an Evangelischen Kriegspfarrern nach dem Stande vom 25.11.1944," BA-MA Freiburg, N282/8.

7. In August 1940, Protestant Military Bishop Franz Dohrmann prepared a "Bericht über die Wehrmachtseelsorge im Kriege." He gathered information from fourteen divisions: all but one division, which did not answer the question, reported that attendance of worship services was good to very good, ranging from 60 to 90 percent in most cases; one divisional chaplain recorded participation of 100 percent after battles. BA-MA Freiburg, N282/v.7. A postwar account by former chaplain Schubring [first name not given] indicates that the winters in the Soviet Union led to an increasing demand for pastoral care; as many as 80 percent of troops participated and surprisingly many took communion. Schubring, "Die Arbeit der Feldseelsorge im Kriege,"

BA-MA Freiburg, N282/v.4. On the basis of interviews with former chaplains, Jörn Bleese makes similar observations in "Die Militärseelsorge und die Trennung von Staat und Kirche" (Ph.D. diss., University of Hamburg, 1969), 190.

8. On German chaplains as witnesses to massacres of civilians in Greece, see Mark Mazower, "Militärische Gewalt und nationalsozialistische Werte: Die Wehrmacht in Griechenland 1941 bis 1944," in Hannes Heer and Klaus Naumann, eds., *Vernichtungskrieg: Verbrechen der Wehrmacht, 1941–1944* (Hamburg: Hamburger Edition HIS Verlag, 1995), 157–90. For a case of chaplains seeing Nazi brutality up close in Ukraine, see reminiscences of former Catholic Chaplain Ernst Tewes, "Seelsorger bei den Soldaten, 1940–1945: Aufzeichnungen und Erinnerungen," in Georg Schwaiger, ed., *Das Erzbistum München und Freising in der Zeit der nationalsozialistischen Herrschaft*, 2 vols. (Munich: Verlag Schnell & Steiner, 1984), 2:244–87; also Bernd Boll and Hans Safrian, "Auf dem Weg nach Stalingrad: Die 6. Armee 1941/42," in Heer and Naumann, *Vernichtungskrieg*, 260–96.

9. See discussion in Gerhard L. Weinberg, "Propaganda for Peace and Preparation for War," in Gerhard L. Weinberg, *Germany, Hitler, and World War II* (New York: Cambridge University Press, 1995), 68–82.

10. See, for example, the death announcement of the military chaplain Franz Albert, born in 1876, and a decorated veteran of the First World War, who had spent thirty-eight of his forty-four years as a priest ministering to soldiers. Catholic Military Bishop's *Verordnungsblatt*, no. 4 (May 3, 1944): 13, AKM Bonn.

11. A detailed description of the Great War as a model of supraconfessionality appears in Armin Roth, *Wehrmacht und Weltanschauung: Grundfragen für die Erziehungsarbeit in der Wehrmacht*, foreword by Hermann Göring (Berlin: E. S. Mittler & Sohn, 1940), 19.

12. A scathing denunciation of religious complicity in the Great War appears in Julien Benda, *The Betrayal of the Intellectuals*, trans. Richard Aldington (Boston: Beacon Press, 1955), chap. 3, "The 'Clerks'—the Great Betrayal," esp. 65–73, 101, 109–11. In much of the book, Benda uses the term "clerks" to mean modern-day intellectuals in general, but these passages refer specifically to men of the church.

13. Paul Fussell, "The Fate of Chivalry and the Assault upon Mother," in Paul Fussell, *Thank God for the Atom Bomb and Other Essays* (New York: Simon and Schuster, 1988), 221–48, notes the intimate connection between "mother" and piety.

14. "'Die Soldatenpredigt im Kriege,' Leitgedanken aus einem Vortrag bei einem Frontlehrgang im Osten von Wehrmachtdekan Schackla," *Mitteilungsblatt des Evangelischen Feldbischofs*, no. 4 (Oct. 10, 1942), 6, BA-MA Freiburg, RW 12 I/12.

15. Dr. Müller, "Vierteljahres (Seelsorge)-Bericht des ev. Divisions-Pfarrers der 7. Pz. Division für die Zeit vom 1.10 bis 31.12.41," p. 1, in T-315/439/303.

16. Fussell, "Killing in Verse and Prose," in Fussell, *Thank God*, 131.

17. For an explicit effort to distance the Second World War chaplains from the supposed stab in the back of 1918, see Catholic Military Bishop Franz Justus Rarkowski, "Heimatgruß des katholischen Feldbischofs der Wehrmacht," with instructions to circulate to all Catholic members of the Wehrmacht, *Verordnungsblatt*, no. 2 (Sept. 1, 1939): 6, AKM Bonn.

18. James Jones quoted in Fussell, "Killing in Verse and Prose," in Fussell, *Thank God*, 144.

19. For discussion, see George Mosse, *The Image of Man: The Creation of Modern Masculinity* (New York: Oxford University Press, 1996).

20. "Anzug der Wehrmachtgeistlichen und Kriegspfarrer a.K.," *Verordnungsblatt*, no. 2 (Feb. 10, 1941): 11, AKM Bonn.

21. See account of Lambert Drink in *Erinnerungen rheinischer Seelsorger aus den Diözesen Aachen, Köln und Lüttich (1933–1986)* (Aachen, 1988), 259.

22. See the accounts by Catholic priests and seminarians serving as orderlies and medics in Brandt, *Priester in Uniform.*

23. Lasch, acting Protestant district chaplain, District XI Hanover, report on the gathering of base chaplains in District XI on May 12, 1943, May 15, 1943; thirty-three base chaplains and fifty-three hospital chaplains attended. BA-MA Freiburg, RH 15/273/119–20.

24. Georg Gründler to Protestant Military Bishop, Münster, Dec. 13, 1940, 2, BA-MA Freiburg, RW 12 I/6, 128. For a similar case involving a Catholic, see Josef Neubauer to Rarkowski (Budweis, Nov. 29, 1943), BA-MA Freiburg, RH 15/272, 83–84.

25. On calls for "manly, powerful, pious, German" music rather than the usual "soft, sweet, sentimental" fare of religious music, see Schieber (Evang. Wehrkreispfarrer V) to Protestant Military Bishop, Ludwigsburg, July 15, 1938, BA-MA Freiburg, RH 53–5/72, 11–13. For a description of how Christmas at the front bound a "childlike sense" with "true manliness," see "Hirtenbrief," "Der Katholische Feldbischof der Wehrmacht Franziskus Justus . . ." Berlin, Advent 1942, 3–4, BA-MA Freiburg, RW 12 II/4.

26. "'Die Soldatenpredigt im Kriege,' Leitgedanken aus einem Vortrag bei einem Frontlehrgang im Osten von Wehrmachtdekan Schackla," *Mitteilungsblatt des Ev. Feldbischofs*, no. 4 (Oct. 10, 1942): 2, BA-MA Freiburg, RW 12 I/12.

27. "Standortpfarrerversammlung im Wehrkreis XI, 12.5.43," report signed Lasch, stellv. Ev. Wehrkreispfarrer XI, Hanover, May 15, 1943, to Army High Command via Protestant Military Bishop, BA-MA Freiburg, RH 15/273, 119–20.

28. "Wesen und Aufgabe der Feldseelsorge," signed Edelmann, [1941], 5, BA-MA Freiburg, RH 15/282, 26.

29. Bauerle, "Gruß zum 12. Sonntag nach Trinitatis," Aug. 23, 1942, 1, NL Bauerle, LKM Ludwigsburg, materials labeled "Sonntagsgruß."

30. Kriegspfarrer Satzger, "Bericht über Kampfhandlungen," Jan. 9, 1942, T-312/419/7995355–56.

31. Death notice for Anton Gerritschen, chaplain with an infantry division, April 6, 1941, *Verordnungsblatt*, no. 4 (Apr. 21, 1941): 21, AKM Bonn.

32. Obituary for Anton Grois, Wehrmachtpfarrer and Divisionspfarrer, *Verordnungsblatt*, no. 4 (April 15, 1942): 21, AKM Bonn.

33. Franziskus Justus Rarkowski, "Heimatgruß an alle katholische Wehrmachtangehörigen," *Verordnungsblatt*, no. 3 (Oct. 18, 1939): 10, AKM Bonn.

34. Günther Kaufmann, (editor in chief of *Wille und Macht*, leadership organ of the National Socialist youth), *Feldzeitung der Moselarmee*, reproduced in *Mann und Kirche*, no. 9, [1940]: 64, one of attachments to letter from chancellery of the German Protestant Church to Hitler, Oct. 28, 1940, in binder labeled "Haltung der kirchlichen Zeitschriften im gegenwärtigen Kriege," 49, BA Potsdam, 51.01/23740.

35. Chaplain Graf, report of activity with the 8th Jäg-Div., France, Feb. 15, 1942, T-315/465/1031.

36. See remarks in appendix to report by Stellv. Ev. Wehrkreispfarrer IX, Karig, "Möglichkeiten und Schwierigkeiten der Truppenseelsorge," for meeting of base chaplains in Kassel, Feb. 17, 1943, 4, BA-MA Freiburg, RH 15/273, 15.

37. There seems to have been considerable confusion as to whether chaplains could be decorated, if so, which chaplains, with what, by whom, and under what conditions. See correspondence regarding the Iron Cross, Second Class, without swords, and lists of proposed names; for example: Bunke, Stellv. Ev. Wehrkreispfarrer III, "Vorschlagsliste 1 für die Verleihung des K. V. K. II. Kl. o. Schw.," Berlin-Spandau, Apr. 18, 1944, BA-MA Freiburg, RH 15/272, 123. On the question of whether base chaplains and chaplains in military hospitals could be decorated, see Army High Command to Military Bishops, Mar. 21, 1944, BA-MA Freiburg, RH 15/272, 104. For a case where several Iron Crosses were withdrawn from base and military hospital chaplains, see Army High Command, Jan. 30, 1945, BA-MA Freiburg, RH 15/270, 13; the same file contains a great deal of related correspondence.

38. See circular from Lasch, Stellv. Ev. Wehrkreispfarrer XI, "An alle Ev. Standort- und Reservelazarettpfarrer im Wehrkreis XI," Hanover, June 28, 1944, 2, BA-MA Freiburg, RH 53–11/71.

39. Ibid.

40. Even members of the "German Christian" movement complained about anti-Christian attitudes in the SA, SS, and army. See, for example, Walter Schultz to Hitler, April 30, 1941, and attached, untitled report, relevant sections entitled "Bekämpfung und Verächtlichmachung des Christentums und der Kirche," and "Angriffe auf Geistliche," 4–5, Bundesarchiv Koblenz (hereafter BA Koblenz), R 43 II/172/fiche 1, 3–6. These materials have been relocated within the German federal archive system since I used them. On German Christians in the chaplaincy, see Doris L. Bergen, "'Germany Is Our Mission—Christ Is Our Strength!' The *Wehrmacht* Chaplaincy and the 'German Christian' Movement," *Church History* 66, no. 3 (Sept. 1997): 522–36.

41. On Hitler's belief in the stab-in-the-back myth and its impact on his behavior during the Second World War, see Weinberg, "Propaganda for Peace and Preparation for War," in Weinberg, *Germany, Hitler, and World War II*, 73–76.

42. On Nazi measures against the Wehrmacht chaplains, see Manfred Messerschmidt, "Aspekte der Militärseelsorgepolitik in nationalsozialistischer Zeit," *Militärgeschichtliche Mitteilungen* 1 (1968), and Messerschmidt, "Zur Militärseelsorgepolitik im Zweiten Weltkrieg," *Militärgeschichtliche Mitteilungen* 1 (1969). See also postwar manuscript by Schubring, "Die Arbeit der Feldseelsorge im Kriege," BA-MA Freiburg, N282/v.4.

43. On absence of chaplains in the Luftwaffe, see guidelines prepared by Group S (Seelsorge) of Army High Command, signed Edelmann, "Wesen und Aufgabe der Feldseelsorge," [1941], 7, BA-MA Freiburg, RH 15/282, 28. For examples of chaplains nevertheless ministering to members of the Luftwaffe or being requested to do so, see the following: Protestant Kriegspfarrer Albrecht, 2nd Mountain Division, "Bericht über die seelsorgerliche Tätigkeit des evangelischen Kriegspfarrers bei der 2. Gebirgs-Division vom Juni 1940–28.2.1941," Norway, p. 4, T-315/99/594; Catholic military bishop Rarkowski to Army High Command, July 9, 1943, 3, BA-MA Freiburg, RH 15/280, 121; SS-Main Personnel Office to Supreme Command, Berlin-Charlottenburg, Sept. 14, 1944, BA-MA Freiburg, RH 15/272, 263.

44. Dohrmann's notes provide a figure of 455, BA-MA Freiburg, N282/1, 163.

45. OKH (Army High Command), signed Jüttner, Dec. 23, 1933, BA-MA Freiburg, N282/3. For complaints about the failure to maintain adequate numbers of chap-

lains or fill vacant positions, see German Protestant Church, Ecclesiastical Chancellery, to Supreme Command, Nov. 13, 1942, Berlin, BA Potsdam, 51.01/23847.

46. Supreme Command, signed Keitel, Mar. 15, 1941, Berlin, "Wehrmachtseelsorge," BA Potsdam, 51.01/21839, 62−63.

47. "Bestimmungen für besondere Dienstverhältnisse der Kriegspfarrer beim Feldheer," June 18, 1941, BA-MA Freiburg, N282/v.3.

48. See ibid.; also earlier memo from Supreme Command to Reich Ministry of Church Affairs, Berlin, Aug. 1, 1940, BA Potsdam 51.01/23158, 254.

49. Army High Command, signed Kauffmann, to military bishops, Oct. 26, 1939, 1, BA-MA Freiburg, RW 12 I/13.

50. Supreme Command, signed Keitel, "Betr.: Richtlinien für die Durchführung der Feldseelsorge," Berlin, May 24, 1942, 1, BA Potsdam, 51.01/21839, 147.

51. On antagonistic officers, see Tomaschek, Catholic chaplain, 2nd Mountain Division, "Tätigkeitsbericht vom 1.11.1940−28.2.1941," Norway, Mar. 1, 1941, 2, T-315/99/601; on unsympathetic nurses who obstructed the work of the chaplains, see report by Pastor Engelbrecht, Fulda, "Die Seelsorge im Res.-Lazarett," summarized in Karig, deputy Protestant military chaplain, District IX, to Supreme Command and Protestant military bishop, Kassel, Mar. 13, 1943, 1, BA-MA Freiburg, RH 15/273, 9.

52. Doerne, "Lazarettseelsorge," report from the conference of base and military hospital chaplains in military district IV, Dresden, July 7, 1943, in copy of *Mitteilungsblatt des Ev. Feldbischofs*, no. 3 (Oct. 15, 1943): 5, BA-MA Freiburg, RW 12 I/13, 5.

53. See list of complaints signed Vicar Werthmann, Catholic military bishop to Army High Command, July 9, 1943, 5, BA-MA Freiburg, RH 15/280, 123.

54. Stempel, report on "Lazarettseelsorge," Feb. 19, 1940, Landau, 5, ZASP Speyer, 150.47/2e.

55. Report on meeting Sept. 12, 1940, on "Besprechung über Schrifttumsfragen," and letter from chancellery of German Protestant Church, signed Werner, Hymmen, Marahrens, and Schultz, to Hitler, Berlin-Charlottenburg, Oct. 28, 1940, BA Potsdam, 51.01/23740.

56. Chaplain Wirtz, "Tätigkeitsbericht über den Einsatz im Westen vom 10. Mai bis 9. Juli 1940," Stettin, Aug. 1, 1940, T-315/87/637−38.

57. To see the approval procedure at work, for example, Ministry of Church Affairs to Supreme Command (OKW), May 22, 1944, BA-MA Freiburg, RH 15/272, 216−17; Church Affairs to OKW, BA-MA Freiburg, RH 15/272, 116; same file, Bunke, "Bericht der Wehrmachtkommandantur Berlin," Dec. 18, 1943; OKW (Gruppe S) memo to military bishops, Mar. 21, 1944, 113; report of Gestapo Hanover on Pastor Friedrich Voges, in Deputy Chief Command, District XI, to OKH, Nov. 17, 1944, BA-MA Freiburg, RH 15/270, 25; and church ministry files re: chaplains, BA Potsdam, 51.01/23846 and 23847.

58. Security Service report on Pfarrer Ernst Müller in Roxförde, Sept. 28, 1940, BA Potsdam, 51.01/23847, 35.

59. Schultz, Bishop of Protestant-Lutheran Church of Mecklenburg, to State Secretary Muhs, Reich Ministry for Church Affairs, July 28, 1942, BA Potsdam, 51.01/23846, 298.

60. Karig, deputy Protestant chaplain for Military District IX, Kassel, "Möglichkeiten und Schwierigkeiten der Truppenseelsorge," copy of speech, attached to Karig

to Supreme Command, report on gatherings of base chaplains in Kassel, Eisenach, and Frankfurt am Main, Mar. 13, 1943, 5, BA-MA Freiburg, RH 15/273, 16.

61. Circular from deputy Protestant chaplain Lasch, Military District XI, Hanover, Advent 1943, "To Protestant Base and Military Hospital Chaplains of Military District XI," 1, BA-MA Freiburg, RH 53–11/71.

62. Catholic divisional priest, 7th Tank Division, entry for May 3–8, 1942, in "Tätigkeitsbericht, 1.1.42–12.5.42," 7, T-315/439/329.

63. Dr. Müller, Protestant divisional chaplain, 7th Tank Division, "Tätigkeitsbericht, 22.6.-30.9.1941," 4, T-315/439/301.

64. Rarkowski to Army High Command, Berlin-Tempelhof, Jan. 5, 1937, 3, BA-MA Freiburg, RW 12 II/5, 6.

65. Edelmann, "Wesen und Aufgabe der Feldseelsorge," [1941], 1, BA-MA Freiburg, RH 15/282, 22.

66. On Stangl, see Gitta Sereny, *Into That Darkness: An Examination of Conscience* (New York: Vintage Books, 1983).

67. See Hans Richard Nevermann, "Warum zog ich nicht die Notbremse? Erinnerungen 40 Jahre nach dem Überfall auf die Sowjetunion," *Junge Kirche*, no. 6 (1981): 282–84.

68. Heinz Keller, "Ob das der Herrgott von uns will?" in Brandt, *Priester in Uniform*, 130–31. Keller was with the 2nd Medical Corps, 46th Infantry Division, in the Crimea and the Caucasus.

69. *Verordnungsblätter des katholischen Feldbischof der Wehrmacht*, no. 6 (Aug. 12, 1944): 30, "Generalabsolution," signed Rarkowski.

70. Omer Bartov, *The Eastern Front, 1941–1945: German Troops and the Barbarisation of Warfare* (New York: St. Martin's Press, 1986).

71. For additional discussion of women's roles in Nazi warfare, see Claudia Koonz, *Mothers in the Fatherland: Women, the Family and Nazi Politics* (London: Jonathan Cape, 1987); Gaby Zipfel, "Wie führen Frauen Krieg?" in Heer and Naumann, *Vernichtungskrieg*, 460–74; and Sereny, *Into That Darkness*, esp. 355–62.

CHAPTER NINE

"*WE* WILL BE"

Experiences of an American Jewish Chaplain in the Second World War

RABBI MAX B. WALL, IN CONVERSATION
WITH THE SURVIVORS OF THE SHOAH
VISUAL HISTORY FOUNDATION, EDITED BY
ELIZABETH E. HAYES

Max B. Wall was born in a small Polish town on July 23, 1915. In 1921, his family immigrated to Denver, Colorado, and moved six years later to New York, where they settled in Manhattan. In 1942, he graduated from the Jewish Theological Seminary in New York and shortly thereafter became a chaplain in the U.S. Army. He arrived in Germany late in 1944 prior to the Battle of the Bulge. In the following interview, conducted on May 12, 1998, in Burlington, Vermont, Rabbi Wall recounts his experiences ministering to soldiers as a Jewish army chaplain during the Second World War. The full interview is recorded on videotape by the Survivors of the SHOAH Visual History Foundation, whose permission to transcribe and publish the sections reproduced here is gratefully acknowledged.[1]

Right after Pearl Harbor, right away, a group of us students from the seminary applied for acceptance as chaplains in the United States army. Whereupon, we were rejected and told we had to have two years of

Rabbi Max B. Wall. Personal photograph. Courtesy of Rabbi Wall.

experience in the rabbinate before we could be accepted as chaplains. I hadn't graduated yet. So I was graduated, and then in September 1942, I went to Temple Beth-el in Woodbury, New Jersey, and there I finally was called by the army and told I could now apply for the chaplaincy. I was interviewed by the Jewish welfare board's commission on chaplains. I was accepted and eventually, I think it was late October or early November 1943, I was admitted as a chaplain for the army of the United States.

Up until that time, what did you know about what was happening in Europe?

Well, the *New York Times* and the Yiddish papers and the Jewish news told us about the tragedy that was beginning. We didn't know the immensity of it because we weren't getting that kind of information publicly. But we knew, and what the mind didn't know, the heart felt. That was the problem. We didn't exaggerate by much, as it turns out, in imagining what was happening to our people. That was the painful thing about it.

Tell me what it was like at the training for the chaplainship.

The chaplaincy school at that time was at Cambridge. They took all of us in buildings at Harvard University. So I can say, "I went to Harvard University"—for five weeks. They trained us in all the military courtesies and military behavior and even involved us in some physical training—marching and running and crawling under barbed wire—and taught us all about military etiquette and that kind of thing. It was a five-week thing, and I was transferred from there to my first assignment at Fort Evans in Massachusetts, not too far from Vermont. There I spent almost a year, until October 1944, and then I went into the process of being shipped overseas. I finally ended up in Europe in mid- or late November 1944 and eventually ended up as a chaplain with the 9th Infantry Division in Germany.

What was your rank at the time?

At that time I reached all the way to first lieutenant, which was exactly where I started, too.

What was the trip over like?

It was the first time I was ever on a plane. I flew from LaGuardia across the Atlantic to Prestwick, Scotland. We stopped, of course, in Newfoundland and the Azores and then ended up at Prestwick at about two-thirty in the morning on a freezing day. They took us to some kind of hotel where we spent the night—there was another chaplain with me—and the next day they flew us to London, where we spent a long period of time, almost two days. Then finally they flew us to Paris, city of lights, where they allowed us to spend one day. Then the next five weeks I spent in a replacement depot—we used to call them repel depots—waiting for assignment, until I finally was given the assignment to the 9th Infantry Division.

What was your company?

Well, it's interesting. The first army chaplain interviewed me and interviewed another Jewish chaplain, Günter Plaut. He said, "I've got several divisions that need you as chaplains. The 9th Infantry Division consists of a lot of Jewish boys from the New York area, so I think I'll send Max Wall there because he speaks Yiddish. And Plaut, I'll send you to the 103rd Division." And that's the way it was. I was sent to the 9th Infantry Division. When I came to the 9th Infantry Division, I was assigned as chaplain of special troops—that was my company. As special troops chaplain I was free to roam around the entire division, whereas the chaplain who proceeded me, Chaplain Tepper, who was killed in August 1944 in France somewhere, had been assigned to the 60th Infantry Regiment, one of the three regiments that made up the 9th Infantry Division. That limited his ability to move around to service all the Jewish men in the division. I was able to move around much more freely because I was assigned to headquarters, in a sense.

I served not only Jewish personnel but all personnel. At chaplain school some of my Catholic colleagues taught me how to say the final prayer, you know, if I happened to be dealing with a wounded soldier who was Catholic. "I baptize you in the name of so and so and so and so and so and so." I taught them the S'hmah, in case they were dealing with a Jewish boy. We worked it out, and I think the chaplaincy was the beginning of a new spirit of interrelationship between Christians and Jews in America. The ecumenical period was long before Pope John XXIII. It started when chaplains got to know each other as human beings. At chaplain school I got up early in the morning to put on my tfillin, and the three other chaplains living with me looked at me. Why, it gave me the opportunity to teach them exactly what the tfillin were, what Jewish prayer was, so we got to know each other very well. It was an intimate relationship in which we were serving American GIs—it didn't make any difference who, what, where, or what color. That was the beginning of a period of a sense of glory, being part of a large element that was out to finish off the Nazis.

When you arrived in Europe in November '44, were you then engaged in any battles or combat duty?

Remember, I was a chaplain, so I was never engaged in military combat. But I used to be surrounded by combat all the time because I was an infantry chaplain.

How close were you to the front troops?

Well, when I was at the aid stations, maybe a quarter of a mile, half a mile, tops, because that's where the wounded were brought in for first aid before they were sent back to where it was felt they would do the most good. So we were very close. My first experience was being driven to the division HQ [headquarters], and I saw bodies and animal corpses lying in the field nearby, all destroyed by shrapnel and by other kinds of fire. And in my heart I said, What am I doing here? I was scared, and I don't think I stopped being scared until the war was over. Fortunately, it said the word "chaplain" on the jeep that I inherited from Chaplain Tepper, and on either side of the word *chaplain* on the windshield—or below the windshield, since we didn't have a windshield— was a *Mogen David* or Star of David. And my first thought was *veh iz mir*, I'm going to be identified as a Jew automatically wherever I go. And the first German who sees me is going to [shoot at me]. And that kept me sane, though I was scared. I was too scared to remove those Stars of David. I was too scared for that, so I kept them and that's what kept me going. I did lots of things . . . because that's what everybody was doing. Everybody was scared. Everyone was doing what he had to do to push ahead in the process of ultimate destruction.

Although I was never wounded, I got lost many times, and I thought we would wind up as POWs. Fortunately, I inherited a wonderful assistant from Amsterdam, New York, Maury Olender, who had been the chaplain's assistant under Tepper. And he sort of guided me carefully to make sure I would not do foolish things. Really, it's interesting: there was no sense of time during combat as long as we were at war because every day was like a brand-new life, very special. Once the war ended, it became a different kind of a story.

Rabbi Max B. Wall in uniform, 1945.
Courtesy of Rabbi Wall.

What were some of the things you had to face as a chaplain?

The very first thing was inexperience. I had an assistant, I had a driver, and I had a jeep. Beyond that, how to conduct services, what kind of services, under what conditions, all these things you had to learn as you moved along. . . . When did we have services? We didn't have them in synagogues, obviously. We had them by a tree, or in a dugout; very often in a trench, or something similar to it. In a truck, in nice times in an open meadow, under all kinds of conditions. During the war, wherever I went for services, as many Jewish people as possible came. They were not really structured services as we had in the *siddur*. There might be a *shema Yisroel* or perhaps if there was somebody mourning we had *kaddish*, stuff like that. I tried to bring whatever goodies I could collect. Cigarettes, because the closer you got to the front, the less the GIs had. In Paris, the GIs wore wonderful jackets and the finest boots, but at the front this wasn't so. Whatever I brought—whether it was a box of Tollhouse cookies from America for me that I shared for everybody—it was a *me-cha-ye*. It was absolutely wonderful; it brought back home to them.

Where were those first experiences? What area?

Probably the most famous city that you would recognize is the city of Aachen, the place where the Holy Roman Empire was started by Charlemagne. I lived near Aachen for a couple of days in this town called

Stolberg, and I went to the various units of the division. When you entered Aachen on any road, American engineers had put up a sign, quoting a statement of Hitler. Hitler had said, "Give me five years and you will not recognize Europe." And they put this sign up in quotes. If you looked at Aachen, it was in total ruins; there wasn't a single building that had a roof on it. As if to say, well you're right, you're absolutely right.

I remember the division in combat was divided into two sections: division rear and division forward. Division forward was the tactical part of the division with the commanding officer and the various active troops. Division rear was the administrative and support units—the quartermaster, the ordinance, the motor pool—it couldn't be right up in the front because if you got hit, you'd be destroyed completely. So the combat units were up front, and division rear was at times as much as twenty-five to fifty miles behind. My office was technically with division rear, with administration, headquarters troops. So in order for me to reach the troops, I was constantly on the move. I covered, even in actual combat, six or seven hundred miles a week. Which was a lot, considering my territory was limited because the enemy was on the other side. But everybody did it.

Were you instructed or was this a part of your training?

Nobody ever told me anything about that. Or I don't remember anybody telling me. You went where you felt you had to.

Where did you feel you had to go?

Wherever the GIs were that needed me. I was once very much embarrassed. It was two days after I joined the division, and I get a note that, I forget the boy's name, let's call him Becker, in the second battalion in the 60th Infantry, wants to see me. Well, I'm gung ho, that's what I'm here for, to be of service to the GIs. I finally find the, oh, it was the 47th Infantry Regiment; I came there in the morning to regimental HQ and I ask for Becker, and they say he's in the 2nd Battalion. It was just about lunchtime and they ask me, would you like to have lunch? And I say, well, I've got to go see him first. But at a certain point there was an MP [military police], and he said you can't go any farther because there's active fighting right beyond there. So I told my assistant to stay back, but my driver and I went on a little way ahead and we got out of the jeep and we finally find the CP [Command Post] for the 2nd Battalion. I went in and the officer asked me what I wanted, and I told him, and he said, you see that field of fire over there, he's in one corner of that field and he'll be back in for lunch soon, so why don't you wait, would you like to have some lunch? No, I might as well wait. About an hour later he comes in with his dripping mess kit, and I introduced myself and took him out of the CP. I asked him, "What's the problem?" He says, "No problem. I just wanted to meet the new Jewish chaplain."

I don't know how this happened, but by the time I got back to regimental headquarters, they all knew about it already. By the time I got to division HQ, the assistant division chaplain, Reverend Propst, came over to me and says, "If you ever do something as stupid as that again and you survive I personally will kill you. We waited almost six months for a replacement for Chaplain Tepper. If you're going to get killed, at least do it for a good purpose, not with stupid behavior like this." Well, I learned, but I was more embarrassed than anything else. I realized how foolish I had been. But I learned.

During active combat I discovered I was less frightened than when we had a period of comparative nonfighting. There were some periods after the Battle of the Bulge, before the next major activity started, when you didn't encounter too much violence. It was the period of lull, of comparative nonfighting, that gave a false sense of security. The first time I heard a shell again, it bounced me up completely, because I hadn't expected it any longer. We were riding along too smoothly. I discovered one other thing—that I wasn't very much concerned with myself, which I thought was a very good experience. I was concerned with my job, my responsibility, and my family back home.

Were you able to write letters? To your wife at home?

Oh yeah, I wrote every single day that I could. And she kept all the letters.

Toward the end of the war, the 9th Infantry Division began to encounter fugitives and refugees from work camps and concentration camps.[2] As they encountered these DPs— "displaced persons"—and the camps and prisons from which they were liberated, Rabbi Wall and others, like Chaplain Abraham Klausener, extended their help. Organizing help of all kinds for refugees in places like Camp Feldafing, Foehrenwald, Landsberg, St. Ottilien; establish-

*ing lines of communication between DPs and their relatives in other countries;
and providing religious services and support, Rabbis Wall and Klausener
expanded their duties as military chaplains to include the victims of the enemies they fought.³*

*To what extent did you know, once you got to Europe, or did you know while
the fighting still continued, what they were doing to the Jews?*

The first experience I had with European Jews was, I think, the first or
second day of Hanukkah 1944. I had not yet been assigned to a division; I was still assigned to First Army Headquarters. After supper a
Jewish officer came over and asked me if I'd like to go and visit a Jewish
family he'd discovered. Of course. I had brought along my Hanukkah
menorah and came to this house where there were a number of women
and some teenage girls. Now I felt kind of weird being alone, not be-
longing to any organization or so on. And I came in there, and I brought
the Hanukkah menorah, and the women said, in Yiddish, "Could you
light the candles?" And I said "yes" and "surely you know about Hanukkah?" They said, "No, we've just been able to come out from se-
crecy a couple of weeks ago since the Americans have come." They
were brought up in a convent, so they didn't get any Jewish education, and that began to tear at me—having to tell Jewish children
about Hanukkah as if they were completely, absolutely ignorant. What
can I say; it was a first.

It was the second night of Hanukkah, and I lit one candle and said
the prayers and told them the story of Hanukkah, and then I said to
them, quoting a Hasidic statement made a long time ago: "A rabbi came
into a shoemaker to have some shoes repaired, and the shoemaker said
to him, 'the candle is almost burned, I won't be able to see very much,'
and the rabbi said to him, 'I'll say it in Yiddish and translate, kol z'man
das lichtl brennt, iz noch als der zejt.'" (So long as the candle is burning, there is still time.) Suddenly it struck me that these few survivors,
whom I had met for the first time—they were the burning candle. I
walked out of there as if I was walking on clouds. Hitler hadn't won, he
hadn't won: the candle was still burning.

Occasionally, we met an individual as we crossed Europe in combat
who was liberated from one slave camp or another—there were so
many. And that's where General Lawton Collins ordered the German
civilians to report for burial detail. When we found trains of cars filled
with corpses, he was so violently angry he forced them all to report for

burial duty and to bury the remains of these people. But I didn't meet any real group of DPs until near the end of the war.

What were you then doing in the late winter and spring of '45?

In the winter of '45 we had the Bulge and it took us a long time to surround it and squeeze it in and destroy it. We then moved across the line into central Germany and had another battle, just short of the Elbe River. During these three major campaigns I was chaplaining, doing what chaplains do. Traveling all over, we happened to come to a line of vehicles on the two days before the bridge—the Remagen Bridge, the railroad bridge—fell in. They had tried to bomb it as soon as we crossed the bridge. The 9th Armored Division found this bridge intact, and they crossed over and were told to take the bridge on the other side. Well, pretty soon they had four or five divisions across there in a narrow, small pocket. We came to this town of Remagen, where the bridge was, and the following day the bridge fell in, but by that time we already had four or five pontoon bridges. And we set up an office in one of the large hotels.

This was in wine country, and, you know, it's like the Catskills, a place where you go for vacations. So this hotel had ample cutlery and all kinds of glassware. This was just before Pesach [Passover], so we decided to observe it, and at that time there must have been close to a thousand GIs in that immediate pocket. I went to Namier, Belgium, in a big truck . . . for the purpose of getting my supply of matzohs and gefillte fish from the Jewish welfare board. By the time I got back, the pocket had broken open. GIs were chasing Germans in tanks and trucks rather than by foot. I had to chase the troops to catch up with them. Rather than the thousand, twelve hundred men that we expected for the seder, there were about seventy who were able to attend the seder. Then we fled. I followed with a tray-load behind my jeep distributing matzohs to all the units. I finally decided that the best thing to do was give it to the quartermaster—as he distributes his rations everyday, he'll distribute matzohs. So wherever I went during the next four or five days, GIs were eating matzoh, Jews or non-Jews, it didn't make any difference.

I came across an interesting city called Dessau where Moses Mendelssohn had once lived. Looked for his grave. Couldn't find it because it was a total wreck of a town. Eventually we settled in a little town called Bitterfeld, and at that point the division rear and division forward decided that it's okay now to merge. So, I met Lieutenant Chambers who was from Wisconsin. He saw me in this town and he said, "Hey Chaplain, I need your help, I need an interpreter. I gotta find suitable quarters for division HQ and if I have to speak to Germans I want you to be with me." We drove around the city, a beautiful little town, hardly touched. There was a beautiful high school, and he says that might be an interesting building for division headquarters personnel. So we went in and looked around, did some measuring, and he says, "Yeah, I think this will do. Now we need an officers' quarters." There's a series of beautiful homes. He knocks on the first door, a woman comes to the door and I said to her in my broken German: "We'd like to come in." She says, "Bitte." There were some people sitting having cognac. One of them turned out to be an actor who had once worked in Hollywood. And Ernie Chambers walked in through all the rooms, sat on the beds, tested the beds. She kept asking questions, he wouldn't say a word. And then he went out, took a piece of chalk, and wrote on the door— he made a figure of the *Mogen David*, Star of David. Went through the next three houses and two houses with three apartment buildings— and each one he examined and said, "Okay, we've got it. I've got to go down to the military government office in order to approve it."

So he went down to the military government office, and there is this fellow who was the classmate of Ernie Chambers from Wisconsin. He says, "What are you doing here?" He [Chambers] says, "I'm setting up division headquarters." So the fellow takes out a large map and says, "Where do you want to be?" "Well, we found this spot right here, right here." He says, "Good, we'll give you a policeman." So a fellow comes out and the badge he was wearing says "Zivilpolizei," civilian police. He gets in the jeep and we drive over, and he asks me, "How much time do you want to give them?" So Ernie figures this and this and this, "It'll take 'em till about 3 o'clock." And he [the policeman] says, "No! One hour, that's all the time they gave me for my home in Amsterdam. That's all they're getting." And he knocked on each door and he told them, "I want you out within an hour. Just take personal belongings—no jewelry, no silver- ware, nothing, no purses, no gold or silver. Report here in the front of the sidewalk and I want your keys. All the keys to the house." He did this to all the tenants in those houses and apartments. Then he turns to me and he gives me all the keys—I was captain by then—and he says, "You're the ranking officer, here. Here are the keys."

So we find five buildings, and I'm three—my assistant, my driver, and myself; Ernie Chambers and his driver, that's five people. So each of us spent that night in one of those houses or apartments because we didn't want to leave them alone. While I was there, I examined some of the furniture there, the closet, and I noticed beautiful garments with labels from Paris and Warsaw, from the best shops in Europe, when the Germans had been victorious and had looted and taken everything. They were civilian clothes, what was I going to do with them? It's the officers' quarters. A few days later, I'm sitting in my office and there's a group of teenagers, fourteen, fifteen teenagers about the ages of fourteen to sixteen years old. Jewish. They were Hungarians who had been liberated from a work camp nearby and were wandering around. They heard I'd be there and came to see me. Suddenly, it occurred to me, they're dressed in these rags. I'd like to do something.

I know where to get clothes. I went to those homes, took out all of the civilian clothes, distributed them; many of them were very useful to them. And I called up the quartermaster and I said, I need food, I need housing, so we went to three nice houses not too far from us. Evacuated the civilians and put these kids into these homes. Loaded up their homes and distributed their food, it wasn't kosher food, but flour, sugar and juices, and meat—all of the food possible. On Friday afternoon, one of the girls and one of the boys came over to me and said, "Rabbiner, thank you. Come to Shabbas," and they had prepared a Shabbas and I got all of the Jewish GIs who were in headquarters at that time. We had a Shabbas—it was almost as celebrated as the celebration of the state of Israel in May '48.

The end of that story is not as pleasant as this part of it. They wouldn't stay in the area. They wanted to go back and see if they could find any relatives, you know, see what happened to their homes. I met two or three of them later on, in Munich, where they ended up in the Deutsches Museum, which was the headquarters for the liberated Jews of Bavaria. Rabbi Abraham Klausener was the head of it at the time. And they told me their story. They got back to their hometown and three of them were killed by former neighbors, townspeople. Several of them had been injured as a result of falling off trucks while hitchhiking back to their homes in Hungary. And the others finally decided that they couldn't find anybody, obviously, and decided that they would get into the basic Jewish underground which was headed to the southern ports of Europe for what was then Palestine. So I met two of them at the Deutsches Museum, and they looked no better than when they were first liberated. They had suffered so much.

Do you remember their names?

No, this is one of the things that's been bothering me all along. I never took down names. But only four of them managed to survive. By the end of April, middle of April, we knew that the war was winding down, and more and more camps were being liberated and more slave camps, not destruction camps, but so-called production camps, and individuals were finding their way to us, they'd heard there was a Rabbiner. These people who survived, survived not simply because of luck, but also because of the certain vitality, brains, you name it. And they would come see me. I remember afterwards I was stationed in Ingolstadt and there was a knock on my door. I look up and there was a fellow in a pajama outfit, couple of people behind him, and he asks "Rabbiner?" and I says, "Yeah." He says, "We're Jews," and I said, "Come in," and I asked, "Why are you still wearing these pajama-type clothes? I understand that the UNRRA [United Nations Relief and Rehabilitation Administration] office had already distributed clothing and rations and even quarters to the DPs in this area." He said, "They wouldn't help us." "What do you mean, they wouldn't help you?" He said, "They wouldn't help us." So I zipped up my jacket and walked across the street to the UNRRA headquarters.

I walked over to the girl at the desk and said, "I'd like to see the person in charge." She says, without even looking up, "He's busy." I looked past her and there's a fellow sitting there with his feet on the desk reading the *Stars and Stripes.* I don't remember his name now, it slipped my mind, let's call him Parker. I said, "I'd like to see Mr. Parker." Without looking up, she says, "Colonel Parker." This guy was sitting in civilian clothes. I said, "Colonel Raymond." She says, "I can't disturb him." So I pushed open the gate and started walking in, and she started getting up. I said, "Fräulein, platzen Sie!" I don't know if it's good German, but she understood it perfectly; she didn't move an inch.

And I walked in, knocked on the door and this time I said, "Colonel Parker, Chaplain Wall here." Down came the feet, down came the paper. "Ah, Chaplain, come in." Technically, I was his landlord, because the 9th Infantry Division was occupying that part of Germany, and he was in our territory. "So what can I do for you, Chaplain?" "First of all, Colonel, you're in civilian clothes?" "Ah yes, I'm a retired officer of His Britannic Majesty's forces in Palestine." ("His Britannic Majesty's forces in Palestine!" I thought.) "What can I do for you?" I said, "Well,

I'm curious, I thought that this office had distributed rations and quarters and clothing to the DPs in this area. How come these people standing out there didn't get any of that?" "Oh," he says, "I wouldn't give anything to those Zionist bastards." I don't know what I felt like, but it was suddenly as if somebody had driven a stake into my head. I pulled down the zipper of my jacket and on my collar I was wearing the sign of the Jewish chaplain. And I said, "You know, Colonel, I'm one of those Zionist bastards and I'll be back."

I walked back to division headquarters. I felt like I was four feet above the ground I was so—not so much angry as frustrated. I walk in, and the adjutant sees me, and he says, "Where're you going, chaplain?" "You better tell the general I'm coming," and I knock on the door. Fortunately, there was nobody there; you don't walk in on a major general just like that. And the adjutant takes one look at me and he says, "What happened?" So I started telling him and began cooling off, and then he starts getting excited. And he said, "Let's see what we can do about this." So he picks up the telephone and says, "Get me Paris." I started to tell him about the DPs in general and what was going on, and as it turned out, it was very good that I told him this. Pretty soon the phone rings, and, "Yup, I'd like to speak to Beetle Smith." Beetle Smith was Lieutenant General Bidel Smith, Eisenhower's chief of staff. He finally gets on the phone. The adjutant tells the story and adds, "I want this fellow out of here. Completely. Okay. See you next week." So he hangs up and then he says to me, "You'll have to wait here."

In a little while the adjutant brings in a kind of cablegram or a telegram or whatever, and he reads it and a smile breaks out on his face. He says, "I don't usually use chaplains as messenger boys, but I think that you would very much like to deliver this message." It was addressed to Colonel so-and-so Parker, retired. "Upon receipt of this telegram you are immediately to be relieved of all duties and responsibility. . . . You will pack all of your belongings and all of your records and report to Paris as soon as possible. No delay whatsoever." Signed by somebody.

I walk across. This time the secretary opened the inner gate for me when I arrived. It was one of the few times I felt good. I walked in and said, "Colonel, I've got something I'm supposed to deliver to you." And I read it to him, plunked it down on his desk, and walked out. Couple of days later, the general sees me in the mess hall and says, "Hey, Wall." "Yes, sir?" "Remember that guy Parker? He's finished. He's out of

Europe; he's out of everywhere. He's completely disassociated. Thought you'd like to know." Closed case. It was one of those rare moments, when a sense of *nekama*—payback—overwhelmed me. I felt guilty about it afterwards, and yet, maybe, that's the way I am.

Why would you feel guilty?

I don't know—I was doing something that I thought was mean. But it worked out all right.

Now this was at the end of April, you said?

It might have been beginning of May.

This is before you got to Dachau?

Yes.

This person who was in the uniform, the pajamas, was it the first time you saw somebody in the pajamas?

No, the kids from Hungary also had those clothes on. Look, end of April and the beginning of May, the camps are really beginning to be liberated, and it wasn't long before we began to see not just the liberatees, but the new category, the DPs. They're liberated, what do you do with them—and that's where the DP designation comes from, "displaced person." Of all the designations, displaced persons.

We were in the Munich area at that time, and we went to Dachau, since that was the big name already at that time. Our division hadn't taken Dachau, another division had taken it. But we were close and we wanted to see. Got there, saw the usual kind of things. I couldn't describe it in any great detail because I think the first moment I walked in, I was hit by a sense of helplessness and a sense of tragedy and lonesomeness. It was overwhelming. It's only looking back on it that makes you realize how overwhelming it was.

What was the first thing you saw? What made you feel this way?

Some gaunt skeletons walking around, very tentatively. I wanted to run away. Didn't know what I could do, I felt totally helpless. I was there with a Protestant chaplain and the two of us sort of held each other and tried to find some strength from each other. It was very depressing, really a depressing kind of experience.

Did any of the former prisoners come up to you?

Inmates? Oh yeah. They spoke to me, spoke in Yiddish, saw the Star of David on my helmet and on my collar. "*Rabbiner? A jude?*" What could I do, it was terrible, a terrible experience.

What did you say to them?

"*Ich bin a jude.*" "Where are you from," he says? I say, "America, Brooklyn." The next few things are a kind of a cloud. I can't remember what I did, where I did it, I knew that I was walking around in a total daze.

Can you describe the setup of Dachau, what it was that you were observing?

Well, by that time already, there were GIs, you know, Red Cross, military medical vehicles were there transporting people, picking up people who couldn't walk, putting them on stretchers and carrying them out or assisting people. It was turmoil. It wasn't the Dachau people see today, you know, everything is set up and labeled and so on. There was a terrible stench, the few who were able to walk were reaching out to all of the servicemen who were there, trying to communicate. We gave them what we could, cigarettes, chocolate, whatever candy we had, whatever we had, we tried to give them. And the first thing they really wanted was to communicate, to start linking up. "From Brooklyn?" "*Ihr kennt mein zede*"; "*Ihr kennt mein kusin.*" Do you know this, do you know that person? And that's the way they did it. As GIs came in they gave them their names, and these GIs who were veterans of combat took their names and wrote them down, and they wrote about them to their parents, and they wrote and they asked them to look up these people. Pretty soon you had a whole network of people who were communicating on behalf of these DPs.

But there was no direct communication. They'd write and say, "I met your cousin. But I'm going home next week." Because you know, the point system started, and if you didn't have enough points, you stayed much longer, as I did. And all of the veterans were sent home two weeks after VE-Day, May 8. So you had one group of people setting up linkages through the United States and Canada and South America. On the other hand, these people couldn't communicate directly because there's no postal system set up for DPs, so in order for them to communicate, they had to communicate with the GI who wrote down their name. But that GI is no longer there, he's home. These GIs went home, and they put into their local papers and their synagogue bulletin and in their homecoming speeches that they gave from various places all about what was going on. And they didn't describe it from a sanitized point of view. They described all the filth and the violence and the carelessness that was being perpetrated on these people even after liberation. And people began to respond to these public requests for help for the DPs. And the GIs from my division went home and they said, you want to help DPs, write or send help through Chaplain Max B. Wall, AP 09. Because they knew I didn't have many points, I would be there a long time.

That's how I started getting letters and packages. Three packages, a dozen letters. What a joy it was. By that time, Chaplain Klausener had already set up Foehrenwald, Landsberg, St. Ottilien, so that it was much easier to communicate with these people. I now became a link as other resident servicemen and chaplains who still had to be there through whom Americans, South Americans, Canadians were able to communicate with their relatives in DP camps. I would get a letter saying, "Please give this to my cousin Shmuel Rabinowitz who is at Camp Feldafing." So I would go to Camp Feldafing and tell that to Shmuel Rabinowitz. And what a great thing that was for me to make up this tiny little link. Can you imagine what a joy it was for Rabbi Klausener, who printed up the names of thousands of survivors and distributed them throughout the camps and was able to establish a linkage among the living. . . . A couple of letters, a package or two, it was a great joy.

I used to look forward to going to this—you'll forgive the expression—stinking camp, occupied by roughly five thousand Jews, to be able make these linkages. Feldafing, Foehrenwald, they were not exactly ideal living quarters. They were barracks, originally used for German troops. And they didn't have the same number of people in them as the German army required. They were packed. In some of the rooms, there were twenty-five or thirty people. With bunk beds, that kind of stuff. The only thing is that they could walk out whenever they wanted to and meander around in a larger area. But they were contained. They didn't want them to be loose in the population. They didn't know how to deal with them. I have a feeling that there was a certain amount of guilt on the part of the authorities, as we discovered later on. They wanted to deal with clean, sweet-smelling people, not with people who brought up all kinds of guilty feelings in them. Why didn't we do more, why didn't we save them earlier, why didn't we bomb Auschwitz or the other destruction camps, or do anything to slow down the process of death and destruction? So it was much easier to deal with Germans, who suddenly were very friendly. The amazing thing was there were no experiences of any kind of hostility toward Americans once the war ended. We could go anywhere, travel at night, in the day, alone. Nobody ever bothered us. It was a very interesting thing. And there were no Germans who I ever met who had ever been involved in any of this miserable, destructive activity. None!

Were there any SS officers in the camp?

No. I was at Camp Feldafing, which was a Jewish DP camp, where I saw what they had identified as a former kapo. Before my very eyes, I mean a large crowd of people, they destroyed him. Literally almost tore him apart limb from limb. The DPs. Nobody could gainsay that. I was there, I was watching. They saw him, and they recognized him, and that was the end. They had nothing to be afraid of. These DPs, they had endured Hitler. Do you think they were going to be frightened by a couple of American MPs? It didn't work that way.

How'd you feel standing there watching that, as a Rabbi?

Well, before I was a Rabbi, I was a Jew. And these were my brothers and sisters behaving in a way I thought at that moment was very natural behavior. They had discovered somebody who had tortured them, who had made their lives as miserable as possible, and he was now trying to hide in their midst. Of course what was interesting, as we discovered later on, as scholars of the Holocaust period have discovered, is that thousands of Germans tried to escape any punishment by the Allies by disguising themselves as DPs. So when they discovered one of these people, there's no question about it, all of their pent-up anger was released. Here I'd come out of a world war, an infantry division that's seen so much violence, and I'd never seen that kind of violence as what happened to that person.

But at the same time, these people were engaged in other kinds of activities as well. They started cultural activities, started developing all kinds of Zionist activities. It was in this period that the world began to realize what was happening, and the full revelation took place. And so you have all kinds of big shots coming from America, from England. To examine, to interview, to see, to communicate.

After the war ended, Rabbi Wall spent two more years in Europe, until spring 1947, working along with Abe Klausener and others to help Jewish survivors rebuild their lives. In the process, he witnessed and participated in the Zionist movement. At the same time, as a chaplain in the U.S. Army, he ministered to troops of all religious backgrounds. He continued his ecumenical activities when he returned to the United States, teaching classes in Judaism at two colleges in Burlington, Vermont.

Among these big shots who came, there were people like David Ben-Gurion, who came to Munich in October. He came, naturally, to speak to the DPs and the growing Zionist movement that was burgeoning in the Allied occupied zones. We had lunch, for Rabbi Klausener had arranged a lunch for him. We sat around, and I happened to be sitting next to Ben-Gurion. I was very pessimistic about the immediate future. And I said to him, "Mr. Ben-Gurion, look around, what do you see, what's missing? What will be?" So he looks at me, you have to remember the little cherubic face, bald head, the rabbit ears on both sides, and he pats his chest and he says, "*We* will be, we will be." It just so happens that many years later I was in Jerusalem visiting the Knesset with my wife. And there was Ben-Gurion, sitting in the well of the Knesset. He was reading the *New York Times* in a short-sleeved shirt. I turned to my wife and I said, "Dear, he was right, he said, '*We* will be.'" And there he was, now the prime minister of the State of Israel.

Those three words enabled me to take up the courage to do what I could do on behalf of my brothers and sisters who were still breathing. It was those moments that I think instilled into me, like an injection, the energy, the spiritual and psychic energy, in order to go on and do, not what I wanted to do for them, that was impossible, but to do what I could for them. It makes a big difference. No one can do everything for everybody, but if each of us does his portion that he can do today, it makes a lot of difference. Look what Rabbi Klausener did. He couldn't do everything. But if he commits murder fifty times he will still be eligible, in my judgment, for immediate entrance into the highest level of *gan eden*—paradise—because of what he did.

How did you first come to meet him?

I met Abe Klausener when I was about seven or eight, and he was about the same age, maybe a year younger. We both lived in Denver, Colorado. We took different paths later on; I came to New York and so on. He eventually became a Reform rabbi. And I met him again overseas. We had never been close friends, and I don't think we became close friends. I don't know what it was. He was so involved with the DPs that everything else was peripheral, not important. I didn't care. I was so grateful to him for holding the reins and doing what could be done and marshaling my efforts and the efforts of other service people to help this process that I didn't care what else he did or how he treated any of us. What he was doing was central. He went AWOL, absent without leave, from his unit, which was a medical unit, for about six months and worked with the DPs. They'd try to reach him and nobody knew where he was. But we all knew where he was. As a matter of fact, I got a call from some military officer, "Hey Rabbi. There's a group of Jewish people just come in from the Russian zone of occupation. Will you tell Klausener that we're sending them over to him?" I'd get a call, "You know where Klausener is? He's AWOL." "Never heard of him." They knew intimately what he was doing, and why he was doing it, and who he was doing it for.

I remember one instance where we went to see the military government officer who was in charge of civilian towns all around Munich. Klausener came to him to ask him for an order to give to the various Bürgermeister—mayors—of the small towns ordering them to assist in printing the lists of survivors, and he said, "I'm not going to do that." So Abe Klausener says to him, "May I speak off the record, sir?" "Yep, chaplain, go ahead." "I understand that you're not regular army. You come from New York City and you've been in politics in New York. How would it appear if it gets around that you refused two New York rabbis help in publishing lists of Jewish survivors in the camps? Do you think you'd have much of a chance for political success in New York City?" The officer says a dirty word and then, "Give me the paper." That's how Abe worked. The important thing was that it was for his cause, and there's absolutely nobody like him at all.

What did you know about the black market in the camps?

The black market was not so much in the camps as it emanated from the camps. Let me give you an example: If you're an inmate in one of the camps and you get a package, fifty pounds, from Rabbi Wall, which comes from Brooklyn or Nevada or wherever, and it's got all kinds of goodies like cigarettes and chocolates and any other kind of food needed in Europe—you know what a cigarette can bring on the black market. Are you going to smoke it yourself? That's burning gold. So then they go out onto the street in local towns or in Munich, and they would start wheeling and dealing. Now I became involved to the extent that I was very frightened by the 3rd Army inspector general because in January 1946, I was called to the inspector general's office and told that I would have to answer all kinds of questions dealing with the black market and the mailing system.

Months earlier, my general called me in one day and said, "Chaplain," he says, "I got a telegram here from the AFL-CIO Labor War Chest, and they want to send help to the Jewish DPs in this area. What shall I tell him? Shall I tell them to send it through the Red Cross? What shall I do?" So I said to him, "Sir, the Red Cross is another military administration, you know what I told you about the way the military behave here. This is your area. Anything I do is by command of you. I work with the DPs on a daily basis. I bring them spiritual help, religious help"—I didn't emphasize the material help—"I'm in the best position to know what and how these people could use help." He says, "Well, I'll think about it." I didn't know, but as it turned out, he thought about it and sent a response to the AFL-CIO Labor War Chest committee telling them, "Send whatever help you wish through Chaplain Max B. Wall APO 9." So I started getting large packages of all kinds, clothing, you know, stuff for people to use. This area was poor—totally poor—of everything. All of this stuff began gradually to emerge into the streets.

So I get this call. As soon as I heard that they wanted to see me, I destroyed any letters that I had asking for help from the UJA [United Jewish Appeal], from various organizations, national organizations, the B'nai Brith, because I thought, they're going to blame me for all the mail that I am getting. I went in, saluted, and reported. They said, "Have you ever heard of the articles of war?" I said, I heard of them when I came into the service. "Well, sergeant, read the articles of war." I read the articles of war again. And then he said; "Now you're under oath. You tell me what you know about these black market materials that are appearing all over Munich." I said, "I don't know, general. GIs saw the tragedy that was here. They went home, and they told their people at home to send help, help through Chaplain Max B. Wall. I have no way of controlling these packages. If people from Australia, from South America, from Canada, from England, and from France are sending me packages, how do I stop it?" He says, "Well, you have to stay here until all the packages stop coming." My wife had had a baby in February 1945, here I am waiting to get home and it's a year later. And for two days he kept drilling me.

His assistant finally said to him, "Sir, I know Chaplain Wall because I was the inspector general at the 9th Infantry Division before I came here. He's a lousy poker player, but he's a very nice man, a very good man, and whatever he's doing is something that I as an American would be proud that he's doing on behalf of the American people. Why don't you give him a chance to tell you off the record what's going on." So he looks at me, "You'd better tell me the truth."

So I told him. Told him what's happening to the DPs, how real help was going out to the DPs. I told him how MPs were pulling them off the street and stripping them of whatever they possessed, and Klausener, most of the time, and I, whenever I had the chance, used to go to get them out of jail. He says, "Why don't I know about these things?" I says, "Sir, you are the major general; things don't get up that far." He says, "You're right." That was the period when Truman was ordering Eisenhower to investigate the lack of treatment and the mistreatment of the DPs in the camps. And it fit right in. He was very angry when I told him about it because he thought I was criticizing the United States. But I wasn't criticizing the United States, I was criticizing the way we were trying to provide help to these people.

I managed to get off. You know, I wasn't put in jail. I thought of Leavenworth already, all kinds of punishment, because I had already used American mail for nonmilitary purposes, and by the time the packages stopped coming, we were receiving anywhere between five hundred and eight hundred packages a day. I couldn't walk into my office. And it was creating a personal problem, a sense of guilt. People would come to me and say, I have a letter from corporal so-and-so that tells me that my sister in Brooklyn is sending me a *Paket*, a package, where's my *Paket?*" I've got six, seven, eight hundred packages coming in a day. How do I know? I had already given the Central Committee of Liberated Jews permission to receive all my mail. And they would send a truck to the Munich post office and receive mail that was addressed to me. They would take these packages, and they would look into them and they would say, "Shmuel Rabinowitz of Feldafing. You have a package here. You have five weeks in which to pick it up. If in five weeks you do not come, we will open the package and put the stuff on the shelves and distribute it to whoever comes in who is needy." So he knows he's got a package because corporal so-and-so gave him a letter from Brooklyn. But the letter said they were sending the package to me. So, "Where's my package? Are you involved in the black market with these packages?" I had a real job. And of course the DPs had not exactly come to be agreeable, they were not real saints. . . . It was an interesting kind of mess. So when they finally took over the packages from me it was a pleasure, except I couldn't get any packages from home either because all packages to me were going to the Central Committee of Liberated Jews.

You mentioned before how you had been writing to your wife at home. To what extent were you able to discuss with her through the mail what you were going through?

Well, I've got one little excerpt here from a letter that I thought might be of interest: "You need not worry about my becoming bitter and cynical. I said that I would never be able to laugh again, but that was when I was in the depth of dejection, when I was so filled with misery because I felt inadequate to the task of helping. Since then I have seen much more and I've become less dejected. I've decided to do what I could within the limits of my position and my abilities. Decided also to do whatever I could, whenever I could, without worrying if I'm doing enough as I should."

You mentioned how you had a child that was born while you were overseas.

Yeah, when I left for Europe, my wife was pregnant. On February 18, 1945, she gave birth to a little girl whom I didn't get to meet until April '46. So I came to the conclusion that any GI who left children at home and went overseas must have had a much rougher time, as a result of not getting to meet my daughter until she was eighteen months old. But the longer I stayed there, the less these things concerned me. I became completely absorbed with my inadequate ability to do what had to be done for my brothers and sisters. It wasn't enough. Whatever I did, it wasn't enough. There was still sorrow, there was still misery, there was still poverty, there was still separation.

Tell me more about your duties as a rabbi there.

We used to hold services in some of the smaller towns where a lot of DPs were living who were not under the control of DP camps. The military government officers in the town of Erding—this is all in Bavaria I'm talking about—we used to have services every Friday night, and there would be sixty, seventy people—most of them were DPs who were living as civilians in the larger community. In addition to the so-called services, we had wine and cake and fruit and candy, whatever we could scrounge up together. We would sing Israeli songs and talk about Palestine.

I have to tell you about the experience I had when I attended the first "Zionist Conference of Liberated Jews in Bavaria" in the city of Landsberg. This was the fortress city where Hitler had been imprisoned in the 1920s, where he wrote his book, *Mein Kampf.* I went there, knowing that as a chaplain I would be called upon to say a few words, and frankly I was so scared because I didn't know what I could say to bolster their spirits or do anything for them. What could I say, standing there in a nice uniform telling them about their experiences, and how could I talk to them? As we got close to the camp—it was some kind of a DP camp or something—I heard noise, singing. As we got closer, it was Hebrew singing, "Am Yisroel Chai"—the Jewish people lives. These people were telling me that I don't have to encourage them. They were firmly convinced in *am Yisroel chai.* We came in there and Dr. Greenberg, an important figure in the Central Committee of Liberated Jews in Bavaria, gave a rousing address. Most of the language was Yiddish. It basically affirmed a simple principle: no matter what happens to us we have an obligation to live, not only because we want to live, but because we have to guarantee the survival of *am Yisroel,* the Jewish people. And no place else in the world can there be that kind of guarantee as much as in our homeland, *Artz'enu,* our land *eretz Yisroel.* There was no Israel at that time, of course.

When was this?

It was October '45. And there were tears, plenty of tears; they were not tears of sadness, they were tears of affirmation, of obligation, right, and the will to live and to rebuild. There was an old song, I think it came from Israel years and years ago. "Anu banu artzah livnot u'lihebanot bah"—"We've come to the land to build and to rebuild." They wanted to come there to build. Whether they would be rebuilding was a side concern for them, they wanted to build, they wanted to guarantee the survival of the existence of liberated, free Israel. I came back full of pep and full of vigor which lasted for at least two weeks!

By the time I was eligible to go home, I don't think they had a point system any longer, at least I wasn't aware of it. But, one day I got a call, "You're going home!" So you have to be relieved of your post and then you join a traveling unit—it was like a vehicle that takes you toward home, except it's a human vehicle, not a truck—you go with that unit gradually till you get back to the States. It so happened that I was relieved of my responsibilities just before Pesach and Easter '46. I was with a group that was meeting in a small town on our way back somewhere in Bavaria. I was the only chaplain, Jewish, and Easter Sunday came along, but I was a U.S. chaplain. So I had to arrange for services for the various GIs and personnel who were with me and stationed in the area where there was no chaplain available.

You can just imagine, a Rabbi trying to arrange Easter services for a group of Christians. But I felt that it was my responsibility, so what I did was I found a couple of people who had been former chaplain's assistants who were considering going into the ministry, and they had a hymnal, so we met in this bombed-out church—it was a beautiful setting, strange to say it was bombed out, but there was something beautiful about it. And here I am, leading a group of Christians who did their own singing, and I was to deliver the "sermon." Easter represents what—the affirmation of life over death—and so I tried to emphasize that aspect of it. And people asked me about the Holocaust—we didn't use that term, of course—and they asked me, where did it all come from? And we talked about that and they said, how can you affirm life? I said the only thing left for us is to affirm life in the face of such death. It struck me later on that here I was in a church speaking to Christians, and we stayed in that church until almost five o'clock. We started at eleven o'clock, talking and analyzing, and I never felt as much at home in any synagogue service that I attended subsequent to that. That's how intimate and loose things were at that time.

What were you talking about?

About the meaning of life, Jews, Christians, Judaism, Christianity, the destruction of the Jewish community in Europe, antisemitism. Suddenly, we felt very uninhibited, and all of us felt that, and they sat there, and when it was all over, one of the GIs came over to me and said this is going to look very silly, but I'd like to kiss you, this is the most memorable Easter that I can recall. You've made me a better Christian. I felt it was a compliment.

Well, I got home and met my daughter, and I came home, it was about 11:30 at night, a Sunday night I think—and they took me into the bedroom, and they woke her and she came right into my arms. Something she hardly ever did subsequent to that, but without crying or nothing, she came right into my arms. Oh, I had received so many pictures of her and so many letters describing her; it was very delicious kind of a feeling. To hold her, to have my wife, to have my parents. I was exhausted. I weighed 119 pounds when I came home. When I left for Europe, I weighed 144 pounds. Most of that weight was lost as a result of working with the DPs. After the war ended, I was a wreck. I had itches and twitches and was smoking three packs of cigarettes a day.

And I had to look for a job. I didn't have a job, and my income from the army was going to end at the beginning of June. So I went to the seminary; they had a list of positions open, and they said, how about Burlington, Vermont, a nice community, so I went there still in my uniform, I didn't have any civilian clothes. The first question they asked me in the interview after my speech was, "How much do you want?" I said, "That's the wrong question, first you should ask me, do I want to come here, and the answer is no, I don't." I left, I wasn't coming back. I got a call from the seminary, "You gotta go again, because there are some people you didn't meet, and they want you very much." I didn't have a job, and I was living with my parents in a New York City apartment, so I went back. This time, I met a group of former GIs who had just come home as I did, all young people who were planning to separate from the congregation and open their own congregation. They looked like good people to me, so I said, "Tell you what, fellas, if you promise to not separate, to keep the unity of this community, if you promise to work with me and not behind me, I'll come for a year, we'll see what's what." And that's what happened. I came for a year in 1946, got stuck in the snow. And I've been here ever since.

I built a synagogue, built a tremendous linkage between the Jewish community and the non-Jewish community. Eventually, I ended up teaching at St. Michael's College, which is an Edmundite Catholic college. Judaism, courses on Judaism. I taught at St. Michael's for twenty-five years. I have never had a greater sense of acceptance of fellowship than I had with these priests and nuns who were my students. I taught at Champlain College for twenty-six, twenty-seven years, all in areas of Jewish religion. I was very much involved in the ecumenical movement I set up. It sounds like a series of I, I, I, it's not really that. These are the moments that have given me a great sense of satisfaction with what I've done with my life.

NOTES

1. Used with permission. For information on the Survivors of the SHOAH Visual History Foundation, see www.vhf.org.

2. See Robert H. Abzug, *Inside the Vicious Heart: Americans and the Liberation of Nazi Concentration Camps* (New York: Oxford University Press, 1985).

3. On the situation of Jewish displaced persons, see Margarete Myers, "The Jewish Displaced Persons: Reconstructing Individual and Community in the U.S. Zone of Occupied Germany," *Leo Baeck Institute Yearbook* 42 (1997): 302–24; Zeev W. Mankowitz, *The Survivors of the Holocaust in Occupied Germany* (New York: Cambridge University Press, 2002); and Michael Brenner, *After the Holocaust: Rebuilding Jewish Lives in Postwar Germany* (Princeton, N.J.: Princeton University Press, 1997).

CHAPTER TEN

CLERGY IN THE MILITARY—
VIETNAM AND AFTER

One Chaplain's Reflections

JOSEPH F. O'DONNELL, C.S.C.

The path that my life has taken would have been considered the stretches of fantasy when I was a youngster. My father had been "of age" for the draft in the Second World War, but he was exempted because our family ran a grocery and meat store in Chicago. He did become an official of the Office of Price Administration (OPA), and all the family spent endless hours counting food stamps during the time of rationing. My two brothers spent two years each in the army during the Korean conflict. I was the innocent, naive, simple, third son, talked out of entering the seminary after high school at the behest of my father, who wanted me to go to the University of Notre Dame in Indiana, where he (and my older brother) had been students. But we had money problems, and that started my life on a very new twist.

In 1951, I applied for a college scholarship through the Naval Reserve Officers' Training Corps (NROTC). I had no idea what it meant to be in the navy, much less to be an officer. But it was a way to college, and hopefully for me, a way to Notre Dame (achieving the scholarship was one step, being accepted into a particular school was a second challenge). I knew I wanted to be at Notre Dame, any way I could get there.

I received an alternate rating on the scholarship exam, and a few weeks later was accepted into the NROTC as a full scholarship student. Acceptance at Notre Dame came within a few days. I spent two years as a midshipman and regular student at Notre Dame. The summer after my freshman year included an eight-week cruise on board the USS *Missouri* (BB-63), the famous battleship built at the end of the Second World War. I was terrified as I went aboard the ship, especially when I learned that I was to be bunked with nineteen other students from the United States Naval Academy, most of them on the Naval Academy's football team. They literally cared for me throughout the cruise, and several friendships continued for thirty years and more after.

At the end of two years as a student, I entered the seminary of the Congregation of Holy Cross, the society that began Notre Dame. I resigned from the NROTC, with a notation on my military record that I had "broken contract" and could never be commissioned as a naval line officer in the future.

I was ordained a Catholic priest in June 1960 and began a year of graduate studies at Notre Dame, followed by seven years of giving parish and school retreats. In 1965, I joined the Naval Reserve, this time as a chaplain, and I laughed heartily when my earlier NROTC "dismissal" came to light. But the paper had not said that I could not become a naval staff officer. I was commissioned in 1965 and spent almost three years in the reserves, performing summer active duty for training and slowly learning the ropes of this new endeavor.

Early in 1968 the Vietnam War was expanding, and the Navy Chaplain Corps was desperately short of Catholic priests. Their office called me and my provincial superior. It seemed the right thing for me to do, and I received permission to begin active duty as a naval chaplain. I received orders to an amphibious squadron of five ships with a total crew of about 2,000, and carrying about 4,000 marines. The squadron was deployed. This was to be my new parish.

It was August 1968. I had been a priest for eight years. At the University of Notre Dame, there already was a distinctly antiwar, anti-Vietnam, antimilitary feeling among some faculty and Holy Cross priests, despite the fact that the school held the largest reserve officers training numbers in the entire country, except for the military academies. One of my brother-priests stopped me the day before I left for active duty and asked me why I was leaving the community. I replied that I did not think I was, but I felt I was following the will of God and my superiors as best I could. His comment has stayed with me until this day. It hurt, but I knew I was doing the right thing.

The air trip from South Bend to Danang took ten days, with brief layovers in California, Hawaii (just time for one Mai Tai at two in the morning) and three days at a naval air station in the Philippines, while a typhoon wandered the area, including Vietnam. I finally landed in Danang on September 6. This was a new world for me, a world of machine guns, mortars, and fear.

It was hot and muggy. My dress khaki uniform coat and tie were horribly out of place. After hitching a ride from the first navy person I saw, I went to several places and tried to check in. In the bewildering array of military "stuff," I finally found the appropriate office, was checked aboard, and assigned to a hotel that was surrounded by sandbags and machine guns. There, I was given a bed in a room with six other beds. In the room, I unpacked more comfortable clothing. I stripped bare, tossing my wet and dirty clothes on the bed. As I turned to reach for dry clothes in my bag, I saw a small, frail, Vietnamese woman sitting on the floor at the end of the bed. I had not heard her come in. She kept waving her hand at me. It took me a minute to realize she was asking for my dirty clothes. So as I stood stark naked before her, I gathered my dirty clothes, gave them to her, and said to myself, "Welcome to war, Joe!"

That night I had dinner, including steak and ice cream, with other chaplains at the officers' club. Afterward I moved to another barracks near a helicopter pad from which I could reach my ship the next morning. The laundry lady never got paid, but she did all my clothes, and I can only hope that she charged the next guy double. I did not sleep; there were mortars in the distance, rockets overhead, and I kept going over in my mind the route to the bomb shelter just outside the door.

While delayed by the typhoon in the Philippines, I became friends with a young navy ensign, who was also brand new to the military and headed for his first assignment aboard another of the ships in the same squadron. We were assigned to the same hotel for that first evening, and when I moved to another barracks closer to the helicopter pad, I went to his room to tell him to come with me. He was as afraid as I was. The other chaplains and I found him asleep, with his brand-new naval sword unsheathed and in his hand. Waking him was a delicate task.

The next morning, after a huge breakfast—when I'm scared, I eat— we went to the helicopter pad to await a ride to the ship. The ship's helo came to pick up mail, and the landing personnel asked the pilot if he would take two passengers. He said no. Then he was told that one of the passengers was the new priest. He gave a thumbs-up for me. At that, I visually gave him "either we both go or we both stay," because the young officer with me was more scared than I, if that were possible. The pilot said okay. The helicopter flew the other officer to his ship, and then landed on my new home, the USS *Tripoli* (LPH-10). Only then did I find out that the pilot was a Notre Dame alumnus, Lieutenant Commander Tom Bartholomew, whose father taught Shakespeare for thirty years at Notre Dame, and had been a classmate of my father in the class of 1927. Among the treasures of the military for me are the friendships that endure until today.

The first day after my arrival on the ship proved to be a literal baptism by blood. I had been unable to obtain the required two pairs of shatterproof eyeglasses before leaving the United States, so the very next morning I flew back into Danang and went to the naval hospital, which had a full optometry laboratory. While I was waiting for my glasses and for one of the ship's dentists who was having his own dental work done, I was called to the triage area, or emergency room. Two helicopters had brought in fifteen marines. They had been ambushed. I anointed each one, no worry then about who might be Catholic. Eight were already dead. I left the area, puked, and cried. "Welcome to war, Joe."

Chaplains are noncombatants. That means that according to the Geneva Convention we are not allowed to carry weapons, though occasionally I heard rumors about chaplains who did so. I did not. I lived on the ship, but flew almost daily trips ashore. If casualties occurred, usually a helicopter would be diverted to pick me up and I would return immediately to the ship and the triage area.

Toward the end of my third month, I was in the field moving from small group to small group, celebrating the Eucharist with those who wished to pray together. That day I had with me a young marine who had been assigned as bodyguard to the chaplain because he had told his colonel that he would not use his M-16 weapon. "Great," I said. Off we went, into the jungle. At one point we became disoriented and got lost. We were in a small village; it was empty and deathly quiet. I was afraid and wondered if I would take this marine's weapon and defend myself, and him, if I had to. Fortunately, within a very short time, perhaps two to three minutes, which seemed an eternity, two very large marines appeared from behind a house. Though we had not realized it, we had

Joe O'Donnell, C.S.C., flying in a helicopter from the USS *Tripoli* to the naval hospital, Danang (South Vietnam). Official U.S.N. photograph. Used with permission.

strayed only some ten yards from the perimeter where the marines were spread out. We continued along the perimeter, arriving within a few minutes at a platoon of about thirty young marines. I offered mass, my seventh that day. I returned to the ship without further incident, though I did inform the commanding officer that I wanted another marine assigned to me in the future. I tried to arrange for that young conscientious objector, or justifiably frightened young man, to be returned to the United States.

The next day, the battalion we were supporting medically and spiritually came under severe attack. The group for which I had celebrated my seventh mass the day before was ambushed. There were many casualties, and they could not be retrieved for two days. On the third morning, aboard ship, the code word for deceased came over the ship's public address system, and I went to the flight deck as three helicopters landed. Eighteen bodies were removed and placed on the huge elevator, which would take them down to the hangar deck for identification and the start of the long journey home to grieving families. About thirty marines and sailors stood around the body bags on the elevator, waiting for me. These eighteen men had been dead for two days; I knew that. The Catholic Sacrament of the Sick is for the living; I knew that too. But I knew what I had to do. One by one, I unzipped each body bag, and anointed whatever I found there. It was not pleasant. But it was the most solemn and powerful prayer service I have ever experienced. In the midst of all the action, there was absolute silence and lots of tears.

This first trip to Vietnam lasted from September 1968 to April 1969. During that time, I flew several hundred hours in helicopters, to other ships and ashore. The squadron spent some time "off line," generally in order to resupply, but also to give us a rest. Finally, the squadron headed for home. We crossed the Pacific in about twenty days, after taking our embarked marines to Okinawa. Arriving home in San Diego was an extremely emotional event. Hundreds of people lined the pier, looking for their loved ones on the ship. At first, I felt very alone, since I did not have any close family in the San Diego area. But when I looked down on the pier, I saw my godfather's son and his wife. He too was a naval officer, and we had met once while we both were deployed. He and his wife made my welcome a tearful one, but tears of joy instead of loneliness.

We stayed in San Diego for about five months while the ship received needed repairs, supplies were received, and most of the crew had

Vietnam, 1968. Father O'Donnell says a prayer for those who have died. Each rifle and bayonet in the ground with a helmet on top represents a marine who gave his life. Personal photograph. Used with permission.

some time at home with their loved ones. In the fall, we hurriedly left again for Vietnam, with only a four-hour stopover in Guam to refuel the ship. We arrived in Danang harbor, for the first time tied up at a pier under full alert wartime conditions, and loaded one of the last marine battalions to take them to Okinawa. This was the beginning of our withdrawal from the Vietnam War. On the way to Okinawa, we encountered a typhoon in the North China Sea. There were few on the ship who were not sick. I set my own record one evening when I celebrated mass for some fifty marines and sailors . . . in six minutes. After leaving those marines in Okinawa, the ship continued operations in the southwest Pacific. I was detached from the ship in the first week of 1970, and headed for a new assignment at the National Naval Medical Center in Bethesda, Maryland. There I would meet hundreds of young victims of the war, as they struggled to get well and return to lives as normal as they could ever make them.

Being a chaplain in the military is not all about war, blood, and guts. Much of the chaplain's work is the same as that of any parish priest. Not every minister, priest, or rabbi is suited to be in institutional ministry, especially in ministry where there can be violence. If I were choosing chaplains, I would look for three qualities.

The first is that he or she have the ability to listen, to listen not only to words, but to, and with, both heart and soul. The ability to listen includes the willingness to accept people where they are in their own understanding of life and faith, not where the chaplain would like them to be. As a chaplain, I must realize that no matter how firm I feel about my own approach to God, I cannot have the last word for anyone else.

This concept of pluralism is perhaps the most significant change in the chaplaincy from earlier times. In the Second World War, chaplains in the United States military included Roman Catholic priests, a very few rabbis, and ministers from six major Protestant denominations. By 1994, my last year in the navy, there were more than 150 faith groups providing chaplains to the military. Ten years later, there are even more.

The second requirement is that the chaplain be credible. I have to live what I believe. I have to be a person of faith, and hope, and love—yes, love—in the midst of war. Over my years in service, there was ample opportunity to give moral input to human situations that were ethically difficult. Part of being credible is also that I realize I have only part of the answer, not all of it. I am a player, a teammate, a consultant, an idealist living in reality. Credibility is not a given in the military, as it may be in civilian churches or denominational institutions. One earns his or her place by being there, by listening, by keeping secrets, by speaking when it is time to speak, and not speaking when it is not. Deciding those times is not always crystal clear.

The third requirement is that a chaplain understand the nature of confidentiality, or Rule of Privilege, as it is called in the *Manual for Courts Martial*, the operative, judicial portion of the Uniform Code of Military Justice. The chaplain is covered by a particular federal law. It is quite restrictive, with a presumption of privilege for almost any one-on-one conversation. As a chaplain, I have to know when to keep my mouth shut. Nothing could be worse for a chaplain than to be labeled someone who cannot keep a secret. If that occurs, his or her ministry is finished. The chaplain's assistant or secretary is also covered by the *Manual for Courts Martial*. That provision is very different from civilian law, in which an assistant or secretary usually is not free to withhold the secret of a confidant in the exercise of official business.

There have been a number of federal court cases involving the Rule of Privilege. In my almost thirty years as a naval chaplain, I never heard of any chaplain deliberately violating this rule. I did see cases where a law seemed to have been broken (but was not), and also cases where an individual chaplain did not interpret the law correctly (those cases eventually were settled by a judge, with the Rule of Privilege maintained).

In 1976, after two years at the National Naval Medical Center in Bethesda, a year as pastor at a combined navy and air force base in Keflavik, Iceland, two and a half years at a naval hospital in Portsmouth, Virginia, and a year of graduate study in medical ethics at the Institute of Religion, University of Texas Medical Center in Houston, I was sent overseas to Okinawa to be the only priest at a large hospital that the navy was taking over from the army. I would share those hospital duties with one Lutheran chaplain, a close friend.

It was peacetime. Okinawa is home to thousands of American military personnel. The United States government controls about 10 percent of the land there, and there have been constant objections raised by the Okinawan people concerning this inundation of American personnel since the end of the Second World War. Most of the duty there would be similar to that at any local hospital—most of the time.

It was the fall of 1976, and a typical, peaceful morning in Okinawa. I had been at the hospital only a few weeks. Naval personnel taking the place of the previous army staff had been arriving each week, until we now had a naval staff of about four hundred personnel. One day, we were scheduled to have a disaster drill, to see if we were ready for a major incident. At lunch, some of us noticed a large CH-46 marine helicopter, capable of carrying forty to fifty people, go by the hospital, fly out over the water, and then dive right into the ocean. We waited only a minute. The coded alarms went off in the hospital. The public address system cut in, "This is not a drill, this is not a drill; prepare for major casualties." Lunches were left on the tables. Visitors were asked to leave. Clinics were cleared of regular patients. All four hundred hospital staff were summoned from bed, or baseball, or lunch, or wherever, and in ten minutes we were ready to receive casualties, having no idea how many people were on the helicopter. As it turned out, there were only four young marines: a pilot, co-pilot, and two crew.

The crash had occurred on a reef just offshore. Other helicopters came to the scene and looked for survivors. Ground personnel and ambulances soon arrived at the shore only a few hundred yards from the helicopter. The victims were removed and flown to us one at a time. The first victim was dead on arrival, yet our doctors worked feverishly to find any sign of life. The man was soaked with gasoline, and I remember our neurosurgeon, a constant smoker, entering the triage area with a lit cigarette. A military policeman literally tackled him and removed him from the area before he blew us all up.

The second and third victims were brought separately by helicopter, both of them already dead. All of their families were back home in the United States, and the difficult job of notification would be done by others. The fourth victim was pinned under the engine of the fallen helicopter. It took three hours to release him. This young officer was engaged to one of our navy nurses. She was at work on the third floor. Everyone in the hospital seemed to know that he was her fiancé. But his death had to be confirmed first by his commanding officer. I was kept apprised by a cell phone. The commanding officer of the squadron finally called me and verified that they had removed the body and identified him. I then walked to the third-floor nursing station. I did not have to say a word. I simply hugged her, as other nurses and doctors waited in the adjoining corridor. As soon as I could, I left and went to my office, sat down, and cried. "My God, how long can I do this?" I said to myself. "Welcome to war, Joe, even in peacetime."

Just about every minister knows that the most difficult part of dealing with grief and loss is notifying the next of kin. In the military, sadly, those calls came frequently during the Vietnam War, as in every other conflict. While on inactive naval reserve duty in the summers of 1967 and 1968, I made a number of "casualty calls" in southern California. Almost every time, the young officer whom I accompanied would say to me, "Chaplain, I've never done this before. Would you take the lead and tell me what to do and say?"

On one occasion it was late evening as our official vehicle stopped in front of a home near Riverside, California. A young marine captain and I were about to notify a family that their son had been killed. We rang the doorbell, and a woman of about forty answered the door, saw our uniforms, and immediately said, "Oh, you must know my son Jimmy." We did not, and we had bad news. After asking her if anyone else was home, and learning her husband was at work, we sat with her in the living room, told her what we knew, and waited—for four hours. The shock was immense. Our job was to help as much as we could.

Those occasions were never easy and never the same. In later years, after the birth of CNN, it became more difficult to make such notifications. The media were and are of absolutely no help and have little concern for the feelings of those affected. On one occasion in 1981, when I was stationed in the Office of the Chief of Naval Operations, one of my staff chaplains and a senior naval officer were rushed by police escort to a home to inform a family of the death of their daughter, a naval officer on the west coast. When they arrived, a CNN truck was already parked near the house. Even though the process of notification went smoothly and quickly, we simply could not get there as fast as the media could.

Notifications of events from home occurred as well. In Japan during my tour at the naval hospital (1976–78), I notified a young marine corporal, after finding him in an off-base bar on a Sunday afternoon, that his brother had been killed by police gunfire in a shootout. His only comment was, "I wondered when it would happen." A great group of marines and a little chaplain savvy made it possible for us to delay an air force C-141 transport plane at Kadena Air Force Base next door, get this young man packed, have his commanding officer issue new orders returning him to the United States, and get him on the plane, all within one hour.

After I completed two years at the hospital in Okinawa, the then navy chief of chaplains, Rear Admiral John J. O'Connor (later John Cardinal O'Connor, archbishop of New York), selected me to be on the staff of the Naval Chaplains School, Newport, Rhode Island. In 1981, the new chief of chaplains, replacing Admiral O'Connor, asked me to become his executive assistant in Washington, D.C. The position is much like that of the chancellor in a Catholic diocese (not the chancellor in an Episcopal diocese; the latter is always a lawyer). Duties included being the office manager for a staff of thirty-five persons, the direct liaison with all the endorsing churches, confidant to the chief of chaplains, and as it turned out for me, being the senior priest in the navy. The job involved a great deal of responsibility and daily contact with the senior officers of the navy and U.S. Marine Corps. It was an administrative position, most of the time.

In 1983, one week after the horrendous explosion at the marine barracks in Beirut, Lebanon, at 7 a.m., I boarded a presidential helicopter at the Pentagon, along with my boss, the chief of chaplains; Admiral Jim Watkins, the chief of naval operations; Watkin's aide; General Patrick Xavier Kelley, the commandant of the Marine Corps; and Kelly's aide. The six of us were flown to Dover Air Force Base, Delaware, for the arrival of the first fifteen bodies of those who had been killed in the Beirut explosion. We were the official welcoming party for the president of the United States. The ceremony was held in a huge hangar. Hundreds of media people were on hand. Fifteen caskets were lined up in impeccable order, each covered by an American flag, each accompanied by a marine in full dress uniform. The ceremony was short and somber. There weren't many words that could be said to express the grief that could be felt in that huge hangar. It hurt, believe me.

Before the ceremony, in cooperation with the United States air force, I set up a twenty-four-hour chaplains' office on the base, because families would be coming there from all over the United States during the following weeks. Protestant, Catholic, and Jewish chaplains from the navy and air force would be available around the clock at the base chapel, which would be the meeting place for the families and also a place where they could be free of the often intrusive media.

On the way back to Washington, the chief of naval operations said to me, "Joe, we have to do something about terrorism. What we do has to be moral, ethical." By the time we landed at the Pentagon, we had laid plans for a series of conferences to be held on the subject, "A Moral Response to Terrorism." I was asked to construct and administer the conferences. Over the next few months, three seminars were held at the Naval War College in Newport, Rhode Island. Attendees included Protestant, Catholic, and Jewish theologians, along with personnel from various security agencies, the military, and the State Department. The written outcome of these conferences became the Reagan policy. It was the most exciting thing I did while in service. The results have only recently been released from their top-secret security status, and at least a couple of attendees have written books on the subject. Such things simply do not happen without credibility, without trust, without the ability and willingness to work within a system.

When I was working on an early draft of this essay in January 2000, the American media wrote about the first military chaplain in the modern Russian armed forces. He is a Russian Orthodox priest. In 1994, during my final tour in the capital, I was part of a team of American military chaplains that hosted a delegation of five senior Russian officers who came to the United States to learn about chaplains. They were former KGB, political, or regular military officers. As part of our briefing, we flew them in air force helicopters from the Pentagon to the United States Naval Academy at Annapolis, Maryland. In the course of our day there, one of them said to us, "Well, you just give us two million Bibles in Russian. We will tell our men that they are orthodox Christians; it will be okay then." It was a challenge to explain to them that times, even within Christianity, had changed, that religious freedom was a precious gift, and that they would have to start from the beginning to bring any form of faith to their personnel.

I do not intend to take up here the issue of religious freedom and religious accommodation. The army faced that challenge thirty years ago when two Harvard law students filed a suit against the army, stating that the military chaplaincy was unconstitutional, a violation of the separation of church and state. It took years, but a federal judge finally ruled in favor of the right of military personnel to have opportunities for worship and prayer, no matter where they might be stationed.

The challenge now, and the most remarkable change that I see in U.S. chaplaincies over the past fifty years, is that of accommodating the increasing numbers of small faith groups, including some single congregations, that desire to be registered as Department of Defense endorsing agencies. These latter are the civilian agencies that approve chaplains for service in the military, stating that they are prepared according to the norms of each faith group. There is currently pressure from diverse faiths to alter the standards for entry into the chaplaincies. Some groups do not have either the preparation time or the experience required for chaplains. Still others are focused on the fertile valleys of young souls for proselytization, forgetting that theirs may be the only chaplain on a ship of six hundred crew, responsible for providing and facilitating worship opportunities for members of many faiths.

The challenge to the system is the necessity of providing religious accommodation for an increasing religious diversity among members of the military service. These diverse religious needs have to be met by recruiting and retaining chaplains or perhaps other religious providers in the necessary numbers and religious orientations, though it will be impossible to accommodate every religious faith in a specific manner. This effort to accommodate as many faiths as possible is a factor directly contributing to the overall readiness of the force.

In 1993 the commanding officer of a ship called me in Washington and asked what to do with a young seaman who stated that he was a Wiccan and who desired to observe the winter solstice, December 22, as a religious holiday. I suggested that he give the young man the day off, but to be sure that he was on the duty roster three days later, on Christmas Day.

Orthodox Jews frequently are discharged if they feel that they simply cannot fulfill their religious requirements, even though the military tries to provide kosher food, at least for the high holy days. Other cases have not been so easy. One of the major concerns for the chaplaincy in the U.S. military is that individual interpretations of spirituality and conscience have become a substitute for creedal confession and denominational guidance. In 1999, a young air force officer was disciplined and eventually removed from his position as a missile silo officer because he said that he could not stand watch alone in a silo with a female, given his religious faith (Catholic), the fact that he was married, and the confined work space. The archbishop for the military services agreed with him. But where will it end? More than one sympathizer has wondered if the outcome would have been different if the young officer had been a Muslim. Some critics feel that the government is willing to accommodate almost everyone.

In 2000 a situation arose involving an air force first lieutenant who told her superior officers that God had informed her, with the guidance of her religious faith, that she must not wear trousers. The problem is that she is a pilot, in whose training the government has invested hundreds of thousands of dollars. She wants to wear a skirt in the cockpit, both a practical impossibility given the structure of the cockpit and a safety factor as well, since military flight suits are fire-retardant. Her church says that they will support her. As of this writing, the case is unresolved.

Catholic priests have served with distinction from the very beginning of American chaplaincies; however, there have never been enough priests to meet the needs of military personnel. At the present time, the shortage is more critical than ever. In 2000 the army chief of chaplains reported that he had only eighty priests for the entire army (active duty members and their families). The military generally reflects the civilian religious census. Approximately 25 percent of all military personnel are Catholic, with the proportion among the marines running much higher. The religious needs of Catholics often are not being met in the services. It is not much better today in many civilian communities as the Catholic Church goes through a long period of renewal and change. For a time during the 1980s and 1990s, the navy accepted priests up to the age of fifty, an exception to the standard of accepting chaplains only up to the age of thirty-six. These older priests forfeited all rights to military retirement, since they would have to leave before they could achieve twenty years of active service; these older men made heroic sacrifices to meet the needs of Catholic personnel. At the same time, adopting this as a full-time policy would unbalance the structure of the Chaplain Corps, and would prevent priests, if all were older when they entered, from becoming senior officers in positions of making policy.

Prior to the end of the Vietnam War, the presence of women in the armed services was limited, more so in combat areas where only nurses served, for the most part. After that conflict, the number of women in the services grew immensely, and in the late 1970s, the navy commissioned its first woman chaplain. She and those who followed her had an uphill battle for years. They were "invading" two almost totally male enclaves, the ministry and the military. The first women chaplains were a wonderful and courageous group. They broke ground for new concepts and new challenges while bringing the best of spirituality to our personnel. The presence of ordained female ministers, however, remains a question for many denominations.

Chaplains are not perfect. Until the 1990s, if chaplains or other professionals such as doctors, nurses, or lawyers got into trouble, they would usually be quietly removed from their positions and discharged from military service. Not so any more. One of the most difficult aspects of my job in Washington (1981–84, 1992–94) was to be a liaison with chaplains who were in trouble, and also a liaison for the navy to the ecclesiastical endorsing agents for the churches. I once gave a talk to a major Baptist conference. As I spoke, I knew that one of the chaplains from this church was in trouble for sexual misconduct. He was standing on the stage with me and other chaplains. Within a few days, I had to visit their bishop and inform him that we wanted to discharge that chaplain and do it quickly. I had received a phone call from a four-star marine general, telling me to get this man off his base and out of his command, which included the entire Pacific, in twenty-four hours. I told the general that even the chaplain had to have his day in court. He did not want to hear that. As quickly as we could, we conducted the proper hearing. One late evening—and there were many— in the Pentagon, I had the discharge paper signed by the secretary of the navy. I then called the general in Hawaii, and told him to "make the chaplain a civilian." That man was fortunate to get out without a court martial. Others have not been so lucky. Most painful for me was the obligation to visit two chaplains as they served time in the federal military prison in Fort Leavenworth, Kansas. Both have now been released and discharged. One even wrote me a letter in early 2000.

Finally, there has been a major shift in the work of the military, and it affects all chaplains. A navy priest friend had the following experience. His helicopter carrier and several other ships loaded with two thousand marines were sent to Chittagong, Bangladesh, after a major typhoon. When they arrived, they saw that hundreds of bodies filled the harbor. The troops helped with body recovery and burial, assisting the local government and the various religions in that predominantly Muslim country, including our own missionaries of the Congregation of Holy Cross. In general, however, the role of the chaplain in humanitarian and peacekeeping operations remains undefined. The possibilities are numerous; for example, navy chaplains stationed with the United States Coast Guard have been deeply involved in the aftermath of recent commercial air crashes—Egypt Air 990 off the coast of Newport, Rhode Island and Alaska Air 261 off the coast of Port Hueneme, California. Both areas have large naval installations.

Let me end where I began, in Vietnam. In October 1968 I had been aboard the USS *Tripoli* only a few weeks. One of the physicians on the surgical team told me that he was ready to return home, and that he had identified 155 bodies during his one-year tour. I used to debrief every evening with the two surgeons and the anesthesiologist, talking over each case, those who lived, those who had died that day. These physicians and surgeons often worked eighteen to twenty hours straight.

One afternoon, the haunting word, "incoming," came over the public address system. My place was on the triage upper level, just above the hangar deck. Several marines were brought to the ship by helicopter, and the most seriously wounded came immediately to where I was stationed. One of the doctors called me to help him. A young staff sergeant had been critically wounded and needed a chest tube. I anointed the sergeant and held him in my arms while a doctor made a small incision and inserted the tube. The man bled out about three pints of blood almost all at once. The doctor's eyes said it all. I just held him, a twenty-eight-year-old husband and father, as he talked of his life. He asked me to write a letter to his wife, to tell her that he loved her, and that he had been faithful. Within a few minutes, he died in my arms. It was most painful to lay him back on the gurney and move on to other patients. Later that night, I wrote his wife a letter, gave it to my clerk to type, and went on to myriad other duties, including celebrating mass for him and for others. The next morning, I signed and mailed the letter and more or less forgot about it in the continual rush of other responsibilities. Several weeks later, we were still on the line off the coast of Vietnam. I received a letter from the young staff sergeant's wife, thanking me for what I had done and telling me that if ever I came through San Antonio, to please call her and visit.

Life went on; there were many other dead, many other maimed, many other injured. But a year or so later, in 1970, I stopped in San Antonio to visit a retired air force chaplain, Father Tom Hewitt, C.S.C. I called the dead marine's wife and told her I was in town for one day. She asked me to meet her and her two children at their parochial school and then go to lunch. We ate at McDonald's, and I told them what I could, what I knew. After lunch, she told me I had to come to the house that evening because the whole family would be there. I already had dinner plans, but felt that I had to say yes. When I arrived at the home, more than fifty people were there: neighbors, parents, cousins, family, friends. Each had brought something for a party. When the group quieted, the woman introduced me: "This is Raymond's priest." I swallowed hard and tried to say something and to pray. Inside the house, in the dining room, a glass cabinet stood in a prominent place. In it were Raymond's picture, his medals and ribbons, and my letter.

I retired from active duty in September 1994 and spent the next two and a half years as superior and administrator of Holy Cross House, a retirement and medical residence for the priests and brothers of the Congregation of Holy Cross, located near the campus of the University of Notre Dame. I was then transferred to a community house in Phoenix, Arizona, where I now reside. In the fall of 1997, I endured my own post-traumatic stress syndrome, and many other things, through a long bout of acute clinical depression. I spent almost nine months "finding myself" and learning that I could never be the perfect human being that I expected of myself and thought others expected of me. I came to understand my own humanness, and I have been able to look back over the last thirty-four years and see the amazing life that I have had during my time in military service. Although I have made many mistakes, I have also become the person I am supposed to be at this time in my life.

One of the primary issues that plagued me were those words that Raymond said to me the day he died, "Tell her I have been faithful." For thirty years, I had carried those words in my conscious and unconscious mind, sure that in my own life as a priest I had not been faithful, and hence creating in myself an immense fear of God and death. Thanks to some very good therapy, I now see life in a much better way. Today, I live and work in Phoenix, as a "semi-retired" priest. I substitute two days a week for the priest at the Veterans' Administration Medical Center, have a daily liturgy in our chapel where I live, do weekend parish work about every other week, volunteer three days a week as senior chaplain for the Arizona Highway Patrol—that's where I am living my "second childhood"—and serve on an Air Disaster Response Team for the National Transportation Safety Board and American Red Cross. I haven't felt this good in more than thirty years. And I would do it all over in a heartbeat.

NOTE

This essay may not contain all the references, footnotes, and professional data that should be here. But it is my story. I am grateful to my fellow-priests who read my paper and made comments, to Doris Bergen for her valuable suggestions, and to Chaplain Russ Gunter (captain, Chaplain Corps, United States Navy), executive secretary to the Armed Forces Chaplains Board, Department of Defense, for his insights and recommendations.

CHAPTER ELEVEN

From Morale Builders to Moral Advocates

U.S. Army Chaplains in the Second Half of the Twentieth Century

ANNE C. LOVELAND

During the second half of the twentieth century, providing religious services so that military personnel could worship God according to their particular faith continued to be the focal point of the U.S. Army chaplains' ministry, as it had been since the beginning of the chaplaincy. However, moral guidance and morale building were also important duties. Although the commander bore the ultimate responsibility for "the religious life, morals and morale within the command," the chaplain, as a staff officer and an adviser and consultant to the commander, was regarded as having "specialized knowledge" and was expected to "display appropriate initiative in recommending policies" regarding such matters.[1]

Chaplains' moral guidance and morale-building duties were more limited in the first half of the twentieth century than they became later on and were only tangentially related to military training. During the Second World War, for example, chaplains gave the mandatory "Sex Morality Lecture" that recruits received during basic training. They also worked closely with Special Service officers in organizing enter-tainment and recreational activities for the troops. Perhaps their most important contribution to morale was counseling soldiers regarding personal and family concerns, as well as the problems they experienced in adjusting to military life.[2]

During the second half of the twentieth century, army chaplains' responsibilities for morals and morale were more broadly interpreted and became more formalized. In the late 1940s, chaplains developed a program called Character Guidance to provide religious, moral, and citizenship instruction to all army personnel. Instituted in 1947, the program was a command responsibility, but the lectures were prepared in the Office of the Chief of Chaplains (OCCH) and presented by army chaplains. In the 1950s, recruits received four lectures during basic training and another two lectures during advanced individual train-ing; all other personnel were required to attend monthly, hour-long presentations. In the 1960s, however, officers and enlisted personnel of grade E-6 (staff sergeant) and higher were required to attend only a "monthly briefing" on the content of instruction presented to lower-ranking personnel.[3]

The religious orientation of Character Guidance was obvious. In-deed, army chaplains claimed that the principles they taught came from the "Natural Law" and the "Moral Law," which in turn came from God. In the same breath, however, they insisted that the program was non-sectarian. The lecture titled, "One Nation Under God," which was the first of the four presentations given to soldiers during basic training in the 1950s and early 1960s, reveals the religious emphasis characteris-tic of many other lectures. According to the chaplain's guide, its basic theme was that *"We as a nation are DEPENDENT upon and RESPON-SIBLE to Almighty God."* In concluding the lecture, the chaplain was directed to "EMPHASIZE: That we must cultivate within ourselves the religious beliefs and attitudes that were a part of those who built our nation."[4]

Although one of the main reasons the army instituted Character Guidance was to reduce the high incidence of venereal disease among soldiers, Character Guidance did not limit chaplains' moral guidance to sexual matters. The lectures prepared by the Army Chaplain Board inculcated a wide range of "personal and civic virtues," including not only religious faith, but also self-reliance, courage, obedience, fair play, and persistence. The stated objective of the program was "to develop the kind of soldier who has sufficient moral understanding and courage to do the right thing in whatever situation he may find himself."[5]

Character Guidance may be seen as the first of several steps the chaplaincy took during the second half of the twentieth century to gain recognition as an essential participant in military training. In September 1947, commenting on the recent establishment of the program, Chief of Chaplains (Major General) Luther D. Miller observed, "The army chaplain is no longer playing guard; he is in the backfield. Commanding officers more and more are making up plays with the chaplain carrying the ball." He predicted that in the future, the chaplain would increasingly be called upon to serve as "a specialist in . . . morale as well as an authority in religion."[6]

The Cold War heightened the importance of the chaplains' programs. Viewing the Cold War as a struggle between godless communism and God-fearing democracy, many Americans believed America's chief weapon in the Cold War was its "moral power." The religious construction of the Cold War exerted a decisive influence on the army chaplaincy and reinforced its claim to a vital role in military training. Chaplains assumed the task of indoctrinating soldiers in the religious and moral principles basic to "the American way of life." As Chief of Chaplains Frank A. Tobey explained in 1959, "An essential deterrent against our enemy must remain the courageous heart, the right conscience, the clear head, the strong body fortified with the truth and obedient to the dictates of moral good."[7]

In the 1960s, the chaplaincy continued to press for recognition as an important participant in military training. For example, in 1961, the OCCH urged the United States Continental Army Command to insure that the army leadership made "full use of religious and spiritual values as motivation factors."[8] Both the 1964 chaplain field manual and the 1968 Character Guidance manual emphasized the way the chaplains' programs improved soldiers' fighting capability. In a discussion of the chaplain's mission, the 1964 manual noted that along with "native bravery and thorough training," the "spiritual sense of obligation to duty," which the chaplain instilled or reinforced, "will produce the very best type of soldier" and a "devoted defender of the nation."[9] The 1968 manual cited army research showing that "under combat pressure it is not the loud-swearing, bravado-soldier of peacetime who does the required job for his country on the battlefield. Rather, it is the man of resolute character and strong moral convictions." In contrast to the "nonfighters" who exhibited "indifference to socially desirable values," the "actual fighters" had "much to fight for and a will to preserve their values," and were thus able to "stand up under enemy fire or under the rigors of POW existence without breaking."[10] Both the 1964 and 1967 chaplain field manuals pointed out the many ways chaplains inculcated the "clear abiding faith in God and strong spiritual and moral convictions" that gave the soldier "a purpose in life and the motivation to faithfully serve his home, his God, and his country whether in combat or in captivity."[11]

The crucible of Vietnam exposed the strengths and weaknesses of army chaplains' efforts to inculcate morality and build morale. The "ministry of presence" they provided to soldiers in the combat zone constituted their most important contribution to morale. Accompanying the men on combat missions, living in the dust and mud with them, eating the same rations, sharing the trauma and losses of battle—that kind of intimate association, apart from their performance of the usual priestly and pastoral duties—earned chaplains the gratitude of many enlisted men and officers.[12]

However, the Vietnam War also revealed deficiencies. The fact that army chaplains overwhelmingly supported the war, even to the point of endorsing it "in the name of religion," alienated many soldiers. After the war, in veterans' counseling programs and investigative hearings, Vietnam veterans offered examples of what they called "chaplain bullshit": "chaplains blessing the troops, their mission, their guns, their killing."[13] A blatant example was provided by the chaplain who, when asked by Colonel George S. Patton III to pray for a large body count, offered the following petition: "Oh, Lord, give us the wisdom to find the bastards and the strength to pile on."[14]

Shortcomings in the Character Guidance program also became apparent. The chaplaincy never achieved the attendance rate it hoped for, and during the Vietnam War, the percentage of enlisted men not receiving regular monthly Character Guidance instruction increased significantly.[15] Those who did attend the lectures reacted with "either bored resignation or bemused cynicism."[16] Commanders' skepticism also increased.[17] Many of them dismissed Character Guidance as "the chaplains' program." Most doubted the chaplains' claims that character education enhanced combat motivation and performance. Commanders believed that soldiers fought more for their buddies and their unit than for their country or ideological or religious convictions; combat effectiveness depended on unit cohesion rather than patriotism or piety.[18] Most important, the inculcation of religious and moral principles failed to prevent the careerism, alcohol and drug abuse, racial animosities, "fraggings," and illegal acts of war that many observers cited as proof of the disintegration of the army.[19]

Just as the chaplains' support for the Vietnam War offended some soldiers, so did their failure to address the moral questions raised by the war. In the United States, the chaplains represented themselves as moral authorities, but in Vietnam they seemed unwilling to respond or incapable of responding meaningfully to the queries their men posed. Some seemed immune to doubts about warfare and killing, perhaps because of their strong support for the U.S. intervention or because they had not been challenged to consider such issues in seminary or at the Army Chaplain School. Whatever the reason, their responses dissatisfied many soldiers. One soldier, who testified at the Dellums Committee Hearings on War Crimes in Vietnam, recalled an occasion when he went to talk with his battalion chaplain because he felt guilty about shooting at an old Vietnamese woman who was probably a civilian:

All he said was, "Well, we all see things in war that we don't like, that we don't want to see."

And he said, "Well, could you help it?"

And I told him that yes, I could, I guess I could. Maybe I shouldn't have shot.

And he says, "Well, it could have been VC, right?"

And I said, "Yes, it could have been."

But he sort of rationalized it away and he gave me the statement of "Let's pray to God that He will give us courage and strength to carry on with the mission."

Now this upset my thinking with the religion. He was praying for God to give us courage and strength to keep doing what we were doing.

Well, from there on I never attended any more services.[20]

Chaplains' performance as advisers and consultants to their commanders on morals within their command also rendered them vulnerable to censure. When news of the My Lai massacre broke, critics of the Vietnam War indicted the chaplains for their "silence . . . in the face of moral atrocities" and their failure to exercise their "special prophetic responsibility."[21] The record shows that a few chaplains did protest successfully against war crimes, either preventing their occurrence or helping to bring the perpetrators to justice.[22] Given the extent of illegal acts of war in Vietnam, it seems likely that more than a few chaplains were aware of such incidents and did little or nothing about them;[23] we will never know for sure.

In the case of the My Lai massacre, however, what the chaplains did and did not do and that they acted inappropriately has been well documented. The two chaplains involved were not so much silent as ineffectual. One of them, Division Artillery Chaplain (Captain) Carl E. Creswell, learned of the massacre from Warrant Officer Hugh C. Thompson, Jr., a helicopter pilot who had witnessed the incident. Creswell advised him to lodge an official protest in command channels (which Thompson did) and said he would do the same through "chaplain channels." Creswell then informed his superior in the chain of command, American Division Chaplain (Lieutenant Colonel) Francis R. Lewis, about the allegation, and Lewis said he would forward it through the operations officer for the division. Lewis claimed he talked with him, as well as two other division staff officers, about the massacre, but at the inquiry conducted by Lieutenant General William R. Peers one and a half years later, all three denied any recollection of his doing so. The U.S. Army's Peers Commission Report concluded that Lewis's discussions with the division officers were so informal and vague that they failed to register on the officers. Lewis also claimed to have spoken with the 11th Brigade chaplain, Major Raymond P. Hoffman, but at the Peers inquiry Hoffman denied it. Hoffman did say that Creswell told him he had reports that "our people had fired into women and children," and that Creswell continually "ragged" him and "pulled his leg," but never offered any specific information or made specific allegations, and so he did not take him seriously.

The army filed no formal charges against the two chaplains. However, the Peers Report did criticize them, saying, "It is clear from the actions—and the acts of omission—of Chaplains Lewis and Creswell, that while both were aware of the serious nature of the charges alleged by WO1 Thompson, neither took adequate or timely steps to bring these charges to the attention of his commander. It should have been evident to both these chaplains that the idea of conducting an investigation of a war crime through chaplain channels was preposterous." General Peers specifically criticized Lewis for conducting his own personal inquiry and then, when it proved futile, failing to ensure that an adequate investigation was conducted; Peers also criticized Lewis for limiting his action at division headquarters to "informal discussions with various staff officers." Peers faulted Creswell for failing to report the matter to his commanding officer (the division artillery commander) or to the staff judge advocate or the inspector general; and for reporting only to Chaplain Lewis and then, upon receiving no satisfactory response, failing to take effective action to ensure that an investigation would be conducted. Creswell, himself, provided perhaps the most acute judgment on his conduct. He was quoted as saying, "In hindsight, I feel I should have done more. . . . God forbid that in a similar situation, any Chaplain should ever be content with the actions I took."[24]

Even before the Vietnam War ended, the army chaplaincy adopted a new approach to morale building and moral guidance. Many factors impelled the reorientation, including the chaplaincy's recognition of the deficiencies of some of its programs and of the problems the army confronted in the last years of the war. No doubt the anti-Vietnam critics' indictment of the chaplains also exerted some influence.

On the one hand, the new approach entailed a gradual reduction of the chaplains' morale-building role. As early as 1970, the OCCH rejected the idea that the chaplain instilled faith in men in order to motivate them in battle. "The chaplain is not an instrument for the conditioning process to make good fighting men," the OCCH declared. It pointed out, "That men of great spiritual strength" were generally "good soldiers" was simply a "bonus" the army received from supporting religious programs for the troops.[25]

On the other hand, the new approach broadened the chaplains' moral-guidance role in several significant ways. Major General Gerhardt W. Hyatt, who became the army chief of chaplains in 1971, led the way by expanding the chaplain's mission to include an "institutional ministry," a ministry to the military as an institution rather than only to individual members of the armed forces. It was also a "prophetic ministry," aimed at "transform[ing] the society in which we live." Hyatt urged chaplains to become "agents of change," exerting influence not only on the members of their congregations, but on the army as a system, "on its institutions, its policies, its practices and its way of life."

Describing the objectives of the institutional ministry, Hyatt declared: "We are in business to help replace social injury with personal wholeness, schism with harmony and dysfunctional behaviors with positive life styles." Under his leadership, chaplains developed programs to address drug and alcohol abuse and to improve race relations. They replaced Character Guidance with two new "nontheological and non-sectarian" character education programs. Instead of imposing a value system on the soldier, as in the Character Guidance program, chaplains who administered the newer programs were supposed to "assist him to develop his own meaningful value system." Chaplains also created another new program, Personal Effectiveness Training (PET), to improve the leadership effectiveness of junior officers and NCOs by training them in communication, problem-solving, and counseling skills.[26]

Although, as mentioned earlier, the chaplaincy in 1970 rejected the idea of chaplains being involved in combat motivation, it did not entirely give up the role of morale builder. One of the purposes of PET, as well as of the Ministry of Human Relations (which counseled commanders on race relations issues and conducted sensitivity training workshops for chaplains and line officers), was to enhance the quality of life in the military community. Indeed, in its continuing campaign to impress upon army leaders the vital role chaplains could play in the armed forces, the OCCH emphasized the way their "ministry to the institution" meshed with the military's efforts to "humanize" the army, first in the experimental "liberalization program" of the early 1970s and then in the All-Volunteer Force instituted in 1973. Among other things, the "liberalization" effort and the All-Volunteer Force promoted a "participatory" as opposed to an authoritarian approach to leadership, with emphasis on "communication" between officers and enlisted personnel. Such "people-oriented" goals impressed chaplains because of their professed interest in "people problems" and "human concerns," and doubtless also because such goals seemed to promise a significant role for the chaplaincy.[27]

Gaining the attention of commanders and approval for chaplains' programs proved much easier in the 1970s than it had been in the 1950s and 1960s. In 1973, speaking at the Annual Command Chaplains' Conference, Hyatt observed: "Commanders are requesting chaplains to develop in their units and on their posts a more rewarding quality of life. This demand is testimony to the confidence they have in us. I am convinced that credence in our professional ability has never been greater, or more deserved."[28] Later, in an interview given after he had retired as chief of chaplains, Hyatt explained military leaders' enthusiasm for the new programs. He pointed out that "the top leadership of the army was looking everywhere. Who can help us? What can we do? They were so open to new things that had any possibility of success. Because the army was down so far, and because morale was so bad, when we took a program [to the army leadership], we got an ear right away. Ten years before they'd have said, 'Well, that's another Character Guidance Program, or something[,] you know.' They aren't saying that now."[29]

Army leaders also welcomed chaplain support in addressing the leadership crisis of the 1970s. Rampant careerism, the inflated "body counts" and the My Lai cover-up during the Vietnam War, and the 1976 cheating scandal at the U.S. Military Academy, all signaled that "something had gone fundamentally wrong with the values and ethics of the officer corps."[30] A series of army investigations, along with an outpouring of books and articles by civilian as well as military commentators, pointed to a broad and apparently growing gap between officers' professed ideals (duty, honor, country) and their self-interested attitudes and actions. The result was a wide-ranging effort to improve the ethical and moral aspects of leadership.[31]

Hyatt seized the opportunity to involve chaplains in the effort. He wrote two friends, the commanding generals at Fort Knox and Fort Benning, and proposed a deal: "If they would put a chaplain on the faculty of their school to teach . . . in the area of ethics and human relations and then also have a course on how a commander should use his chaplain, then I would give them the best chaplain we had in the corps to do this job." The overture worked. "Within days, I had a letter back— 'Send him!'" Soon, other commandants heard about what was going on at the Armor School and the Infantry School and requested chaplain instructors. By mid-1973, chaplains were teaching courses in nine branch service schools. In 1974 the number rose to fourteen, and when Hyatt left office the following year, chaplains held instructor positions in twenty schools.[32]

Hyatt's successors in the OCCH, Major General Orris E. Kelly (1975–79) and Major General Kermit D. Johnson (1979–82), continued to make the placement of chaplain instructors at branch service schools a matter of priority. During Kelly's administration, the U.S. Army War College instituted a twelve-session course in ethics as part of its regular curriculum. In the newly organized Sergeants Major Academy, a chaplain was responsible for more than half of the moral leadership coursework. During the 1980s, chaplain instructors (including two female chaplains) were also teaching at West Point, the Command and General Staff College at Fort Leavenworth, and some twenty branch service schools throughout the United States. The content of their courses varied widely. In addition to "moral leadership," most chaplains taught ethics, counseling, and human relations. Chaplain Joseph Beasley, the first chaplain instructor assigned to the U.S. Military Academy in the twentieth century (in 1971), offered a course entitled "History of Western Ethics," which considered classical ethical theories and their application to "moral problems concerning race, poverty, politics of dissent, the sanctity of life, war and international relations." One of his successors in the 1980s, Chaplain John W. Brinsfield, taught a popular course known as "The History of the Ethics of Warfare: From Plato to NATO." At the U.S. Army War College, Carlisle Barracks, Pennsylvania, Chaplain Charles Kriete dealt with such subjects as the moral dimensions of strategic planning. In addition to placing chaplain instructors at the branch service schools, the OCCH also sponsored various workshops, seminars, and conferences on the ethical and moral aspects of leadership, which involved not only chaplains, but also service school faculty, as well as unit commanders and staff and line officers.[33]

At the same time that the chaplaincy expanded its involvement in leadership training, it also broadened its definition of the chaplain's ethical responsibilities and his role vis-à-vis the commander. Like Hyatt, both Kelly and Johnson believed the chaplain had a duty to offer "moral and prophetic guidance" to the military community.[34] During their administrations, the chaplain field manual (*The Chaplain*, later entitled *The Chaplain and Chaplain Assistant in Combat Operations*) and army regulation 165–20 (*Duties of Chaplains and Commanders' Responsibilities*) were revised so as to assign the chaplain a clearly defined moral advocacy role that went beyond advising and consulting with the commander regarding religion, morals, and morale in the command to criticizing, when necessary, his decision making, policies, and leadership.

The 1977 chaplain manual, for example, added a new aspect to the chaplain's relationship with the commander. Besides serving as an "advisor and consultant," he was expected to "assist the commander to implement policies and leadership practices that are in keeping with moral and ethical, [sic] and humanitarian standards by providing periodic evaluation to the commander on the moral and spiritual health of the command." The manual specified that the evaluation "will include ethical and humanitarian dimensions of command policies, leadership practices and management systems."[35] The chaplain manuals issued in 1984 and 1989 extended the chaplain's purview to include illegal, immoral, or inhumane practices during combat. Not only was he supposed to aid the commander in preventing such practices, but he also was specifically directed to report to him possible violations of the laws of war, as well as such practices as "dehumanizing treatment of friendly troops, enemy prisoners of war (EPW), or civilians; violations of codes of morality; illegal acts, desecration of sacred places, and disrespect for human life."[36]

By the latter part of the twentieth century, army chaplains in the United States had fashioned morale-building and moral-guidance roles very different from those of the late 1940s and 1950s. Instead of combat motivation, their morale-building effort concentrated on the quality of life in the military community. The leadership ethics of the officer class, rather than the personal morality of enlisted personnel, became the focus of their moral-guidance effort. In addition, chaplains assumed a moral advisory role vis-à-vis commanders that was much more significant than the one previously assigned to them. As a result of such changes, chaplains acquired greater influence within the military as an institution (particularly in the area of military training) and were authorized to play a more decisive moral-guidance role in the combat zone than they ever had before.

At least theoretically. For no matter how much the chaplain's role had expanded, his influence remained limited. In the areas of leadership and ethics, the army assigned proponency to the Infantry School at Fort Benning and the deputy chief of staff for personnel; the chaplaincy was to provide resources and support.[37] The personal inclination of many chaplains was also a limiting factor. A significant number preferred the priestly–pastoral role to the moral-guidance role.[38] And, as one chaplain admitted, even those who accepted the challenge of moral advocacy found it to be "at best, difficult," not a task they were "willing to tackle with the same enthusiasm as adventure training, personal counseling, or running the chapel."[39] Chaplains also faced commanders' continuing indifference or skepticism. Those serving with a combat-arms battalion in combat confronted perhaps the greatest challenge when it came to evaluating "the ethical and humanitarian dimensions of command policies," as directed by the 1977, 1984, and 1989 chaplain manuals. As the editor of *National Guard* pointed out in the introduction to a series of articles on the chaplaincy: "Since the mission of any maneuver-unit commander is 'to close with the enemy and destroy him,' any chaplain's advice to the contrary is not productive or appropriate and certainly not welcome."[40]

Such limitations may explain why the official history of the army chaplaincy for the period from 1975 to 1995 mentions only one instance where a chaplain felt constrained to challenge command policies.[41] The instance is significant, not only because of its singularity, but also because it reveals another limitation on the chaplains' moral-guidance role. In 1982, at a time of acrimonious public debate over the U.S. government's nuclear policy and its support of the government of El Salvador, the army chief of staff, General Edward C. Meyer, asked his staff for a paper on the moral aspects of the two issues. The task fell to Chief of Chaplains Kermit Johnson. In a memorandum for the chief of staff, entitled "Moral Issues of Nuclear War and of Conflict in El Salvador," Johnson used just-war criteria to raise questions about the morality of such things as limited nuclear war, the use of strategic nuclear weapons, and nuclear deterrence, as well as U.S. support (including military assistance in the form of equipment, advisers, and training) for "a regime whose military forces systematically and spontaneously engage in violence against its own people[.]" Although formulated as a series of "Socratic questions," the memorandum clearly revealed Johnson's disagreement with the Reagan administration's policies regarding nuclear weapons and El Salvador. His views were the product of several years of "soul-searching," during which time he decided that the chaplaincy should extend its moral guidance "beyond 'in-house' ethical issues" to "the ethical implications of nuclear warfare." The memorandum was part of his larger effort to expand the scope of chaplains' prophetic ministry beyond the army as an institution to the larger issues facing the nation as a whole.

Meyer circulated Johnson's memorandum to other military leaders. Johnson later recalled that when it reached the Office of the Deputy Chief of Staff for Operations, Lieutenant General William Richardson, "it angered his 'Iron Majors.'" On the question of El Salvador, he and the director of the army staff, Lieutenant General James Lee, "went head to head." As John Brinsfield observes, Johnson "was increasingly being perceived as 'out of step' with the army and with many of the senior leaders in the Chaplaincy who totally supported the policies of President Reagan as the surest and strongest deterrence to 'the evil empire' of Communism." In May 1982, faced with the choice of working "inside the box" (remaining within the army chaplaincy and subject to its constraints) or going "outside the box" to engage in the more broadly focused prophetic ministry he believed God required of him, Johnson announced that he would retire early, one year before the conclusion of his four-year term as chief of chaplains.[42] As Johnson himself recognized, his opposition to Reagan administration policies regarding nuclear weapons and El Salvador had placed him in an untenable position. His case reveals the ultimate limitation on army chaplains' prophetic ministry: as active-duty officers in the armed forces, they are not free to criticize publicly the policies of the U.S. government or the president as commander in chief.

NOTES

1. Department of the Army, *The Chaplain*, FM 16−5 (Washington, D.C.: U.S. Government Printing Office, 1952), 13; Headquarters, Department of the Army, *The Chaplain*, FM 16−5 (Washington, D.C.: U.S. Government Printing Office, 1958), 6−7.

2. Robert L. Gushwa, *The Best and Worst of Times: The United States Army Chaplaincy* (Washington, D.C.: Office of the Chief of Chaplains, Department of the Army, 1977), 122, 125, 132−35; Daniel B. Jorgensen, *The Service of Chaplains to Army Air Units, 1917−1946* (Washington, D.C.: Chief of Air Force Chaplains, n.d.), 195−99.

3. For a longer, more comprehensive discussion of the Character Guidance program, see Anne C. Loveland, "Character Education in the U.S. Army, 1947−1977," *Journal of Military History* 64 (July 2000): 795−812.

4. Department of the Army, *Character Guidance Discussion Topics: Duty, Honor, Country*, Department of the Army Pamphlet 16−5 (Washington: U.S. Government Printing Office, Jan. 14, 1966), vii.

5. The Chaplain School, *The Army Character Guidance Program*, ST 16−151 ([Carlisle Barracks, Pa.]: Chaplain School, Mar. 1, 1950), 4, 14, 15.

6. Luther D. Miller, "The Chaplains in the Army," *Army and Navy Journal*, 85 (Sept. 20, 1947), 74.

7. Frank A. Tobey, "Character Guidance Program," *Army Information Digest* 14 (Oct. 1959): 6. See also, for the chaplaincy's statement to the Senate Preparedness Investigating Subcommittee claiming that the Character Guidance program helped combat communism "by positively promoting a healthy response to American virtues, principles and ideals," Office of the Chief of Chaplains, "Historical Review, 1 July 1962 to 30 June 1963" (typescript at Washington National Records Center, Suitland, Md.), 77.

8. Department of the Army, Office of the Chief of Chaplains, *Summary of Major Events and Problems 1 July 1960 to 30 June 1961* (Washington, D.C.: n.p., n.d.), 26.

9. Headquarters, Department of the Army, *The Chaplain*, FM 16−5 (Washington, D.C.: U.S. Government Printing Office, 1964), 1.

10. Headquarters, Department of the Army, *Character Guidance Manual*, FM 16−100 (Washington, D.C.: U.S. Government Printing Office, June 26, 1968), 10.

11. Headquarters, Department of the Army, *The Chaplain* (1964): 41; Headquarters, Department of the Army, *The Chaplain*, FM 16−5 (Washington, D.C.: U.S. Government Printing Office, Dec. 26, 1967), 40. See also OCCH, *Summary of Major Events and Problems 1 July 1960 to 30 June 1961*, 26.

12. Henry F. Ackermann, *He Was Always There: The U.S. Army Chaplain Ministry in the Vietnam Conflict* (Washington, D.C.: Office of the Chief of Chaplains, Department of the Army, 1989), 5, 15, 19. Based on a 1985 survey of enlisted men and officers in the

army, Henry F. Ackermann observed that chaplains were remembered as being "always there" to offer comfort and reassurance (p. 15). One respondent described his chaplain as "an island of stability, tranquility, and strength in the midst of chaos and turmoil" (p. 149). For other testimonies from the survey, see 104, 112, 123, 132, 139, 142, 168, 169. See also Rodger R. Venzke, *Confidence in Battle, Inspiration in Peace: The United States Army Chaplaincy, 1945–1975* (Washington, D.C.: Office of the Chief of Chaplains, Department of the Army, 1977), 152, 153, 163.

13. William P. Mahedy, *Out of the Night: The Spiritual Journey of Vietnam Vets [sic]* (New York: Ballantine Books, 1986), 135, and see also 133; Robert Jay Lifton, *Home from the War: Vietnam Veterans: Neither Victims nor Executioners* (New York: Simon and Schuster, 1973), 163–64; Vietnam Veterans Against the War, *The Winter Soldier Investigation: An Inquiry into American War Crimes* (Boston: Beacon Press, 1972), 8, 161. On chaplain support of the Vietnam war, see Anne C. Loveland, "Prophetic Ministry and the Military Chaplaincy during the Vietnam Era," in Karen Halttunen and Lewis Perry, eds., *Moral Problems in American Life: New Perspectives on Cultural History* (Ithaca, N.Y.: Cornell University Press, 1998), 249.

14. Quoted in *Washington Post*, Dec. 4, 1970, p. 18.

15. Loveland, "Character Education," 805, n. 29.

16. Charles C. Moskos, Jr., *The American Enlisted Man: The Rank and File in Today's Military* (New York: Russell Sage Foundation, 1970), 99. See also John Sack, *M* (New York: The New American Library, 1966), 8–10, and Peter Tauber, *The Sunshine Soldiers* (New York: Simon and Schuster, 1971), 108–10, 160.

17. Loveland, "Character Education," 805–6, 815–17.

18. See, for example, Loveland, "Character Education," 805–6, and Ronald H. Spector, *After Tet: The Bloodiest Year in Vietnam* (New York: The Free Press, 1993), 59–61.

19. See, for example, Richard A. Gabriel and Paul L. Savage, *Crisis in Command: Mismanagement in the Army* (New York: Hill and Wang, 1978), esp. x–xi, 17–22; Cincinnatus, *Self-Destruction: The Disintegration and Decay of the United States Army During the Vietnam Era* (New York: W.W. Norton and Company, 1981); and Edward L. King, *The Death of the Army: A Pre-Mortem* (New York: Saturday Review Press, 1972).

20. The Citizens' Commission of Inquiry, ed., *The Dellums Committee Hearings on War Crimes in Vietnam: An Inquiry into Command Responsibility in Southeast Asia* (New York: Vintage Books, 1972), 212.

21. See Loveland, "Prophetic Ministry," 247, 250.

22. Ackermann, *He Was Always There*, 181–82; Clarence L. Abercrombie, *The Military Chaplain* (Beverly Hills, Calif.: Sage Publications, 1976), 98; Venzke, *Confidence in Battle*, 159.

23. See Spector, *After Tet*, 202–3.

24. Seymour M. Hersh, *Cover-Up: The Army's Secret Investigation of the Massacre at My Lai 4* (New York: Random House, 1972), 138, 177; United States, Department of the Army, *The My Lai Massacre and Its Cover-up: Beyond the Reach of the Law? The Peers Commission Report with a Supplement and Introductory Essay on the Limits of Law* (New York: The Free Press, 1976), 267–68, 312, 334, 337–38. Creswell quoted in Venzke, *Confidence in Battle*, 159, and Earl F. Stover, "Army Sponsors Ethics Workshop," *Christian Century* 93 (Oct. 20, 1976): 904.

25. Office of the Chief of Chaplains, "Historical Review, 1 July 1970 to 30 June 1971" (typescript at U.S. Army Center of Military History, Washington, D.C.), 62–63.

26. On Hyatt's reforms, see Loveland, "Prophetic Ministry," 250–51, 253–56, and Loveland, "Character Education," 812–16.

27. "Humanizing the U.S. Military," *Time*, Dec. 21, 1970, 16; Gen. Bruce Palmer, Jr., "The American Soldier in an Equivocal Age," *Army*, 19 (Oct. 1969), 31; William M. Hauser, *America's Army in Crisis* (Baltimore: Johns Hopkins University Press, 1973), 133–37, 139; Robert K. Griffith, Jr., *The U.S. Army's Transition to the All-Volunteer Force, 1968–1974* (Washington, D.C.: Center of Military History, United States Army, 1997), 63–65, 67–68, 70–74, 76, 84–85, 102–4; Office of the Chief of Chaplains, "Annual Report of Major Activities: Historical Review, 1 July 1973 to 30 June 1974" (typescript at U.S. Army Center of Military History, Washington, D.C.), 49; *The Chaplain and the Modern Volunteer Army: Lesson 2 of FY72 Chaplain Training Packet* (U.S. CONARC: August 1971), 1–5, 7, 9, 10.

28. Hyatt quoted in OCCH, "Annual Report of Major Activities" ([1974]), 65.

29. U.S. Army Military History Institute (USAMHI), "Senior Officers Debriefing Program: Interview with Major General Gerhardt W. Hyatt (U.S. Army Chief of Chaplains, Ret.) by Chaplain Colonel J.H. Ellens, 19 July 1976" (typescript in Archives Branch, USAMHI, Carlisle Barracks, Pa.), 58, 59.

30. J.A. Fallows, "A Military Without Mind or Soul," *Washington Monthly*, Apr. 1981, p. 20.

31. See John W. Brinsfield, Jr., *Encouraging Faith, Supporting Soldiers: A History of the United States Army Chaplain Corps, 1975–1995* (Washington, D.C.: Office of the Chief of Chaplains, Department of the Army, 1997), pt. 1, 41; John P. Lovell, *Neither Athens Nor Sparta?: The American Service Academies in Transition* (Bloomington: Indiana University Press, 1979), 224–25; Samuel H. Hays, "The Growing Leadership Crisis," *Army* 20 (Feb. 1970), 39–43; *New York Times*, July 22, 1973, IV, p. 14, and Apr. 21, 1985, pp. 1, 27; James Jay Carafano, "Officership, 1966–1971," *Military Review* 69 (Jan. 1989): 45–52; David J. Woehr, Anthony Longval, Jr., and Paul W. Morgan, Jr., "Ethics, Values, Which Way?" *Air Defense Magazine* (Apr.–June, 1979): 27; Robert A. Fitton, "Leadership Doctrine and Training: A Status Report," *Military Review* 65 (May 1985): 29–41.

32. USAMHI, "Senior Officers Debriefing Program," 23–6 (Hyatt was Deputy Chief of Chaplains when he made the overture); Office of the Chief of Chaplains, "Annual Report of Major Activities: Historical Review of the Office of Chief of Chaplains, 1 July 1972 to 30 June 1973" (typescript at U.S. Army Center of Military History, Washington, D.C.), 43, 104; Office of the Chief of Chaplains, "Annual Report of Major Activities: Historical Review, 1 July 1974 to 30 June 1975" (typescript at U.S. Army Center of Military History, Washington, D.C.), 40, 55.

33. On chaplain instructors in branch service schools and OCCH-sponsored workshops, seminars, and conferences, see Office of the Chief of Chaplains, Department of the Army, "[Historical Review], 1 July 1975 to 30 September 1976" (typescript at U.S. Army Center of Military History, Washington, D.C.), 22, 23; Office of Chief of Chaplains, "Historical Review, 1 October 1976 to 30 September 1977" (typescript at U.S. Army Center of Military History, Washington, D.C.), 30; Office of Chief of Chaplains, "Historical Review, 1 October 1977 to 30 September 1978" (typescript at U.S.

Army Center of Military History, Washington, D.C.), 24, 20; Office of Chief of Chaplains, "Annual Historical Review, 1 October 1978 to 30 September 1979" (typescript at U.S. Army Center of Military History, Washington, D.C.), 19; OCCH, "Annual Report of Major Activities" ([1975]), 40, 55; OCCH, "Annual Report of Major Activities" ([1973]), 42; OCCH, "Annual Report of Major Activities" ([1974]), 48; and Brinsfield, *Encouraging Faith*, pt. 1, 41, 66−67, 133−34, 136, 265, 381. On the content of the courses taught by chaplain instructors, see Joseph Hodgin Beasley, "Implications of Teaching Ethics: The West Point Experience" (Ph.D. diss., University of North Carolina, 1985), 82−83, 92−94; John Wesley Brinsfield, Jr., "Developing a Ministry of Teaching the History of Ethics and World Religions at the United States Military Academy, West Point, New York" (D.Min. thesis, Drew University, 1983), 56−67, 77−78, 82−84, 94−96, 181−204; Richard H. Whaley, "Training Support Package Teaches Military Ethics," *Air Defense Magazine* (July−Sept. 1982): 25−26; Jerry D. Autry, "The Chaplain in the Military Service School," *Military Chaplains' Review* (spring 1975): 18−21; Department of the Army, *Moral Leadership/Values: Responsibility and Loyalty*, pamphlet 165−15 (Headquarters, Department of the Army, Dec. 15, 1986); and Brinsfield, *Encouraging Faith*, pt. 1, 42, 67, 134, 136.

34. OCCH, "Historical Review" ([1977]), 30−31; OCCH, "Annual Historical Review" ([1979]), 21; Office of the Chief of Chaplains, "Annual Historical Review, 1 October 1980 to 30 September 1981" (typescript at U.S. Army Center of Military History, Washington, D.C., [1981]), 5; Brinsfield, *Encouraging Faith*, pt. 1, 67−68; 1979 Chaplain Professional Development Plan for the Army quoted in Robert Vickers, "The Military Chaplaincy: A Study In Role Conflict," *Military Chaplains' Review* (spring 1986): 83.

35. Headquarters, Department of the Army, *The Chaplain*, FM 16−5 (n.p., July 1977), 1−3. See also, for slightly different or briefer phrasing, *Army Regulation 165−20, Religious Activities: Duties of Chaplains and Commanders' Responsibilities* (Washington, D.C.: Headquarters, Department of the Army, Aug. 22, 1972), 3; *Army Regulation 165−20, Religious Activities: Duties of Chaplains and Commanders' Responsibilities* (Washington, D.C.: Headquarters, Department of the Army, June 15, 1976), 2−1; *Army Regulation 165−20, Religious Activities: Duties of Chaplains and Commanders' Responsibilities* (Washington, D.C.: Headquarters, Department of the Army, Oct. 15, 1979), 2−1.

36. Headquarters, Department of the Army, *The Chaplain and Chaplain Assistant in Combat Operations*, FM 16−5 (Washington, D.C.: U.S. Government Printing Office, Dec. 1984), 12, 21, 22; Headquarters, Department of the Army, *Religious Support Doctrine: The Chaplain and Chaplain Assistant*, FM 16−1 (Final Coordinating Draft, Apr. 1989), 3−8 to 3−9, 1−14. See also U.S. Army Chaplain Center and School, *U.S. Army Chaplain Officer Basic Course: Chaplain Values Training 1, Subcourse No. CH 0555* (n.p.: U.S. Army Training and Support Center, Aug. 1988), 5−1 − 6−16.

37. Brinsfield, *Encouraging Faith*, pt. 1, 66−68, 134; OCCH, "Annual Report of Major Activities" ([1973]), 43, 104−5; OCCH, "Historical Review" ([1977]), 32.

38. See Loveland, "Character Education," 817; Loveland, "Prophetic Ministry," 257−58.

39. Ford F. G'Segner, "A Chaplain's Perspective On the Application of Values," *Military Chaplains' Review* (fall 1986): 56.

40. "What Do Chaplains Do Besides Pray?" *National Guard* (Mar. 1987): 32.

41. Even during the Gulf War, except for some complaints about being prohibited from wearing branch insignia (crosses and tablets) in an Islamic country, chaplains had nothing but praise and offerings of spiritual reassurance for their commanders, as illustrated by VII Corps chaplain, Colonel Dan Davis, who told Lieutenant General Fred Franks "that God had revealed to my heart that he was anointed to lead the VII Corps in battle and that the forces he commanded would be an instrument of God's righteousness," and who reassured Major General Ronald Griffith, commander of the 1st Armored Division, by saying that God had spoken to his heart and assured him that there would be "victory without great casualties." Brinsfield, *Encouraging Faith*, pt. 2, 54, 59–61, 138, 158.

42. Memorandum for Chief of Staff, Army, from Kermit D. Johnson, Chaplain (Major General), USA, Chief of Chaplains, March 31, 1982, in File 701–01 Chaplain Instruction Files (82), Record Group 247, Acc. No. 247–88–001, Washington National Records Center, Suitland, Md.; Kermit D. Johnson, *Realism and Hope in a Nuclear Age* (Atlanta: John Knox Press, 1988), 12–14, 108–14; Kermit D. Johnson, "A New Stage: Beyond 'In-House' Ethical Issues," *Military Chaplains' Review* (spring 1982): v; Brinsfield, *Encouraging Faith*, pt. 1, 144–48.

CHAPTER TWELVE

IN PLACE OF AN AFTERWORD

My Argument with Fr. William Corby, C.S.C.

MICHAEL J. BAXTER, C.S.C.

On the lawn in front of Corby Hall at the University of Notre Dame stands a statue of Father William Corby, C.S.C., who served as president of the university from 1866 to 1872 and again from 1877 to 1886. He is more widely known, however, for his service from 1861 to 1864 as military chaplain for the 88th New York Volunteer Infantry Regiment of the Irish Brigade of the Army of the Potomac, and in particular, for a remarkable act of heroism he performed on July 2, 1863, the second day of the Battle of Gettysburg. Most of that day had been taken up with the Union and Confederate armies hurrying to move tens of thousands of men and hundreds of cannons into position, so it was not until late in the afternoon that the opposing forces were ready for battle. As the Confederate troops advanced, the Irish Brigade, which had been posted that morning on Cemetery Ridge, was ordered to repel the attack. It was at that moment, as the soldiers of the Irish Brigade were about to move forward, that Fr. Corby, as Gardiner Shattuck tells it in his essay in this collection,

climbed onto a nearby boulder and, exposing himself to enemy fire, stood up and pronounced the absolution of sin on every man he saw. He later claimed that all the soldiers in the brigade,

whether Catholic or not, knelt solemnly in front of him as cannonballs exploded and bullets whistled over their heads. Sustained
by their own prayers and by the priest's benediction, the troops
then joined the battle and bravely risked death in defense of the
Union position.

The Irish Brigade helped repel the Confederate attack that day,
which contributed to the Union victory at Gettysburg, the most decisive battle of the Civil War. Given this unfolding of events, it is not
surprising that the veterans of the Irish Brigade long remembered
Fr. Corby's act of heroism. Nearly fifty years later, the Brigade's surviving members memorialized it by placing a bronze statue of Corby
right on the spot where he gave his priestly blessing. The statue in
front of Notre Dame's Corby Hall is a replica of the one on Cemetery
Ridge on the Gettysburg battlefield.

Corby Hall is the center of community life for the Holy Cross priests
and brothers who work at the University of Notre Dame, the place
where some of us live (most of us live in the student residence halls)
and where all of us come together for morning and evening prayer,
mass on Wednesday afternoons, and meals. So I walk by Fr. Corby's
statue on a regular basis. Every so often, I stop and look at him standing on that boulder: hat and gloves set on the ground beside him,
priestly stole draped over his shoulders, right arm raised in blessing,
his eyes gazing heavenward as he gives absolution to the soldiers kneel-
ing beneath him. From time to time, I ask myself—and him—how he
could justify giving absolution in the name of Christ to soldiers preparing to kill other soldiers in battle? How could you justify ministering to Christian soldiers when Christ instructed His followers to follow His teaching and example of peacemaking? How do you reconcile
serving as a military chaplain with the Sermon on the Mount, with
Christ's commands to love our enemies, to do good to those who per-
secute us, and to turn the other cheek? How do you justify being a
chaplain to Christian soldiers when their so-called enemy soldiers are
also Christians, also members of the body of Christ?

I first asked Fr. Corby those questions in the early 1980s as a Holy
Cross seminarian. At the time, I was taking theology courses from
Stanley Hauerwas and John Howard Yoder, two ethicists and compelling articulators of Christian pacifism. I was also counseling students in
the ROTC program at Notre Dame who were conscientious objectors.

Father William Corby, C.S.C. Courtesy of the Archives of the University of Notre Dame.

In the years since, I have continued to ask these questions, either when visiting campus or, for the past six years, while living here. Throughout, I have remained involved in various aspects of Christian peacemaking: counseling conscientious objectors in the military, demonstrating against nuclear weapons and twice committing acts of civil disobedience, studying the theology of Christian pacifism, and now teaching and writing about it.

Contrary to what one might expect from conversation with a statue, my questions to Fr. Corby have not gone entirely unanswered. Since I was ordained a priest in 1985, I too have been obliged to administer the sacraments no matter what the circumstances, simply because the faithful want, need, and have a right to them. This experience has helped me appreciate Corby's work as a military chaplain. Futhermore, since coming to Notre Dame I have learned the importance of working within large bureaucratic institutions, with their inevitable tendencies toward compromise and corruption, because of the good that can be accomplished in spite of the constraints. This experience has also enhanced my appreciation of his ministry. But my questions have not gone away. As a result, for the past two decades or so, I have continued a running conversation, indeed an argument, with Fr. Corby.

In recent months my argument with Fr. Corby has been enlivened by reading his reminiscences of his life and times as a military chaplain during the Civil War, *Memoirs of Chaplain Life: Three Years with the Irish Brigade in the Army of the Potomac.*[1] Constructed largely from memory almost three decades after the Civil War, Corby's *Memoirs* is an account of his service as chaplain of the Irish Brigade from the fall of 1861, when he first joined the brigade at its encampment in Alexandria, Virginia, to the fall of 1864, when he was called back to Notre Dame for the election of a provincial superior. There are reflections interspersed throughout this account on the value of religious faith in the midst of war, as well as a concluding essay on the importance of the military chaplaincy and personal portraits of several chaplains. Corby devotes much of the book to the details of life in the field during his three years with the Irish Brigade: the discipline, camaraderie, hunger, disease, tedium, wood ticks, summer heat, winter cold, exhausting marches, fighting, killing, and dying. However, the purpose of the memoirs is not only to provide a realistic account of the hardships and heroism of military life. It is also, as he states in the preface, "to show the religious feature that existed in the Army." This "religious feature" is crucial to Corby's understanding of his ministry as a military chaplain.

In the preface to his *Memoirs*, Corby explains that "in the presence of death, religion gives hope and strength. The Christian soldier realizes that his power comes from the 'God of battles,' not from man."[2] In the *Memoirs* themselves, Corby shows how he and his fellow chaplains imparted religion to the Union soldier, mainly by means of the sacraments, especially confession, anointing, Eucharist, and, when necessary, baptism. His *Memoirs* are replete with stories of confessions heard and masses said in encampments, on marches, amid battles, whenever and wherever possible. His paramount concern is the soldier's soul at the moment of death. If a soldier dies unrepentant, it will cost him eternal life; if he dies in genuine repentance of his sins, he will be received into God's merciful hands. Thus, if a soldier is dying on the battlefield, Corby and the other chaplains will risk life and limb to hear his confession and give him absolution.[3] The same is true for the soldier succumbing to a fatal fever and for a deserter awaiting the firing squad or the hangman's noose. Their bodies may die, but so long as they repent and trust in God's mercy, their souls will be united with God forever. It is the chaplain's task to impress this religious truth upon the soldier facing imminent death and thus, God willing, to save his soul.

Corby insists that by attending to the religious well-being of individual soldiers, a chaplain also contributes to the performance of the army as a whole. The concluding reflections of the *Memoirs* emphasize this point. "The religious feature in an army," he notes, "is, indeed, no small matter. 'Conscience doth make cowards of us all' is quite applicable in a very forcible manner in this connection." But applicable in what sense? For Corby, "men who are demoralized and men whose consciences trouble them make poor soldiers"; by contrast, "moral men—men who are free from the lower and more degrading passions—make brave, faithful, and trustworthy soldiers," as can be seen in an example from ancient history. According to Corby, "Rome stood proudly mistress of the world while she held morality sacred." He marshals three examples of the moral strength of Rome, all having to do with chastity, to demonstrate that "when . . . morality was practiced and held up for admiration . . . the Roman soldier had no equal in the world." But, he adds, "when these same Romans were pampered with the luxuries of every clime; when the wealth of nations poured into Rome and enabled them to indulge every appetite, every passion, then the dauntless Roman became effeminate, in the presence of the enemy a coward, and great Rome sank into oblivion."[4]

As Corby sees it, "the religious feature" was an altogether salutary contribution to army life, not only on religious grounds, but also for military reasons. The two go hand in hand: religion makes for virtue and virtue makes for good soldiers, soldiers not controlled by their passions nor given over to weakness, but temperate, courageous, and conscientious soldiers. This is the lesson he draws from ancient Rome, a lesson that refutes any Clauswitzian interpretation of the adage, "con-science doth make cowards of us all." For it is not conscience itself that turns soldiers into cowards, but bad conscience; by contrast, good con-science turns soldiers into heroes. Thus, for Corby, there is an intrin-sic connection between religion and the kind of morality that wins wars, and this connection is made possible by the military chaplain whose concern with life after death exerts a palpable effect on military life *before* death. In other words, the chaplain's care for soldiers' souls dis-poses soldiers to give their bodies over to the cause to which the mili-tary is devoted. Hence, the central point of the book: by ministering to the religious needs of the soldiers of the Irish Brigade, Corby and his fellow chaplains served the nation.

Making this point was important for Corby for two reasons. First, Corby had been a military chaplain, and military chaplains in the Ameri-can Civil War were often seen as detrimental to the cause. Second, Corby had been a *Catholic* military chaplain, and in the United States of the nineteenth century, Catholics were widely regarded as disloyal. Did they not pledge their allegiance to the Church in a way that called into question their commitment to the nation? More specifically, did they not pledge allegiance to the Roman pontiff in a way that compro-mised the freedom from religious authority that was a hallmark of U.S. political life? Corby confronts these familiar charges directly in chap-ter nine. In doing so, he reveals how his *Memoirs* were deeply shaped by an assimilationist or Americanist agenda.

The chapter is titled "Bigots—True Freedom, etc." Corby begins by pointing to an anti-Catholic bias in the press, "which holds out to the American people the great power of the Pope, and tells them that by his power and office he directs Catholic politics in the United States, and that our great American free institutions are in danger!" Then, in the most emphatic prose of the book, he attempts to refute this charge by noting that it was a Catholic, Christopher Columbus, who "discovered this country" and that no Catholic since has ever "failed patriotism." Ex-panding on this point, Corby reviews the roles of Irish, French, Polish, and other Catholics who fought in the Revolutionary War, and so it has been, he insists, ever since:

> In no struggle into which our dear country has been precipi-tated, either with England, Mexico, or the late conflict of the re-bellion, can you find a lack of gallant generals, officers of every rank, with tens of thousands of brave, hardy sons of the Catholic

Church in the ranks and at the front, the place of peril, called in war times the "post of honor."[5]

On the basis of this record, Corby excoriates "the bigots," as he calls them, "for their ingratitude," their "lack of a sense of justice," and their readiness to cast "dishonor on the memories of the men who saved their lives and the honor of this country!" Corby emphasizes that such bigotry does not emerge from the citizenry at large, but only from certain quarters, and he aims his concluding criticisms accordingly:

Once more, let bigots cease their useless vituperation; let the Gospel, not scandal, be preached from the pulpit. Let the press temper its language and be inspired by the noble, manly spirit of our forefathers. Let the legislative bodies allow no bigotry, but deal only in justice, equity, and truth with all men. Then, and not till then, can we call ourselves a free people, bound together by the most sacred ties that patriotic blood is able to cement.[6]

Throughout this chapter, Corby works his rhetoric so as to depict a United States of America in which Catholics completely belong. By isolating the sources of anti-Catholic propaganda to people in the pulpit, in the press, and in politics, and then distinguishing such people from the general population, Corby is able to characterize anti-Catholicism as an aberrant rather than a normal feature of U.S. society (even though there was plenty of evidence to suggest otherwise). This move allows him to reassure Catholics that, despite the pronouncements of the cultural elites of the day, they do have a home in the United States. At the same time, it enables him to admonish those who would refuse Catholics a place in America with the countercharge that they, in fact, were denying the principles of religious freedom on which the nation was founded, in which case it is they, and not the Catholics, who are un-American. Thus, we are given a vision of fundamental harmony between Catholicism and the United States, a vision that is verified in the historical record, in that Catholics contributed to the founding, building, and defense of the nation from Columbus on through to the Civil War; a vision that is verified legally in the U.S. Constitution, which guarantees that Catholics are free to practice their religion just like everyone else.

However implausible it may have seemed to non-Catholics, Corby's picture of harmony was rather common among Catholic thinkers in the United States in the nineteenth century. It figured prominently in

Catholic intellectual life toward the end of the century, as the dispute arose and intensified over the extent to which Catholics should adapt their religious beliefs and practices and their cultural mores to U.S. culture. In fact, when Corby's *Memoirs* were first published commercially in 1894, two aspects of this general controversy had recently come to a head: the so-called school controversy and the controversy over what was known at the time as "Cahenslyism." These debates concerned whether or not immigrant Catholic schools and parishes should discard their ancestral languages and customs in order to assimilate into the new culture. Catholic leaders in the United States were divided between assimilationists or "Americanizers," who were mainly clerics of Irish descent (either foreign-born or second-generation), and "Cahenslyists" or conservatives, who came from non-English-speaking immigrant groups, especially Germans. Nowhere do the *Memoirs* mention this controversy, but Corby makes clear his sympathies by dedicating the book to one of the most prominent Americanizers, James Cardinal Gibbons, archbishop of Baltimore, whom he describes as "the Great Major-General of Christ's Army in America."[7] The spirit of that dedication fits the description of chaplain life presented in the pages that follow. Catholics need forfeit nothing in assimilating to America, Corby maintains. Like the Catholics in the Army of the Potomac, they can serve both church and nation.

Corby's *Memoirs of Chaplain Life* creates the impression that there is no tension whatsoever in being Catholic and being American, in serving both God and country. To be sure, Corby is careful to say that God takes priority. For example, he states that "a true Christian soldier has for [a] motto: 'Fidelity to God *first*, and to his country next': and no man can be a true, reliable patriot who is a traitor to his Maker."[8] However, he also carefully avoids any suggestion that there might arise a conflict between serving God and country, that being a true and reliable Catholic might even make one a traitor to one's country. Such an idea would contradict the central theme of the *Memoirs:* The Catholics of the Irish Brigade were loyal to God, and this loyalty to God empowered them to serve their country with deep devotion, in many cases, with their full measure of devotion unto death.

There is a problem with Corby's theme, however. It overlooks an important fact about Catholic participation in the Civil War: Catholics were devoted not only to the Union, but also to the Confederate cause. Although fewer in number, Catholics in the South readily served as officers and soldiers in the Confederate military. The same is true of Catholic priests. More than forty priests were chaplains in the Union armies and about thirty served with Confederate forces.[9] In a real sense, therefore, Southern Catholics demonstrated a commitment to their "country"— namely, the Confederate States of America—that was comparable to that of Northern Catholics. Throughout the Civil War, Catholics faced each other in battle. Catholics from the North fought Catholics from the South; "Union Catholics," so to speak, fought "Confederate Catholics." Even though this fact could undermine the theme of Catholic loyalty to country, the *Memoirs* register it not once but twice. The two passages in question reveal a central problem in Corby's understanding of the military chaplaincy. The first reference occurs in Corby's account of the general absolution he administered at Gettysburg. "That general absolution," he writes,

> was intended for all—*in quantum possum*—not only for our brigade, but for all, North and South, who were susceptible of it and who were to appear before their Judge. Let us hope that many thousands of souls, purified by the hardships, fasting, prayers, and blood, met a favorable sentence on the ever memorable battlefield of Gettysburg.[10]

The second passage appears in Corby's account of meeting a Mrs. Semmes of Warrenton, Virginia. He explains that many of her daughters and other female relatives had married Union officers, but most of the men in her family were fighting on the Confederate side. "Mrs. Semmes herself," Corby continues,

> had strong secession proclivities. She had charge of the church, and gave me a small altar stone and also baked some altar breads for me, and, although she thought I was on "the wrong side," as she expressed it, we parted good friends, united in holy Faith which no war can disrupt, and against which even "the gates of hell can not prevail."[11]

In both passages, Corby portrays himself administering a sacrament to those on opposite sides of the Union-Confederate divide. At Gettysburg, as he makes clear, he intended to absolve Southerners as well as Northerners, under the assumption that the grace of absolution would work its saving effects on the Confederate soldiers advancing from Cemetery Ridge, or at least on those disposed to receive it. So too with the mass; it establishes a bond between Fr. Corby and Mrs. Semmes that is not broken even by their dedication to opposing sides of the war. Sacramental grace crosses battle lines, so to speak, and keeps the members of the Church "united in holy Faith" even in the midst of a horrifying, destructive war. For Corby, this is a strength of Catholicism, a sign that nothing can sever the bonds established by Christ and His Church. But Corby's claim here depends upon a theology in which the grace of the sacrament somehow operates independent of earthly allegiances; it flows in and through historical events without impinging on them in a concrete way, and its effects are felt in a sphere beyond materiality, a purely spiritual sphere of the soul.

The problem this theology creates is that, when the communion of souls enjoyed by members of the Church is confined within a purely spiritual sphere, the Church loses its capacity to be an actual body distinct from other earthly bodies. On this score, what Corby perceives as the strength of the Church is, in fact, a source of weakness. For although it is true that no conflict among earthly powers can tear asunder a purely spiritual communion, it is also true that such a communion is powerless to challenge the divisive and destructive dynamics of earthly bodies. As a communion held together by purely spiritual bonds, it is insulated from all earthly bodies.

I am not suggesting that Corby was indifferent to matters of the body. Cussing, illicit sexual activity, and the like were serious pastoral concerns for Corby, and he tried to dissuade the men under his charge from misbehavior in these areas. In this respect, Corby cared about matters of the body—matters pertaining to soldiers' personal bodies—because they had definite bearing on the salvation of their souls. In respect to another earthly body, however, Corby displayed little, if any, pastoral concern. I refer to the body of the state. When it came to soldiers' behavior in relation to this body, Corby apparently thought it had nothing to do with salvation of their souls. For him, the political body, or body politic, of the state occupies a space removed from the sphere of the soul. Political identity and allegiance thus have little to do with the communion of souls that Catholics share. Hence, Corby was not troubled by the fact that Catholics from the North and South, whose competing political allegiances defined each other as enemies, could nevertheless go to mass and be "united in holy Faith."

With regard to politics, then, Corby's thought shows a conceptual dualism between the concerns of the body and the concerns of the soul. That dualism made it possible for him to think of his ministry to Confederate soldiers and sympathizers not only as unproblematic, but also as a sign of the Church's resilience and strength in the face of political rivalry. Politics, classified as pertaining to the body, had no immediate relevance to the soul, at least not to the soul's salvation. So for Corby, the Church has nothing pastoral to say about the activity of politics, and thus nothing pastoral to say about waging war.

It is not surprising, therefore, that Corby never seriously takes up the question of whether or not the Union cause is just. And yet, it is puzzling that he does not do so, for he could have argued that the Union went to war to defend those who were suffering and dying under slavery. After all, many Christians in the North, in particular many African Americans, fought for the Union because they saw it as the only hope for doing away with "the damnable institution." As a Catholic, Corby could have drawn on the Church's just-war tradition to claim that the war was fought in defense of the innocent. No such claim is found in the *Memoirs*. Or again, Corby could have argued that the Union cause was justified on the grounds that the integrity of the nation had to be preserved. He articulates no such position. Granted, at one point Corby states that the Civil War had been fought on behalf of liberty, and at another point, he says that the war's purpose was to preserve the Union.[12] In neither case, however, does he argue his position; it is as if the justice of the Union's cause is self-evident, despite the fact that it was precisely in the name of liberty that the Confederate states seceded in the first place.

Admittedly, Corby wrote the *Memoirs* almost three decades after the Civil War had ended. Still, it is odd that nowhere do we see him or the other chaplains discerning the morality of the war. Nowhere do we see them expressing outrage at the suffering of slaves in the South or concern over the integrity of the nation. Nowhere is the just-war teaching of the Church even mentioned. Corby does not bring forth Augustine's view that Christians may go to war to defend the innocent or to preserve political peace; nor does he refer to Aquinas' position on the need to defend the common good against the discord that comes with acts of sedition; nor does he discuss the principles set forth by the Scholastics in order to determine the justice of a nation going to war and of military operations within a war; nor does he address just-war teaching as it was presented in the moral manuals of the day.[13] He shows no interest in using the Church's traditional teaching on just war in critically analyzing the morality of the Civil War, even though it could have strengthened his position. His approach is simply to assume, rather than argue, the justice of the Union cause.

To be fair, Corby does mention the moral dilemma of soldiers being ordered to participate in unjust actions. But he does so only in passing, and even then his overriding concern is to preserve the military chain of command. "Among officers and veterans," he writes, "it is an axiom to obey first, and if there be a supposed injustice, to speak of it afterward; not, however, before showing absolute obedience to the order given, be it right or wrong."[14] Corby could have marshaled support for his axiom from the writings of Augustine and Aquinas, both of whom arguably hold that the culpability for unjust actions lies primarily with commanding officers.[15] Nevertheless, Corby eschews this line of reasoning, perhaps because it would have involved acknowledging that the justice of a war must be determined on the basis of natural law; and to acknowledge the authority of natural law as antecedent to the authority of the state could suggest a conflict between the dictates of justice and the dictates of the U.S. government. So instead of delving into the intricacies and implications of just-war theory, Corby simply passes over the matter of the morality of the war in silence.

My point is this: The body/soul dualism that shapes Corby's thought, wherein the activity of war pertains to the body rather than the soul, insulates the practice of waging war from critical moral judgment. As a result, the premium is placed not on adherence to the Church's teaching on just war, but on loyalty to country. The fact that Catholics supported the Confederate side of the Civil War presents no problem for Corby because "Southern" Catholics *were* loyal to their country, which from their perspective was the Confederate States of America. In this case, however, Catholics would be loyal to their country no matter what it stands for, no matter what causes it sponsors, no matter what crimes it commits.

Certainly, loyalty to country is not necessarily a vice. On the contrary, as we see in Aquinas, it can be listed under the general heading of the virtue of *pietas*, that is, the virtue of offering fitting devotion and faithful service, in this case to one's fatherland or *patria*, as suggested in the word "patriotism."[16] But, as we also see in Aquinas, *pietas* toward one's country—patriotism—must be guided by the virtue of justice.[17] And yet, a serious account of how patriotic service to the Union during the Civil War constituted a service to justice is missing from Corby's *Memoirs*. As a result, he gives the impression that the justice of the war has nothing to do with the moral and religious lives of soldiers and thus has no bearing on the work of military chaplains. Their primary duty is the care of soldiers' souls: providing soldiers with the opportunity to confess their sins, receive absolution and perform the assigned penance, and thus be in a state of grace so that, should they die in battle, they are assured of eternal life.

Corby, I have argued, understands the work of a military chaplain to be caring for soldiers' souls. In his view, that care does not include providing soldiers with guidance as to whether or not or to what extent they should participate in the war being fought. As a result, it is difficult to see how Corby could refute the charge that a military chaplain uncritically supports the policies and operations ordered by military command, even those that violate natural law, and that therefore, one key function of the chaplaincy as an institution is to subordinate the work of the Church to the purposes of the nation.

To this charge, Corby would likely have responded that the work of the Church is not antithetical to the purposes of the United States of America. On the contrary, he might have said, the two go hand in hand. By prohibiting the establishment of any particular religion and protecting the free exercise of all faiths, the U.S. Constitution provides the Catholic Church with the freedom it needs to accomplish its mission. For that reason, he might conclude, it is to be regarded as a just political order that should be defended. This was the general argument of Cardinal Gibbons, Archbishop Ireland, and the other Americanists whom Corby and his confreres at Notre Dame held in high regard.

In contrast, I argue that the United States exacts a price from the Catholic Church for the religious freedom it purports to provide: it requires that Catholic beliefs and practices reinforce the political order of the nation. Corby would doubtless counter that Catholic beliefs and practices do indeed uphold the political order of the nation, and that this is a good thing. But this contention only goes to show how deeply Corby internalized an Americanist worldview. In this worldview, the Church is not a concrete, flesh-and-blood community whose mission is to embody the life of Christ in the lives of its members, but rather is an abstract, invisible communion, which provides its members with the means to the salvation of their souls while calling upon them to offer up their bodies in war. In Corby's Americanist worldview, the Church supplies the army with a "religious feature," but this is the feature of a false religion, a civil religion whose primary function is to serve the nation-state.

My argument with Fr. Corby and his understanding of the military chaplaincy has significance far beyond the battlefields of the Civil War. Military chaplains have long cared for the souls of soldiers facing battle, and they have done so out of loyalty to God and country. Indeed, as the essays in this book demonstrate, Corby's vision of the military chaplain, who both ministers to soldiers' souls and serves his country, has remained remarkably stable over the course of centuries in many different settings: from ninth-century Gaul to twelfth-century Northumbria, from nineteenth-century Prussia to Nazi Germany. The problem with Corby's vision of the military chaplaincy has remained similarly constant. Working under a body/soul dualism, most military chaplains have not encouraged soldiers to make critical judgments about the justice of the war being waged or the tactics employed, even when such judgments bear on whether or not soldiers commit murder and thus on whether or not they attain eternal life.

Doris Bergen's essay on German military chaplains during the Second World War poignantly captures this dilemma. As Bergen shows, the approximately one thousand Catholic and Protestant clergymen who served as military chaplains for Nazi Germany exhibited deep dedication both to ministering to the needs of the soldiers in their charge and to furthering their nation's cause in war. This dual service compelled them to try to make religious sense out of the most heinous crimes. Hence, the Catholic priest's recollections of an exchange with a wounded soldier who had taken part in a mass execution of Jews. Devastated by the experience, the soldier described how men, women, and children were lined up, stripped naked, and then gunned down so that they fell backward into a trench—forty thousand Jews in all. The soldier, assigned to man one of the machine guns, claimed he shot his weapon into the air and never hit anyone; still, he was desperate to know what he, an enlisted man with a wife and family, should have done. The priest was at a loss. Should he have told the soldier that he should have disobeyed his orders? What if the soldier too had then been shot? "Is that what God wants?"

Without denying the genuine moral anguish marking this scene, this last question should be taken more seriously than it was by the priest who posed it. For his assumption seems to be that the answer to the question is clear: God does not want the soldier to refuse orders, get executed, and never see his family again, then to be replaced by another soldier who will finish the job. But is it so clear? What about the forty thousand people whom these soldiers lined up and shot? They too had families; in many cases, entire families were murdered. What about the six million Jews killed under the Nazi regime? And the millions of non-Jews who were also killed? Many of these atrocities would not have been possible without the cooperation of Catholics like the soldier above.

It is also important to remember the teaching of the Catholic Church on this matter. The Church teaches that intentionally taking the lives of the innocent is an intrinsically evil act, that is to say, evil in itself (*in se*), evil always, everywhere, and without exception, including in war. According to the teaching of the Church, therefore, committing an evil act should be avoided at all cost, even at the cost of one's life, and also at the cost of others (for example, one's spouse and children) who will suffer due to the loss of one's life.[18] Based on this teaching, the answer to the priest's question—Is this what God wants?—may very well be, "Yes, that is what God wants."[19] For while it is true that God does not will death to be visited upon those who refuse to cooperate in the slaughter of the innocent, it is also true that those who do refuse, and die for their refusal, embrace God's will by loving others as God loves them: fully and freely, unto death.

Had Catholics in Germany collectively refused to cooperate with the evil deeds of the Nazi regime, many lives might have been saved; indeed, there might have been no Holocaust. Presumably, many Catholics would have died. But then again, many Catholics did die. The difference is that they would have died not for the Fatherland and the Führer, but for God. In any case, those who offered their lives in resistance to evil are rightly revered as martyrs, as beacons of light in a dark time.

For this reason, many in the Church remember the life and death of Franz Jägerstätter, a contemporary of the German priest and soldier just discussed. An Austrian Catholic, farmer, husband, and father of three, Jägerstätter refused to be conscripted into the Nazi-controlled military. His wife pleaded with him to acquiesce. His local pastor and bishop urged him to do so as well, but he resisted their advice. Eventually, he was arrested, tried by a military tribunal, convicted, and on August 9, 1943, beheaded.[20] What is noteworthy about Jägerstätter's witness is that he refused to cooperate with the Nazi-controlled military precisely in order to gain eternal life. As he puts it in one of his letters from prison, "We must do everything in our power to strive for the Eternal Homeland and to preserve a good conscience."[21] Jägerstätter saw a truth that his priest and bishop, and also the military chaplain who "counseled" him shortly before his death, did not see: that body and soul are so inextricably linked that to use one's body to commit evil acts during war causes the death of the soul and can destroy one's capacity to attain eternal life.

Jägerstätter's witness stands as a judgment on those Catholics—lay people, priests, bishops—whose accommodation to the Nazi regime during the Second World War led them into doing evil. It is also a judgment on Catholics who, in waging war against the Nazi regime, were likewise led by their military and civilian leaders into committing evil deeds, such as dropping atomic bombs on Hiroshima and Nagasaki. Indeed, it stands as a judgment on Catholics of every time and place whose loyalty to country has led them to do things during war that are evil in the eyes of God. But in a particular way, Jägerstätter challenges the military chaplaincy as an institution. For chaplains consistently instill into the minds and hearts of Christian soldiers the notion that doing such things is justified, and then later, when faced with their moral anguish, they provide them with the false consolation that they had to do what they did—for God and country.

My argument with Fr. Corby is critical not only of him and his account of the military chaplaincy, but also of the entire tradition that justifies Christians going to war. This tradition emerged around the time when the Roman emperor Constantine converted to Christianity and undertook the task of Christianizing the empire. It has been embodied in the lives of many Christians ever since who, one way or another, see it as their mission to Christianize the social order, whether it be an ancient empire, a medieval fiefdom, a renaissance kingdom, or a modern nation-state. The tradition has retained its central claim in all these contexts: For the sake of social order, Christians are sometimes obligated to go to war. Accordingly, critics refer to the "Constantinian tradition" in which the Church sets aside the task of embodying the peace of Christ in the world in favor of providing a social ethic for the predominant *imperium*.[22]

Corby's place in this tradition is probably best illustrated when he argues for the importance of "the religious feature that existed in the Army" and invokes the example of ancient Rome. Just as religion in ancient Rome fortified the imperial troops in battle, so religion in the United States strengthens its military. It does not seem to occur to Corby that this religion offers sacrifice to Mars, the Roman god of war, not to the God and Father of Jesus Christ. Christians do not take part in bloody sacrifices through the works of war. They offer spiritual sacrifices through works of mercy.

Corby would probably respond that there are times when, owing to sin, Christians are obligated to defend the innocent—a tragic necessity, as Augustine argued. To which I would answer that such arguments from "necessity" are often the false myths of empires that wage wars out of a lust for domination, as Augustine also argued.

Here, I conclude the latest installment of my argument with Fr. Corby. It is not an argument with him alone, but with all the other Holy Cross priests who served as military chaplains in the Civil War, the First and Second World Wars, the Korean War, the Vietnam War, and the Gulf War, as well as those serving now as military chaplains. I believe they would all view their task much as Corby did, as bringing the sacraments to those who risk harm to defend the rest of us. And I regard their service much as I do Corby's, as service to a strange warrior god, not the God and Father of Jesus Christ, who calls His followers to embody His peace, not to take other lives to preserve the peace of this world.

I must confess, however, that it seems too easy to write this way. I have never faced cannon fire as Corby did that day on Cemetery Ridge. I have never absolved a soldier of his sins with bullets whizzing overhead, nor given last rites to someone whose body is mangled beyond repair. I have not blessed the human remains placed in a body bag like Joseph O'Donnell did in Vietnam. Corby and the other military chaplains have to face the challenge of supporting the waging of war. But those of us who renounce violence in the name of Christ have a challenge to face as well: the challenge of criticizing military chaplains for legitimating war while respecting them for having sacrificed more for their beliefs than most of us have sacrificed for ours; the challenge of standing up in our own way for innocent victims of injustice. This admission does not mean that Fr. Corby wins the argument, but it does reveal a need for more truthfulness on my side. Perhaps my argument with Fr. Corby would be more compelling if I were writing from a refugee camp in Afghanistan rather than from my office at the University of Notre Dame.

Not far from Corby's statue in front of the hall that takes his name, within earshot of a rifle report, as he might have put it, is the cemetery for Holy Cross priests and brothers of the Indiana Province. Corby is buried there amid the rows of gravestones, each shaped like a cross. Simple engravings are cut into the stone: name, date of birth, date of death. As I write this, on Memorial Day, May 27, 2002, flags adorn the graves of the chaplains and other veterans in Holy Cross. The custom has taken on added meaning since September 2001, during the so-called war on terrorism. The flag signifies allegiance to the Republic for which it stands, an allegiance much narrower than the cross of Christ who died for all people: Union and Confederate; American, Afghani, and Iraqi; U.S. Marines and agents of al-Qaeda. I look forward to making this point with Fr. Corby in an argument that will not cease until we see each other and God, face to face.

NOTES

1. William Corby, C.S.C., *Memoirs of Chaplain Life: Three Years with the Irish Brigade in the Army of the Potomac*, ed. Lawrence Frederick Kohl (New York: Fordham University Press, 1992).

2. Ibid., 6.

3. Ibid., 71–79.

4. Ibid., 271–72.

5. Ibid., 69.

6. Ibid., 70.

7. Ibid., 3.

8. Ibid., 51.

9. John Tracy Ellis, *American Catholicism*, 2d rev. ed. (Chicago: University of Chicago Press, 1969), 98.

10. Corby, *Memoirs*, 184.

11. Ibid., 206–7.

12. Ibid., 214, 316.

13. See, for example, Augustine, *Letter 189: Augustine to Boniface*, in *Augustine: Political Writings*, ed. E.M. Atkins and R.J. Dodaro (Cambridge: Cambridge University Press, 2001), 217; Augustine, *The Free Choice of the Will*, I, 5, in *Saint Augustine: The Teacher, The Free Choice of the Will, Grace and Free Will*, trans. Robert P. Russell, O.S.A., vol. 59 of *The Fathers of the Church* (Washington, D.C.: Catholic University Press, 1968), 80–83; Augustine, *City of God*, XIX, 12–13, in Augustine, *City of God*, trans. Henry Bettenson and introd. John O'Meara (New York: Viking Penguin, 1972), 866–72; Thomas Aquinas, *Summa Theologiae* II-II, 37, 42 (I am working with the three-volume translation of this text by the Fathers of the English Dominican Province [New York: Benziger Brothers, 1947]); and Franciscus de Vitoria, *On the Indians, or on the Law of War made by the Spaniards on the Barbarians*, in Ernest Nye, ed., *De Indis et de Ivre Belli Relectiones* (Washington, D.C.: Carnegie Institution, 1917), 163–87.

14. Corby, *Memoirs*, 155.

15. See, for example, Augustine, Reply to Faustus the Manichaean, XXII, 75, in *St. Augustine: The Writings Against the Manichaeans and Against the Donatists*, vol. 4, *Nicene*

and Post-Nicene Fathers of the Christian Church, ed. Philip Schaff (Grand Rapids, Mich.: Eerdmans, 1989), 301, and Aquinas, *Summa Theologiae* II-II, 64.3; II-II, 64.6 ad 3.

16. On the virtue of piety, see Aquinas, *Summa Theologiae* II-II, 101.1. On patriotism as the most fitting word for pietas toward one's country, see Charles E. Sheedy, C.S.C., *The Christian Virtues* (Notre Dame, Ind.: University of Notre Dame Press, 1949), 293.

17. As Sheedy writes regarding the virtue of patriotism, "There is an excess of patriotism to be avoided, excessive nationalism, sometimes called 'chauvinism' or 'jingoism': the attitude summed up in the expression, 'My country right or wrong.' If my country is wrong, I should do all that in me lies to put it right" (Sheedy, *Christian Virtues*, 294).

18. This teaching has been clearly laid out by Pope John Paul II in his encyclicals *Veritatis Splendor* (Boston: Pauline Books and Media, n.d.) and *Evangelium Vitae* (Boston: Pauline Books and Media, n.d.).

19. Regarding this particular case of the German soldier's connection to the mass killing of Jews in Sevastopol, a careful discernment as to his moral culpability would require using the categories of traditional Catholic moral theology to determine the nature and degree of his cooperation with those evil actions, whether it was material or formal, proximate or remote, mediate or immediate, or some combination of these. These categories are often criticized as too abstract and analytical, but they have the capacity to address precisely this kind of moral case in precisely such a context, that is, a confessional context. It should be noted that the principles comprising the Church's teaching on just war originated out of confessional contexts, as priests and canonists attempted to discern whether or not or to what degree a soldier had sinned in warfare. The fact that these principles are not used in such pastoral contexts reflects the extent to which most military chaplains neglect key pastoral duties. Of course, such a pastoral encounter might have brought down a sense of God's judgment on the soldier, but it would then have opened the way for God's mercy. Only through God's mercy and the tears of compunction it incites can one achieve the peace the soldier sought. The possibility of such moral discernment and transformation is cut short by the priest's false sympathy, generated, it seems, by his own acquiescence to evil. Thus, the scene is marked by moral helplessness and hopelessness, as if there were nothing else one could do, giving rise to yet another sin: the sin of despair.

20. The story is told and analyzed in Gordon Zahn, *In Solitary Witness: The Life and Death of Franz Jägerstätter* (Boston: Beacon Press, 1964).

21. Zahn, 215. This theme is articulated throughout the letter Jägerstätter wrote to his godson Franz Huber (209–16).

22. See, for example, Stanley Hauerwas, *A Community of Character* (Notre Dame, Ind.: University of Notre Dame Press, 1981), esp. 72–110, and Stanley Hauerwas, *Dispatches from the Front: Theological Engagements with the Secular* (Durham: Duke University Press, 1994), esp. 116–52; John Howard Yoder, *The Original Revolution* (Scottdale, Pa.: Herald Press, 1971), and John Howard Yoder, *The Politics of Jesus*, 2d ed. (Grand Rapids, Mich.: Eerdmans, 1995).

BIBLIOGRAPHY

Periodicals Dealing with Military Chaplains

United States

Military Chaplains' Review. Professional Bulletin of the U.S. Army Chaplain Corps.
The Chaplain. Department of the Army. Washington, D.C.: U.S. Government Printing Office.

Europe

Beiträge aus der Evangelischen Militärseelsorge. Bonn-Bad Godesberg: Evangelisches Kirchenamt für die Bundeswehr.
Europäisches Militärseelsorge-Jahrbuch.
Militärseelsorge. Bonn: Katholisches Militärbischofsamt.

Scholarly Works and Studies of Particular Chaplaincies

Books and Pamphlets

United States and Canada

Abercrombie, Clarence L. *The Military Chaplain.* Beverly Hills: Sage Publications, 1976.
Abrams, Ray. *Preachers Present Arms.* Scottdale, Pa., and Philadelphia: Herald Press, 1933, 1966.
Ackermann, Henry F. *He Was Always There: The U.S. Army Chaplain Ministry in the Vietnam Conflict.* Washington, D.C.: Office of the Chief of Chaplains, Department of the Army, 1989.
Armstrong, Warren. *For Courageous Fighting and Confident Dying: Union Chaplains in the Civil War.* Lawrence: University Press of Kansas, 1998.

Bergsma, Herbert L. *Chaplains with Marines in Vietnam, 1962–1971*. Washington, D.C.: History and Museums Division, Headquarters, United States Marine Corps, 1985.

Beringer, Richard E., et al. *Why the South Lost the Civil War.* Athens: University of Georgia Press, 1986.

Brinsfield, John W., Jr. *Encouraging Faith, Supporting Soldiers: A History of the United States Army Chaplain Corps, 1975–1995*. Washington, D.C.: Office of the Chief of Chaplains, Department of the Army, 1997.

Brown, W.Y. *The Army Chaplain: His Office, Duties, and Responsibilities, and the Means of Aiding Him*. Philadelphia: William S. & Alfred Martien, 1863.

Castonguay, Jacques. *Unsung Mission: History of the Chaplaincy Service (RC) of the R.C.A.F.* Montreal: Institute de Pastorale, 1968.

Chesebrough, David B. *"God Ordained this War": Sermons on the Sectional Crisis, 1830–1865*. Columbia: University of South Carolina Press, 1991.

Councell, Gary R. *Chaplain Roles in Humanitarian and Civic Assistance Operations*. Carlisle Barracks, Pa.: U.S. Army War College, 1994.

Cox, Harvey Gallagher, ed. *Military Chaplains: From Religious Military to a Military Religion*. New York: American Report Press, 1973.

Crerar, Duff. *Padres in No Man's Land: Canadian Chaplains and the Great War.* Montreal: McGill-Queen's University Press, 1995.

Crosby, Donald F. *Battlefield Chaplains*. Lawrence: University Press of Kansas, 1994.

Drazin, Israel, and Cecil B. Currey. *For God and Country: The History of a Constitutional Challenge to the Army Chaplaincy*. Hoboken, N.J.: KTAV, 1995.

Fowler, Albert. *Peacetime Padres*. St. Catharines: Vanwell, 1996.

Fuller, James. *Chaplain to the Confederacy: Basil Manly and Baptist Life in the Old South*. Baton Rouge: Louisiana State University Press, 2000.

Groh, John E. *Facilitators of the Free Exercise of Religion: Air Force Chaplains, 1981–1990*. Washington, D.C.: Office of the Chief of Chaplains, United States Air Force, 1991.

Gushwa, Robert L. *The Best and Worst of Times: The United States Army Chaplaincy*. Washington, D.C.: Office of the Chief of Chaplains, Department of the Army, 1977.

Haberek, Jerome. *The Chaplaincy in the Army after Next*. Carlisle Barracks, Pa.: U.S. Army War College, 1998.

Honeywell, Roy J. *Chaplains of the United States Army*. Washington, D.C.: Office of the Chief of Chaplains. Department of the Army, 1958.

Hutcheson, Richard G., Jr. *The Churches and the Chaplaincy*. Atlanta: John Knox Press, 1975.

Huerta, Carlos C. *Religious Accommodation in the Military*. Patrick Air Force Base, Fla.: Research Directorate, Defense Equal Opportunity Management Institute, 1995.

The Impact of Religious Belief in Military Operations Other Than War. Newport, R.I.: Naval War College, 1998.

Jablin, Julian N., and Azriel Louis Eisenberg. *The Jewish Military Chaplain.* New York: Jewish Education Committee of New York, 1962.

Jones, William J. *Christ in the Camp; or, Religion in the Confederate Army.* New ed. Atlanta: Martin and Hoyt, 1904.

Jorgensen, Daniel B. *Air Force Chaplains, 1947–1960.* Washington, D.C.: Office, Chief of Air Force Chaplains, 1961.

———. *The Service of Chaplains to Army Air Units, 1917–1946.* Washington, D.C.: Office of the Chief of Chaplains. Department of the Army, n.d.

Jorgensen, Daniel B., and Martin H. Scharlemann. *Air Force Chaplains.* United States: Air Force. Office of the Chief of Chaplains, 1961.

Kehoe, Joseph A. *Holy Cross Military Chaplains in World War II.* Notre Dame, Ind.: Holy Cross College, 1995.

Kelman, John. *The War and Preaching.* New Haven: Yale University Press, 1919.

Klug, Eugene F. *The Military Chaplaincy Under the First Amendment.* Fort Wayne: Concordia Theological Seminary, 1980.

Lamm, Alan K. *Five Black Preachers in Army Blue, 1884–1901: The Buffalo Soldier Chaplains.* Lewiston, N.Y.: Edwin Mellen, 1998.

Lee, Douglas. *The United States Army Reserve Chaplaincy in the Army after Next.* Carlisle Barracks, Pa.: U.S. Army War College, 1998.

Levi, Gershon, ed. *David Golinkin. Breaking New Ground: The Struggle for a Jewish Chaplaincy in Canada.* Montreal: National Archives, Canadian Jewish Congress, 1994.

Loveland, Anne C. *American Evangelicals and the United States Military, 1942–1993.* Baton Rouge: Louisiana State University Press, 1996.

McChrystal, Herbert J. *Spiritual Fitness: An Imperative for the Army Chaplaincy.* Carlisle Barracks, Pa.: U.S. Army War College, 1998.

MacIntyre, D.E. *Canada at Vimy.* Toronto: Peter Martin, 1967.

Mahedy, William P. *Out of the Night: The Spiritual Journey of Vietnam Vets.* New York: Ballantine Books, 1986.

Moorhead, James H. *American Apocalypse: Yankee Protestants and the Civil War, 1860–1869.* New Haven: Yale University Press, 1978.

Norton, Herman. *Rebel Religion: The Story of Confederate Chaplains.* St. Louis: Bethany, 1961.

———. *Struggling for Recognition: The United States Army Chaplaincy, 1791–1865.* Washington, D.C.: Office of the Chief of Chaplains, 1977.

Pitts, Charles F. *Chaplains in Gray: The Confederate Chaplains' Story.* Nashville: Broadman, 1957.

Robinson, Jerry L. *A Chronological Record of Historical Events Relating to Diversity in the U.S. Army Chaplaincy as Viewed by Chaplain (Major General) (Retired) Matthew A. Zimmerman, Jr.* Carlisle Barracks, Pa.: U.S. Army War College, 1997.

Shattuck, Gardiner H. *A Shield and Hiding Place: The Religious Life of the Civil War Armies.* Macon, Ga.: Mercer University Press, 1987.

Slomovitz, Albert Isaac. *The Fighting Rabbis: Jewish Military Chaplains and American History.* New York and London: New York University Press, 1999.

Silver, James W. *Confederate Morale and Church Propaganda.* 1957; reprint. New York: W.W. Norton, 1967.

Soldiers Christian Aid Association. *Army Chaplains: Of What Use is a Chaplain in the Army?* New York: U.S. Soldiers Christian Aid Association, 1897.

Steven, W. T. *In This Sign.* Toronto: Ryerson, 1948.

Stover, Earl F. *Up from Handyman: The United States Army Chaplaincy, 1920–1945.* Washington, D.C.: Office of the Chief of Chaplains, Department of the Army, 1977.

Thompson, Parker C. *From its European Antecedents to 1791.* Washington, D.C.: Office of the Chief of Army Chaplains, Department of the Army, 1978.

Townsend, Jim. *The "General Protestant" Problem: Reflections on General Protestant Chaplain Ministry.* Nashville: Board of Higher Education and Ministry, United Methodist Church, 1991.

Venzke, Rodger R. *Confidence in Battle, Inspiration in Peace: The United States Army Chaplaincy, 1945–1975.* Washington, D.C.: Office of the Chief of Chaplains, Department of the Army, 1977.

Wilson, Charles Reagan. *Baptized in the Blood: The Religion of the Lost Cause, 1865–1920.* Athens: University of Georgia Press, 1980.

Europe

Bachrach, D.S. *Religion and the Conduct of War c. 300 to 1215.* Woodbridge: Boydell and Brewer, 2003.

Bamberg, Hans-Dieter. *Militärseelsorge in der Bundeswehr. Schule der Anpassung und des Unfriedens.* Cologne: Pahl-Rugenstein, 1970.

Becker, Annette. *La guerre et la foi: de la mort à la mémoire, 1914–1930.* Paris: A. Colin, 1994.

Beese, Dieter. *Seelsorger in Uniform.* Hanover: Lutherisches Verlagshaus, 1995.

Black, Johann. *Militärseelsorge in Polen: Analyse und Dokumentation.* Stuttgart: Degerloch, 1981.

Blankmeister, Franz. *Die sächsischen Feldprediger. Zur Geschichte der Militärseelsorge in Krieg und Frieden.* Leipzig: Fr. Richter, 1893.

Blaschke, Peter H., ed. *Zum Frieden berufen: Notizen aus der evangelischen Militärseelsorge.* Bonn: Lutherisches Verlagshaus, 1989.

Bock, Martin. *L'assistance spirituelle aux militaires en égard à la separation de l'Eglise et de l'Etat: l'organisation de l'aumônerie militaire en France.* Strausberg: Sozialwissenschaftliches Institut der Bundeswehr, 1996.

———. *Soldatenseelsorge in Österreich und Frankreich.* Munich: Sozialwissenschaftliches Institut der Bundeswehr, 1994.

Boniface, Xavier. *L'aumônerie militaire française, 1914–1962.* Paris: Cerf, 2001.

Borovi, Jozsef. *A magyar tabori lelkeszet tortenete.* Budapest: Zrinyi Kiado, 1992.

Brandt, Hans Jürgen, ed. *. . . und auch Soldaten fragten. Zu Aufgabe und Problematik der Militärseelsorge in drei Generationen.* Paderborn: Bonifatius, 1992.

Brock, P. *The Military Question in the Early Church: A Selected Bibliography of a Century's Scholarship, 1888–1987.* Toronto: 1988.

Brumwell, P. Middleton. *The Army Chaplain.* London: A.C. Black, 1943.

Cavaterra, Emilio. *Sacerdoti in grigioverde: storia dell'ordinariato militaire italiano.* Milan: Mursia, 1993.

Dokumentation zur evangelischen Militärseelsorge; Dokumentation zur katholischen Militärseelsorge: Gesetze, Verträge, Weisungen, Vorschiften. Edited by Evangelisches Kirchenamt für die Bundeswehr and Katholisches Militärbischofsamt. Bonn: das Kirchenamt; das Militärbischofsamt, 1991.

von Domaszewski, Alfred. *Die Religion des römischen Heeres.* First published, Berlin, 1895; New York: Arno Press, 1975.

Dow, Alexander Crawley. *Ministers to the Soldiers of Scotland: A History of the Military Chaplains of Scotland Prior to the War in the Crimea.* Edinburgh and London: Oliver and Boyd, 1962.

Fontana, Jacques. *Les catholiques français pendant la Grande Guerre.* Paris: Cerf, 1990.

Franzinelli, Mimmo. *I cappellani militari italiani nella Resistenza all'estero.* Rome: Ministero della difesa, Rivista militare, 1993.

———. *Il riarmo dello spirito: i cappellani militari nella seconda guerra mondial.* Paese, Treviso: Pagus, 1991.

———. *Stellette, croce e fascio littorio. L'assistenza religiosa a militari, balilla e camicie nere, 1919–1939.* Milan: Franco Angeli, 1995.

Gramm, Reinhard. *Frieden zwischen Waffen: kleine Typologie des Soldatenpfarrers im Spiegel literarischer Texte.* Stuttgart: Kreuz, 1975.

Güsgen, Johannes, *Die katholische Militärseelsorge in Deutschland zwischen 1920 und 1945: Ihre Praxis und Entwicklung in der Reichswehr der Weimarer Republik und der Wehrmacht des nationalsozialistischen Deutschlands unter besonderer Berücksichtigung ihrer Rolle bei den Reichskonkordatsverhandlungen.* Cologne: Böhlau, 1989.

Hambye, Edward René. *L'aumônerie de la flotte de Flandre au XVIIe siècle, 1623–1662.* Louvain: Editions Nauwelaerts; Paris: Beatrice-Nauwelaerts, 1967.

Harnack, Adolf von. *Militia Christi: The Christian Religion and the Military in the First Three Centuries.* Translated by David M. Gracie. Philadelphia, 1981; originally published in 1905.

Hendrickson, Kenneth E. *Making Saints: Religion and the Public Image of the British Army, 1809–1885.* Madison, N.J.: Fairleigh Dickinson University Press, 1998.

Herspring, Dale R. *Soldiers, Commissars, and Chaplains: Civil-Military Relations since Cromwell.* Lanham, Md.: Rowman and Littlefield, 2001.

Johnstone, Tom, and James Hagerty. *The Cross on the Sword: Catholic Chaplains in the Forces.* London and New York: G. Chapman, 1996.

Katholische Militärseelsorge in der Bundeswehr: Ein Neubeginn (1951–1957). Edited by Katholisches Militärbischofsamt. Cologne: J.P. Bachem, 1986.

Koeniger, Albert Michael. *Die Militärseelsorge der Karolingerzeit: Ihr Recht und ihre Praxis.* Munich: Lentner, 1918.

Kreutz, Benedict. *Militärseelsorge im Ersten Weltkrieg.* Mainz: Matthias-Grünewald, 1987.

Kulp, Johannes. *Feldprediger und Kriegsleute als Kirchenliederdichter.* Schloeßmann, 1941.

Langhäuser, Julius. *Das Militärkirchenwesen im kurbrandenburgischen und königlich-preußischen Heer: seine Entwicklung und derzeitige Gestalt.* Metz: P. Müller, 1912.

Laurence, Anne. *Parliamentary Army Chaplains, 1642–1651*. Suffolk: The Boydell Press, 1990.

Leconte, Jacques Robert. *L'aumônerie militaire belge: Son évolution de l'époque hollandaise à l'organisation actuelle*. Brussels: Musée royal de l'Armée et d'histoire militaire, 1966.

Lipusch, Viktor. *Österreich-Ungarns katholische Militärseelsorge im Weltkrieg*. Horn, Austria: Berger, 1938.

Marchisio, Francesco. *Cappellani Militari, 1870–1970*. Rome, 1970.

Martin, Karl, ed. *Frieden statt Sicherheit: Von der Militärseelsorge zum Dienst der Kirche unter den Soldaten: Positionen und Beiträge*. Gütersloh: Gütersloher Verlagshaus Gerd Mohn, 1989.

Mauro, Achille. *Cappuccini e la Croce rossa italiana: i cappellani del Corpo militaire della C.R.I. nel 1° centenario*. Napoli: Giannini, 1987.

May, Georg. *Interkonfessionalismus in der deutschen Militärseelsorge von 1933 bis 1945*. Amsterdam: B.R. Grüner, 1978.

McCormick, Michael. *Eternal Victory: Triumphal Rulership in Late Antiquity, Byzantium, and the Early Medieval West*. Cambridge and New York: Cambridge University Press, 1986.

Mit Gott für Volk und Vaterland: Die Württembergische Landeskirche zwischen Krieg und Frieden, 1903–1957. Edited by Haus der Geschichte Baden-Württemberg and Landeskirchliches Museum Ludwigsburg. Stuttgart: 1995.

Moynihan, Michael, ed. *God on Our Side*. London: Secker and Warburg, 1983.

Morozzo della Rocco, Roberto. *Fede e la guerra: cappellani militarie preti-soldati (1915–1919)*. Rome: Edizioni Studium, 1980.

Pohl, Heinrich. *Die katholische Militärseelsorge Preußens, 1797–1888*. Amsterdam: P. Schippes, 1962; originally published Stuttgart: F. Ehnke, 1926.

Richter, Martin. *Die Entwicklung und die gegenwärtige Gestaltung der Militärseelsorge in Preußen: historisch-kritische Denkschrift*. Osnabrück: Biblio, 1991.

Rudolph, Hartmut. *Das evangelische Militärkirchenwesen in Preußen: Die Entwicklung seiner Verfassung und Organisation vom Absolutismus bis zum Vorabend des I. Weltkrieges*. Göttingen: Vandenhoeck & Ruprecht, 1973.

Russell, Frederick H. *The Just War in the Middle Ages*. New York: Cambridge University Press, 1975.

Schild, Erich. *Der preußische Feldprediger I: Bilder aus dem kirchlichen Leben der preußischen Armee älterer Zeit*. Eisleben: Otto Maehnert, 1888.

———. *Der preußische Feldprediger II: Das brandenburgisch-preußische Feldpredigerwesen in seiner geschichtlichen Entwicklung*. Halle: Eugen Strien, 1890.

Schubel, Albrecht. *300 Jahre Evangelische Soldatenseelsorge*. Munich: Evangelischer Presseverband für Bayern, 1964.

Smyth, John G. *In this Sign Conquer: The Story of the Army Chaplains*. London: Mowbray, 1968.

Solt, Leo F. *Saints in Arms: Puritanism and Democracy in Cromwell's Army*. Stanford: Stanford University Press, 1959.

Speidel, M.P. *The Religion of Iuppiter Dolichenus in the Roman Army*. Leiden: Brill, 1978.

Thomson, T.B. Stewart. *The Chaplain in the Church of Scotland*. The Baird Lecture, 1947.

Vest, Hieronymous. *Der deutsche Feldprediger im XVIII. Jahrhundert*. Basel, 1868.

Worte der Kirche an Soldaten: Päpste, II. Vatikanisches Konzil, Deutsche Bischöfe (1965–1984). Edited by Katholisches Militärbischofsamt. Cologne, 1984.

Zahn, Gordon Charles. *The Military Chaplaincy: A Study of Role Tension in the Royal Air Force*. Toronto: University of Toronto Press, 1969.

General and International

Bock, Martin. *Religion within the Armed Forces: Military Chaplaincy in an International Comparison*. Strausberg: Sozialwissenschaftliches Institut der Bundeswehr, 1998.

Gaona, Silvio. *Capellandes de la Guerra del Chaco (1932–1935)*. Asunción: 1964.

Garcia de Loydi, Ludovico. *Los cappellanes del Ejercito; ensayo historico*. Buenos Aires: Direccion de Estudios Historicos, 1965.

Gonzaléz Errázuriz, Juan Ignacio. *Iglesia y Fuerzas Armadas: estudio canónico y jurídico sobre la asistencia espiritual a las Fuerzas Armadas en Chile*. Santiago de Chile: Universidad de los Andes, 1994.

Herspring, Dale R. *Soldiers, Commissars, and Chaplains: Civil-Military Relations since Cromwell*. Lanham, Md.: Rowman and Littlefield, 2001.

McKernan, Michael. *Australian Churches at War: Attitudes and Activities of the Major Churches, 1914–1918*. Sydney: Catholic Theological Faculty; Canberra: Australian War Memorial, 1980.

Pham, Quang Hao. *The Buddhist Chaplain Branch of the Republic of Vietnam Armed Forces*. Saigon: Buddhist Chaplain Directorate, 1968.

Articles in Periodicals and Chapters in Books

United States and Canada

Autry, Jerry D. "The Chaplain in the Military Service School." *Military Chaplains' Review* (spring 1974): 18–21.

Bliss, M. "The Methodist Church and World War I." *Canadian Historical Review* 49, no. 3 (1968): 213–33.

Burchard, Waldo W. "Role Conflicts of Military Chaplains." *American Sociological Review* 19 (1954): 528–35.

Crerar, Duff. "Bellicose Priests: The Wars of the Canadian Catholic Chaplains, 1914–1919." *Canadian Catholic Historical Association Historical Studies* 58 (1991): 21–39.

Daniel, W. Harrison. "Southern Protestantism and Army Missions in the Confederacy." *Mississippi Quarterly* 17 (1964): 179–83.

Faust, Drew Gilpin. "Christian Soldiers: The Meaning of Revivalism in the Confederate Army." *Journal of Southern History* 8, no. 1 (1987): 63–90.

Gauvreau, Michael. "War, Culture and the Problem of Religious Certainty: Methodist and Presbyterian Church Colleges, 1914–1930." *Journal of the Canadian Church Historical Society* 29, no. 1 (Apr. 1997).

Gordon, A.M. "A Chaplain at the Front." *Queen's Quarterly* 27 (1919): 169–79.

Greenwood, Charles L. "Studies of the Military Chaplaincy: Rank, Uniform, Pay, and Role." *The Chaplain* 31 (1974): 48–49.

Hughes, Andrew S. "For God and Country: Military Chaplains Fulfill Traditional Duties even as Military Changes." *South Bend Tribune* (June 1, 2000): C1–2.

Loveland, Anne C. "Character Education in the U.S. Army, 1947–1977." *Journal of Military History* 64 (July 2000): 795–812.

————. "Prophetic Ministry and the Military Chaplaincy during the Vietnam Era." In *Moral Problems in American Life: New Perspectives on Cultural History*. Edited by Karen Halttunen and Lewis Perry. Ithaca, N.Y.: Cornell University Press, 1998.

Marshall, David. "Methodism Embattled: A Reconsideration of the Methodist Church and World War I." *Canadian Historical Review* 66, no. 1 (Mar. 1986).

Miller, Luther D. "The Chaplains in the Army." *Army and Navy Journal* 85 (Sept. 20, 1947): 47.

Norton, Herman. "Revivalism in the Confederate Army." *Civil War History* 6 (1960): 410–24.

Silver, James W. "The Confederate Preacher Goes to War." *North Carolina Historical Review* 33 (1956): 400–509.

Watson, Samuel J. "Religion and Combat Motivation in the Confederate Armies." *Journal of Military History* 58 (1994): 29–55.

Wight, Willard E. "The Churches and the Confederate Cause." *Civil War History* 6 (1960): 361–73.

Europe

Apold, Hans. "Feldbischof Franz Justus Rarkowski im Spiegel seiner Hirtenbriefe." *Zeitschrift für die Geschichte und Altertumskunde Ermlands* 39, no. 100 (1978): 86–128.

Bergen, Doris L. "'Germany Is Our Mission—Christ Is Our Strength!' The Wehrmacht Chaplaincy and the 'German Christian' Movement." *Church History* 66, no. 3 (Sept. 1997): 522–36.

————. "German Military Chaplains in World War II and the Dilemmas of Legitimacy." *Church History* 70, no. 2 (June 2001): 232–47.

————. "Witnesses to Atrocity: German Military Chaplains and the Crimes of the Third Reich." In *In God's Name: Religion and Genocide in the Twentieth Century*. Edited by Omer Bartov and Phyllis Mack. New York: Berghahn Books, 2000.

Drühe, Wilhelm. "'Instrumentalisierung der Religion zu militärischen Zwecken.' Zur Auseinandersetzung um Bundeswehrgelöbnis und Militärseelsorge." *Junge Kirche* 41, no. 10 (1980) 429–35.

Egli, Eugen. "Die Aufgaben des Feldpredigers werden immer anspruchsvoller." *Schweizer Soldat* 6 (1985): 5–7.

Finckh, Ulrich. "Militärseelsorge am Rubikon." *Junge Kirche* 37 (1976).

Fleckenstein, Bernhard. "Gruppenseelsorge in der militärischen Großorganisation." *Militärseelsorge* 13 (1971): 155–66.

———. "Zur Situation der Militärseelsorge in der Gegenwart." *Militärseelsorge* 12 (1970): 252–65.

Gounelle, Yves. "Französische protestantische Militärseelsorge." *Europäisches Militärseelsorge-Jahrbuch* 3 (1993): 58.

Jones, A. H. M. "Military Chaplains in the Roman Army." *Harvard Theological Review* 46 (1953): 239–40.

Leonard, Jane. "The Catholic Chaplaincy." In *Ireland and the First World War*. Edited by David Fitzpatrick. Dublin: Trinity History Workshop, 1986.

Liedke, Gerhard. "Sorge um die Militärseelsorge: Bemerkungen zu einem Konferenzergebnis." *Junge Kirche* 38, no. 6 (1977): 334–36.

Löffler, Roland. "Militärseelsorger im Ernstfall. Einsatz von Bundeswehrgeistlichen auf dem Balkan." *Neue Zürcher Zeitung*, int'l ed. (Aug. 25, 2000, no. 197): 8.

Lynn, John A. "Towards an Army of Honor: The Moral Evolution of the French Army, 1789–1815." *French Historical Studies* 16, no. 1 (spring 1989): 152–73.

McCormick, Michael. "The Liturgy of War in the Middle Ages: Crisis, Litanies, and the Carolingian Monarchy." *Viator* 15 (1984): 1–23.

McHardy, A. K. "The English Clergy and the Hundred Years War." *Studies in Church History* 20 (1983): 171–78.

Mathisen, Ralph. W. "Barbarian Bishops and the Churches in 'barbaricis gentibis' during Late Antiquity." *Speculum* 72 (1997): 664–97.

Messerschmidt, Manfred. "Aspekte der Militärseelsorgepolitik in nationalsozialistischer Zeit" and "Zur Militärseelsorgepolitik im Zweiten Weltkrieg." *Militärgeschichtliche Mitteilungen* (1/1968 and 1/1969).

Reese, Günter. "Seelsorgerliche Bedenken gegen eine bedenkliche Seelsorge." *Junge Kirche* 43, nos. 7/8 (1982): 351–58.

Schild, Erich. "Ursprung und erste Gestalt des preußischen Feldpredigeramts." *Beiheft zum Militär-Wochenblatt* (1880): 399–430.

Senin, Aleksandr S. "Russian Army Chaplains during World War I." *Russian Studies in History* 32 (1993): 43–52.

Snape, Michael. "British Catholicism and the British Army in the First World War." *Recusant History* 26 (2002): 314–58.

———. "Keeping Faith and Coping: Belief, Popular Religiosity and the British People." In *The Great World War, 1914–1945*, vol. 2, *The People's Experience*. Edited by Peter Liddle, J. M. Bourne, and Ian R. Whitehead. London: Harper Collins, 2001.

Zienert, Josef. "'Lass ihren Dienst gesegnet sein.' Kleine Geschichte der deutschen Marineseelsorge von 1674 bis 1945." *Beiträge aus der ev. Militärseelsorge* (Bonn: Evangelisches Kirchenamt für die Bundeswehr) 43 (Aug. 1983).

General/International

McKernan, Michael. "Clergy in Khaki: The Chaplain in the Australian Imperial Force, 1914–1918." *Journal of the Royal Australian Historical Society* 64, no. 3 (1978): 145–66.

Sheils, W. J., ed. "The Church and War." *Studies in Church History* 20 (1983): 111–27.

Vickers, Robert. "The Military Chaplaincy: A Study In Role Conflict." *Military Chaplains' Review* (spring 1986): 83.

Dissertations and Theses

Bachrach, David Stewart. "Priests at War and Soldiers at Prayer: A History of Military Religion from the Concilium Germanicum (742) to the Fourth Lateran Council (1215)." Ph.D. diss., University of Notre Dame, 2001.

Beasley, Joseph Hodgin. "Implications of Teaching Ethics: The West Point Experience." Ph.D. diss., University of North Carolina at Chapel Hill, 1985.

Bick, Rolf. "Der Lebenskundliche Unterricht der Evangelischen Militärseelsorge als Arbeitsfeld christlicher Ethik und kirchlicher Erwachsenenbildung." Ph.D. diss., University of Münster, 1977.

Bleese, Jörn. "Die Militärseelsorge und die Trennung von Staat und Kirche." Ph.D. diss., University of Hamburg, 1969.

Boyles, Lemuel M. "Pluralism in the Air Force Chaplaincy." D. Min. thesis, Dayton, Ohio, United Theological Seminary, 1993.

Brinsfield, John W., Jr. "Developing a Ministry of Teaching the History of Ethics and World Religions at the United States Military Academy, West Point, N.Y." D.Min. thesis, Drew University, 1983.

Burchard, Waldo W. "The Role of the Military Chaplain." Ph.D. diss., University of California, Berkeley, 1953.

Doyon, Pierre. "Aumôniers Catholiques dans la marine royale du Canada de 1939 à nos jours." M.A. thesis, University of Ottawa, 1968.

Germani, Aidan Henry. "Catholic Military and Naval Chaplains, 1776–1917." Ph.D. diss., Catholic University of America, 1929.

Gilbert, Ernest Williston Sheraton. "The Spiritual, Moral and Social Problem Work of a Chaplain in the Royal Canadian Air Force." M.A. Thesis, Union College of British Columbia, 1946.

Hardy, Margaret. "Priests and Soldiers Too: Military Chaplaincy in the Australian Infantry Forces 1901–1909." Ph.D. diss., Australian Catholic University, in progress.

Hoffmann, Kurt. "Evangelische Militärseelsorge als didaktisches Teilkonzept kirchlicher Erwachsenenbildung." Ph.D. diss., University of Munich, 1978.

Marschke, Benjamin A. "The Development of the Army Chaplaincy in Early Eighteenth-Century Prussia," Ph.D. diss., University of California, Los Angeles, in progress.

O'Brien, Karen, "Making the War Personal: Chaplains, Continental Soldiers, and Revolutionary Obligations," paper presented at The Newberry Seminar in Early American History, 2001.

Risch, Helmut. "Der kurbrandenburgisch-preußische Feldprediger und seine Bedeutung für das Heer, 1655–1806." Ph.D. diss., University of Jena, 1942.

Sandgren, Per Anders. "'Det är bra med en präst liksom.' En undersökning kring några förutsättningar för andlig vård vid militära förband." Lunds Universitet, Teologiske institutionen, Kyrko och Samfundsvetenkap. Survey (licentiatsuppsats) about military chaplains in Sweden. English summary. 1999.

Strizek, Daniel C. "Ella Elvira Gibson Hart: Spiritualist/Civil War Chaplain: 'If Mrs. Hobart is Suited, We Ought to Be.'" M.Div. thesis, Iliff School of Theology, 1991.

DIARIES, CORRESPONDENCE, BIOGRAPHIES,
AND PERSONAL NARRATIVES

United States and Canada

Bennett, William W. *A Narrative of the Great Revival Which Prevailed in the Southern Armies.* Philadelphia: Claxton, Remsen, and Haffelfinger, 1877.

Betts, A.D., and W.A. Betts. *Experience of a Confederate Chaplain, 1861–1864.* Chapel Hill: Academic Affairs Library, University of North Carolina at Chapel Hill (Internet), 1996.

Brodsky, Gabriel Wilfrid Stephen. *God's Dodger: The Story of a Front Line Chaplain, 1905–1945.* Sidney, B.C.: Elysium, 1993.

Chunn, Floyd H. *Memoirs of a World War II U.S. Army Chaplain.* Seymour, Tenn.: *Tri-County News,* 1973.

Clint, Mary. *Our Bit: Memories of War Service, by a Canadian Nursing Sister.* Montreal: Barwick, 1934.

Conference of Army Chaplains. "Minutes of the Conference of Army Chaplains: Held at Leavenworth, Kansas, May 13–18, 1891." Cincinnati: Cranston and Stowe, 1891.

Corby, William, C.S.C. *Memoirs of Chaplain Life: Three Years with the Irish Brigade in the Army of the Potomac.* Edited by Lawrence Frederick Kohl. First published 1893; New York: Fordham University Press, 1992.

Daniel, Eugene L. *In the Presence of Mine Enemies: An American Chaplain in WW II German Prison Camps.* Attleboro, Mass.: Colonial Lithograph, 1985.

Denison, Frederic. *A Chaplain's Experience in the Union Army.* Providence: The Society, 1893.

Kettler, Earl C. *Chaplain's Letters: Ministry by "Huey," 1964–1965.* Cincinnati: Cornelius Books, 1994.

Koedel, Craig. *The Sky Pilot Said It: Memoirs of an Air Force Chaplain, 1953–1956.* Pittsburgh: R. Craig Koedel, 2001.

Landes, Aaron, and George M. Goodwin. *The Reminiscences of Rabbi Landes.* Providence, R.I.: Temple Beth-El, 1943.

Langellier, Phillip J. *Chaplain Allen Allensworth and the 24th Infantry, 1886–1906.* Tucson: Tucson Corral of the Westerners, 1980.

Livazer, Hersh. *The Rabbi's Blessing: From the Memories of a Chaplain in the U.S. Army (1943–1965).* Jerusalem: H. Livazer, 1980.

"M. Donald. Holocaust Testimony (chaplain's assistant in the U.S. Army, World War II, interviewed by Warren H. Robinson and Edwin A. Hiscock, March 3, 1994)." Kansas City, Mo.: Midwest Center for Holocaust Education, 1994.

Videorecording in Fortunoff Video Archive for Holocaust Testimony, HVT-2355.

Maher, William L. *A Shepherd in Combat Boots: Chaplain Emil Kapaun of the 1st Cavalry Division.* Shippensburg, Pa.: Burd Street Press, 1997.

Martin, Tyrone G. *The USS Constitution's Finest Fight, 1815: The Journal of Acting Chaplain Assheton Humphreys, US Navy.* Mount Pleasant, S.C.: Nautical & Aviation Publishing Company of America, 2000.

May, James W., ed. *Ministry in Uniform: Correspondence of an Infantry Chaplain, 1944–1945.* [S.I.:s.n.], 1985.

O'Connor, John Joseph. *A Chaplain Looks at Vietnam.* Cleveland: World, 1968.

Rogers, J. B. *War Pictures, Experiences, and Observations of a Chaplain in the U.S. Army, in the War of the Southern Rebellion.* Chicago: Church & Goodman, 1863.

Sampson, Francis L. *Look Out Below! A Story of the Airborne by a Paratrooper Padre.* Sweetwater, Tenn.: 101st Airborne Division Association, 1989.

Schumacher, John W. *A Soldier of God Remembers: Memoir Highlights of a Career Army Chaplain.* Winona Lake, Ind.: Grace Brethren North American Missions, 2000.

Smith, Wilford E. *A Mormon "Holy Joe."* Provo, Utah: W.E. Smith, 1981.

Springer, Francis, and William Furry. *The Preacher's Tale: The Civil War Journal of Rev. Francis Springer, Chaplain, U.S. Army of the Frontier.* Fayetteville: University of Arkansas Press, 2001.

Stroup, Russell Cartwright, and Richard Cartwright Austin. *Letters From the Pacific: A Combat Chaplain in World War II.* Columbia: University of Missouri Press, 2000.

Stuckenberg, J.H. W, David T. Hedrick, and Gordon Barry Davis. *I'm Surrounded by Methodists: Diary of John H.W. Stuckenberg, Chaplain of the 145th Pennsylvania Volunteer Infantry.* Gettysburg, Pa.: Thomas Publishing, 1995.

Tissot, Peter. *A Year with the Army of the Potomac: Diary of the Reverend Father Tissot, S.J., Military Chaplain.* New York: Catholic Historical Society, 1903.

Tonne, Arthur. *The Story of Chaplain Kapaun, Patriot Priest of the Korean Conflict.* Emporia, Kans.: Didde Printing, 1954.

Wall, Max B. "'I Served not only Jewish Personnel.'" In *The Holocaust: Personal Accounts.* Edited by David Scrase and Wolfgang Mieder. Burlington, Vt.: Center for Holocaust Studies, 2001.

White, Henry S., and Edward Drewry Jervey. *Prison Life Among the Rebels: Recollections of a Union Chaplain.* Kent, Ohio: Kent State University Press, 1990.

Workman, W.T. *The Canadian Catholic Church Chaplain Overseas, 1918–1919; A Report Presented to the Canadian Army Bishop by the Assistant Director of Chaplain Services, Overseas Military Forces of Canada.* London: n.p., 1919.

Europe and Europe's Colonies

Alberti, Rüdiger. *Als Kriegspfarrer in Polen: Erlebnisse und Begegnungen in Kriegslazaretten.* Dresden and Leipzig: C. Ludwig Ungelenk, 1940.

Badré, Jean. *Un homme d'église dans l'histoire: entretiens avec Michel Fourcade.* Paris: Nouvelle Cité, 1990.

Baedecker, Dietrich. *Das Volk das im Finsternis wandelt: Stationen eines Militärpfarrers, 1943–1946.* Edited by Evangelisches Kirchenamt für die Bundeswehr. Bonn, Hanover: Lutherisches Verlagshaus, 1987.

Berg, Ludwig. *Pro fide et patria! Die Kriegstagebücher von Ludwig Berg 1914/18: katholischer Feldgeistlicher in Grossen Hauptquartier Kaiser Wilhelms II.* Edited by Frank Betker and Almut Kriele. Cologne: Böhlau, 1998.

Bickersteth, John, ed. *The Bickersteth Diaries, 1914–1918.* Introduction by John Terraine. London: Leo Cooper, 1995.

Bilder und Texte aus der Soldatenseelsorge, 1550–1945. Edited by Evangelisches Kirchenamt für die Bundeswehr. Bonn: 1983.

Brandt, Hans-Jürgen, and Katholisches Militärbischofsamt, ed., *Priester in Uniform: Seelsorger, Ordensleute und Theologen als Soldaten im Zweiten Weltkrieg.* Augsburg: Pattloch, 1994.

Cortese, Carmine. *Diario di Guerra (1916–1917).* Soveria Mannelli (Cantanzaro): Rubbettino, 1998.

Creighton, Owen. *With the 29th Division in Gallipoli: A Chaplain's Experiences.* London: Longman's Green, 1916.

Eich, Franz Maria. *Auf verlorenem Posten? Als Marinepfarrer im Zweiten Weltkrieg.* Aschaffenburg: P. Pattloch, 1979.

Elbin, Gunther, ed. *Mit der Armee am Niederrhein (1793).* Anonymous. Duisburg: Mercator, 1999; originally published as *Reise eines preussischen Feldpredigers mit der Armee durch Westphalen über Cleve nach Holland und Flandern.* Stendal, 1824.

Gabel, Charles A. *Aumônier français à la prison de Spandau: Conversations interdites avec Rudolf Hess, 1977–1986.* Paris: Plon, 1988.

Gache, Louis-Hippolyte. *A Frenchman, a Chaplain, a Rebel: The War Letters of Père Louis-Hippolyte Gache, S.J.* Chicago: Loyola University Press, 1981.

Galli, Lodovico. *I dimenticati: Brescia, 1943–1945: i caduti della Repubblica sociale italiana, cappellani militari in Francia.* Montichiari (Brescia): Zanetti, 1997.

Gethyn-Jones, Eric. *A Territorial Army Chaplain in Peace and War: A Country Cleric in Khaki, 1938–1961.* East Wittering, West Sussex: Gooday, 1988.

Humenski, Julian. *Wspomnienia wojenne kapelanow wojskowych.* Warsaw: Caritas, 1969.

Ihlenfeld, Kurt, ed. *Preußischer Choral: Deutscher Soldatenglaube in Drei Jahrhunderten.* Berlin: Eckart, 1935.

Keding, Karl. *Feldgeistlicher bei Legion Condor. Spanisches Kriegstagebuch eines evangelischen Legionspfarrers.* Berlin: Ostwerk, 1937.

Kestell, John Daniel. *Through Shot and Flame: The Adventures and Experiences of J.D. Kestell, Chaplain to President Steyn and General Christian de Wet.* London: Methuen, 1903; originally published in Dutch. Amsterdam: Hoveker and Wormser, 1902.

Klein, Félix. *Hope in Suffering: Memories and Reflections of a French Army Chaplain.* London: A. Melrose, 1916.

Klier, Johann. *Von der Kriegspredigt zum Friedensappell: Erzbischof Michael von Faulhaber und der Erste Weltkrieg.* Munich: Kommissionsverlag UNI-Druck, 1991.

"Ein Kriegesmann und guter Christ—": Historische Skizzen aus der Soldatenseelsorge, ed. Evangelisches Kirchenamt für die Bundeswehr. Hanover: Lutherisches Verlagshaus, 1990.

Kunst, Hermann, ed. *Gott läßt sich nicht spotten: Franz Dohrmann, Feldbischof unter Hitler.* Hanover: Lutherisches Verlagshaus, 1983.

Lehmann, Hannalore. "August Hermann Franckes Potsdambesuch im März 1725: Tagebuchaufzeichnungen über seine Initiative bei der Einrichtung des Militärwaisenhauses." In *Potsdam, Märkische Kleinstadt—europäische Residenz: einer eintausendjährigen Geschichte.* Edited by Peter-Michael Hahn. Berlin: Akademie Verlag, 1995.

Lehmann, Paul Gerhard. *Der Feldgottesdienst: Betrachtungen eines Frontoffiziers.* Göttingen: Vandenhoeck & Ruprecht, 1917.

Leonhard, Hans. *Wieviel Leid erträgt ein Mensch? Aufzeichnungen eines Kriegspfarrers über die Jahre 1939 bis 1945.* Amberg: Buch & Kunstverlag Oberpfalz, 1994.

Lummis, William Murrell. *Padre George Smith of Rorke's Drift.* Norwich: Wensum Books, 1978.

Macintosh, Neil K. *Richard Johnson: Chaplain to the Colony of New South Wales, His Life and Times, 1755–1827.* Sydney: Library of Australian History, 1978.

McClelland, Robert. *Heroes and Gentlemen: An Army Chaplain's Experiences in South Africa.* Edinburgh: John Menzies, 1902.

McLuskey, J. Fraser. *Parachute Padre behind German Lines with the SAS France.* London: SCM Press, 1951.

Mensch, was wollt Ihr denen sagen? Katholische Feldseelsorger im Zweiten Weltkrieg. Edited by Katholisches Militärbischofsamt. Augsburg: Pattloch, 1991.

De Miramont, J. T. *Soldat et apôtre: André Denjoy, aumônier militaire à Madagascar (1852–1895).* Tours: Alfred Mame, 1899.

M. L'abbé Charles Morance, aumônier du 33e mobiles et du Ive corps d'armée. Le Mans: Leguicheu, 1889.

Peifer, Rudolf. *Den Menschen ein Angebot: Erinnerungen eines Seelsorgers.* Cologne: Styria, 1993.

Perau, Josef. *Priester im Heere Hitlers: Erinnerungen, 1940–1945.* Essen: Ludgerus, 1963.

Rogge, Bernhard Friedrich Wilhelm, and George Gladstone. *The Chaplain in the Field of War: Being the Experiences of the Clerical Staff during the Prussian Campaign of 1866.* London: Bell & Daldy, 1870.

Rozen, Leon S. *Cry in the Wilderness: A Short History of a Chaplain: Activities and Struggles in Soviet Russia during World War II.* New York and Tel Aviv: Om Publishing C., 1966.

Schabel, Wilhelm. *Herr, in Deine Hände: Seelsorge im Krieg.* Bern: Scherz, 1963.

Schlunk, Rudolf, and Wilhelm Wibbeling, eds. *Wir Pfarrer im Kriege: Kriegserlebnisse des renitenten Pfarrers Rudolf Schlunk.* Kassel: Neuwerk, 1931.

Schneider, Kurd, ed. *Quellen und Beiträge zur Geschichte der deutsch-evangelische Militärseelsorge vom 1564 bis 1814.* Halle: Waisenhaus, 1906.

Schneider, Thomas Martin. *Reichsbischof Ludwig Müller: Eine Untersuchung zu Leben, Werk und Persönlichkeit.* Göttingen: Vandenhoeck & Ruprecht, 1993.

Tyczkowski, Franciszek. *Wspomnienia z pierwszej i drugiej wojny swiatowej w Polsce.* Bronx, N.Y.: Tyczkowski, 1972.

Van Heck, F., ed. *De soldatenpastoor: P. Henricus Verbraak S.J., aalmoezenier van het Ned.-Ind. Leger te Atjeh.* Amsterdam: N.V. de R.K. Boekcentrale, 1924.

Watkins, Owen Spencer. *Chaplains at the Front; Incidents in the Life of a Chaplain during the Boer War, 1899–1900.* London: S.W. Partridge, 1901.

Wollasch, Hans-Josef, ed. *Militärseelsorge im Ersten Weltkrieg: Das Kriegstagebuch des katholischen Feldgeistlichen Benedict Kreutz.* Mainz: Matthias-Grünewald, 1987.

Latin America and the Pacific

Harker, Jack S. *Soldier, Sailor, Priest: Biography of the Reverend George Trevor Robson, OBE, MC, RNZN, 1887–1979.* Auckland, New Zealand: Challenge Communication Foundation, 1992.

Mafezzini, Angel V. *Diario de un cura soldado: el factor espiritual en la guerra de las Malvinas.* Buenos Aires: A.V. Mafezzini, 1982.

MANUALS AND GUIDES

Circular for the Information of Persons Desiring to Enter the Chaplain Corps of the Navy. Washington, D.C.: Government Printing Office, 1917.

Handbook for Chaplains, India. Calcutta: Compiled by the Metropolitan's Chaplain, Bishop's House, Calcutta, n.d.

Headquarters. Department of the Army. *The Chaplain and Chaplain Assistant in Combat Operations.* FM 16–5. Washington, D.C.: U.S. Government Printing Office, Dec. 1984.

———. *Character Guidance Manual.* FM-16-100. Washington, D.C.: U.S. Government Printing Office, 1961.

———. *Religious Support Doctrine: The Chaplain and Chaplain Assistant.* FM 16-1 (Final Coordinating Draft, Apr. 1989). Washington, D.C.: U.S. Government Printing Office.

Kunze, Gerhard. *Evangelisches Kirchenbuch für Kriegszeiten.* Göttingen: Vandenhoeck & Ruprecht, 1939.

RELEVANT FICTION

Goes, Albrecht. *Unruhige Nacht.* Hamburg: Friedrich Wittig, 1950.

Hašek, Jaroslav. *The Good Soldier Švejk.* Translated by Cecil Parrott. London and New York: Penguin, 1973.

Heller, Joseph. *Catch 22.* New York: Scribner, 1996.

For God & Country. Movie from Warner Bros. starring Ronald Reagan, 1943. New York: Goodtimes Home Video, 1985.

Man of the Cross (L'uomo della croce). Roberto Rossellini, dir., 1943.

Melville, Herman. *Billy Budd, Sailor.* Chicago: University of Chicago Press, 1962.

Young, Robert Clark. *One of the Guys: A Novel.* New York: Cliff Street Books, 2000.

CONTRIBUTORS

DAVID S. BACHRACH is assistant professor of history at the University of New Hampshire. His monograph, *Religion and the Conduct of War c. 300–1215* (2003), explores the interrelation of military and religious history during the Middle Ages.

MICHAEL J. BAXTER, C.S.C., a Holy Cross priest, teaches theology at the University of Notre Dame and is the national secretary of the Catholic Peace Fellowship, an organization that supports conscientious objectors to war by education, counseling, and advocacy. He lives and works at Peter Claver House, a house of hospitality for the homeless in South Bend, Indiana.

DORIS L. BERGEN is associate professor of history at the University of Notre Dame. She is the author of *Twisted Cross: The German Christian Movement in the Third Reich* (1996); *War and Genocide: A Concise History of the Holocaust* (2003); and numerous articles and essays on religion, gender, and ethnicity in twentieth-century Europe.

DUFF CRERAR studied at the University of Western Ontario and Queen's University. In 1995 he published *Padres in No Man's Land: Canadian Chaplains in the First World War*, with McGill Queen's University Press. He is the author of several articles on the Canadian military chaplaincy and the history of Presbyterianism in Colonial Canada.

ANNE LAURENCE is professor of history at the Open University, U.K., and author of *Parliamentary Army Chaplains 1642–51*, Royal Historical Society Studies in History (1990); *Women in England 1500–1760: A Social History* (1994); and many articles on the English civil war and on gender relations in the seventeenth century.

HARTMUT LEHMANN received his Ph.D. from the University of Vienna and the habilitation at the University of Cologne. He served as professor of modern history at the University of Kiel from 1969 to 1987; as founding director of the German Historical Institute in Washington, D.C., from 1987 until 1993; and as director of the Max Planck Institute for History in Göttingen since 1993.

ANNE C. LOVELAND is T. H. Williams Professor Emerita at Louisiana State University. She is the author of *American Evangelicals and the U.S. Military, 1942–1993* (1996) and, with Otis B. Wheeler, *From Meetinghouse to Megachurch: A Material and Cultural History* (2003).

RALPH W. MATHISEN specializes in the study of Late Antiquity and teaches in the Department of History at the University of Illinois at Urbana-Champaign. He is the author and editor of numerous works dealing with religion, law, society, and culture in Late Antiquity.

MICHAEL MCCORMICK received his Ph.D. from the Université catholique de Louvain (Belgium). He is the Goelet Professor of Medieval History, Harvard University, and recent recipient of the Andrew W. Mellon Foundation Distinguished Achievement Award.

JOSEPH F. O'DONNELL, C.S.C., a priest of the Congregation of Holy Cross for almost forty-four years, retired in 1994 from active duty as a chaplain in the U.S. Navy after twenty-nine and a half years of service. He currently resides in Phoenix, where he serves as a volunteer chaplain for the Arizona Department of Public Safety, in addition to other ministerial responsibilities.

GARDINER H. SHATTUCK, JR., is the author of *A Shield and Hiding Place: The Religious Life of the Civil War Armies* (1987) and *Episcopalians and Race: Civil War to Civil Rights* (2000), and a co-author of the *Encyclopedia of American Religious History* (1996; 2d ed., 2001) and *The Episcopalians* (2003). An Episcopal priest in Rhode Island, he has also served as a lecturer in church history at Andover Newton Theological School and the Episcopal Divinity School.

MAX B. WALL graduated from the Jewish Theological Seminary in New York in 1942 and subsequently became a chaplain in the U.S. Army. He served in Europe from November 1944 until April 1946. Later in 1946 he took a position as rabbi in Burlington, Vermont, where he still resides. Rabbi Wall has taught courses on Judaism at St. Michael's College and Champlain College.

INDEX